A SPLENDID INTELLIGENCE

ALSO BY CATHY CURTIS

Alive Still: Nell Blaine, American Painter
A Generous Vision: The Creative Life of Elaine de Kooning
Restless Ambition: Grace Hartigan, Painter

A
SPLENDID
INTELLIGENCE

The Life of Elizabeth Hardwick

CATHY CURTIS

W. W. NORTON & COMPANY
Independent Publishers Since 1923

To T.R.M.,
with love and gratitude

CONTENTS

AUTHOR'S NOTE

This biography of Elizabeth Hardwick includes only as much information about her famous husband, the poet Robert Lowell, as is necessary to tell the story of her life. Anyone looking for additional details can consult the three full-scale Lowell biographies by Ian Hamilton (1982), Paul Mariani (1994), and Kay Redfield Jamison (2017).

In response to my letters, Elizabeth's daughter, Harriet Lowell, wrote that she is "a very private person" and declined to be interviewed. After Harriet came of age and lived independently, Elizabeth rarely mentioned her in letters to friends. For these reasons, she appears more frequently in this biography during her early years.

A SPLENDID INTELLIGENCE

Prologue

Sometimes I resent the glossary, the concordance of truth many have about my personal life. . . . Such fact is to me a hindrance to memory.

— Elizabeth Hardwick, *Sleepless Nights*

On July 27, 1973, the novelist, essayist, and critic Elizabeth Hardwick turned fifty-seven. Soon after arriving in New York from Kentucky decades earlier, she had become a fixture of the literary scene. A slender, attractive woman, always elegantly dressed, she had a captivating personality and a distinctive Southern drawl. Elizabeth was best known for her short stories and essays, written in an allusive yet strikingly insightful style that dazzled her readers. Now divorced from the poet Robert Lowell, who had left her for a younger woman, she nonetheless remained deeply invested in his brilliant career.

Lowell's poems about the end of the marriage were published in *For Lizzie and Harriet* earlier that year. But nothing had prepared Elizabeth for his new book, *The Dolphin*. Without her knowledge, he had written poems that lifted, modified, and even invented emotional passages from her letters. This staggering invasion of her privacy led to reviews that treated her behavior as grist for—as she wrote in a letter to Lowell's editor—"general disparagement and rebuke."[1] There could be no way to dispute the facts, she added, because they had been turned into poetry. Several of Lowell's fellow poets—notably Adrienne Rich and his good friend Elizabeth Bishop—protested his decision to use this material, in reviews and in letters to him. But other writers, mostly male, saw no problem with this method of turning life into art.

The photo of Lowell's new family with British writer Caroline Blackwood, published in the July 16 issue of *Newsweek* to accompany a review of the book, piled insult on injury. The child with uncombed hair and a sullen affect was misidentified as "Harriet," Elizabeth's and Lowell's teenage daughter. There was also a separate, unflattering photo of Elizabeth that contrasted with the waiflike allure of Caroline.

Yet, throughout her remaining decades, Elizabeth continued to affirm Lowell's greatness as a poet. She also steadfastly asserted that the loving, stimulating aspects of her life with him far outweighed the troubled times when repeated bouts of mania led him to reject her and pursue other women. Meanwhile her star continued to rise in the literary firmament. Ranging over a broad territory—from the depiction of women in classic novels to the civil rights movement, from theater in New York to life in Brazil, Kentucky, and Maine—her essays remain strikingly original and insightful. Elizabeth's Southern charm cloaked a rapier wit. Her friends, who included Mary McCarthy, Adrienne Rich, and Susan Sontag, appreciated her relish for gossip, progressive politics, and great literature.

In this first biography of Elizabeth Hardwick, I seek to go beyond the glimpses that a famously private person revealed in her published writing to present a portrait of an exceptional woman who emerged from a long, troubled marriage with the clarity and wisdom that illuminate her brilliant novel *Sleepless Nights*.

CHAPTER 1

Lexington

(1916–1939)

WHEN ELIZABETH BRUCE HARDWICK was born, on July 27, 1916, she was the eighth child of Eugene Allen and Mary Ramsey Hardwick, whose family would expand even further, with two more girls and a boy. The houses they rented—first at 299 East Sixth Street and then at nearby 264 Rand Avenue—were part of the run-down North End of Lexington, Kentucky.[1] It was a neighborhood of chance juxtapositions made permanent by inertia. Whites and African Americans coexisted but rarely acknowledged each other. Elizabeth would recall how the old garden of a historic house overlooked a plot heaped with "old pipes, broken clothesline, Coke bottles, and the debris of hope . . . washing machines . . . toilet bowls, rusting tire rims."[2] Safe by day, the area had an aura of danger at night. As a young Halloween trick-or-treater, she would run down the dark lane adjacent to her house, grateful for the dim illumination of the old streetlight on her road.

Looking back, she was fascinated by the way "decent and wage-earning" people lived side by side with "the anarchic and bill-owing." She recalled the "vexatious, crummy family next door" that was nonetheless an intrinsic part of the neighborhood: "you would be alarmed if they weren't all there on the front porch the next day."[3] One young woman, the daughter of kindly, hardworking people, fell into prostitution after high school and was both pitied and shunned by the neighbors. Her story found its way into part two of *Sleepless Nights*. Elizabeth would always be interested in marginalized people—how they managed to get by or lost their grip. Not to her taste was the placid and prosperous tree-lined East End of town, which "lacked any compromising hint of history."

A Southern woman who didn't fit the Southern sensibility, she viewed her origins as both a form of sustenance and a trial. "How can you be from here, and think like you do?" people would ask. She disdained the mementos (ashtrays, barroom paintings of turf scenes) that enshrined Lexington as the thoroughbred horse-breeding center of the United States. And yet she treasured memories of a particular horse farm—the "damp, dark, olive green of its lawns, the shaded black trees, the paths rolling here and there brushed with sunshine"—and the great racehorse Man o' War, king of thoroughbreds. The golden stallion (made of copper) on the old courthouse weathervane was an emblem that played a role in one of her early short stories. One of Elizabeth's brothers worked as a "timer" at the Kentucky Association Race Track at Race and Fifth streets, a half-mile from the Hardwick home.[4] Seared into her memory was a fire when "the horses screamed all night."[5] The narrator in *Sleepless Nights* recalls a day spent at the track, from "the early sun, the tranquil curve of the empty grandstands" to "the pain and pleasure of the outrageous effort" so quickly expended by the horses and jockeys.[6]

As an adolescent, Elizabeth used to sit on the front porch and flirt with the jockeys, who boarded with families in the neighborhood during the autumn and spring. Decades later, she explained that the "horse magic" of Fayette County was believed to be the result of the limestone-enriched earth that promoted bone growth and the bluegrass, good for grazing.[7] In her unromantic description, thoroughbred racing was "the melancholy contract between an animal of over 1,000 pounds and a skinny little fellow dieting, fasting, and vomiting to meet the ordained weight." She recalled the "owners' wives in large hats of floral and feather decorations" and "crowds arriving in shirt-sleeves and old cars at dawn." Calumet Farm, on Versailles ("Ver-sales") Road—a spoke extending from central Lexington into the countryside—became a noted thoroughbred breeder in the 1930s. In contrast to the old farms, with their "mysterious, somber life like that of the absentee owners," the newer ones were "fresh, clear acres with white fences on the road, white barns, sunlit fields."

Tobacco was another defining element of Lexington, which boasted of being "the largest loose leaf tobacco market in the world" and "the greatest burley tobacco producing center."[8] The fields and warehouses (huge single-story buildings where auctions were held in the winter months), the bargains made with tenant farmers and country agents, and the men who gathered to gossip about sales were part of a historic agrarian world that Elizabeth likened to scenes in the novels of George Eliot. She wrote that she would "rather see the full-grown plants in a field than the quivering, wavering beauty of a new foal."[9] But her own family was not involved with the tobacco industry, other than as consumers of the cigarettes her parents smoked constantly.

Elizabeth's mother, Mary Elizabeth Ramsey, was born in 1880 to Scotch-Irish parents in the cotton-farming town of Huntersville, North Carolina.[10] One of her grandfathers was James Gettys McGready Ramsey (1796–1884). A physician, banker, railroad booster, amateur historian, and ardent Confederate in Knoxville, Tennessee, his secessionist views alienated fellow townspeople, causing him to relocate temporarily to Georgia and North Carolina.[11] After the early deaths of her parents, Mary went to live with one of her sisters in Ashville, the first of several childhood moves to live with different siblings.[12] Although Mary's own education stopped after high school, her mother had attended college in Greensboro. This family history may have contributed to her insistence that her own children get a college degree and teach school before getting married. "Sort of the worst thing you could do [in her mind] is get married," Elizabeth recalled, noting her mother's disappointment when some of the children failed to obey her edict.

Another strong belief of Mary's—which Elizabeth inherited— was never to owe anyone money: "That was important because on our street were all these . . . much more uprooted people who were constantly in debt." But when it came to her children's welfare, she was "very casual and generous," Elizabeth said. "You could always steal a quarter, if she had one, out of her pocketbook. And she'd say, 'Where's my quarter? I knew you were going to take that.' In a very kindhearted way." Years later, after meeting the rigid, chilly parents of some of her New York friends, with their secrecy about finances and need to "account for every penny," Elizabeth felt she had gotten the better deal: "When there's so little, you can ask for what you can get."

Petite and stout, after so many pregnancies, with a face Elizabeth described as "a boneless, soft prettiness, with small brown eyes,"[13] Mary spent her days in a constant whirl of cooking and cleaning, with little time or inclination for socializing. A certain friction— typical of mother-daughter issues—characterized Elizabeth's relationship with Mary. In later years, she would receive "upsetting letters" from her mother, "and when I'd rush to answer she'd say, 'Oh, I didn't mean anything to worry you!' "[14] But the primary target of Mary's wrath was her husband. The fireworks between them repeatedly launched and fizzled out, which Elizabeth accepted as the normal course of family life. With this background, she likely viewed her quarrels with Lowell—the "shrill verve / Of your invective" that he found so wounding—as simply part of married life, not a sign that anything serious was amiss.[15]

Reviewers of *Sleepless Nights* were tempted to see the woman depicted as the mother of the narrator as the author's mother. It is likely that "her weight on a stepladder washing windows, her roast and potatoes and fat yeast rolls" and the "peculiar, helpless assertiveness" that reflected "her profound acceptance of the things of life" were true to the facts. In *Sleepless Nights*, the narrator is perplexed that her mother was "so indifferent to the past. . . . as if she did not know who she was." But Mary was simply living the life mapped out for her by habit and tradition. (A "relentless finality" haunted Elizabeth's earlier autobiographical fictional character, Marian Coleman, when she considered the possibility that her life would duplicate her mother's.)[16] By removing herself from the narrative that had been handed to her by family and community, Elizabeth was obliged to reckon with the past and figure out who she really was.

Mary and her children worshipped at First Presbyterian Church, described in *Sleepless Nights* as "agreeable in winter, with its damp cloakrooms and snowy haired superintendents, its subdued hymnal and discreet baptism."[17] But if the account in this novel reflects the facts of Elizabeth's young life, she preferred her "surreptitious visits" to "itinerant evangelical tent meetings" where she was "saved" time and time again, in the company of desperate people. "Perhaps here began a prying sympathy for the victims of sloth and recurrent mistakes," she wrote about herself, "sympathy for the tendency of lives . . . to sink downward." Elizabeth would also remember "the mad preachers in front of the courthouse saying things like, 'Christ don't care about cute, remember that, folks.'"[18] The lengthy scene of an illegal cockfight in her first novel, *The Ghostly Lover* ("the thin bird threw himself up in the air like a puppet on a string"), suggests that she had also managed to sneak off to witness this nocturnal event held under a full moon.

Elizabeth was close to Eugene, her amiable, leisure-loving father, whom she described as tall and good-looking. Friends and family knew him as "Bruce," possibly the source of her curiously unfeminine middle name. Born in 1875 in Lynchburg, Virginia, Eugene, like his wife, became an orphan at a young age. He left school after the seventh grade. The next chapter of his life, before his military service in the Spanish-American War in 1898, remains a blank; perhaps he was learning his trade as a plumber. During the war, he was a member of the Colonel's Quartet, which (according to a note on the back of an old photograph) "later traveled as Dixie Quartet with black face comedy minstrals."[19] On Christmas Day 1900, Eugene married Mary in Durham, North Carolina. Although the date suggests a romantic outlook, it might have been the only day he had free. By 1903, when their first child was born, the Hardwicks had moved to Roanoke, Virginia. None of the seven children born there had birth certificates, likely because these would have been home births.[20]

In 1915 the Hardwicks relocated again, to Lexington, a move no doubt prompted by Eugene's search for work.[21] A prosperous city of 38,318 residents, with a modern sewage system and homes far more likely to have bathrooms than outhouses would have been a promising place to pursue his trade. Still, Eugene's fortunes waxed and waned over the years. By 1923 he owned a plumbing and heating shop on West Main Street, installing fixtures that included Williams-Oil-O-Matic Burner Furnaces. The ads he ran as "exclusive dealer" in the *Lexington Leader* touted this brand as the "absolutely dependable" heater, "burn[ing] cheap fuel oil without soot, smoke or odor." When Elizabeth's mother wanted one, he charged the family two or three hundred dollars over the list price, secretly keeping the extra money. Mary and the siblings who were paying the bills in those days didn't learn about this until much later. The 1927 city directory (which shows the family's new address at 264 Rand Avenue) no longer mentions Eugene's shop; he is listed simply as "plmbr." In the directories of the early 1940s, no profession appears after his name; the 1943–44 edition listed him as a Fayette County plumbing inspector.[22]

Elizabeth recalled that in his later years, he spent most of his time at home puttering or going to the fire station on Sixth Street to play pinochle and chew the fat while his older sons and some of the daughters supported the family.[23] (During the Depression, the Hardwicks also took in a roomer, a middle-aged woman, to help with finances.)[24] She remembered her father constantly smoking, beginning early in the morning as he surveyed the staked plants in the garden—tomato, dahlia, gladiolus. An avid fisherman whose preferred reading matter was *Field & Stream*, Eugene wrote doggerel about "Mr. Newlight," a type of bass. Elizabeth loved hearing him sing hymns and popular songs of the late nineteenth and early twentieth centuries in his "baritone-tenor" voice. But she would annoy him by asking to switch to the Metropolitan Opera radio broadcasts on Saturdays rather than listen to the "nightmare of baseball games and jazz, [Jack] Benny, and *Amos 'n' Andy*."[25] News was another matter. The two of them listened to the radio account of the fall of Madrid to Franco's armies on March 28, 1938, "with tears in our eyes."[26]

Eugene was also "a passionate [Franklin D.] Roosevelt person," she said. But he was not necessarily a friend of labor. In 1925, when Elizabeth was too young to understand what was at stake, members of the plumbers union, who were making one dollar an hour, petitioned for fifty cents more per day, increasing to an additional dollar a day after six months. As a member of the Master Plumbers' Association representing the employers, Eugene voted to deny the increase, which led to a walkout.[27] There was also the matter of his underhandedness. After he died of a heart attack in 1944, at age sixty-nine, two men came to the house. They asked about buying his fishing equipment and his boat, docked at a lake. His boat? Its existence was news to the family. No one had known how expensive the fishing rods were, either. Mary made four or five hundred dollars, serious money in those days, from the sale. But it was clear that Eugene had paid for these items with the money he skimmed from the heater sale. It is a testament to Elizabeth's loyalty to her father that she was amused by his deception. As someone who used personal charm to deflect criticism from his indolence and self-indulgence, his influence on Elizabeth was complex. She had seen how little financial or emotional support he was able to offer her mother, yet at the same time, he was irresistibly attractive and likeable.

In *Sleepless Nights*, Elizabeth wrote that she was reminded of her father by the "handsome" workmen who came to the house she owned in Maine, with their "sunburned faces . . . their strong fingers yellowed by nicotine"—men who awakened "a flirtatiousness" on her part. What, she wondered, "would it be like to be married to such a man, to see him coming out of the shower, to sit at dinner at six o'clock, turn off the lights at nine, embrace, make love frequently in honor of a long day of working, get up at five, visit with the relations on Sunday, never leave town." For both her parents, sleeping in their separate beds, "night is good because it leads to the day, to shoes and stockings, to coffee, to drudgery and repetition." These are people, she is telling us, who do not question their lives or obsess about the past or the future.

Hers was the kind of family in which each member went his or her own way, leaving the house early in the morning to "wander around town."[28] Thursday-night band concerts at whites-only Duncan Park, a block from home, were the only public events the Hardwicks attended as a family. (Elizabeth recalled the performances as amateurish, rife with wrong notes.) Back at the house, as the *Sleepless Nights* narrator says, the family's presence could be comforting: "the solace of opening the door and finding everyone there." On Sundays, the Hardwicks gathered for a big dinner at midday, the kind that left everyone feeling sleepy by three p.m. "You're gossiping all the time about the neighbors and other members of the family," she said later. "But anything you're a little shaky about yourself, you don't go and ask their advice." Not that they didn't offer it anyway.

The two local papers, the *Lexington Herald* and the *Lexington Leader*, published news of large and small events in the lives of the Hardwick family. At age eight, Elizabeth formed a club with two friends at Duncan Park, where she learned to play tennis. In 1925 the *Leader* ran an article headlined "Party at Duncan Park" to announce that the Girls' Club—which had just three young members, including Elizabeth—"will entertain with a party, each member bringing a friend as a guest for the afternoon."[29] Seven years later the paper announced that Elizabeth, now a sixteen-year-old, was one of the "charming young girls" who would "entertain their friends with a progressive New Year's eve dinner" at four homes, ending at five-thirty a.m. with breakfast at the home of a fifth girl.[30] Twenty-one girls and forty-one boys were invited. Elizabeth, who likely would have been unable or unwilling to offer her own modest home for the occasion, was listed as one of the "associate hostesses."

A regular visitor to the Lexington Public Library—a mile from home, at the edge of Gratz Park[31]—Elizabeth read her way through the classics, discovering Thomas Mann's *Death in Venice* because it was shelved under Mysteries. In *Sleepless Nights*, the narrator recalls the thirty-year-old man—"tall and good looking and not very truthful"—who was intrigued to see this eighteen-year-old select a book by Mann from the library shelves. Soon thereafter, on a Saturday afternoon, he had sex with this young woman in a house in "a sodden, threatening part of town." She had fallen under his spell, and now she felt disgraced. Perhaps something similar happened to Elizabeth, who also describes this man (or someone much like him) in an early short story.

Elizabeth's bookish tastes made her an anomaly in her family.

Her oldest sister, Margaret Allen, was elected secretary of her senior class, played on the all-state basketball team at local Transylvania College (now Transylvania University), and became director of the Duncan Park playground.[32] Annette—whose gymnastic cup in high school and college reign as Miss Transylvania were duly reported in the paper—became a high school teacher and married a lawyer. William, the oldest Hardwick brother, worked as a plumber and later as a foreman and superintendent at a heating company; his obituary described him as a "steamfitter, farmer, and horseman."[33] Eugene Thomas ("Joe"), whose youthful sport was the high jump, became a racehorse owner. He may have been the brother who hoped Elizabeth would be successful when she left home, so that she could "follow"—i.e., bet on—the races.[34] He was the only sibling who never married; at age thirty-eight, he petitioned to change his name to Joseph Bird, because that's how he had been known "for many years." Fred Hardwick was a teacher at Lexington Business College and an accountant at Kentucky Ignition Company before serving in the army during World War II. Elizabeth's younger brother, Robert, was a twenty-year-old college student in 1939 when he married a local woman. The ceremony was held at the Richmond home of the minister with only one reported witness, not a family member. (Mary was displeased with this early marriage.) He went to work as a carrier at the post office and was promoted to clerk.

Mary Nell and Florence Hardwick, both tennis champs, faced off for the Lexington girls' tennis title in 1925.[35] A March 1954 ad in the *Lexington Leader* announced that Mary Nell and two other young women were the "skilled beauticians" working at the Beauty Salon "(Formerly Permanent Wave Shop)," at the Hernando Building on Main Street.[36] Florence, whose education ended with high school graduation, married and moved out of state. Jane Tarleton and Frances were Elizabeth's two younger sisters. Jane, a member of the Delta Rho sorority at the University of Kentucky, worked as an assistant cashier for a druggist and as a clerk at Southeastern Greyhound Lines before marrying a local man. Frances, who also graduated from the university, became a schoolteacher; she was the last survivor of the siblings, dying in 2015 at ninety-five. Elizabeth stayed in touch with her sisters throughout their lives, spending time with them when they came to visit, speaking by phone, and sending Christmas wreaths from Maine in her later years.

* * *

In *Sleepless Nights*, the narrator calls "store clerks and waitresses . . . the heroines of my memories," the women who "light up the night on Main Street." The Hardwicks' home was a short walk from this hub of daily life, glamour, fantasy, and illicit pleasure. Elizabeth retained fond memories of the "5 & 10 cent store" (S. S. Kresge), Fayette Cigar Store (which sold newspapers and magazines), Moford's Drug Store (serving "sandwiches on soft, white Kleenexy bread"), Embry's (women's clothing), and the Wolf Wile Department Store, adjacent to Union Station. Built in 1923, this nearly thirteen-thousand-square-foot emporium featured marble floors, walnut woodwork, and two eighteen-passenger elevators.[37] The Hardwick sisters waited all year for the July sales; most of the time the girls had to make do with borrowing each other's clothes. In an era before TV, movie theaters were everyone's prime entertainment, though Black patrons were restricted to the upper balconies. Main Street boasted the resplendent Ben Ali, the palatial Strand, and the mood-lighted Kentucky, each with a Wurlitzer organ. In *Sleepless Nights*, the narrator recalls a "very nice-looking old man . . . with a kind and courtly smile," who paid the admission for young girls, bought them chocolate, and then "ran his hand up our thighs, under our dresses," in the dark. Main Street was also the location of the stately Phoenix and Lafayette hotels, the latter known as "a meeting place for many of the social and civic organizations."[38] In *Sleepless Nights*, the hotel lobbies are described as "sensual" environments "where the wastebaskets contained memorandums of assignations and the hyperbolic, misshapen prose of illicit love letters." It's not clear whether this detail came from local gossip, personal experience, or the author's imagination.

Still a small city in the 1920s and '30s,[39] Lexington contained genteel landmarks, mostly reserved for whites, as well as tawdry and violent areas. Stately Federal-style, Greek Revival, and Queen Anne homes built by civic leaders in the late eighteenth and nineteenth centuries still border the grassy rectangle of Gratz Park, along with buildings owned by Transylvania University. Less than a mile away were the Black saloons on Race Street; the "race fights" that erupted on Fifth Street, and the damaged-looking women displaying themselves in the sprawling red-light district. The Lexington police turned a blind eye to crime in African American neighborhoods. A vice commission report issued in 1915 counted twenty-eight "parlor houses"—buildings entirely used for prostitution—where liquor flowed and young men abandoned themselves to "indecent dances" with the girls to the "cheap and trashy music" of a player piano.[40] Despite civic crackdowns during World War I, when servicemen were stationed in town, the whorehouses returned after the war. The madams and house owners boasted that no city authorities bothered them. Racial violence was shockingly common, even sanctioned by "legal lynchings"—execution by hanging in racially biased cases.

Elizabeth would remember the atmosphere of such a hanging. "On the morning a Negro was to be hanged in the courthouse yard, other Negroes stayed at home from their work for fear of the way the wind might blow," she wrote.[41] A relative of hers visited a department store that day, when the Black operator was not present, and fell down the elevator shaft, "suffer[ing] ghastly damage to her body and her mind." This scrap of family history was Elizabeth's way of demonstrating that the impact of a lynching reached beyond the Black community.

In the summer, when tuxedo-clad Black musicians played at the huge dance pavilion at Joyland Park, all the dancing couples were white. Elizabeth described the scene in an essay about Billie Holiday. "The bands were also part of Southern drunkenness," she wrote, "couples drinking coke and whisky, vomiting, being unfaithful, lovelorn, frantic."[42] The music was "simply there to beat out time for the stumbling, cuddling fox-trotting of the period." Elizabeth described the amusement park in unflattering terms, with its "hot dog stands, the fetid swimming pool heavy with chlorine, the screaming roller coaster, the old rain-splintered picnic tables, the broken iron swings."

Yet summer was a longed-for season in those days. As she wrote, "The congratulation of summer is that it can make the homely and the humble if not exactly beautiful, beautifully acceptable."[43] At home, there was a great bustle to get ready for the warmer weather: "The furnace is shut down . . . windows washed, everything aired . . . doors latched back and covered by a flapping screen—with a hole in it and rusty hinges." In July, "all [was] slow and somnolent except for the supersonic hummingbird in the browning hydrangea bush at the edge of the porch." The front porch—"so unsightly and useless and awful in the winter with the gray of the splintered planks and the soggy sag of the furniture often left out to hibernate in public view"—was now the spot where you could observe passing cars, still an unusual sight. (Elizabeth's family did not own one.) Some had out-of-state license plates that instilled "a primitive pleasure . . . like stamping your palm at the sight of a white horse." The neighbors would be busy barbecuing in their backyards: "There is pleasure in all this, in the smoke, in the luscious brown of the chicken leg—on your own little plot where you fed the chickadee last winter."

* * *

As a sixth-grader at Johnson Elementary School, Elizabeth took her first trip beyond the limits of Fayette County—an excursion to the

Music Memory Contest in Louisville. Public school music classes were given a diet of "musical masterpieces" that were to be identified at the contest, including the "Anvil Chorus" from Verdi's *Il Trovatore*, Dvořák's "Humoresque," and Franz von Suppé's "Poet and Peasant Overture." The intention was to develop an appreciation for classical music in young people, to counter the growing popularity of jazz. (Elizabeth, who later realized that the "masterpieces" were really just light classics, developed an eclectic taste that embraced the folk airs sung by John Jacob Niles as well as jazz, opera, and orchestral music.)

Elizabeth was literary editor of her class newspaper at Lexington Junior High School, but the only event she recalled from this period was a field trip to the home of Annie Fellows Johnston, author of *The Little Colonel* series of children's novels. The romantic setting of the mansion struck the young writer-to-be—unaware as yet of the false picture of the Old South in Johnston's books—as absolutely enchanting. Elizabeth continued her schooling at Henry Clay High School, named in honor of the statesman, which was on Main Street in those days. Built in 1928, it boasted an acoustically sophisticated fifteen-hundred-seat auditorium with a "motion picture machine," built-in lockers, a fire gong on every floor, and other up-to-the-minute accoutrements; it was also one of the top schools in the country in terms of both academic and athletic achievement. Elizabeth believed that her highly condensed writing style began with her practice of writing exams in school: "I'd be the first one finished. . . . I didn't want to tell the teacher what he already knew but to try to get at things from an angle—nothing very grand, just a little twist. That little twist always got me an *A minus*."[44] Attempting to be seen as clever and sophisticated, she would also recall her frustration ("I . . . cried myself to sleep") when she was voted "the best-natured member of the class," an unwanted honor that she had also received in grade school.[45] Elizabeth would recall high school dances in winter: "our curls, our taffeta dresses, satin shoes with their new dye fading in the rain puddles and . . . our ferocious hope for popularity."[46] The great Fats Waller was at the piano, but his music just served as a backdrop for the teenagers' own concerns.

In 1934 Elizabeth entered the University of Kentucky. Living at home—there was no money for a dorm room—did not prevent her from taking full advantage of college life. She would look back at this period as "very happy and alive," a time of making new friends and deepening her interest in literature, history, politics, and philosophy. The opening of the student union building the following year was "a kind of break in the provincialism," she recalled, with prints of works by modern artists on the walls and a room where phonograph records could be played. The first wave of European émigré professors also made the campus a more intellectually engaged place than it had been previously.[47] Thrilled at her exposure to the books that formed the freshman English curriculum, she also read a great deal on her own. "We were intensely literary," she said later, speaking of herself and her friends.[48] They devoted their spare time to keeping up with contemporary literature, from *Partisan Review* to the novels of Stephen Spender and the poetry of W. H. Auden and T. S. Eliot.

Among her professors, she was especially fond of Francis Galloway, a scholar of eighteenth-century literature who "knew everything." She admired what she saw as his "bohemian" aspect; he was divorced at the time, which she viewed as an indication of his delightful lack of respectability. Galloway, an assistant professor, taught a survey of poetry and prose beginning with Milton.[49] Seventeenth-century literature was in vogue during these years— largely because T. S. Eliot had inspired renewed interest in the poetry of John Donne—and Galloway's class inspired Elizabeth to pursue a Ph.D. in the subject at Columbia University.

She later claimed to be the only student at the University of Kentucky who signed up for an honors program that involved purchasing and reading at least fifty books and appearing before the English department to be questioned about their content. In fact, there was at least one other entrant for the inaugural Samuel M. Wilson Library Prize in 1937—the young woman who took second place. Elizabeth won the top prize, thirty dollars.[50] Knowing what she would need to do to win, she had bought "very highbrow things," not easy to afford at a time before serious literature was published in paperback. The university files contain her thank-you note to the judge—shrewdly informing him that the prize money gave her "the opportunity to buy new books"—but not the titles that won the prize. Decades later she told an interviewer that the only ones she recalled were Proust's *Remembrance of Things Past* and Goethe's *Faust*, which she found very difficult.[51] But she insisted that the many books she read were the answer to the question, "How did I get to where I am today from Rand Avenue?"

Her sense of herself as an intellectual and an unconventional person led her to avoid all extracurricular activities at the university. Unlike her sister Jane Tarleton, Elizabeth had no interest in joining a sorority or even knowing the women who belonged to one. She would later boast, "When I graduated, there was not one thing under my name. I didn't belong to any groups, respectable groups"—by this she meant official campus organizations—"and I never have." Indeed, her yearbook entry has no information other than her name. Of course, there were times when her veneer of self-possession fell away. Standing on a receiving line for Frank McVey, the university president, who was in his late sixties, Elizabeth meant to introduce herself the usual way, but for some reason what came out of her mouth was, "President McVey, I'm Mrs. McVey." Gazing at this lovely young woman, he said, "That's good news!"[52]

What really mattered to Elizabeth were the friends she made, "the literary people and the political people," with whom she spent evenings talking and drinking whiskey. The literary people, fellow English majors, were "just interested in books and the theater." Susan Turner, who went on to earn a Ph.D. in English literature from Columbia University and teach at Vassar College, possessed the sort of cultivated mind and lively personality that appealed to Elizabeth. Another college acquaintance, Jay Hazelwood, was a tobacco-chewing Georgian with whom she struck up a friendship because of the alphabetical proximity of their last names. He later ran a bar that was a hub of Beat activity in Tangier, where he befriended the novelists Paul Bowles, Truman Capote, and William Burroughs.

The "political people" were a group of clever young Jewish men from New York who revved up the political atmosphere on campus. Elizabeth later realized that they were probably unable to get into an Ivy League college because of the quotas that existed then. Influenced by these vociferously socialist students, "I was . . . very much anti-Russia and the tyranny in Russia," she recalled. "I thought of myself as a Trotskyite and not a Stalinist. . . . Particularly, the [Moscow] Trials were a nightmare to me, when they killed off all the Old Bolsheviks."[53] Although overwhelmingly conservative, the campus had a small chapter of the American Student Union, a national left-wing organization, founded in 1935 by a merger of Communist and Socialist student organizations. The ASU would split apart four years later after the Soviet invasion of Finland, defended by the Communists but opposed by the Socialist faction.

Other student political activities promoted the unionization of America's autoworkers and combated racism and the exploitation of Southern tenant farmers. At least one major political demonstration was held in Lexington during this period, to protest a WPA administrative order that docked pay for lost time even if the worker was not at fault. In the summer of 1937, nearly one thousand people marched through the city, organized by the Kentucky Workers Alliance, a division of the Workers Alliance of America. The spirit of the times was intensely political, and Elizabeth was caught up in the fervor. "If

you were in school," she said, "unless you were dead, I guess you'd
be interested." Decades later, a local newspaper columnist who had
been a fellow classmate would remember her as a radical student
living in a world apart from his own.[54]

In the summer of 1938, after she graduated, Elizabeth took a
university course in contemporary poetry taught by the poet and
critic John Crowe Ransom. "So this small and very precise man
came in . . . this very refined, very complex man . . . whom I came
to know very well later . . . and it was utterly thrilling to me."[55] He
taught her how to read a poem, 'how you get at the sense of it."
Her paper was a Marxist interpretation of a poem by C. Day Lewis,
which he marked A-plus despite holding political beliefs diametri-
cally opposed to hers. The rest of the class was composed of high
school English teachers from small towns who were seeking education credits. "I have a memory of sitting there and feeling smug . . .
the terrible smugness of youth," she said later, believing that she was
the only one in the room who knew who Ransom was and what he
was talking about. Yet her smugness was really a form of aspiration,
Elizabeth's effort to become the cultured, sophisticated person she
wanted to be.

Little is known about Elizabeth's romantic life during these
years, other than her decision to break up with a boyfriend when
she learned that his father was a coal mine owner. ("I felt they were
murderers. He didn't like me much either.")[56] Another boyfriend may
have been the model for the devoted swain in one of Elizabeth's
early short stories, "Yes and No." Although the narrator describes
him as having a "generous, warm nature," she constantly criticizes
him, "from his soul to his clothes." She thinks of him as her "sweetheart," yet she never wants to see him when he shows up. Although
he is a political science faculty member at the university, "his views
seemed to me flat and impersonal." What keeps her in his thrall is
his unshakable affection for *her*, obliging her to duck his constant

proposals of marriage while keeping him on a string. She confesses that his green Chevrolet convertible—in which they drive to taverns where she drinks too much and baits him mercilessly—is one of his major attractions. The kicker, at the end of this short tale, is that she acknowledges "what pleasure we have all received from someone we imagined 'not quite good enough' for us."

* * *

In the 1938 University of Kentucky yearbook, Elizabeth's photo reveals a strikingly beautiful woman with a heart-shaped face, classic features, and a simple hairdo swept off her forehead and flipped up at the ends. Her serene expression suggests a certain self-possession—a woman who had come to know what set her apart from others and what she wanted from life.

After earning a master's degree in English the following year,

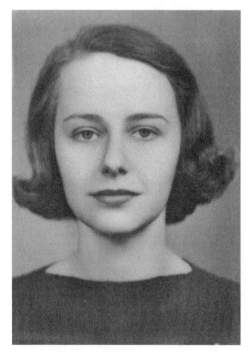

University of Kentucky yearbook photo, 1938.

she won a fellowship to Louisiana State University. It was the home of *The Southern Review*, whose pages contained work by Ransom, Eudora Welty, Robert Penn Warren, Allen Tate, Randall Jarrell, Wallace Stevens, Muriel Rukeyser, W. H. Auden, Delmore Schwartz, Philip Rahv, Sidney Hook, and other significant writers of fiction, poetry, and criticism. Some would become good friends of hers a few years later. But during that summer, the LSU president was charged with embezzling a half-million dollars, and "the whole place sort of collapsed."[57]

Elizabeth said later that she took this as her cue to leave the South for New York City, like "some provincial [character] in Balzac, yearning for Paris."[58] This decision was, she told an interviewer, "a critical, defining moment" that led her not to become a Southern writer: "Being a Southern writer is a decision, not a fate."[59]

CHAPTER 2

Discovering New York

(1939–1947)

In September 1939, Elizabeth took a Greyhound bus to New York to pursue a doctorate in seventeenth-century English literature at Columbia University. A few years earlier she had visited the city with two high school friends, staying at the Hotel Taft in Times Square. The women's accents had piqued the curiosity of people, who asked where they were from.[1] This time Elizabeth hoped to save money by staying with her older sister Margaret. The first in the family to venture far from home, she lived on Staten Island with her husband, a Lexington man who directed the physical education program at a high school in that borough. But after about a month of enduring the long and exhausting commute by ferry and subway to the campus on 114th Street, Elizabeth realized that she had to live in the city. Rooming houses near the university ("those bricky towers in the smoky air" with "the marigold odor of multiple occupancy. . . the greasy couches and scarred table tops")[2] were the only places she could afford. To pay the bills, she worked part time at the National Youth Administration, a New Deal agency, and in the university registrar's office, jobs she hated.

Elizabeth was attracted by the idea of graduate school. As she said later, "I am one of those people who feels going to school beats the rest of your life, at least it beats working."[3] But her courses at Columbia were a disappointment. She was not inspired by F. A. Patterson, editor of *The Works of John Milton*, or by most of his colleagues on the English faculty. The university was useful to her mostly as a place to meet interesting people, including Morton White, a young professor of philosophy; Richard Volney Chase, later a distinguished critic; and Robert Snyder, who became a documentary filmmaker.[4] Home for the summer of 1940, she gave a talk to a luncheon meeting of the Lexington Altrusa Club, at which her mother was a guest. Elizabeth's topic was Richard Wright's novel *Native Son*, which she discussed in terms of its "psychological significance and . . . the controversies aroused among some reviewers."[5] She was already edging away from the seventeenth century to contemplate the literary world of her own time.

Back at Columbia for her second year, Elizabeth received a resident scholarship that paid for her room and board.[6] Living in a dormitory was a new experience. Her letter to her friend Sally Alexander was filled with pointed remarks about the women in Johnson Hall and news about everything except her studies.[7] At a concert by the University Choir, "the music was charming; the unspiked wassail was terrible." Elizabeth was practicing "a neat little pas de deux" with another woman, in case a man might ask her to a dance. She did have a boyfriend, "Jerry with the dark black hair," who was "as nice as ever," and she was "still beautiful in the morning"—a reference to their sexual intimacy. For six years, she would have an on-and-off relationship with Jerry Felder, a medical student.[8] ("He has that merry, optimistic psychology of the chronically ill.")[9] After studying at New York University Medical School, he interned at several hospitals in the city. There must have been a strong physical or emotional attraction to keep the affair going so long—he told her later that the relationship was the best thing that ever happened to him—but he lacked the intellectual interests that were so important to Elizabeth.

She was attempting to teach herself German, traditionally the primary language of scholarship, but soon realized she lacked sufficient ambition to earn a Ph.D. She did not want to write "some dull little textual thing." Learning was enjoyable, but she wasn't really intent on becoming a scholar. Another consideration was that women were not getting college teaching jobs in New York in those days, and she was determined to stay in the city. After skipping the required oral examinations ("I just couldn't face it," she said later), Elizabeth dropped out of the program. From then on, she planned to devote her time to writing. But she felt like a fraud and found it difficult to explain to her family that she had had "all that education" but was not going to be a university professor. "They said, 'When are you getting a teaching job?' And I said, 'Leave me alone.'"[10] The stress of trying to pursue a writing career made her "defensive, nerve-wrung and spiteful."[11]

To support herself, she worked for a publishing company that did not require her to show up at the office. Elizabeth was hired to condense "very bad" detective novels to about 128 pages, suitable for pulp fiction paperbacks. Without even bothering to read the books, she would take about two hours to edit each one to the desired length. Decades later, she claimed she had "always hated mystery stories."[12] Another job during these years was teaching English to young women from the South at an understaffed "academy" on Riverside Drive. "I couldn't stand it," she said, "and they couldn't stand me. . . . I wasn't sentimental enough." Elizabeth described the students as "kind of feeble minded from well to do families." She lasted just half a term. At one point during this period, she wrote to Sally about another part-time office job she hated that was supposed to be over, though she wasn't actually sure.[13]

Now living in a single room, she was "on the threshold of starvation," with money for just one month's rent. (In *Sleepless Nights*, the narrator mentions having to make a choice among "the woeful macaroni . . . bready meatloaf . . . drying sandwiches" at the Automat, with its "deformed diners and their revolting habits.")[14] Dinner that night was an egg and mushroom soup. Her poverty and loneliness made her look forward to dining with her boyfriend's parents ("the food is an important item") and spending time in a home redolent with the warmth of family life. "I suppose I don't like to face the reality of myself," she mused to a friend, "which is that I am solely dependent on my own ability to support myself." She felt "estranged" from her own family now, unable to look to them "for consolation" if she could not make her own way. They were becoming a burden "not in the physical but in the mental sense," and this was "destroying" her. Elizabeth failed to describe the problem more fully, but her hints in this letter and other evidence suggest that financial support from one of her brothers was making her feel guilty for not being able to take care of herself. Adding to her concerns, an unidentified full-time job (this might have been the teaching position) had led to a period of bad health. Elizabeth wrote that she was feeling "anchorless and . . . a little bit afraid," concerned that she had "much less physical endurance than I had imagined—and I never thought I had much."

She would allude to this period of her life in a semiautobiographical short story. "The Temptations of Dr. Hoffmann." It opens with a lonely young woman living in a building where the other residents were women of a certain age, "mostly quite mad." (In *Sleepless Nights*, Elizabeth described the older female occupants of rooming houses as reminiscing about the houses in which they grew up, secretive about their jobs, and filling their wastepaper baskets with "cracker boxes, candy wrappers, hot-dog cartons.")[15] An acquaintance from Kentucky invites the young woman to meet Dr. Hoffmann, a German theologian devoted to radical causes. She becomes friendly with Hoffmann and his wife, an atheist like herself, who is in poor health.

The couple's devout teenaged daughter reminds the woman of her own efforts at piety at age twelve, giving up dancing and movies. The daughter reveals that Hoffmann's mother faked a heart attack to take him away from his wife's bedside when the daughter was born. After Hoffmann's wife leaves for Arizona to recuperate, the daughter continues to attack her father, accusing his mother of being a Nazi. Hoffmann is shaken. The young woman, who had wondered about the strength of his faith, now thinks his mother-dominated life caused him "to seek his fulfillment in a Heavenly Father." The strangeness of this rather clumsy story—so dominated by the narrator's fascination with the mysterious figure of Hoffmann—is that for all its grandiose notions, it is ultimately about a lonely person in a metropolis who attaches herself to a substitute family and becomes enmeshed in the dramas of their lives.

* * *

Elizabeth went home during the summers to work on short stories set in Lexington and two early novels; the advantage of free room and board undercut by her emotional stress. "I was frightened of getting trapped there," she recalled. "I was always maneouvering to come back."[16] (In those years, it was easy to find another room or apartment in New York to replace the one given up for the journey home.) She realized that her first novel was not worthy of being published. But by working on it, as she said later, "you get rid of a lot of childish things and you learn a good deal about how to write." Elizabeth was too insecure about her hoped-for career to announce it to her family. "I have dreams of stories in mind if I can ever get around to doing them," she confided to her friend Sally.[17] "Right now"—after typing the first draft of her novel—" I never want to see a typewriter again." In this undated letter, Elizabeth wrote that she planned to return to New York in early September, staying with Margaret for a while and with friends. ("If I don't get to New York, Mama is petitioning to have me put in the Asylum for the Crazy and Mad," she joked.) Sally was evidently planning to stay in Manhattan, too, and Elizabeth hoped to find an apartment in a residence club, which would allow each of them to have a room as well as kitchen privileges. One problem, besides their up-in-the-air plans, was that she had "exactly $1.98." Maybe, she added wistfully, one dollar could serve as a deposit.

In another letter written from home, Elizabeth informed Sally that she was "sleeping like a fool. . . . Sometimes I wake up in the middle of the night and say: Watch it Hardwick, you don't want to sleep your life away."[18] Throughout her life, Elizabeth seemed to tire fairly easily; she would often write to friends about taking pleasure in being able to get to sleep early. This summer she arose at seven o'clock in the morning to start writing. (Although Daylight Savings had begun a month earlier in Lexington, her mother stubbornly chose not to put the clocks ahead. "What are you hurrying for?" she asked, to Elizabeth's irritation.) Turning to the topic of suitors, Elizabeth reported that the phone was not ringing, which "isn't the complete joy I expected." If the date drought kept up, she would be calling her New York boyfriend long-distance "just to talk"—which would have been an expensive luxury in those days. "Walking down to the drug store alone to drink my evening coke" and playing pin-ball "with the masses," she missed Manhattan "terribly."

Elizabeth also spent Christmas back home during these years. Wearing the fur coat she had purchased at a thrift shop, she would travel to Lexington on the George Washington passenger train of the Chesapeake & Ohio Railway.[19] It rumbled through West Virginia's mining country (hauling coal was C&O's prime source of income) and small-town Kentucky: Morehead, Owingsville, Mount Sterling, Ledges, Winchester, Pine Grove, Combs Ferry. Decades later, she described "a stinging, green stillness along the way, the hills rising up on either side to cradle the train as it slipped through the valleys."[20] In an undated letter to Sally about one of these Christmas visits, she wrote, "There aren't words to describe the Marx brothers comedy that's going on here."[21] While the woman she refers to is never named, it is clear that this is her mother. Mary had wanted bedroom slippers, but Elizabeth decided to buy something much nicer: "I thought the sense of guilt would be touched by such an act from one so poor." She asked her mother, "Do you think $16.95 is too much for me to pay for your present?" Meant as a joke— Elizabeth hadn't actually bought anything yet—this remark was taken seriously. Her mother felt she had to reciprocate, bringing home a bounty of pigs' feet, sausage, figs, Limburger cheese, and other unwanted food. Despite Elizabeth's own need for new clothes, she felt called upon to up the ante, so she bought her mother a nine-dollar dress. "I had to do it," she wrote. "I had to win."

Elizabeth in her fur-trimmed outfit, 1945.

In Elizabeth's short story "Evenings at Home," the push-pull of the narrator's feelings captures her (and the author's) struggle to become independent from her family and its expectations. She is startled that her first visit home from New York is not the horror she imagined; her mother "carries no whips," and the family "accuse me of no crimes, made no demands upon me."[22] The woman had been involved with a local man years earlier, heedless of her family's efforts to end the romance. Despite his apathy and mediocrity—in school, in sports—she slept with him (an event only fleetingly alluded to) and pledged her love. Thank goodness she finally spurned him. To her relief, old friends see her only as a former "radical," not as this man's sometime lover. But now he is waiting for her on the steps of the family home. Why hasn't her mother tipped her off to his presence in the neighborhood? Unable to confront her mother directly, she picks a silly quarrel with her. (" 'If there is something wrong with me it's your fault,' I said triumphantly. 'Mine!' she called back. 'What madness!' ") To her mother's bewilderment, the woman decides that she must leave home the next day. Launching into one more quarrel makes her feel better. Then, on a visit to the family's cemetery plot, graced by flowering dogwood, her mother points to the space reserved for the young woman. The last line of the story reinforces the narrator's conflicted emotions about her family, attesting to the comfort of "roots."

When Elizabeth's mother visited her in New York, they would go to the uptown branch of Café Society, a nightclub that featured Black musicians and (unusually, in those days) welcomed patrons of both races, as well as to Broadway hits like *Oklahoma!* and *Tobacco Road.* Another standby of these visits was dinner at the Latin Quarter, "a large Hungarian sort of place with a large menu featuring the splendid oxymoron, baked Alaska, and a long, florid floor show."[23] According to one New York friend, Elizabeth would tell her city acquaintances that they "didn't want to know" the people from back home who came to see her.[24] It was obviously important to the urban persona she was creating to keep the two parts of her life separate.

* * *

In the spring of 1943, Elizabeth moved to the shabby Hotel Schuyler, at 57 West 45th Street, where the residents—unlike the forlorn souls she had known in other furnished rooms—were "restless, unreliable, changeable, disloyal. . . . They drank, they fought, they fornicated; they ran up bills, they lied; they had furtive, mild debaucheries."[25] The air-conditioned hotel advertised itself as "A Home Away from Home. Off Fifth Avenue and Radio City," offering rooms, suites, and apartments "with or without kitchens or kitchenettes."[26] Elizabeth's room had a kitchen; she shared the bath with Greer Johnson, the occupant of the apartment's other room. He was—as she described him decades later—"a red-cheeked, homosexual young man from Kentucky" whom she had known all her life.[27] He had many traits that irritated her, including his compulsive neatness and a habit of brushing his teeth right after dinner. But as a publicist for Billie Holiday, he opened up a new world to Elizabeth. She accompanied him on nocturnal visits to the "blaring shops" that sold old jazz records and to the jazz clubs on 52nd Street, where the great musicians of the day performed.

Elizabeth's essay on Holiday, written many years later, evokes the quiet nights early in the week during wartime ("wandering soldiers, drunk and worried, musicians, couples, hideously looking into each other's eyes, as if they were safe") when the singer's presence transformed the bleak setting with "her talents and the brilliance of her mind."[28] An invitation to join her for chili offered a peek into a life of pain and addiction. In her hotel room in Harlem, Holiday's presence was reduced to her voice on a record that was playing and "groans and coughs from the bedroom." During her sole visit to Elizabeth and Johnson's apartment, "we sat there in the neat

52nd Street jazz club, Christmas 1945. From left: unidentified man, Madeline Capp, Greer Johnson, Mel Powell, Elizabeth, Robert Snyder.

squalor and there was nothing to do and nothing to say and she did not wish to eat."

After Johnson moved out, a call girl from Tennessee moved in with her pimp. As Elizabeth wrote later, Miss Chadwick was "rather pretty in a bow-legged, fair-skinned, blue-eyed Southern way."[29] One night while Chadwick was out, probably servicing a client, the pimp accosted Elizabeth in the hallway leading to her room. "He smiled at me in his empty, handsome, dead way. . . . He pressed me against the wall and, eyes rolling, rubbed off on my coat." Disgusted, she moved out the next day, ending nearly six years of exposure to a sordid world of "unreal hopes and activities." She imagined that the middle-aged woman living across the hall—a pianist in a bar who had once borrowed fifty dollars ("like five hundred then") and called Elizabeth a "dirty cunt" when she dared ask for repayment—was saying "good riddance."

* * *

Elizabeth had submitted *The Dyer's Hand*, a novel written during this period, to Knopf. (The title comes from Shakespeare's Sonnet 101, which blames Fortune for actions that brought him disgrace, because he has to work for a living: "my nature is subdued / To what it works in, like the dyer's hand.")[30] Nothing is known about this manuscript other than her impatience to learn what the publisher thought of it and the rejection letter she received in April 1943.[31] The first positive sign for her writing career occurred the following spring, when she received a contract from Harcourt, Brace "on the strength of the hundred or so pages I've done [on *The Ghostly Lover*] and they are advancing me enough money to go home for the summer and complete it."[32] This was especially good news, because the Rosenwald Fellowship she had applied for didn't come through, "which almost caused a breakdown."[33] More devastating was her father's fatal heart attack on May 29; by the time the fire department's first aid squad arrived at the house, he had died. Still, she was able to finish the book.[34]

In the summer of 1944, Elizabeth responded to a letter from Grant C. Knight, a literature professor at the University of Kentucky whom she had not particularly liked, telling him that New York was "fine" now that she was no longer working at a full-time job. ("Not that I can afford to be without gainful employment—I merely can afford the nerve to be without a settled income.") She wondered what the university was like during the war, with so few male students: "Literature classes have always been dominated by girls with well-guarded sentiments and now their tyranny must be complete."[35] Two years later Knight wrote to suggest that she write a novel about a Kentucky mining town. She replied that she would consider this idea, but "in many ways one can't choose a fictional idea; it chooses you rather."[36]

When Elizabeth went home for Christmas this year, she was thrilled to receive a letter from *New Mexico Quarterly* accepting her short story "The People on the Roller Coaster." (It would be reprinted in *O. Henry Memorial Award Prize Stories of 1945*.)[37] The story begins with the scene of a fortune-teller couple setting up shop near a Southern amusement park with a roller coaster (a stand-in for Joyland). The dark-skinned woman is married to an albino Black man. A genteel middle-aged white woman who lives nearby "had always liked Negroes" but is frightened that her "colored girl" (her servant) has suddenly shown signs of rebellion. When the woman asks the fortune-tellers why this is happening, the husband keeps asking what the servant has done, frightening the woman, whose fear redoubles when she sees that the servant has left. This haunting evocation of race relations is somewhat in the Flannery O'Connor mold but with the sort of imaginative swerve that only Elizabeth could provide. In the evenings, when the roller coaster is moving, the fortune-tellers' small daughter imagines that she can make the riders, with their blurred faces, "a new race, something neither alive nor dead."

The Yale Review published another of her short stories, "Saint Ursula and Her Eleven Thousand Virgins," in its 1945 issue. An elderly academic who once dabbled in left-wing politics but was never one of the "ravaged, fanatical fellows" is now comfortably retired in Florida. He remembers his guilt at the sight of human suffering as he walks alongside a funeral procession in a poor Black neighborhood. When his daughter dismisses a story he tells his grandson about Saint Ursula's eleven thousand virgin martyrs—she says some of them were surely "just masquerading"—he sees himself as "only a masquerader, a not-quite-pure lover of purity who, nevertheless, joined in the march." And yet "that too was a privilege, he thought. Perhaps even better than being an accredited member." Despite Elizabeth's convincing portrayal of this character's conflicted moral superiority, the story suffers from a heavy-handed quality.

A third early story, "The Golden Stallion," appeared in *The Sewanee Review* in 1946. The stallion of the title is mounted on a weathervane on top of the courthouse in a Southern city (a feature Elizabeth borrowed from Lexington). Mentioning it is the conversational gambit of a shy, wealthy, "strikingly handsome" woman to attract the attention of a serviceman. She is in a loveless marriage to a doctor serving in the army. When the serviceman comes to see her, she finds him "guarded, feeble, second rate," with "savage little eyes." She learns that he is mysteriously troubled and that what he wants but doesn't think possible is to fall in love. On subsequent visits, she is aware of "a kind of corrosion they both had to undergo." One day he arrives at her house just before dawn, bleeding from a fight and claiming that he wanted his attackers to hurt him. By now, for reasons that are never clear—perhaps, as he suggests, because she just needs to care for someone—she is in love with him. The reader has begun to suspect that he is actually gay, but this fraught topic is never even hinted at. She tells him she could support him so that they could live together after the war. He curses her, telling her she could meet "lots of golden stallions." Still believing he will wait for her, "she walked forward to meet him in the darkness." Once again, Elizabeth has written a character study, in this instance, of two lost souls struggling to connect. It could almost be a synopsis of a (nonexistent) play by Tennessee Williams. Yet the theater reviews Elizabeth wrote later would strongly condemn his focus on his characters' delusions and extreme emotional states.

* * *

Elizabeth dedicated her novel *The Ghostly Lover* to John Woodburn, her Harcourt, Brace editor. Like her author, protagonist Marian Coleman is from Kentucky. (As Elizabeth said later, "Everything is you when you have a girl about your age; it's something that comes out of you. But her life and her family are not mine.")[38] Marian is haunted by memories of her feckless parents, who left her and her hand-some, indolent brother, Albert, with her grandmother, occasionally paying unsatisfactory visits. Marian has a relationship with Bruce, a divorced man (Elizabeth mischievously gave him her father's nick-name)[39] and is supported by him when she attends college in New York. As Elizabeth wrote in the preface to the 1985 edition, with a first novel, "one is saying to the family and old acquaintances: Well, I guess I haven't been thinking what you might imagine about these streets and faces. . . . If no personal offense is given, there is always the offense of subject matter."[40] Marian shares Elizabeth's belief as a young woman that marriage meant being taken care of. She had told a suitor from Lexington that if the novel was not published, she would marry him, "a wild offer brought on by anxiety" that she felt compelled to gainsay when she returned to New York.

The novel received a mixed reception. One reviewer found the introspective aspect and style of the novel "somewhat removed from reality."[41] A writer at Elizabeth's hometown paper grappled earnestly with the "troubled and mystifying" plot, focusing on the woman's "excruciating longing for emotional security."[42] Aware of the prob-lems involved in writing a first novel, the sympathetic *Partisan Review* critic noted that Elizabeth had only "moderate" success in balancing her own "obsessive early experience" with the require-ments of a novel, but he praised her "skill at characterization."[43] In *The New York Times,* Gertrude Buckman (soon to be a short-term lover of Robert Lowell) singled out the "tremulous richness of tex-ture" of the writing and the "forthright and delicate" perception guiding Elizabeth's portraits of the characters.[44] On the debit side was the book's structural weakness, the vagueness of the settings (New York seems a lot like the unnamed Southern city), and the sense that the characters are "strangely suspended in air." But Buck-man astutely identified the quality that would be a hallmark of Eliz-abeth's best fiction: her ability to recognize "our evasions, the hints and revelations we give one another . . . the strange, fearful sadness that surrounds and informs us."

Professor Knight, who maintained voluminous scrapbooks that display both his vanity and his prickly personality, accused Elizabeth of not believing in the subject of her novel. She responded that "honest writing is a long and tedious process in which the writer is utterly alone." While admitting to having "not very great" confidence and conceding that certain aspects of the book did not satisfy her own standards, she informed him that he had misunderstood the character of the grandmother. Rather than being a dominating figure, "the main spring of her character is listlessness of a profound sort. . . . She is almost a moron." Although Elizabeth was in Lexington at the time, she told Knight—who had suggested a visit—that she couldn't see him because of her "many dark inhibitions about returning to places."[45]

Elizabeth later told an interviewer that Marian was partly based on the life of a young woman, a good friend of hers, who lived in a large, attractive house in Lexington. In the early 1970s, this woman happened to be in New York. When they got together, Elizabeth asked what had happened to her mother. "She said, 'What do you think?' And I said, 'I haven't any idea.' And she said, 'My father died and one year my mother committed suicide. Just as you might have thought.'"[46] The interviewer suggested that Marion's frustrations must have reflected Elizabeth's. "Oh certainly," she responded. "Of course that's me." But Albert, Marian's brother, was "totally made up."

Philip Rahv, co-founder and editor of *Partisan Review*, read the novel and sent her a letter praising it ("exceedingly well written and beautifully felt").[47] She had also sent him a short story, which he called "a fine piece of work"; it would be published in the spring 1945 issue. "Perhaps we could get together for lunch someday soon," he added. "We like to meet our new contributors and talk with them." Was she free on Saturday, February 17, for a meeting at the

PR office? Of course she was. Elizabeth had discovered the magazine during her years in Lexington and was an ardent fan. According to its editors, *Partisan Review*'s ideal reader was "receptive to new work in fiction, poetry, and art . . . aware of the major tendencies in contemporary criticism . . . concerned with the structure and fate of modern society," and curious about psychoanalysis "and the other humanistic sciences."[48]

Years later Elizabeth joked to an interviewer that her Southern background made the staff dubious about her "mental qualifications." Rahv was "quite astonished that I was very political and critical." But she felt comfortable with the literary bent of New York intellectual life and soon became a regular contributor of book reviews.[49] Rahv "was one of the main movers of the Henry James Revival," she said. "James, Kafka and Dostoievsky were the [novelists] he liked." Elizabeth had what she later described as "a brief encounter" with Rahv; she would not dignify it with the word "affair."[50] He was then married to Nathalie Swan, an architect and Vassar graduate from a wealthy family. Born in Ukraine as Fevel Greenberg and raised in Palestine, Rahv came to the United States as a young teenager. Unlike most of his peers, this imposing, bearlike man with "a very strange sort of gruff, swallowed way of speaking" was an autodidact who had never attended college. A former Marxist who renounced Communism at the time of the Moscow Purge Trials in 1937, he remained strongly committed to the anti-Stalinist left. His co-editor, William Phillips, was a graduate of City College with a master's degree in English literature from Columbia University. Phillips's political journey mirrored Rahv's.

Partisan Review was founded in 1937 by Fred Dupee, literary editor of *The New Masses*, and a group of writers that included Rahv, Phillips, Dwight Macdonald (an associate editor at *Fortune*), and Mary McCarthy.[51] An abstract painter, George L. K. Morris—a friend of Dupee's and Macdonald's, and a fellow Yalie—was also part of the group; they hoped to tap him for money. Dupee had become frustrated with the bureaucracy and Communist Party line of *The New Masses*. Although each of the founders had a different idea of what was needed, they managed to agree on editorial independence from conservative thought as well as from the shibboleths of both Stalinists and Trotskyites, the dominant left-wing political groups. Yet while the Marxist-influenced political dogmatism of the 1930s had mellowed by the early '40s, the journal still reflected a strong link between the writing of fiction and the exposure of sociopolitical realities.

Other members of the *PR* inner circle in the 1940s were Lionel Trilling, Sidney Hook, Irving Howe, Meyer Schapiro, and Delmore Schwartz. With the exception of Macdonald, Dupee, and McCarthy, the *PR* coterie was Jewish. In an often-quoted remark, Elizabeth once said that she had wanted to be "a Jewish intellectual," in the sense of being skeptical of received ideas and values—the distinguishing trait of this disputatious group. Elizabeth admired their feisty exchanges and their commitment to the political causes they believed in. (Two decades later Macdonald's showboating style can be heard in a recording of a symposium on literary criticism in which he constantly interrupts the other panelists, including Elizabeth, and keeps insisting on his point of view.)[52]

Phillips later described Elizabeth as "one of our most cutting minds," the person who made the group "aware of our faults as well as our virtues."[53] The faults were "super-rationalism, a competitiveness, an intellectual hardness, and an indifference to loyalty that was humanly destructive." He believed that "the oral culture of the South" accounted for the ease with which Elizabeth fit into the "verbal, cosmopolitan culture of New York." She was "a marvelous talker," he wrote, who was usually "charming even when most devastating or malicious."

Much the same could be said about Mary McCarthy. She had

burst onto the scene after a childhood of upheavals—orphaned at age six, years of abusive treatment from relatives in Minneapolis, rescue by wealthy and doting maternal grandparents in Seattle—and an illustrious career at Vassar College. One week after graduation, she married a young aspiring playwright whom she treated worshipfully while writing witty theater reviews for *The Nation* that raised her profile far above his faltering career. Divorced in 1936, she lived briefly with Rahv. Now she was the theater editor for *Partisan Review*. Her autobiographical short story "The Man in the Brooks Brothers Shirt," published in *PR* in 1941, was a succès de scandale, with its frank depiction of casual sex from a woman's point of view. Elizabeth met her in the mid-1940s at Rahv's apartment. Being a guest at one of these *PR* social events involved "enter[ing] a ring of bullies, each one bullying the other"[54] while imbibing "awful" blended whiskey.[55] At first, the two women paid no attention to each other. But after Mary became involved with the amiable Bowden Broadwater, whom she married in 1946, the three of them got together socially. That year Elizabeth came to visit them in the upstate New York village of Red Hook. "All couples like unmarried friends," she remarked.[56]

During the 1940s, a few more women became part of the inner circle at *PR*, notably Hannah Arendt. A petite, chain-smoking German Jew, Arendt was thirty-six in 1941 when she immigrated to New York. She lived with her husband and mother in a shabby rooming house, stretching a seventy-five-dollar monthly stipend from a Zionist organization to pay for rent and food cooked in a communal kitchen. Arendt soon began to publish essays in English, with halting grammar smoothed out by editors, on such crisis-laden topics as the condition of stateless refugees and on German Existentialism, a topic new to American readers. Arendt was a brilliant student of philosophy who had had a romantic and intellectual affair with her professor, Martin Heidegger, a leading philosopher, later a member of the Nazi Party. As her biographer wrote, at cocktail parties and other

events, she was soon "dazzl[ing] the tight-knit group of Jewish intellectuals, most notably the men, with her brains."[57] After an initial
misstep by Mary McCarthy—whose shockingly breezy joke about
Hitler at one of Rahv's parties alienated Arendt—the two women
became the closest of friends.

Arendt's self-assured persona rubbed some people the wrong
way, including Lionel Trilling's wife, Diana, who was eleven years
older than Elizabeth. A Radcliffe graduate from a troubled family, she
had switched her career goal from art historian to opera singer while
battling depression after a sexual assault by a friend of her father's.
She met Lionel when they were both twenty-two years old; they married two years later. Diana made valiant attempts to be judged the
equal of the men, but she was hobbled by self-doubt rooted in a
fear of success instilled by her mother and by her father's warnings
against self-display. Even her professional retention of her husband's
last name was a liability. Diana felt out of place at *Partisan Review*
gatherings; before she started publishing reviews in *The Nation*, she
was merely the "wife of," snubbed by both Hannah and Mary and
never on a secure footing with Elizabeth—who later "look[ed] back
with a good deal of shame on how I never addressed a word to those
wives."[58] As an outsider, Diana's only recourse was to present herself
in an imperious manner, backed by her rigidly logical mindset.

In her patronizing review of *The Ghostly Lover*, Diana began by
dismissing it as "lacking drama or even a coherent story direction"
and offering mainly "dull reading." Then, after knocking Elizabeth
down, she patted her on the head, suggesting that certain pages in
the novel demonstrated "the quite fierce creativeness of which Miss
Hardwick is capable . . . a rare imaginative intensity."[59] Diana cred-
ited certain scenes in the novel that take place in the South—a region
with which she was personally unfamiliar—as more accomplished
than Eudora Welty "at her beguiling best" and "close to the slashing
courage of D. H. Lawrence." But in her view, the New York section

was "merely accurate, sensitive social reporting." Her most valuable remark was that Elizabeth "must use her powers of observation in the service of her powers of imagination." Toward the end of her life, Diana's aggrieved tone in a letter to Elizabeth revealed the bitterness of someone who never felt she had been taken seriously. In her autobiography, she wrote, "my marriage may have detracted from my literary recognition," because "people will celebrate one member of a household but not two."[60] That would have been news to Elizabeth.

During these years Elizabeth had a string of lovers in New York—two affairs resulted in abortions, one of which she alluded to in *Sleepless Nights*[61]—but none were serious enough for her to contemplate marriage, and some of the men were already married. (The "Alex" of the novel is likely a composite portrait.) An affair was a risky thing for a woman in those days; in addition to the fear of pregnancy, having a male guest in her apartment at night could result in her being thrown out. Elizabeth once recalled how, "if a man left your place at three in the morning you felt quite nervous in case anyone had noticed."[62] Intriguingly, the *Sleepless Nights* narrator says, "In those years I did not care to enjoy sex, only to have it."[63]

One of Elizabeth's sometime lovers was Allen Tate, who had divorced novelist Caroline Gordon in 1945, remarrying her the following year. He wrote to Elizabeth in the autumn of 1947, entrusting her with a poem he wrote, his first in four years, and asking her not to mention it to anyone. He hoped to see her the following weekend, promising to call, and closed with "Love."[64] Elizabeth's mother met Tate during his one visit to Lexington; her blunt verdict was that he was too old for her daughter—and his head was too big. Elizabeth, who later claimed that the affair was not particularly intense, described him as "*excessively* convivial" and "disreputable in a funny kind of gentlemanly way."[65]

* * *

Debuting in the spring 1945 issue of *Partisan Review* as both short story writer and reviewer, Elizabeth was in the company of such major authors as Jean-Paul Sartre, Stephen Spender, Hannah Arendt, George Orwell, Delmore Schwartz, Lawrence Durrell, Arthur Koestler, Robert Frost, Thomas Merton, and Herbert Read, and rising fellow Southern writers Randall Jarrell, Allen Tate, and Peter Taylor. In her short story "The Mysteries of Eleusis," she drew on her memories of life in a poor neighborhood.[66] A twenty-one-year-old woman—we eventually learn that she is a waitress in New York who is about to be married to a man she hardly knows—dreams that she is revisiting the family home from which she has fled. Much of the story is taken up with the setting and characters of the dream: the rotting porch, the hideous wallpaper, the undefinable smell in the kitchen, the stern older sister, the athletic younger one, the secretive brother, the mother's pink eyes ("from sewing and crying"). Awake, the woman watches people in a factory through her window, "struck by the dreadful and yet appealing calm of drudgery." In pursuit of "freedom," she has had "many male heads beside hers on a limp, greyish pillow." Implausibly, she nearly forgot that this was the day of her wedding. Despite her impulse to back out, "she was powerless to divert the direction of her life." This statement reflects the politically conscious underpinning of the story: an uneducated working-class woman unable to break out of the cycle of poverty. Essentially a character study, what lifts it out of mere agitprop is the vividness of the descriptions and Elizabeth's awareness of how a move from the family home to an ugly furnished room could seem like progress: "Perhaps it was the privacy, if nothing else."

Elizabeth's reviews in this issue were of Richard Wright's memoir *Black Boy* and two novels featuring "the pampered, fast living, rebellious girl," a trope with "inexhaustible appeal to both writers and readers."[67] Elizabeth's arresting first sentence—"To be a Negro in America is a full-time job"—leads to a thoughtful account of the difficulties involved in attempting to be "an individual artist" as well as a spokesman for one's race. She celebrates Wright's success in presenting an African American character in *Native Son* who is neither "lovable" nor "suffering" and salutes the novel's "courageous and stubborn kind of integrity." Taking on two female characters in recent fiction, Elizabeth wrote about Hopestill Mather in Jean Stafford's novel *Boston Adventure* and Sue Murdock in Robert Penn Warren's *At Heaven's Gate*. Elizabeth has some fun with the symbolic qualities of the characters' passionate relationships with horses as well as with the women's significant alcohol consumption and their need to become involved with men of a lesser social position. Unable to conform to society's requirements, these cynical young women are obliged—by the unwritten rules of the genre—to die, either by their own hand or by another's. (Mather, secretly pregnant by her fiancé and trying to induce a miscarriage, gets herself thrown from a horse; Murdock, a financier's daughter, is strangled by her bohemian lover.)

Stafford's miserable childhood in Boulder, Colorado, and lifelong string of bad luck helped form her acerbic outlook. After graduating from the University of Colorado, she received a fellowship from the German government to study Anglo-Saxon literature at the University of Heidelberg. The year was 1936, but Stafford, drinking heavily, was mostly untroubled by the Nazi regime. She spent her time in Germany working on her own writing rather than studying. Back in the United States the following year, she was hospitalized with a painful ailment no doctor initially could diagnose. In July she managed to attend the Colorado University Writers' Conference in Boulder, where she befriended Robert Lowell, a gangly, bashful twenty-year-old poet from a storied Boston family, who was unhappily enrolled at Harvard. After a brief, disappointing stint as a literature instructor at Stephens College in Missouri, rejection from publishers, and torment about her decision to marry a man she wasn't sure she loved, Stafford met with Lowell again. Driving with him in Boston when he drunkenly crashed the car into a wall, she suffered major injuries to her nose, skull, and jaw. He had already asked her to marry him, much to the horror of his Boston Brahmin family. After several painful surgeries, a severe headache that interfered with her writing, and a slow-moving lawsuit to pay for her treatment, she fled to New York. But Lowell was persistent, and they finally married in April 1940. Of course, when Elizabeth wrote her review, she had no way of knowing that she would one day become Lowell's second wife.

* * *

In 1947 Elizabeth debuted in *The New York Times* with a review of a New Directions anthology, noting that editor James Laughlin's "false pride" in excoriating debased popular culture "makes our best art self-righteous and less original and profound than it should be."[68] With the exception of Mary McCarthy, Elizabeth did not spare anyone—even friends—in her book reviews. Peter Taylor was devastated when she published a dismissive review of his first short story collection, *A Long Fourth and Other Stories*, calling him "a kind of A student, modest . . . and traditional," with "more talent than ambition."[69] While praising his "delicately individual creation of particular families" and his "superb" dialogue, she found his low-key stories about middle-class families in Tennessee "too serene" and declared that she sometimes longed for "harshness, indiscretion, and that large early ugliness a young writer can well afford, a battle with the inexpressible." Referring to the title story—in which a white woman's hostile relationship with the family's Black servants is a key plot point, and the son's female guest comments negatively about his racial views—Elizabeth wrote that the South was an impossible subject to bring off convincingly in terms of larger social themes. Taylor later wrote to Robert Lowell that he had "never realized how truly dreadful she is until I saw her mind and her prose style at work on my own dear stories."[70]

In the same "Fiction Chronicle," Elizabeth also delivered a harsh verdict on a story collection by the "mercilessly pretentious" Anaïs Nin. While granting her "a fierce foolishness that is not without beauty as an act," Elizabeth snatched away this grudging praise by adding, "it is too bad her performance is never equal to her intentions."[71] The most noteworthy aspect of this review is its discussion of the way Nin's penchant for using vague, mystical phrases to create a spurious aura of sexual revelation was typical of women writers of the era. They offer "the illusion of having opened the bedroom door without involving the performer in a recognizable scandal." Elizabeth would have much more to say about sex in women's novels in future decades.

She could be equally dismissive in reviews of major American writers. In her *Partisan Review* essay "Faulkner and the South Today" she explained why she believed *Intruder in the Dust*—about the exoneration of a Black farmer accused of murdering a white man—does not achieve the level of Faulkner's great novels. She saw this book as a "plea that the South be allowed to redeem itself." Yet she found it "historically ridiculous in terms of America today," citing the migration of Black Americans to the North and the lack of sympathy among those who remained in the South to the "destiny" of the region. "It is the end . . . of Faulkner's imaginary kingdom," she wrote, "and he is terrified by it."

* * *

Philip Rahv, writing to Mary McCarthy, suggested that Elizabeth was no longer "very poor"; he thought her brothers must have been sending her money, since she was surely unable to live on the pittance she received for her writing. This subject came up because Elizabeth had insisted on paying her share for a drive upstate to visit Mary and her husband.[72] Afterward, Elizabeth wrote to Mary to reminisce about the view, the fun, and the "breakfasts on the porch." Protesting that her friend had been "much too generous and hospitable," she enclosed a check (amount unknown) and suggested that Mary use it to get drunk at a local bar.[73] It wasn't that Elizabeth had cash to spare; rather, she had an inbred sense of appropriateness and a determination not to take people for granted. It would serve her in good stead when her life became entwined with the scion of a famous family.

CHAPTER 3

Love and Torment

(1948–1950)

As an attractive single woman in postwar New York, Elizabeth had no shortage of attention from men. Writing to her college friend Sally Alexander about dancing at the Biltmore Hotel with a man Sally had dated, she described him as "really a nice fellow, but I suspect great selfishness beneath that avuncular surface. . . . Of course, it's the most fantastic arrogance for me to be analyzing him on such short acquaintance, but I never let that stop me."[1]

Elizabeth first encountered the handsome, imposing figure of Robert Lowell in the summer of 1947, at a party given by the Rahvs in their Greenwich Village apartment.[2] A dozen years later, in his poem "Man and Wife," he described this night as the one when he "outdrank the Rahvs in the heat / of Greenwich Village, fainting at your feet— / too boiled and shy / and poker-faced to make a pass, / while the shrill verve / of your invective scorched the traditional South."[3] For her part, Elizabeth later claimed to recall little about the meeting, except that she also met the poet Allen Tate, and that Lowell was with his novelist wife, Jean Stafford, whose troubled history with her husband Elizabeth knew nothing about.[4] A year would pass before they met again.

Robert Traill Spence Lowell IV was known as "Cal" ever since his obstreperous prep school days. The nickname embodied aspects of both the cruel Roman emperor Caligula, whose marble image he resembled, and Caliban, the half-human, half-monster in Shakespeare's play *The Tempest*. He was an only child, the scion of an old and storied Boston family that included a president of Harvard, eminent men in politics, law, the military, and the clergy, and several writers famous in their day (including Amy Lowell and James Russell Lowell). It would be hard to imagine a background and upbringing more radically different from Elizabeth's. Like most only children, he was the object of focused parental attention, especially from Charlotte Winslow Lowell, his insecure, highly conventional mother, who constantly sought to rein in his emotional, rebellious behavior. As Kay Redfield Jamison has written, this was a family line riddled with dark moods, suicidal episodes, and what was formerly known as "nervous exhaustion."[5] Cal's father, Robert Traill Spence Lowell III, was a distant, ineffectual figure. Charlotte had bullied him into abandoning his career as a naval officer—she viewed it as a lowly occupation—causing him to flounder in useless retirement. As Elizabeth wrote later, he found Cal "a balky intrusion, an unrewarding expense of energy and concentration."[6] Yet this unruly son, who had once knocked him down in a rage over a parentally thwarted romance, possessed a great gift. At thirty, Cal was already a major poet. Among his honors were the Pulitzer Prize (for *Lord Weary's Castle*), a one-thousand-dollar award from the American Academy of Arts and Letters, a Guggenheim Fellowship, and an appointment as poetry consultant at the Library of Congress.

Elizabeth would win her own Guggenheim Fellowship in 1948—one of seven novelists, including Stafford and Saul Bellow, who received the honor. In May of that year, she applied to Yaddo, the artists' colony in Saratoga Springs, New York, with the plan of spending July and August revising the first draft of her second novel.[7] Founded in 1926 by the financier Spencer Trask as a gift to his writer wife, Katrina, Yaddo is a retreat for artists, writers, and composers. The majestic, four-hundred-acre estate contains hundreds of thousands of coniferous and deciduous trees and gardens patterned after Italian and French Renaissance aesthetics, graced by fountains and marble statuary. Most guests stay in the fifty-five-room turreted Victorian mansion, where they work in seclusion every day from ten a.m. to four p.m., according to the rules of the colony. All meals are provided, with a packed lunch delivered at noon.

As references, Elizabeth listed John Woodburn, her Harcourt, Brace editor (who wrote that the press considers her "one of the majors of the young writers"); Lambert Davis, a fellow Southerner, also an editor at Harcourt; *PR* co-editor Philip Rahv; and *Time* magazine drama critic Louis Kronenberger, whom she probably knew from her graduate school years at Columbia, where he was a visiting professor.[8] Because she had applied so late in the year, Yaddo was unable to honor her choice of dates, offering the months of June and July or August and September instead.[9] Elizabeth chose August and September. This was a more momentous change of plan than it seemed at the time, because the last days of her stay coincided with the arrival of Robert Lowell. Exactly what transpired between the two of them at that time is unknown. But the spark was lit.

She saw him again in November, at a poetry reading at Bard College that featured, among others, Elizabeth Bishop, Richard Wilbur, Louise Bogan, William Carlos Williams, Jean Garrigue, Richard Eberhart, and Kenneth Rexroth, with a young James Merrill among the attendees. In a possibly apocryphal story, Cal had too many glasses of punch at this hard-drinking event and was helped to his room by the two Elizabeths. After Elizabeth Hardwick loosened his tie and opened his shirt, she reportedly exclaimed, "Why, he's an Adonis!" Her behavior prompted Bishop—who became close to him at the conference—to suggest to Merrill that Elizabeth would be the next Mrs. Lowell. Yet in a postscript to a letter to Cal, apropos Elizabeth's imminent arrival at Yaddo, Bishop warned, "Take care."[10]

Newly divorced from Stafford in the spring of 1948,[11] Cal had asked Elizabeth to return to the artists' colony, which she did in early January 1949, after being interviewed for a potential teaching position at Sarah Lawrence College. ("The idea is distasteful because I've just gotten settled and am working well," she wrote to Mary McCarthy and her husband, "yet I cannot refuse. I must face the fact of my vanishing finances.")[12] In a friendly note to the young author, signed "my love to you," Yaddo director Elizabeth Ames suggested that she "come prepared to stay through February if you can."[13] Ames had no inkling of the way Elizabeth and Cal would join forces to drastically undermine Yaddo's peaceful way of life.

A month before Elizabeth's arrival, Cal's friend Peter Taylor had warned him, "She's dangerous for you."[14] It's not clear why he felt this way, since he scarcely knew her; perhaps he was still nursing a grievance about her negative review of his work. Cal responded flippantly that he might be able to interest her in Taylor's brother-in-law, also due to arrive at Yaddo. Instead, the affair between Elizabeth and Cal began in earnest. He wrote to Taylor that "Miss Hardwick" was "slipshod, good humored, malicious (harmless), and humorous— full of high-spirits[,] rattling a lot of sense . . . very good company."[15] To his mentor, the philosopher George Santayana, Cal mentioned that there were "two new people here to liven things," including "a Southern girl (a New York character now) full of gossip—which alas I enjoy."[16] Philip Rahv joked to Elizabeth that Yaddo "must be very good for you if you are planning to stay on till the end of March."[17] She wrote to Richard Volney Chase, an English professor she had met at Columbia University, that social life—with Alfred Kazin, Lowell, and others whose names she didn't mention—had become "so much like New York that we had to ban elevated conversation in favor of a more natural, light-headed communication."[18]

Despite the augurs of an exciting romance, a giant impediment loomed. Cal was an Episcopalian who had converted to Catholicism in the early 1940s and left the church in 1948; now he insisted on returning to the faith, making wild announcements about his piety. As a Catholic, he believed he could neither remarry nor commit adultery. Unbeknownst to Elizabeth, he was in the grip of escalating mania, a recurrent sign of the bipolarity that plagued his adult life. At a meeting of the Yaddo trustees in early February, he demanded that they fire Ames on the grounds of tainting Yaddo with subversive ideas, because she had allowed her journalist friend Agnes Smedley to stay at the colony. Smedley, who was under investigation by the FBI, was indeed a "fellow traveler," with a checkered career that included German-funded activities for Indian revolutionaries during World War I and spying on behalf of the Soviet Union. But Ames was innocent. Yet Elizabeth went along with the witch hunt, getting in touch with people she knew to warn them to stay away from Yaddo until Ames was gone. Dwight Macdonald, who had been invited to stay at the colony, fired off an angry letter to Ames denouncing her and rejecting his appointment. Elizabeth later said that she didn't remember contacting Macdonald, but his letter to Ames mentions having had a conversation with Elizabeth about the situation.[19] FBI investigators converged on Yaddo, seeking information about Ames from Malcolm Cowley, Flannery O'Connor, Edward Maisel, and Elizabeth and Cal. (The director was finally "cleared" on February 18.)

Alfred Kazin described Yaddo in winter as "a thorny mysterious return to another century on the rim of the Adirondacks, a mixture of primeval woods and the genteel tradition."[20] For writers who could deal with the Victorian atmosphere, "a few winter weeks of solitude put you chapters ahead, gave you back to yourself." He recalled Cal and Elizabeth as "a brilliant couple," although Cal was "just a little too dazzling . . . in a state of grandeur not negotiable with lesser beings . . . handsome, magnetic, rich, wild with excitement about his powers." Kazin and Eleanor Clark, another writer at Yaddo, tried to rally many of the writers, composers, and artists who had spent time at the estate to support Ames. Kazin wrote with disgust about those who refused to help, especially indicting "lesser poets . . . concerned with Lowell's power to affect their reputations even when they had no reputations."[21] Allen Tate and his wife, Caroline, were well acquainted with Cal's mercurial behavior. Caroline bemoaned his liaison with Elizabeth, and Allen wrote to her to ask how she could have jumped on the anti-Ames bandwagon.[22] Elizabeth, struggling to work on her novel during this unsettled time, seems to have explained her role in a convincing way. Allen sympathized with the strain she had been under.[23]

By March 26, Cal had sufficiently recovered his equilibrium to attend the Cultural and Scientific Conference for World Peace at the Waldorf-Astoria Hotel with Elizabeth and a number of other prominent Americans in the arts, including Lillian Hellman, Dashiell Hammett, Leonard Bernstein, Aaron Copland, Frank Lloyd Wright, and Marlon Brando. In the complicated politics of the day, the sponsoring organization was believed by some to be a Communist front with a pro-Soviet agenda. Under the banner of Americans for Intellectual Freedom, the philosopher Sidney Hook organized a group of New York intellectuals and labor union representatives to invade the conference and discredit it. Cal and Elizabeth, accompanied by Mary McCarthy and Dwight Macdonald, decided to hijack the panel on writing and publishing to demand information about Stalin's treatment of dissident Russian writers.[24] The two women, advised that they would be treated harshly, brought umbrellas as props, planning to pound them on the floor of the Starlight Roof Ballroom to attract attention and to wield them against potential attackers. As things turned out, this maneuver was unnecessary: each of the four was granted two minutes to speak during the question-and-answer period. Elizabeth recalled later that the Communists responded by accusing the American South of persecuting Black people.

Whether as a result of the inflamed passions aroused by this intervention or as part of his ongoing struggle with bipolarity, by the end of March Cal was in a weak and tormented state. He managed to travel to Kenyon College in Ohio, where Allen Tate reported that Elizabeth's phone call had "calmed him no end."[25] But by early April, he unraveled again at the Tates' home, insisting on telling Caroline about her husband's earlier lovers. After Cal grabbed Allen and held him out the window, the police were called to subdue him; he soon left for the Bloomington, Indiana, home of Peter Taylor and his wife. Allen wrote to Elizabeth to warn her that Cal was "dangerous," with homicidal tendencies.[26] "You must not let him live in your apartment," he added. In a letter to Cal on April 7, she chose to avoid mentioning the episode, assuring him that she was safely keeping a manuscript of his and offering to send books or anything else he wanted.

But more bad news was to come. While visiting the Taylors, Cal assaulted a policeman at a movie theater and was arrested. On April 10 he was admitted to Baldpate Hospital in Georgetown, north of Boston. Elizabeth wrote him a newsy letter, suggesting that she might send him a chocolate rabbit for Easter, which fell on the following Sunday. She had been frightened by the extent of Lowell's illness—she likened it to the behavior of deranged characters in a Russian novel—but after he was sequestered at Baldpate, she wrote that she looked forward to seeing him if his doctor allowed it. Despite, or more likely because of, the gravity of the situation, she wrote to Tate that she was extremely unhappy that he and Taylor had let others know about Cal's condition. In those days, mental illness was considered a shameful condition that should be kept private. Tate replied, "I quite realize that your instinct is to conceal the whole thing (it always is with you, my dear!)"—the latter remark probably a reference to their own brief affair.[27]

In her letters, she told Cal she was "busy reading all of Elizabeth Bowen" for a *Partisan Review* article and promised that she would take his "general advice . . . and not be as 'bad'"—as severely critical—"as I was in the past, in this or other more important things."[28] (Cal's irritation at her negative remarks and her subsequent promise to reform would surface periodically over the years.) Elizabeth's mother had called, wondering if she was coming home for the Kentucky Derby, but she "didn't at this moment find that a very diverting idea."[29] By June 14 she had made no summer plans, "mostly because I can't bear the thought of staying more than a week with friends."[30] The very next day, to her great joy, she learned from a mutual friend that Cal would be released soon. She asked him to call collect and offered to come and see him, "unless you want relief from human kind for a while." While telling him she had washed some of his things—clearly a labor of love—she also kept a certain distance, asking if he was still planning to go to Europe in the autumn.

Elizabeth traveled to visit Cal for two weeks, apparently telling only Mary McCarthy where she was. In an eerie foretaste of her future life, she wrote, "I've at last found the proper scene for my peculiar temperament: I was a gratifying hit with doctors and patients at Baldpate and for most purposes have gotten Cal committed to my care!"[31] Before she left, her mother had sent a letter to the New York apartment (apparently with an enclosed check or cash) that required an immediate answer and became worried when there was no reply. The reason for Elizabeth's silence is that this money had paid for the trip to Boston—a visit she didn't want her mother to know about. Since money was a constant worry for both Cal and herself, she tried to assure him that being together wouldn't cost either of them more that summer than if they were alone. "At the worst," she wrote to him, "one can start all over in the fall, financially."[32] Nathalie Rahv had offered to let the couple stay in her house until August 15, but that "would only be a last resort."

On her return from Massachusetts, she called Cal's editor and various friends, to tell them of his recovery. She informed the poet John Berryman that "Cal has recovered completely, marvelously. He looks wonderful and is well in every way."[33] Elizabeth likened the convalescent wing of the hospital to "a small country club." Cal was now doing normal things—walking, swimming—but the doctors told her he would need psychotherapy, and he refused to go anywhere by himself. Unsaid was that her own nerves were on edge, and she was sleeping badly. Learning that the Lowells were going to stick him with the hospital bill, she reassured Cal that Blair Clark would figure out how to get the money. "The important thing is that you shouldn't have to worry about money for a year at least," she wrote. "And as I told you, I can take care of myself, as I've always done."[34] In a passage indicating that marriage was in the offing, she explained that she was going to see a lawyer about "an honest pre-engagement settlement," including the amount she would be expected to contribute.

Days earlier she had assured Mary, "we are not thinking of getting married."[35] That was probably because Cal was tortured by the belief that his marriage to Jean remained valid in the eyes of the Catholic Church.[36] But it seems that he had set his heart on a life with Elizabeth. Back in April, he wrote to Peter Taylor to ask how his friend felt about her, adding, "we want to be together."[37] Cal's brief, newsy July 1 letter to Elizabeth concluded, "*Gosh* your visit was wonderful and *saning*. Hope you can stand me still."[38] On the July Fourth weekend, he wrote that his mother "has finally accepted our arrangement—with cordial (?) diffidence."[39] He asked Elizabeth if she would like to be engaged "like a debutante," and he assured her ("my heart is with you") of his concern as she dragged around Manhattan in the summer heat, trying to rent out her apartment and find a place for the two of them to live when he left the hospital a few days later. "How happy we'll be together writing the world's masterpieces, swimming and washing dishes," he wrote. It was a joyous, mixed-up vision of the life they would actually lead.

Less than two weeks before the wedding, Elizabeth wrote to Mary that she still didn't know when it would be, that the Low-

ells were "behaving barbarously," and that she and Cal had no idea
where they would live.[40] They were "exhausted by idleness and the
inevitable chaos" of trying to sort out their "practical affairs." Elizabeth and Cal had decided to marry in Boston without any of their
friends or family members in attendance, "because neither of us felt
up to planning any kind of wedding, and we couldn't afford it." But
the Lowells announced that they would host it at their country house
in the oceanfront community of Beverly Farms.

Because the July 28 wedding was organized on just two days'
notice, there were few guests: Cal's uncle Cotting, Mary McCarthy,
and the couple's friends Blair and Holly Clark and Frank and Leslie
Parker. (Dr. Merrill Moore, Charlotte's and Cal's sometime therapist,
pointedly was not invited, and Elizabeth had decided not to inform
her family until afterward.) Mary was the maid of honor; Frank was
the best man. Elizabeth, wearing an ill-fitting blue silk dress purchased the day before and a black Balenciaga hat loaned by Mary,
was unable to speak above a whisper. It was one hundred degrees
inside the house—probably one reason she apologized to Mary a few
days later "for the rigors" of the event.[41] The glum mood was apparent to the clergyman, who told the assembled group that "we are
here for a wedding, not a funeral."[42] After a honeymoon in Glouces-
ter, Massachusetts, the couple rented a house in upstate New York
that belonged to Fred Dupee and his wife, Barbara.

Elizabeth's thank-you letter to the senior Lowells was a model
of polite phrases and upbeat remarks. Describing the Revolutionary
War–era house as "just about perfect for us," she praised Cal's return
to writing and, in a wifely manner keyed to the recipients of her letter, his handling of "the garbage and lawn problems."[43] Charlotte was
initially hostile to Elizabeth, as she had been to Jean, whose plebe-
ian, West Coast background was not what she had in mind for her
son. While Elizabeth's background and opinionated personality were
not to Charlotte's liking, she had come to appreciate her daughter-

in-law's Southern manners and realized that she would take care of Cal. Charlotte was still a difficult person to deal with. Her insecurity often made her hysterical, her snobbishness led her to value things Elizabeth found laughable, and her misplaced sense of frugality coexisted with a taste for suffocating luxury.

Writing to Sally Alexander, Elizabeth joked about her new stage of life. "On the electric range," she wrote, "I prepare one failure after another. . . . I try to make up for it by a great deal of dusting and moving about of small objects, a procedure I call housekeeping."[44] She was "wildly happy," and she and Cal were both back at their writing. Decades later, Elizabeth would remark to an interviewer that age thirty-two was late to marry "even for a Bohemian," and that she had been afraid of marriage because she was "afraid of losing something."[45] That "something" was primarily her ability to continue dedicating her life to writing, which—despite other travails—her marriage never placed in doubt. (Elizabeth would retain her maiden name for her writing, while becoming "Mrs. Lowell" in private life.)

A few weeks later, in a letter to Mary, Elizabeth—who was accustomed to living near friends in Manhattan—mentioned her disappointment at being isolated in the country, with no connection to the community.[46] By mid-September, she had something else on her mind: Cal was feeling depressed, and they went to see a doctor in New York, who advised hospitalization for intensive psychotherapy. Elizabeth believed that it was important for him because he "cannot function without a set of principles or attitudes."

From Payne Whitney Psychiatric Clinic, Cal wrote to Elizabeth that he thought of her constantly "and worry so about all I have dumped on you." He added, "We are going to work it out, dear, be as wonderful as you have been."[47] Alone in the house, she tried to keep working and "not alarm or disturb anyone."[48] She claimed that she didn't want to return to Manhattan because it would be too expensive. More to the point, she saw herself "in a little room . . . without books, too unsettled to work . . . drinking, etc." Marriage had helped her recover from a terrible feeling of loneliness, and now, she wrote, "I cannot bear to be unsettled again."

But in a letter to Cal a few days later, she announced that she was going to give up the house and had asked friends to help her find prospective tenants.[49] That morning, she wrote, a man staggering out from the local bar—an anomaly in this rural setting—reminded her of the Lower East Side. As always, literature filled her days. Reading Dickens's *Nicholas Nickleby*, she found herself unable to respond to the cruelty of Mr. and Mrs. Squeers, proprietors of a ghastly boys' school. "This book," she wrote, in a sentence that could have come from one of her essays, "is a terrifying monument to those Siamese twins, cruelty and sentimentality." In another letter to Cal, written after a dinner of cold roast beef in the snug house ("I think your furnace work warmed it up for the rest of the fall"), she told him that she missed him "terribly" and asked him not to be depressed about having to stay in the hospital.[50] Much as she wanted to see him the following weekend, she would wait one more week, "but my noble resolves may break down for want of a look at you." Probably out of fear that an impending move would upset him, she wrote that she did want to stay in the house "if possible" and "how nice it will be when you come back." But in reality, the Red Hook idyll would not be repeated.

When a package of S. S. Pierce canned goods arrived from the senior Lowells, she thanked Charlotte, adding that Cal "had to go into New York"—reason unstated—but that she would "be hearing from him soon."[51] (A month later Dr. Moore wrote to Elizabeth that she was right not to inform the Lowells about the hospitalization, but that they had found out by themselves. He claimed to have "thoroughly convinced" Charlotte that Elizabeth was handling the situation well and that Cal was simply having "follow up treatment.")[52] To Elizabeth's dismay, when Mary received her letter about Cal's hospitalization, Dwight Macdonald and his wife were present, and he insisted that she read it aloud. Mary said that they promised not to repeat the news, as Elizabeth had requested in the letter, but as she knew, gossip was catnip to the New York literary world.

In late September, Elizabeth was once again living in a single room without a bath, this time at "an awful hotel" with one advantage: it cost only twenty dollars a week.[53] "Nothing could be more unreal and depressing than wandering around looking for a furnished apartment that rents for $75 or less," she wrote to Mary. "It gives you a Rip Van Winkle feeling."[54] She had put her books and records in storage in Poughkeepsie and did not want to retrieve them until she had a permanent place to live. By late October, Cal was able to leave the hospital during the afternoon and was about to be granted permission for an overnight stay on Saturdays. Cal and Elizabeth spent their afternoons going to the movies, museums, City Center Opera, and the Betty Parsons Gallery exhibition of Jackson Pollock's recent drip paintings, where the couple "felt again the breath of avant-garde life."[55]

Now that they would be reunited in the coming months, Elizabeth rented "an unspeakable apartment" at 29 West 104th Street, in the heart of Spanish Harlem. It was a one-bedroom walk-up "high in the clouds," with "a few pieces of indescribable furniture."[56] The Rahvs sounded horrified at the location, but the monthly rent was sixty-five dollars, and the apartment received good light. Although Elizabeth wrote that the building was "fairly respectable and not too depressing"—just two blocks from Central Park West—she found the neighborhood "frightfully unappetizing" and felt "like a gangster in hiding." Still, she realized that she would "feel just as forlorn in [Greenwich] Village" if she lived alone there. She spent a few dollars on necessities at Macy's, but her sheets, towels, and cooking utensils remained in storage, awaiting a move to more promising lodgings. Charlotte Lowell (who knew nothing about New York neighborhoods) wrote to Elizabeth to approve her decision to move the household to the city, to offer "any help we can give," and to express her pleasure that the couple agreed to celebrate Thanksgiving at Beverly Farms.[57] Two weeks later Cal praised Elizabeth to his mother as "marvelously brave, ingenious and sympathetic" and told her that despite "little money and much uncertainty," their life would lead to "sense and happiness."[58]

Money was a problem, and Cal hoped to pull his weight by teaching. There was some hope of finding him a position at Bard College; Allen Tate had been promoting this idea with a poetry instructor there. Now Paul Engle, head of the writing program at the University of Iowa, offered the possibility of a temporary position from February to June 1950. Perhaps partly out of guilt for allowing Macdonald to hear the contents of Elizabeth's letter, Mary mailed her a ten-dollar check. (For some reason, it was never cashed.)[59] Allen Tate also came through with a check from what he called the Relief Fund Committee, asking Elizabeth not to tell Cal that he was involved.[60] Cal's relative Sarah Winslow Cotting—who was trying ("I am quite bewildered") to read Kafka's novel The Castle, presumably at Elizabeth's suggestion—conveniently sent bed linens as a belated wedding present.[61]

Cal was finally released from the hospital in mid-December. The couple still had no literary social life to speak of. Elizabeth had invited the Berrymans to dinner but received "a strange and cold refusal." A dinner for the Rahvs was cut short when they had to cart home bags of melting frozen food that they had brought with them, for some reason. But the good news was that the Iowa offer was definite. (The letter from Engle crossed with a letter Elizabeth wrote to Tate expressing her worry that Cal would take rejection very badly, because "he'll feel all teaching jobs are closed to him for the same reason." There was no need to spell out what this was.)[62] Elizabeth sent ahead their clothing, household goods, and her typewriter in two wooden trunks, which she worried were packed too carelessly. She was relieved when these items arrived safely at the small, unfurnished apartment at 728 Bowery Street in Iowa City.

Despite the inauspicious street name (Manhattan's Bowery was a slum district), the apartment offered consolations. It had a private bath, a bonus in those days, and the kitchen—"the center of home life here," Elizabeth wrote—had a new linoleum floor, a new stove, cabinets, and sink.[63] She soon realized that in Iowa City, "the love of the spotless stove and kitchen floor is infectious." Willing to do her part to maintain appearances, she drew the line at other "native folk ways, such as doing your husband's shirts." To Eleanor Taylor, Elizabeth professed being "quite content" with "the calm, sober, quiet life," though "it is impossible to speak of liking Iowa," where there were no bohemians.[64] The other families in the Lowells' building were always asking her if she had done "the week's baking yet and other normal and embarrassing questions." Even the students— "stolid, dependable people"—were married; husbands hung out at the Laundromat while doing the family wash.

The Lowells socialized mostly with the novelist Robie Macauley, a fellow faculty member, and his wife. "You feel more likely to meet a buffalo at a party than a person with temperament," Elizabeth wrote to Elizabeth Bishop.[65] "That there should be a writing school here shows that the pioneer belief in the impossible is still active." The poet W. D. Snodgrass, then a graduate student in the writing program, recalled meeting Elizabeth a few times, mostly when he and Cal had returned to the house at night. She seemed depressed and ill, asking guests to see her in her bedroom. "Usually languid and exhausted, she could occasionally be encouraged to don a robe, get up, and 'do' some well-known, eccentric acquaintance," he wrote. "These imitations were delicious, crackling with energy."[66]

* * *

Philip Rahv informed Elizabeth that Gambier, Ohio—where the
Lowells would move in the summer, for Cal's six-week teaching
position at Kenyon College—was a similar environment, with the
difference that a number of literary "characters" would be livening
things up.[67] Rahv wrote that he hoped she had been writing more
short stories, since *Partisan Review* was desperate for good work. She
sent "The Friendly Witness"—Rahv deemed it "very fine"—which
appeared in the April 1950 issue. This story, about the bookish, progressive mayor of a city accused of having accepted $500 from an
old friend who owned a nightclub with illegal gambling rooms, was
a look back at the world of her youth. The mayor needs the money to
fulfill his daughter's dream of attending a Southern boarding school.
A woman he admires, a fellow progressive with a high local profile,
has witnessed the transaction and told others; now he is in the cross-
hairs of local evangelicals who demand that gambling be ended. In
the end, the high-minded woman saves the mayor from disgrace—
an ending too pat for good fiction but one in tune with the political
spirit of the magazine.

     Elizabeth's first "Fiction Chronicle" reviews had been published
in *Partisan Review* in January: a look at novels by Italo Svevo, Elio
Vittorini, Paul Bowles, and Frederick Buechner. This was a noteworthy beginning for a critic whose interests would always include
literature from beyond American shores.[68] Svevo, she wrote, was "a
master of motive and fluctuating feeling because he was perhaps
rather ashamed of his own vacillations and doubt." Bowles's *The Shel-
tering Sky* struck her as "a peculiar blend of the ambition of [E. M.
Forster's] *A Passage to India* and the mood of [Hemingway's] *The Sun
Also Rises.*" Cal wrote to George Santayana that he would send him
some of Elizabeth's writing "almost over her dead body—so passionate is her modesty."[69]

     In March, Elizabeth wangled accreditation from the *New York
Post* so that she could be a daily visitor to the three-week murder trial

of a fraternity boy accused of killing his fiancée, which gripped the whole city. Cal wrote to Peter Taylor that she "talked a book" about the proceedings.[70] A book was indeed forthcoming: it would be a novel. Elizabeth wrote to Sally that, according to Cal, "my theories, speculations & curious deportment alarmed the town much more than the murderer."[71]

A cheering thought for the Lowells was their decision to travel to Italy in the autumn and stay for a year. In a high-spirited letter to Elizabeth Bishop in early May, Elizabeth announced that she and Cal had decided on the trip a week earlier, and suggested that Bishop join them in the cheap lodgings they hoped to rent.[72] ("I trust the stories about 'living like a king' are true.") She confided that the plan was "a sort of subterfuge of mine to keep Cal from becoming head of the Department of English at the University of Iowa." She knew that he wasn't cut out to be one of those men climbing "the academic ladder."

But first came the Kenyon experience. Elizabeth wrote to the Macauleys that she was "thoroughly traumatized" by her solo ride to Gambier, Ohio—Cal had gone to Boston to see his parents and speak at Harvard—with a "brutal and disgusting" man and his "leaden" wife, whose company she had to put up with for nearly a week.[73] Then it turned out that the housing the Lowells were allotted was her "worst apartment yet," which was saying a lot. It was so dark, the lights had to be kept on all day, "the bedroom is a sweltering attic; the kitchen is the size of a sheet of paper." She railed against moving "to a small town" offering accommodation similar to "the slums of Chicago." Cal had given her a silver dollar "to promise to behave this summer," she added, "but I've only accepted fifty cents and expect to have to return a quarter of that." The promise no doubt involved reining in her tendency to be anxious and critical.

In contrast to the apartment, Elizabeth found Kenyon "exciting and stimulating." The college was the home of the celebrated *Kenyon*

Review, and the literary illuminati included William Empson, Delmore Schwartz, and her former teacher John Crowe Ransom. She also was working on arrangements for the European trip, including booking passage on a freighter. Practical matters like this were always her department. Whether because of the stress of managing the details, the heat, or simply lack of exercise (there was no place to swim), Elizabeth was "developing humorous hypocondriacal [*sic*] complaints," Cal informed Peter Taylor, as well as a "24 hour dieting program."[74] In August, when Cal's teaching stint concluded, the Lowells paid a brief visit to Elizabeth's family in Kentucky (he jokingly described them as "Elizabeth's mother and thirteen brothers") and spent time with the Taylors in North Carolina and the senior Lowells in Beverly Farms.

Cal and Elizabeth had booked passage on a ship embarking on August 30, 1950, but the night before their boat sailed, a telegram arrived with the news that Cal's father had died of a heart attack. Fortunately, the couple's suitcases were allowed to remain at the pier, and Fern Lines agreed to defer their passage for the original amount they paid—"the same as the lowest on a commercial boat, where we would have traveled dormitory style," Elizabeth noted.[75] For the next few weeks, they stayed with Charlotte to deal with the funeral arrangements and keep her company. Life with her was "so orderly neither of us can get anything done," Elizabeth wrote.[76] "I've given some thought to the problem of getting a cup of coffee at eleven in the morning or maybe three in the afternoon, but it couldn't be done without a great deal of disarming explanation." Cal was upset to learn from his mother that he was not even mentioned in his father's will. (He did receive a small trust fund.) When he tried to talk to her about her financial situation, she fainted "and crumpled down on the stairs"—which Elizabeth skeptically viewed as the sort of dramatic display her mother-in-law liked to indulge in.[77]

During this period of suspended animation, she vented her irritation at Mary McCarthy and her husband for being "a little too amusing about Payne Whitney" and "recounting some doctor's dire picture of shock treatment" when the Lowells had visited the couple in New York months earlier.[78] Elizabeth missed city life terribly; a day's outing in Boston temporarily filled her need to wander around urban streets. She also felt that she had "lost touch with the past," because other than basic articles of clothing, she and Cal had none of their belongings with them during their months of teaching exodus. It was fortunate that she had no idea how long it actually would take them to be able to settle in one place. Elizabeth's mother, who knew the pain of bereavement, wrote a condolence note to Cal in which she advised, "the best way to find consolation is to keep busy and find some outside interests."[79] She also suggested that the couple might put off their European trip for "a year or so." Of course, that idea had no appeal.

CHAPTER 4

European Immersion

(1950–1952)

As THEY COUNTED the days until they could leave dreary Iowa City, Elizabeth and Cal were sustained by dreams of their grand adventure: "a frugal year abroad," financed by the money he had made from teaching and what remained of his $2,500 Guggenheim Fellowship. "We plan to be in Italy until June," Cal wrote to George Santayana, "with only a comfortable blur of plans."[1]

Postwar Europe was awash with young Americans—most prominently, artists and writers seeking a different life, or simply a more adventurous one. For Black artists and musicians, and novelist James Baldwin, who moved to Paris in 1948, the object was to escape a racist society. For others, the lure—beyond the acknowledged virtues of great museums and cities steeped in history—was the more relaxed pace of café society, cheap hotels, and a less puritanical view of sexual relations. Unlike the earlier exodus of creative people from the United States in the 1920s, many of the new émigrés were men using their G.I. Bill money to return to a part of the world they had come to know during the war. But the Lowells were more like members of the previous generation, seeking an immersion in the cultural traditions they had learned to esteem during their college days.

Elizabeth and Cal were finally able to begin their trip on September 28, sailing on the *Hopeville*, a freighter that arrived at Genoa on October 10. It was a pleasant voyage. There were only seven other passengers—at first, it was hard to know what to say to them at dinner—and the quiet double cabin allowed the couple to do "an immense amount of sleeping."[2] Peering at the captain's maps and trying out the radar instruments captivated both of them, as did the whale sightings. ("We . . . felt the advantage, not shared by the other passengers, of having read *Moby-Dick*," Elizabeth informed Mary McCarthy.)[3] When the boat stopped in Tangier, they ran into fellow Americans James Caffery—a friend of Jean Stafford's who lived with his aristocratic English lover, David Herbert[4]—and Jay Hazelwood, Elizabeth's friend from the University of Kentucky, who ran a bar called Parade–Parada.[5] Spotting the composer and author Paul Bowles on the street, the Lowells learned that he was irritated at the Americans and Europeans who were invading his paradise. The couple had such a good time that they had to be rowed back to their boat— which had pulled away from the dock—at nine o'clock at night.

Burdened with many heavy suitcases during their first week in Florence, Elizabeth and Cal were anxious to rent a place quickly. They sprang for a furnished apartment on Lungarno Amerigo Vespucci, alongside the Arno River, with a view of a statue of the witty eighteenth-century playwright Carlo Goldoni. (Cal thought he resembled Alexander Hamilton.)[6] The "embarrassingly luxurious" flat—five rooms plus a bath and maid's quarters—came with sheets, towels, silverware, and dishes for the equivalent of seventy-five dollars a month. Central heating, which would not be switched on until December, cost another seventy-five dollars.[7] Elizabeth—always mindful of the hard work of women who cleaned houses—increased the live-in maid's monthly wage from $12 to $13.50 "because of Cal's shirts." She confessed that despite her "proletarian sympathies" and dismay at "not being able to say much except <u>grazie</u> and <u>buono</u>," she quickly got used to having someone who did the daily marketing (there was no refrigerator) and all the cleaning, cooking, washing, and ironing.[8] (Months later, when the maid was hospitalized with appendicitis, the Lowell household was thrown into a state of chaos. "I missed our tin-can, refrigerator civilization . . . and the hot running water most of all," Elizabeth wrote to a friend. "Living in a foreign country is complete hell unless you have someone to do the work.")[9] Food for the Lowells and the maid cost about $2.15 a day, "including table wine." They would be careful not to turn on lights at night in rooms they were not occupying, because she couldn't quite understand the costs she was quoted. The myth back home was that you could live like a king in Italy for one hundred dollars a month, so it was a relief to be assured by American art historian Sam Hunter and his housemate, English critic Anthony Bower, that "we had an unusually cheap situation!"[10] Cal wrote to Elizabeth Bishop about their good deal: "a maid, wine and lovely furniture for what a moderately good apartment would cost in New York."[11] He was dazzled by the "abundance in every direction, so that it seems one's energy and interest would never tire."

Now that they had a place to stay for the winter, Elizabeth and Cal decamped for the Hotel d'Inghilterra in Rome, near the Villa Borghese. On a postcard to Peter Taylor, she noted two sobering discoveries: "Italy very expensive and they really don't speak English."[12] (Rome, she learned, was considerably more costly than Florence—$160 for their two-week visit[13]—and restaurant meals and clothes were pricey in both cities.) Another discovery was that the Italian literary figures to whom they had been given letters of introduction no longer lived in the Eternal City. But that hardly mattered once they encountered the heady mix of Americans living abroad, including writer Gertrude Buckman, Cal's old flame (and fellow poet Delmore Schwartz's former wife); *Harper's Bazaar* literary editor Pearl Kazin; poet Dunstan Thompson; composers Harold Shap-

Elizabeth and Anthony Bower
at a restaurant in Italy, 1951.

ero and Lukas Foss; and "a boy named Weaver"—William Weaver, who would soon embark on his career as a gifted translator of Italian literature. Attending a cocktail party at the American Academy, Elizabeth saw friends from Yaddo "who no doubt . . . after the Academy palazzo think Yaddo is a modest housing project."[14] Although the Lowells uncharacteristically skipped the Vatican and Capitoline museums—perhaps dodging tourists who had come for the Holy Year[15]—they spent a day at the ancient seaport of Ostia Antica and visited the town of Tivoli, site of Emperor Hadrian's villa and the gardens of the Villa d'Este. An American friend of Mary's husband, Bowden Broadwater, drove the Lowells to Pisa, where the three of them climbed the famous leaning tower "and took pictures of each other at angles." In a letter to a friend, Elizabeth exulted that Italy seemed "much more beautiful, pleasant and, yes, inspiring than I would ever have believed." She and Cal hoped they could stay in the country for two years.[16]

Back in Florence, she loved being able to walk everywhere, guidebook in hand. Cal's determination to immerse himself in the culture of the cities they would visit meant that their baggage included books by nineteenth-century cultural authorities Walter Pater and John Ruskin. "Cal was born for [sightseeing]," she reported. "He climbs every tower."[17] But unlike Elizabeth, who spent her first week immersed in language study, he didn't want to learn Italian, whimsically proposing that he could make himself understood "simply by tossing about bizarre words and phrases."[18] It amused him that he could say things to the maid "that no one can understand." But Elizabeth had no trouble deciphering his cutting remarks about her shortcomings. According to her, every night he told the maid, "La Signora tries to cook this, but it didn't turn out so well."[19] Still, by early December, they had settled into what they viewed as an ideal way of life. Cal wrote to Elizabeth Bishop that they were now thinking of staying abroad for three years. In a letter to Mary, Elizabeth exulted, "We feel very stimulated and excited and yet very serene."[20]

When she wasn't "roaming the streets . . . window-shopping, looking at the buildings"—and dodging the streams of bicycle and motor scooter traffic—she was working on a novel based on the trial she had witnessed in Iowa City. Elizabeth had not been able to write during the previous two years, and it was "a pleasure to feel the mysterious clouds lift."[21] Her satire on expatriate life in Florence—in which "the indescribable splendor of Florentine snobbery" bumped up against the brash pragmatism of an American photographer—would be published in *Partisan Review* the following spring.[22] But there was also a steady stream of visitors. Eighty-five-year-old art historian Bernard Berenson invited the couple for lunch, eliciting Elizabeth's tart remark that meeting him was like "seeing the matinee of a play that had been running for eight decades."[23] He "pets you on the knee and gives you his word of honor that Italy"—where the Partito comunista italiano was a major force—"will never go Communist."[24]

One Sunday, she and Cal visited the British writer Harold Acton and his parents, a household she skewered in a letter to Mary as a place where "the old folks pulverize you with their queerness." There were parties at the country home of Marjorie Ferguson, head of the United States Information Service (USIS) and a former girlfriend of art critic Clement Greenberg. Luminaries the couple encountered in Florence included Stephen Spender, W. H. Auden, the philosopher A. J. ("Freddie") Ayer, and the composer Samuel Barber. With his wife, Natasha ("very intelligent, tall and dark," in Elizabeth's view), Spender would meet up with the Lowells the following year at London's Royal Opera House for a performance of *Wozzeck*. At dinner afterward, artist Peter Watson and Sonia Orwell, widow of the author, joined their table. "I suppose it's all being in a foreign country," Elizabeth wrote to Mary. "But one seems to get along with everyone [one] meets."[25] Inevitably, there were also a few undesirable new acquaintances: British snobs, "rather bitter and complaining"; a young woman from Boston who detested homosexuals and the "lower class"; and the "glowering," rabidly anti-Semitic American wife of Lord Desmond Harmsworth, a witty Englishman the Lowells were fond of.[26] Lubricated with martinis, Elizabeth had a "grand fight" with Lady Harmsworth at their last dinner with the couple, unaware that she would meet up with her again the following year in England.

Generous checks sent by Cal's mother and Cousin Harriet for Christmas funded clothing purchases and a three-day New Year's trip to Monte Carlo. After driving to the gambling mecca with Tony Bower and his mother and sister, "who had more money to spend than we had,"[27] the Lowells met up with Frank Parker, an artist and longtime friend of Cal's, and his English wife, Lesley. Instead of gambling, they settled for sightseeing and meals featuring "gallons of red wine, tons of raw red steak." The city, Elizabeth wrote, was "still elegant looking but by now as plebian [*sic*] as a baseball game and a lot cheaper since it only costs about 25 cents to get into the casino."[28] After this holiday, marred by frostiness between Elizabeth and Lesley, "jealous as a snake,"[29] Elizabeth returned to Florence, and Cal traveled to the village of Luynes in southern France, where the Parkers lived. "Miss my pretty girl," he wrote to her, promising "not to run you ragged again."[30]

During this period Elizabeth was happy in Florence, though she would confess a few months later that life there was "too pleasant and exciting for writing" and less stimulating intellectually than what they were used to at home.[31] Cal concluded that Rome was "much more lively socially and intellectually than Florence."[32] Next summer they hoped to travel to Venice, Vienna, maybe Paris, "Spain certainly," and perhaps Yugoslavia and Ischia, while storing most of their possessions in Florence.[33] As the months went by, the couple's travel plans kept changing—mostly at Cal's insistence. Venice would have to wait until September, when his mother would join them.

Late January marked General Eisenhower's arrival in Rome, with thousands of police stationed along his route to protect him from Communist Party demonstrations. Elizabeth heard that many shops were closed that morning as "a phony strike, which was really a protest."[34] Surprised that people interpreted this as a Communist "weakness," she was fascinated by the chaotic state of Italian politics and hoped for the development of "a real socialist movement." One night Cal drank too much and wandered the streets of Florence until four a.m., when he came home and launched into an argument with Elizabeth. Shortly afterward he went to Rome for a few days, while she stayed in Florence to work on her novel. Despite this incident and their temporary separation, Elizabeth wrote to Mary that Cal was "in wonderful shape and is a joy to be with." He liked her novel about the trial in Iowa "very much and encourages me to keep at it constantly."[35] It probably helped that Cal was trying to live a more orderly life while revising his long poem *The Mills of the Kavanaughs*.

In April, the Lowells took brief trips to Pisa, Siena, and San

Gimignano, where Elizabeth sadly noted that even "wonderful works of Art . . . are beginning to go dead on me."[36] They also spent ten days at the Roman villa of Marguerite Caetani, Princess of Bassiano, a trilingual elderly American art patron whose conversation rarely strayed from her literary journal *Botteghe oscure*.[37] To Cal, the princess was "a mad, sympathetic aristocratic" version of Yaddo director Elizabeth Ames. She was an ideal subject for Elizabeth's dutiful letters to Charlotte Lowell. "A most luxurious and wonderful visit," her daughter-in-law reported, "with even a chauffeured car at our disposal for sightseeing in Rome!"[38]

After another visit to Rome in May, where they saw Spender and Auden, the Lowells sailed from Puglia to Istanbul and on to Greece. "I'd love to live in Athens," Elizabeth wrote, "except that it's more expensive than New York."[39] Turkey—"the only place about which I feel I have something interesting to say"—inspired "Two Recent Travellers." Her gimlet eye for the clash of romantic first-world presumptions with the harsher reality of Turkey gives the short story its ironic tone. Visiting the country to see its ancient ruins and bask in its quaintness, a young woman and a male employee of an export credit agency are bemused at "the squalid, inspired frenzy of the new"—the Westernizing reforms of Atatürk.[40] Hardwick finished the piece the following year and sent it to *The Kenyon Review*. The editor, John Crowe Ransom, wrote that "it was a very handsome job of writing," but suggested that it should be "a little more of a story and less of a travelogue." Weighing the journal's need for more fiction against his doubts about Elizabeth's efforts, Ransom added that he would hang on to the piece for potential publication; it would appear in the summer 1953 issue.[41]

In a letter to her mother-in-law, Elizabeth mentioned that Cal was walking doggedly along the ancient Roman walls of Constantinople, investigating mosques and church ruins, while she would run out of steam, needing to "come home and lie down and read."

Appealing to Mrs. Lowell's notions of frugality, Elizabeth noted that they were given an "excellent" empty cabin on the ship despite traveling third class and had moved from an expensive hotel with no running water to a cheaper one with a view of the Bosporus and a good restaurant. In Greece, they declined the services of a taxi driver in favor of taking public transportation to the Acropolis that cost a mere three cents.[42]

After two weeks in Paris in July, they toured the Loire Valley and Germany in a rented Renault with their friends Robie and Anne Macauley. Paris in the summer got on Elizabeth's nerves, what with "the boring young Fulbrights, hundreds of couples talking about bargains on the flea market," and the hordes of young Americans hanging out in cafés: "As you go down the street, some one [sic] yells at you, 'Hey, Elizabeth, meet Shirley!'"[43] Months of constant traveling were beginning to take their toll on her. "We've had fantastic troisième classe tours of half the world," she wrote to Mary, "& I'm crosseyed especially from our last 15 chateaux on the Loire."[44] While Cal went to England, she would be in Paris "to accomplish a month of hand laundry." All such chores fell to her normally, but the real reason she did not accompany him was her exhaustion from Cal's relentless sightseeing.

Cal wrote to Elizabeth from London to apologize for "all the fret and harrying of the last 3 days."[45] He felt "ridiculous and guilty and lonely." If she wanted him back "in a hurry," she should send a wire, and he would return "in a few hours." In another letter from London, he asked her to try "not to get all nerve-wrung and hysterical" and suggested that she needed a "check-up," presumably with a doctor.[46] He insisted that they needed each other "so desperately— at least I need you," adding a promise to be "more considerate from now on and take care of you and myself in doing so." This is a troubling letter, in which he sounds not only needy but also arrogant and manipulative. Why couldn't he see that traveling with another person meant not always doing everything your driven personality demanded? (Months later, in a letter to novelist Flannery O'Connor, he snidely remarked, apropos of Elizabeth's lack of interest in sightseeing on his terms, that she "expects the wonders of the world to file past her on a news film, a short one at that with lots of politics.")[47] Perhaps realizing that his tone in the letter to Elizabeth was off-putting, he added an olive-branch postscript informing her that he had "learned to wash his socks and send out laundry."

By early August, it was clear that something had snapped between the two of them. Elizabeth wrote to Mary that she was "absolutely paralyzed with hysteria" after Cal left her "weeping on the floor of a horrible hotel in the Rue Montmartre."[48] She moved to another hotel, but it proved to be a "wretched, dark cave . . . that literally belongs to the devil." She couldn't even work on her book, because the manuscript was in a suitcase at the Excelsior Hotel in Florence. "At the last minute there were too many suitcases, and we had to leave one behind," she explained. But why was *that* the one they didn't take with them? What with Lowell's mother due to arrive in a fortnight ("I'll be in a strait-jacket," Elizabeth moaned), exhaustion from constant travel, and the grim situation in Paris, she wrote, "My soul is rumpled." Yet she felt lonely without Cal, urging him not to stay away too long. Elizabeth hoped that moving on to Majorca "and the challenge of a Spanish phrase-book" would "iron me out again." But she prophesied that "by next Christmas, we'll probably be settled again in some freezing house somewhere, nervously smiling our way through another language we can't speak." Sure enough, Cal had a new plan.

Having fallen under the spell of John Lothrop Motley's *The Rise of the Dutch Republic* and Eugène Fromentin's classic survey of Dutch painting, *The Masters of Past Time* (*Les maîtres d'autrefois*), he wanted to visit Holland. It was time to leave "the Latin cultures," he wrote to Elizabeth from the Hotel Bristol in Pau, a village in southwestern

France where he was staying briefly with friends.[49] Holland would provide "novelty, the freedom to pick and choose and the privacy which is so necessary for reactions that are at all personal or profound." (What he probably meant was that in Italy, as soon as they left the apartment, they had to engage with people—by then the Lowells had numerous acquaintances—whereas in the Netherlands, they would be more anonymous.) He would accept "sight-unseen anything that *satisfies* you in Amsterdam." Elizabeth now had the chore of finding a new place to live in an unfamiliar city where she didn't speak the language, while burdened by an array of heavy suitcases. How was she to board a train with so much luggage? "Trying to keep our belongings together has nearly wrecked me," she wrote to Cal. "I have tried, because I wanted it myself, to make some sort of situation for us during all the moves of the last two years, but I have only caused myself paralyzing anxiety and haven't been able to suit you and so shan't do it again." Half-jokingly accusing him of not loving her and not "conceiv[ing] that anything might be painful" to her, Elizabeth explained that she was trying to do a " 'wife's part' " in arranging his affairs, but that it took a toll on her well-being.[50] She urged Cal to "take it easy, calm down before things get any more absurd & destructive. Living side by side as we do, without friends to advise & help, I get caught up in the whirl, utterly worn, bewildered & irritable & so can't help you because my life becomes a nightmare."[51]

Amsterdam was a grim place to put down roots so soon after the end of World War II. There was a serious housing shortage, food was scarce, heating was insufficient, and people on the street were bundled up almost to unrecognizability in layers of clothing. The shabby forty-dollars-a-month apartment Elizabeth managed to find at Nicolaas Witsenkade 17, near the Rijksmuseum, overlooked a canal at the city center. There were two large rooms, separated by a curtain, with dark walls and ugly furniture, and a kitchen with a stove (stoked with coal at eight dollars a bag), but no oven, no hot water, and no dishes or cutlery. The bathroom was in the hall, shared with others. Electricity and gas ran on coin-operated meters, and coal stoves were the sole source of heat. There was no telephone or radio. Granting that Amsterdam had attractive areas, Elizabeth wrote to Mary that she and Cal were on "a junky McKinley period street"—the reference was to the turn-of-the-century American president. "Everything is purple melancholy, deathly quiet, and freezing breezes slipping through the windows."[52] Although she felt "wretchedly lonely," Elizabeth mused that Holland seemed curiously "unforeign," perhaps because it shared the "Protestant" habits of "provincial America," including the six p.m. dinner service at restaurants. Trying to look on the positive side, she noted that the Concertgebouw was not far away, so she looked forward to "excellent music all winter." And there was always the prospect of "warm[ing] up on gin."[53]

That fall, she joked, the two of them were "pretending this is the only place in Europe where a typewriter works."[54] But as far as she was concerned, Amsterdam was utterly depressing. Cal had passed out invitations to their apartment at a reception the British Council held for the Lowells, but how could you have a dinner party without basic kitchen equipment? In early October, Elizabeth informed Mary that she was "now back at the grind, like a Buffalo housewife, except that I don't speak the language."[55] Her daily hour-and-a-half shopping trip for food—which had to be conducted in whatever halting Dutch she could muster—"gives you the kind of anxiety usually felt only for the last judgment." She sometimes came home with strange cuts of meat in "uncookable shapes."[56] It was demoralizing not to be able to pronounce Dutch words or understand what people on the street were saying. And then there were "the extraordinary household chores this primitive place demands."[57]

Adding to her woes was lack of access to their suitcases of clothes (en route from Florence by "slow freight") and being able to obtain only a half-pound of coffee every six weeks, with a ration card. She asked Mary to send a few jars of Nescafé. Elizabeth had asked Cal to bring this brand of powdered coffee from Paris but feared he would forget, since he now preferred Dutch hot chocolate. She also requested Hannah Arendt's new book, *The Origin of Totalitarianism*, which she and Cal would find deeply absorbing, a companion piece to their reading of official proceedings from the Nuremberg Trials.[58] Avoiding restaurants, she and Cal were eating at what she called hotdog (*frikandellen*) stands, where they observed the "indescribably, brutally homely" people leading a life that was all "family, washing, cleaning, heavy, heavy, dark discomfort."[59] In a way, although she didn't put it in so many words, her own life had become uncomfortably similar to her mother's. What she did compare it to was her early married life on 104th Street, in that "unspeakable apartment."

Cal, who had no responsibilities for chores or shopping, was delighted with the Dutch city, "and if I complain he kicks me," Elizabeth joked to Mary. He praised their new digs in a letter to his mother, happily announcing that they "had two home-cooked meals" (no mention of who did the cooking).[60] Pleased that "life is like it is in America and one feels more in control," he wrote to Charlotte that they were "very lucky to get an apartment that has a good kitchen, is clean and not remote." Granted that Cal was at pains to send his mother good news, it seems that he and Elizabeth were not on the same wavelength. He also apparently did not miss what she passionately lacked—friends with whom to discuss personal problems. As far as she was concerned, the only bright side of their current life was "reading English books and talking as though we weren't here, but at home."

The personal problems she wanted to discuss likely concerned Cal. Inevitably, quarrels would erupt between them—what he would call "domestic argument and sabotage."[61] Cal proudly told his mother that he was "a power-house of help about the apartment." But his readiness to pitch in was a sometime thing. A few months later he remarked to Elizabeth Bishop that "household chores" were among the things he was avoiding, along with his own writing.[62] In a letter to her that spring, he described what he called "a comic strip scene." He was lying on the sofa with a glass of milk while his "nervous, puzzle-faced wife [was] standing by a chair piled with books."[63] She was about to try to fix the window shade. Rather than offering to help, he told her to get a stepladder instead of trying to stand on the books, because she might fall. The humor he perceived in this situation seems strained, to say the least. His joking always had an aggressive edge. Elizabeth would remember how he used to say that he would send her back to Kentucky: "If you don't behave, I'm going to put you in a crate with a glass of water and a copy of *Partisan Review*, and I'm going to put on it One Way."[64] As far as Cal was concerned, everyday life in Amsterdam was almost completely over-shadowed by his deep and thrilling immersion in European history, literature, and art. The only drawback was a certain difficulty in tearing himself away to pursue his own writing.

Meanwhile Elizabeth fretted over her many unfinished projects, including her "nearly completed novel" about the trial (which would be published in 1955 as *The Simple Truth*). Maybe there was no point in putting work aside, she mused: you either had to try to publish it upon completion or toss it.[65] She had written a story based on the unfinished novel, which she sent to *Partisan Review*. Philip Rahv would reject this piece, praising "some excellent writing" but noting that it seemed "much too patently part of something else to stand by itself."[66] Elizabeth's essay about the false "snow queen" archetype of Amer-ican women met with a better reception: it would be published in the December issue of *Commentary*.[67] In this piece, she compared the "heavy-lidded coquetry of the middle-aged French couple" to the spu-rious airs and graces of a Southern belle. Elizabeth decried the artifice and calculation involved in European romance as compared to the

American ideal of love as "a noble possibility." Mary McCarthy especially liked "the image of the European woman—so funny, so exact."[68]

* * *

In January 1952 Elizabeth wrote, "We groan away these cold, dark,
paralyzing Dutch nights and days too, because it is always night here."
She longed for a villa in Tuscany "where we can have two servants
and there will be no cooking, no laundry, no cleaning—breakfast in
bed, lunch outside until December—and the magnificent scenery."[69]
The south of Italy would be "more boring" than Florence, she figured, and therefore more conducive to work." But with the exception
of a quick trip to London, Cal's plan was to stay put until March 1
"and, heaven forbid, probably longer." According to him, there was no
money to go elsewhere until spring.[70] Adding to his financial worries,
the cost of making his obsessive revisions on the proof of his recently
published book of poetry, *The Mills of the Kavanaughs*, nearly canceled
out his royalties.

Charlotte Lowell's visit that summer had been "a disaster worse
than could have been predicted."[71] Elizabeth and Cal were obliged
to spend time with her on the Basque coast, near Biarritz ("big and
brassy like Atlantic City I suppose" was Elizabeth's verdict). Writing to Peter Taylor, Cal described the "long meals comparing food
and hotels, or silent or arguing about whether we could afford a
cup of filtered coffee."[72] Now Mrs. Lowell was headed to Amsterdam
for a week's visit. Cal described his mother as "a very competent,
stubborn, uncurious, unBohemian woman with a genius for squeezing luxury out of rocks, who was accustomed to a pre-war level of
service that was no longer on offer.[73] He and Elizabeth were "fum-
ing inside like the burning stuffings of an overstuffed Dutch chair"
during her months-long sojourn in Europe.

But there were other reasons Elizabeth was, as she admitted,
"powerfully depressed." During the three months when she waited

for the delivery of her and Cal's clothes from Florence, she had only one change of clothing. How demoralizing that must have been, especially for someone who prided herself on her appearance! When their clothes finally arrived, she was dismayed to see that they were "worn out from packing and wrinkled beyond repair." Perhaps that hardly mattered, because venturing outdoors involved swaddling herself in "layers of underwear and sweaters under my suit." The uncomfortable flat was another dismal aspect of everyday life. It took an enormous effort to enter their freezing bedroom at night and to get out of bed in the morning and wash. "I can see why the Dutch are famous for clean houses and dirty faces," she wrote to Mary.[74]

In a *Sleepless Nights* passage marked "Holland, 1951," the narrator invokes the "squat black stove" that "tormented our days and nights," the "complaining letters" she wrote, and "how we fight after too much gin." (The other member of that "we" is not named.) Night was also the time when, "feeling uprooted because so much was familiar, we would tell each other the story of our lives." That odd twist in the sentence—how could a feeling of dislocation be evoked by a sense of familiarity?—seems to refer to the couple's itinerant life, setting up households in a succession of places that were not their own. Amsterdam, in this light, was scarcely different from Iowa City. A few aspects of this novelized version of the Amsterdam months seem to contradict the author's reality—in particular, the narrator's declaration that living in Holland was "one of the happiest periods of my life." Perhaps, in looking back after Cal's death, Elizabeth felt that their enforced togetherness in the stuffy room, spending their nights talking about their families (as they do in the novel), was actually a high point in the tumultuous history of her marriage.

There were some things Elizabeth could do to cheer herself up. By late October, she had treated herself to a permanent wave and bought a sofa for the living room and a bedspread and pillows. (Thinking about the other sofas and bedspreads she had bought during the past few years that were now "in Iowa, 104th Street, or lying around in storage houses" did give her a pang.)[75] She also invested in a secondhand radio, a "little smile from God" that supplied "excellent music all day and all night" as well as BBC Third Programme lectures and the U.S. election returns. Elizabeth found the paintings in the Mauritshuis in The Hague "a constant joy." And she came to realize that the Dutch people were "so extremely nice and obliging that you feel emotional about it." (Cal viewed them as "people who put you at your ease.")[76] Musing about the Protestant backbone of the Dutch, she wrote that the country "is so much in my bones that it's like a threat." Her mother "would fit in perfectly," she thought. "I wish she were here[,] for it takes a woman like that to keep us going!"

As the months went by, Elizabeth and Cal began to meet Dutch intellectuals and invite them for cocktails and dinner. These people were acquainted with a surprising breadth of American literature and wanted to discuss the poetry of Marianne Moore and the New Criticism.[77] Cal described them as "very loving, urbane and hard-headed about each other."[78] One acquaintance—"dry, enthusiastic, exact, and with a terrifying knowledge of German philosophy"— would "talk intellectual shop" from eleven a.m. to one o'clock the next morning. On a visit to a country home, the Lowells were taken aback by an "expert reading" of Joyce's *Finnegans Wake* and a recitation of Chaucer's *Canterbury Tales*.[79] But few people returned the Lowells' hospitality. "This is the European way, I suppose," Elizabeth remarked, "partly poverty and partly a horror of having a stranger en famille. . . . Furthermore there is a general suspiciousness about our being here in the first place. . . . The young Dutch intellectuals stand rather on their dignity, afraid you're making fun of them." The Lowells' lack of familiarity with current Dutch literature also hampered their efforts to befriend the literati. Yet at least one Dutchman, the novelist H. van Galen Last, genuinely enjoyed their company, envious of all the free time they had "to talk, to drink, to read and to travel." Elizabeth "seemed to have read as much as [Cal], and she talked with more ease and greater enthusiasm."[80] Van Galen Last and his wife thought of Cal as "a friendly walrus with a toy" when he rode their son's scooter. They recalled that Elizabeth had mentioned "the inequality" of being a slender woman married to "a giant who can't imagine that someone else gets tired."

As with many aspects of living abroad, Elizabeth found conversations with the Dutch "a little bit off center," like a radio station that wasn't properly tuned in.[81] Not that American expats were necessarily more compatible. After spending an evening with Americans who were living in Salzburg, Elizabeth airily dismissed them as "an awful collection of drips" in a letter to Mary.[82] Summing up her feeling of alienation, she added, "Not knowing another America[n] whom you've known before or who knows something you know is a terrible thing." It helped that she was basking in praise from Cal for the story she'd just finished, which she sent to *Partisan Review*.[83]

Intervals of European travel also brightened the picture. Cal had become voraciously interested in music, which led to a banquet of opera at the Royal Opera House in London in January 1952 (*Der Rosenkavalier, Fidelio, Wozzeck*) and five Mozart operas in six nights in Brussels the following spring. Despite his new passion, he was having trouble, as he wrote to Elizabeth Bishop, "convincing the cynical and skeptical Eliz. H. Lowell that I am not tone-deaf."[84] (Her sarcasm is palpable in a letter to Mary in which she observes that he "has great difficulty telling a low note from the higher, but he seems to think that no detriment to a man of grit.")[85] Curiously, neither Lowell seems to have commented about the extensive war damage in London. Instead, Elizabeth described taking tea with T. S. Eliot at his flat: "I fell quite in love with him, the way Eleanor Clark and I both started blushing and competing for the favors of a great tall handsome man in California who turned out to be seventy-four."[86]

There were excursions to Cambridge and Bath, and Elizabeth spent time with the Harmsworths again. If nothing else, they provided good gossip: their daughter, a Sarah Lawrence graduate, "just had her second illegitimate child." The family's story reminded Elizabeth of Ford Madox Ford's novel *The Good Soldier*, about a tangled web of marriage betrayals.

When the Lowells returned to Amsterdam, Elizabeth found the apartment "more pleasant," with "two stoves going" and "several new plants."[87] In a letter to Randall Jarrell, who had recently been divorced, Cal wrote that he and Elizabeth "have long been wanting to ask you to come and live with us."[88] But plans for a spring trip to Germany and Austria were clouded by Mrs. Lowell's announcement that she was planning a return visit. Telling the Macauleys that "Cal has tried to stave her off," Elizabeth joked that she and Cal would have Mrs. Lowell's passport revoked "so that we could have a wonderful summer with you. (She really and profoundly is subversive.)"[89]

By late February, the strain of working a few feet from each other in one room for months began to fray the couple's nerves again. Cal wrote to Elizabeth Bishop that his and Elizabeth's political outlooks were now opposed, conservative versus liberal. They liked to read aloud to each other, but they both "detest listening." After discussing other subjects, he came to the point: "Sometimes, I suspect we see too much of each other."[90] He had already opted for four days of bachelordom on a houseboat borrowed from a Dutch psychiatrist acquaintance, Huyk van Leeuwen. Elizabeth, who would use the three days living on her own to catch up on laundry, wrote to Peter and Eleanor Taylor that living in Amsterdam made her "permanently immune to guilt feelings about luxurious living! I feel I have known the bottom of drudgery and ugliness."[91] (Washing clothes involved heating water on the stove and then waiting weeks for everything to dry in the damp climate.) She also expected to have to scrub the deck of the houseboat after Cal returned, "so that the owner won't be disgraced."[92] Van Leeuwen's first wife, Judith, later recalled Elizabeth as "frighteningly severe and intellectual." and the Lowells as "always intense." They sounded like "a bear and a bird, even when they talked at the same time, which they often did."[93]

In March, Elizabeth wrote to Mary mainly to discuss *The Oasis*, which she thought "a bit too long" and slightly marred by "too many foreign phrases."[94] Elizabeth's larger objection to this problematic novel about academic life was that Mary's talent was so original, yet she was "pushing this uniqueness into an 'established form'"—a novel—whereas her real gift was for something else: "a portrait, an argument, a memoir." At least none of the characters were recognizable figures, which was a good thing. Elizabeth added that "everyone in Amsterdam" was reading Mary's short story collection *Cast a Cold Eye*. By now, the Lowells had a circle of Dutch friends who discussed such matters at gatherings lubricated by *oude genever* (an aromatic gin).

Always seeing life through a literary lens, she compared herself in this letter to a character in a Knut Hamsun novel after washing "a huge batch of winter underwear." An excursion to Leyden—where the Lowells were guided by an anthropology professor "who is sort of an anthropological fact himself, being Negro, Jewish & Dutch!"—leavened the "cramped, hard, dark and unproductive" days they spent indoors in Amsterdam. After a visit to the city's war-devastated Jewish quarter, Elizabeth wrote, "To see the bare spots where their houses had been was terrible, because there is never an unoccupied spot in Holland." But other forms of sightseeing could be boring. "I felt I'd go mad if I ever heard myself exclaiming again about lovely old Dutch houses and streets," she wrote. "I am swollen with the enthusiastic visitor platitude."

It was finally time to leave the Netherlands. "The day of May 4th will be the happiest of my life," Elizabeth wrote.[95] "Free of the ashes, the rug beater, the Dutch market at last."[96] After traveling to several cities in Belgium ("Antwerp is positively sinister . . . prix fixe meals for $5.00, sans service, wine or coffee"),[97] the Lowells were headed for Paris, Germany, and Vienna, en route to Salzburg, where Cal would be teaching in July and August. He wrote to Elizabeth Bishop that the apartment "was now full of half-opened suitcases . . . and each [of] us knows that if he can only stall long enough the other will do the packing."[98]

In May, the Masterpieces of the Twentieth Century Festival was in progress in Paris, organized by the Congress for Cultural Freedom.[99] Cal had imagined that the conference would be "pompous and exciting."[100] Participants included Allen Tate, William Faulkner (who "uttered a few inadequate sentences," according to Elizabeth), Katherine Anne Porter (who had been ill but said "a few vapid words about 'working artists'"), and W. H. Auden.[101] Elizabeth found the proceedings to be "a fantastic combination of friends, gossip, complaints, speeches, concerts, receptions, cocktail parties," but with "very little atmosphere of political debate."[102] There was "much dashing about in taxis, long luncheons, meetings at the [Café] Flore," and she worried that she wasn't "quite 'brilliant' enough." Not to mention feeling "woefully underdressed," having thought the event would be like one of the "sweaty debates" she had attended in New York. For her, the high points were cultural events, including performances by the New York City Ballet; Jean Cocteau reading his libretto for the oratorio *Oedipus rex*, conducted by its composer, Igor Stravinsky; and Benjamin Britten's new opera *Billy Budd*. Tate, a recent and fervent convert to Roman Catholicism, entertained the Lowells in other ways. He was "gloriously effervescent and unacademic," Cal wrote,[103] and helped them put up with another visiting American writer whom they found a bore.

In Germany, Elizabeth dismissed Cologne and Mainz as resembling "a dinky little boardwalk of shops Coney Island style."[104] The older part of Heidelberg, which had not been bombed by the Allies, was "brown, baroque & magnificent," yet she just didn't like the city. It's a good bet that her dyspeptic responses to this leg of their travels were due to fatigue. By now, no matter how compelling the sights were, Elizabeth was "utterly fed up" with the stresses of travel. "My life is just one long grimace of misunderstanding," she wrote.[105] She had to keep packing and unpacking, storing and shipping their possessions, and fixing up each rented apartment, only to disassemble her homey touches when the couple moved on. This exercise was one in which Cal apparently took no part.

Irritated at once again having to shop for basic household goods, Elizabeth was also "sick at heart for the sound of my own language." So starved was she to hear English spoken that she was rooted to the spot in an Amsterdam flower shop, listening to an American woman say "Listen, do yuh ship . . . flowers to airplanes?" The problem wasn't only language; she also missed what she called the American "temperament," in a world seemingly ruled by "thrift and caution and indifference and humorless pride."[106] Meanwhile the American who shared her life got to hear her unvarnished opinion about marriage: "You can be as gross, slovenly, mean and brutally verbose as you want."[107]

* * *

Since 1947, the Salzburg Seminar had presented programs on diverse topics, with the twin goals of introducing the range of American cultural achievements and promoting cultural exchange. Young Europeans were invited to the Schloss Leopoldskron, a dazzling white rococo castle, to initiate what was envisioned as a center of intellectual thought. Participants received a travel stipend and room and board.[108] In July 1952 the seminar hosted one hundred poets, artists, and musicians. Cal spoke about American poetry "from Emerson to [Randall] Jarrell" and gave seminars on Chaucer, Pope, and Wordsworth. Students adored his passionate commitment to the poets.

"Cal was a huge success," Elizabeth wrote to Charlotte. "But the whole thing was exhausting simply because it was so stimulating, and he responded to nearly every one of the 100 students."[109]

In retrospect, Cal's intensity in the classroom was a tip-off that another manic phase was beginning. More worrisomely, another sign was his sudden attraction to Giovanna Madonia, a music student. As he had done in the past with Jean, he expected Elizabeth to acquiesce to a blossoming affair with a younger woman. His now-dormant, now-revived passion for Madonia would thread through the remaining decades of his life, even after her marriage and his marriage to Caroline Blackwood. Madonia left Salzburg several weeks before the seminar ended, but Cal remained on the boil. One day in August, he went missing and was discovered wandering near the German frontier. After he was brought back to the castle, the police arrived, and he barricaded himself in his room, wearing only his shorts. Austria was still under American occupation, and the director of the seminar felt that he would do better among English speakers. With some difficulty, Cal was coaxed into an ambulance that drove him to a local military hospital. But he was allowed to stay there only one night because the rooms that housed violent patients were filled. It was decided to move him to the U.S. Army hospital in Munich, but no ambulance would take him to Germany, so the seminar director and his assistant smuggled Cal across the border in a private car. Elizabeth and the director's wife followed in another car.

In Munich, more chaos ensued. Cal insisted that his real problem was a fracture in his leg, and he was denied admission because he was a civilian. Only after the seminar leader and his assistant described Cal as "America's natural treasure" did the admissions sergeant agree to accept this patient, who was moved to a locked ward of mentally ill military personnel. Elizabeth, who stayed at a hotel, visited him every day. The hospital was "a terrible place for him," she wrote to the Macauleys, who had been in Salzburg and were aware of his recent behavior.[110] He seemed to confuse the other patients with his students and, despite their hostility, tried to converse with them about Goethe's *Faust*. For Elizabeth, he had a different tone. "Everybody has noticed that you've been getting pretty dumb lately," he told her.[111] Racked by a dreadful combination of worry and terror, she had no idea how to respond to his outbursts. If his insults didn't make her cry, he "would become anxious and suspicious." The long days of painful conversation were so exhausting that she would fall asleep as soon as she returned to her hotel at eight p.m.[112] Yet for Cal's sake, she believed it was a good thing that she was the person he treated most harshly. "It's been my experience that nobody holds a man's brutality to his wife against him," she wrote. (Not completely unaware of her martyrdom in this instance, she remarked that her father-in-law would have thought her "an outstanding example of Christian charity.") She insisted that she had "no hard feelings at all" but only wanted "that wonderfully rich, alive and extraordinary person to be well again."

One day the head of the hospital asked her for information about Cal's army record. When she explained that he had been a conscientious objector, the man flew into a rage. It was all she could do to insist that her husband remain in the hospital for lack of any other place to go. Despite all these struggles, Elizabeth was determined to keep this episode as private as possible, certain—or trying to be— that Cal would be well again soon after his electroshock therapy treatments at the hospital.[113] She cautioned the Macauleys against saying anything that would provoke gossip: "please just say it was overwork and exhaustion." But she was stuck in Munich with no one to confide in, and letters were the only outlet for her feelings. "I pity Cal from the bottom of my heart, and I fear for him in every way," she wrote. "Needless to say, I have reached the lowest point in my life."[114] In a letter to John McCormack, another friend of Cal's, her anxieties extended to a vision of "landing penniless in New York City."[115]

When he seemed to recover, a tussle ensued about whether to give her power of attorney so that she could cash a letter of credit. Cal agreed, but the doctors said they weren't sure he was in his right mind. Finally, "Cal rushed up to me and began to weep and apologize for <u>everything</u>." He was "utterly exhausted and ashamed, completely calm and rational however." Yet although he was ready to do whatever she wanted, she was in a quandary. Flying home, she wrote, would cost nearly eight hundred dollars for each of them.[116] She knew he needed to be in a hospital, but the thought of trying to find one at home, where they also had no place to live, was overwhelming. On August 31, when Cal was released, she wrote to McCormack, who had visited her, to apologize for being "so exhausted and hysterical." To the Macauleys, she wrote that Cal could now recall having only friendly feelings toward Giovanna. Unaware of how many times this scenario would be repeated in the coming years, Elizabeth was experiencing "a joy beyond description to have Cal himself again."[117] Months later, in a letter to his mother, Cal would praise "my dear and intelligent Elizabeth" for her efforts on his behalf.[118]

Although the doctors advised her that Cal need not move to another hospital right away, she wanted him "to be talking to a doctor every day for a while."[119] She finally decided that the Binswanger Sanatorium in Kreuzlingen, Switzerland, was the best option. Despite Cal's apparent good health, Elizabeth had to struggle with their suitcases by herself as they stepped aboard the third-class train car. Once they arrived at the sanatorium, she realized that this was the right choice, providing "connecting beautiful rooms . . . deep baths . . . four meals a day," all for fifteen dollars a day for both of them. In early September, she wrote Blair and Holly Clark that Cal "just keeps saying, 'gosh that's wonderful.'"[120] After ten days in this luxurious setting, they traveled to northern Italy.

Elizabeth had been worried about the plans she and Cal had

made to join Allen Tate in Venice in late September, during the International Conference of Artists sponsored by UNESCO.[121] Although they looked forward to seeing their old friend, neither of them was in the mood for days of heavy socializing. Yet somehow it all worked out, and the Spenders and the Clarks, who were then based in Paris, also joined them. Afterward, the Lowells spent time sightseeing in Venice, Padua, Verona, and Torcello. "It was all marvelous," Elizabeth reported later. "Even I never got tired because I was completely enchanted."[122]

The Lowells' new plan was to spend the winter in Rome. It seemed more affordable than Paris, especially because they needed a more spacious flat after having been "cooped up in one room . . . since last May."[123] On a postcard to the Clarks, Elizabeth described the Eternal City as "splendid—sky so clear, so crowded & noisy we feel a little dizzy."[124] They were staying at the Pensione California, Via Aurora 43, steps from the Borghese Gardens, "overlooking pine trees & the entire city & far too expensive." (Writing to his Boston-centric mother, Cal described the apartment as "two smallish . . . immaculate rooms in a sort of Beacon St. going into the Fenway part of Rome . . . so proper that I fear we'll turn into two nineteenth century spinsters.")[125] Elizabeth explained to the Macauleys that the pensione was "just what we need, no household, no puttering about all day & real privacy for working."[126]

A few days later she wrote John McCormack that she and Cal were "suddenly and amazingly wildly contented & for the simplest reason. . . . We have settled ourselves in two quite separate rooms."[127] As she explained, "ever since we've been married we've been breathing on each other's necks like dragons in various wretched apartments in which you slept, ate, worked & argued in the room. The sudden privacy is overwhelmingly exciting." They were "writing, reading & studying all the time," and when they went out for a meal, "it's like going to your first party." The weather was "wickedly balmy," and for once, she didn't "feel bewildered & tense in a foreign city." Italy was now relatively familiar territory.

They had eased into a comfortable routine, visiting their "neighborhood restaurant, coffee bar & newspaper seller." When they went out for a cappuccino in the morning, Elizabeth would order while Cal would go in search of *The New York Times* and *Herald Tribune*. Cal, she reported, read "all the speeches of all the candidates [for U.S. president] & likes to say that Stevenson is over his head & Truman is really his speed." (This was just a pose; when Eisenhower won a landslide victory, the Lowells—like other American intellectuals—were devastated.) "We're working like monks . . . much harder than we've ever done since we've been married," Cal wrote to Allen Tate. "Elizabeth has a good draft of a long story that's starting to become a novella and ought to be her master-work."[128]

The only problem with their lives, Elizabeth told the Clarks, was that "we are poorer than we even admit to ourselves" and thus unable to wander too far in Rome. Their social life was "a vicious game of solitaire, double, in the evening, after the trattoria."[129] Eventually, according to Cal, they found themselves lying in bed two hours later than usual, nursing hangovers. The magic had begun to drain away. That fall every Fulbright grantee apparently expected to have dinner with them, which involved returning to the pensione on buses at one a.m. ("It's too dull and exhausting for words.") When the McDowells, friends from Kenyon College, visited in November, the Lowells took them on a tour of Rome. At dinner "with too much wine," Elizabeth "with devastating charm and mobile face" lectured their visitors that they were too talkative—which caused the couple to leave the restaurant and walk "into the Roman dark and out of our lives."[130] But the Lowells now presented a united front. In his letter to Tate, Cal declared, "I don't think I could live a month without Elizabeth."[131]

Months earlier he had received a letter proposing a teaching position at the University of Iowa, to replace a faculty member who had a year-long grant, for a salary of $5,000. "That would mean actually leaving Europe, being on the boat, no later than the 1st week in January!" Elizabeth wrote to Blair Clark.[132] They desperately needed money, and they couldn't afford to return to the United States without a job for Cal. Still, they decided against a contract to teach the entire year, and Elizabeth wrote, "The best thing that could happen is for the job not to materialize." But by December 8, the die was cast. Cal would teach a course on European poetry in translation at Iowa. They would leave Rome in late December and spend a week in Paris before the boat sailed on January 9. (Although their books were still stored in Amsterdam, they decided to let American Express handle the shipping rather than return to Holland.)

Now that the immediate future was settled, the young Americans who wanted to have dinner with the Lowells seemed "rather fun," what with "Greenwich Village parties and dinners in trattorias for 10 people."[133] Elizabeth was "ready to die from fatigue in the last hour" of these meals, when everyone had to figure out his part of the check. "Rome," she concluded, "is wearing both of us out."[134] On December 27, the Lowells took the train to Paris, where they stayed at the Hôtel des Saints-Pères, "right off the Boulevard St. Germain." In a letter to the Clarks, with whom she and Cal were about to meet up, Elizabeth gossiped about Jean Stafford (her second marriage, to *Life* magazine writer Oliver Jensen, was on the rocks) and Eleanor Clark's surprising recent marriage to the novelist Robert Penn Warren, "whom no one ever expected to be 'available.'"

Unlike the Lowells' outbound voyage, their return trip on the *Samaria* was a "fearful" experience, with hundreds of immigrants to Canada, "all sick the entire way." On January 19, 1953, the couple arrived in New York, more than two and a half years after they had left. Their time in Europe had resulted in a roller coaster of emotions and experiences, given them new perspectives on each other, and in many ways set a pattern for their remaining years together. When they landed, Elizabeth was reminded of the triumphant feeling she had the first time she took the C&O train from Kentucky to New York. To celebrate their return, she prevailed on Cal to take her to the Plaza Hotel bar for a drink; when the bill came to nine dollars "before we had hardly eaten a potato chip, . . . we knew we were home."[135]

CHAPTER 5

Boston

(1953–1958)

BACK IN BOSTON temporarily, Elizabeth wrote to the Clarks that she found the city "enchanting," except for the "horrid reality" of Charlotte Lowell. There was also a martini-enriched dinner party at which Cal's cousin Alfred drunkenly "kissed and pinched and mauled" Elizabeth and other women. The Lowells had one "thrilling moment, delirious personally and financially," when they talked to a realtor about buying a house in Boston.[1] But nothing came of it, and in February they returned by train to Iowa City for the winter term at the university.

In a letter to Charlotte, assuring her that Cal was writing "brilliant" poetry and that his courses would not occupy too much of his time, Elizabeth described their surroundings as "flat and ugly," with "the air and look of a temporary town."[2] She scoffed that "anything over fifty years old is a landmark." (Of course, she knew that Charlotte would be sympathetic to this criticism.) With a population of just fifty thousand in the early 1950s, Iowa City had a compact downtown with small stores, "taverns with pool tables in the back, and restaurants that served meat and potato meals."[3] Flannery O'Conner wrote to the Lowells that she remembered the "sooty tubercular-looking houses" and "the zoo with two indifferent bears in it."[4] Outdoors it was zero degrees Fahrenheit, but the Lowells' new apartment was large and pleasant enough, with three rooms plus kitchen and bath. The luxury of taking a bath three times a day after the deprivations of Amsterdam had not yet lost its appeal. After unpacking and making multiple visits to the five-and-dime and hardware stores, it was as though they had never been away. During the weeks before the term started, the couple caught up with the literary magazines and books they had missed out on during the past two years. Elizabeth wrote to Mary that they were "reading aloud with horror to each other" from book reviews "written in the unknown tongue of Sewanee,"[5] and that she was baffled at the negative response to Mary's novel *The Groves of Academe*.

The Lowells were also busy with their writing; Cal reworked poems he had written in Rome, and Elizabeth made final revisions to her story set in Turkey. ("I'll never again try anything with 'exotic climes' in it," she declared.)[6] In March, she finished what Cal called "a wonderful polemic" on the English translation of Simone de Beauvoir's bombshell, *The Second Sex*, for the May–June issue of *Partisan Review*.[7] Calling this long book "madly sensible and brilliantly confused," Elizabeth found that de Beauvoir had packed it with a "bewildering inclusiveness" of information and opinion. "There is a nervous, fluent, rare aliveness on every page," she wrote, as well as "discipline, learning and doggedness." But the French author's forceful intellectual stance often ignored everyday reality. Claiming that women's subservient behavior was largely the result of men's actions, particularly with regard to private property, de Beauvoir wrote that "the domestic cares of maternity imprisoned" women in a kind of eternal repetition that "produced nothing new." Elizabeth's response was that "housework, child rearing, cleaning, keeping, nourishing, looking after—these must be done by someone, or worse by millions of someones day in and day out." (As always, she was mindful of the legion of cleaners and carers that made middle-class lives possible.) She pointed out that "most men, too, are doomed to work of brutalizing monotony."

Writing about de Beauvoir's insistence that women were "the equal" of men, Elizabeth wished for a more nuanced evaluation. In her view, women's physical differences from men could not be overcome, accounting not only for women's inability to "build bridges, conquer foreign lands," but also for situations in which men could dominate simply by virtue of their size and strength and aggressive sexual drive. "Any woman who has ever had her wrist twisted by a man recognizes a fact of nature as humbling as a cyclone to a frail tree branch," she wrote—a startlingly vivid image no doubt drawn from personal experience. "After she has been conquered [i.e., become a girlfriend or wife] she has to 'pay' the man to restrain his appetite, which he is so likely to reveal at cocktail parties, and in his pitifully longing glance at the secretary—she pays with ironed shirts, free meals, the pleasant living room, a son." This exchange typified the life of the average American woman, but it was remote from de Beauvoir's own experience with Jean-Paul Sartre—an open relationship in which she did not tend to his household needs. One of de Beauvoir's "most brilliant" statements, in Elizabeth's view, is that artistic women are concerned with disrupting the status quo. Yet she noted that the Frenchwoman had failed to mention a major factor that limited women's breadth as writers: their inability—largely because of cultural taboos—to pursue the tremendous variety of experience vouchsafed to men. Even so, Elizabeth insisted, "the *best* literature by women is superior to *most* of the work done by men."

Rahv praised this piece, and so did Blair, Diana Trilling, and Robert Giroux.[8] Cal half-jokingly wrote to Peter Taylor that Elizabeth "proves with all the eloquence of Shelley that no woman can ever be as good as a man. It's quite gone to her head[;] she walks around with

her head in the clouds and I am dirt under her feet."[9] Robie Macauley
teased Elizabeth that because de Beauvoir's book was so expensive,
it was "plenty cheaper to mistreat your wife and then listen to her
complain."[10] Clearly, a belittling view of women was no less present
in progressive circles than it was elsewhere. In a rare change of heart,
Elizabeth would later reject her initial response to *The Second Sex*.
Without specifically crediting the women's movement of the 1970s,
she realized that the book was a landmark effort and that women
were now able to live much fuller lives, even "go[ing] to Arabia in
your jeans [with a] knapsack."[11]

* * *

During the spring term, Elizabeth audited Cal's class on French, German, Italian, and Latin poetry (Five Poets in Translation). The couple
planned to spend the summer in Bloomington, Indiana, where Cal
would teach at the School of Letters before returning to Iowa in the
fall.[12] Afterward, from January to June 1954, he would occupy the
endowed poetry chair at the University of Cincinnati. Elizabeth was
pleased that for the next year he would not need to look for a new
job every time they needed money, or when he felt like teaching as
a break from writing. By April, she had even become "rather fond"
of Iowa City, believing that it had taken the place of Lexington in
her life. (She had just flown back home for Easter, after not having
seen her family for several years.) There was even "another horrible
murder," though it was not the sort of thing that she wanted to write
about.[13] Meanwhile her work on *The Simple Truth* continued.

Elizabeth still had her heart set on buying a small house in Boston.
With luck, this could happen while Charlotte Lowell was sojourning
in Europe, to avoid her interfering advice. Of course, Elizabeth never
admitted as much in her chatty letters to her mother-in-law ("Are you
still thinking of Rapallo or Portofino, heavenly places").[14] In June she
wrote that Cal would be sure to visit Charlotte before she left, but that

the cost of hotels in the high season and their lack of a car would keep them from spending the summer in New England.

They actually did buy a car that month, a 1937 Packard. Cal got a new license after fifteen years away from the wheel—the aftermath of the terrible accident that disfigured Jean—but more than a decade would pass before Elizabeth took the driving test.[15] Cal wouldn't let her practice driving, claiming that it would be "hard on the car."[16] The hot weather revived Elizabeth's dislike of Iowa, but visiting friends from the Netherlands pried the Lowells out of the house for several days of "camping, swimming and boating"—an interlude that left them both "suntanned and rested."[17] She did not accompany Cal to Indiana after all, because no apartment could be found, and she didn't want to have to stay in a dormitory for the six-week course. After his teaching stint was over, he spent August in a Gambier, Ohio, house loaned by a friend and filled with more friends—including the Taylors, the Ransoms, and the Macauleys—before visiting his mother in Boston.

Elizabeth was initially unsure whether she and Cal could afford to buy a house. "It was my plebian [sic] fear," she wrote to him, "and your . . . caution that made me think we had to work and save the entire house money."[18] But that autumn she was in "the most happy mood," because "all of a sudden it was clear that we could do it easily." The solution, as she presented it to Blair in a letter, was to ask if he could lend them $10,000 "to be paid back in ten years." She explained that Cal's Winslow trust had repaid a debt, freeing about $1,000 a year, which the Lowells could ask to have sent to Blair. With this loan for the house, she argued, they could use their savings to buy furniture, create an emergency fund, and allow Cal to turn down the Cincinnati position—which she fervently hoped he would do. Elizabeth stressed that Cal was "just as eager" as she was for this house, which would mean being able to keep their books in one place "and have a free, more spacious life."[19]

To Cal, she wrote that she had to purchase new glasses while recovering from convergence insufficiency, a misalignment of her eye muscles when focusing at close distances. (Elizabeth actually described this as "conversion deficiency," a misheard diagnosis—or perhaps a deliberate play on words—that amused her. The understood reference was to Cal's religious conversion and her lack of interest in it.) She was reading "morbid and obscure plays by Pirandello," but she had also been wandering around Montgomery Ward, looking at household furnishings and "barely" refraining from purchasing items for the future house.[20] Elizabeth regretted that the Iowa City apartment did not look its best ("I ought to buy little things to make it more cheerful and comfortable"), but her heart wasn't in it, especially since the décor of all their other rentals was packed away in trunks.[21] In a plaintive letter to her husband after he had been gone nearly two weeks, she announced that she had "arrived at a little principle of my own—a week of separation is the limit." Elizabeth vetoed Cal's suggestion of looking for a house on Cape Cod because "it would be Greenwich Village in the summer," with too many people coming through.[22] She missed having him there to drive her on errands ("I . . . nearly wept bringing about 10 books for my review home on foot yesterday").

Picking up the thread of a discussion they had had, she admitted that she hadn't fully explained her thoughts about the "famous marriage" of the poets Robert and Elizabeth Browning, because it was "not at all propitious for writing in his case—he did most of his work before and after."[23] She added that the Brownings' relationship, "intense as it was, was very peculiar," because when Robert told his wife that he put himself in her hands, she insisted it was she who wanted to put herself in *his* hands. "But," Elizabeth concluded, "one should not draw private lessons from public history!" Married life was uppermost on her mind during this brief separation. "Mostly it's that baffling question of why one should torture the person he most loves in all the world and upon whom his happiness depends," she wrote. (Elizabeth always used *he* in the traditional way in referring to an individual, even when—as in this case—she was writing about herself.) While she figured that "all married people" did this, she worried that she was always letting him down: "I should be calm and sensible about trifles, indifferent to them, instead of anxious and jabbing." She promised to improve, adding that she knew she could, because she had already moderated her drinking "to a reasonable extent, unless I flatter myself."

The house the Lowells decided to buy was in Duxbury, Massachusetts, forty miles south of Boston. Built in 1740 and sitting on three acres that included a stream (and a flagpole), it was shingled in red cedar and equipped with an up-to-date oil furnace, but the roof was in poor condition.[24] Blair had declined Elizabeth's request because he lacked the resources for such a large loan, but he subsequently said he could manage to send $2,000.[25] In mid-November she told him that they didn't need his loan after all—they had obtained a bank mortgage—and that the roof repairs would be put off until spring. The Lowells planned to move in after Cal finished his teaching. "The house has made the most enormous difference to us somehow," she wrote. Life in Iowa seemed bearable because "we know we'll be in our own little love nest in May."[26] (The move-in date was later shifted to June.) Her new worry was that Charlotte would return from Europe for the housewarming. "We want our shabbiness to be intact and irrevocable before she sees us settled," Elizabeth deadpanned. "Nothing is more terrifying to me than to try to execute Mrs. Lowell's interior decoration ideas on no money—even with money perhaps."[27]

During the unseasonably hot and dry autumn in Iowa City, she sat in on a class Cal taught, with a member of the classics department, on Homer in the original Greek, and she was one of the few students who showed up to take the final exam. "It's wonderful fun," she told Blair, "but I now understand why it's impossible to write when you're teaching." She and Cal had "organized record listening afternoons" and were playing checkers at the cocktail hour in lieu of drinking. The two of them had even become "great fans of the Iowa football team." She also was trying to improve her cooking skills (though Blair had praised her "serious cooking" when she had lived on 104th Street). "And so I . . . don't get any of my writing plans finished, even though I have done short things."

One of these things was her wide-ranging essay "Memoirs, Conversations and Diaries," published in the September–October issue of *Partisan Review*. In the decades since that 1953 essay, memoir writing has undergone a sea change; the widespread avoidance of intimate personal details that Elizabeth described has been superseded by raw outpourings she likely would have detested. Still, understood in context, her point of view remains compelling. Apropos of the "sinful appeal" of revelations about the famous or infamous, she wrote, "We can hardly imagine the malice of writing, 'I have met Gide but he was distracted by the sight of a beautiful young boy on the beach.'" Yet some aspects of celebrity have remained constant. Elizabeth noted that magazine and newspaper profiles had become "an unyielding bore of joshing flattery" and "the piling up of a benign lump of fact." She skewered the new fashion for articles composed entirely from quotes by a famous person as "a monstrous crossbreeding of indifference and total recall" with "no more relation to . . . the interview or the conversation . . . than a cough to a song recital." The casual references in this essay to James Boswell, Paul Valéry, Stéphane Mallarmé, the Goncourt brothers, André Gide, Alfred Jarry, Edmund Wilson, Ben Jonson, Thomas De Quincy, Frank Harris, T. S. Eliot, Henry James, Charles Augustin Sainte-Beuve, Emily Dickinson, Herman Melville, and other literary figures would pose a significant challenge to today's magazine readers. Throughout her writing life, Elizabeth never provided identifying information for the authors she wrote about, on the assumption that she was addressing peers equally steeped in classic and modern literature.

In November, Rahv wrote to ask for permission to include "The Mysteries of Eleusis"—her short story about the waitress—in *More Stories in the Modern Manner: From Partisan Review*, to be published by Avon in 1954.[28] Royalty payments (one cent per copy) would be made in two installments: half in January and half in April. Apparently responding to her request that the anthology include "Evenings at Home"—her semiautobiographical story about a woman who returns to her Kentucky home—he promised to try to persuade the publisher to add it. (They did, but they omitted "Mysteries," which was published in 1953 in *The New Partisan Reader*.) Rahv apologized for not including her piece on Faulkner in the *Reader*: the book was too long, and it was decided to omit work by most of the authors who contributed more than one piece.[29] He hoped she could write an article for a new *Partisan Review* compilation—maybe a piece about younger American writers, or current opinions about Freud, or "the specific achievement and characteristics of women novelists."[30]

In the meantime, Elizabeth published "Anderson, Millay and Crane in Their Letters," a review of three recent compilations of literary correspondence. "Letters are above all useful as a means of expressing the ideal self," she wrote. "In letters we can reform without practice, beg without humiliation, snip and shape embarrassing experiences to the measure of our own desires." Private correspondence tends to show "that people do not live their biographies." (Yet her own letters, especially when she was deeply upset and writing to people close to her, are nakedly revelatory.) Elizabeth regretted that the letters of Sherwood Anderson (best known for his short story collection *Winesburg, Ohio*) had been chosen "upon a principle of reckless high-mindedness," as if only his "literary life" and not his personal life—which included four marriages—were important. In her view, Anderson was interesting "*as a case . . . the peculiar rising* and waning star, this man who brought to literature almost nothing except his own lacerated feelings." Reading Edna St. Vincent Millay's letters, she found that the poet she thought she knew (the one who "kissed so many lips") turned out to be "Meg in *Little Women*, resourceful, sensitive, devoted," cutting off her hair "not to be a flapper, but to pay for Father's illness." Elizabeth wrote that Edmund Wilson (a lover of Millay's who had written about her) "undervalue[d] the spectacular pain of the sort of success she had." Success came too soon, giving her a "hopeless, killing bitterness about her own place" in literature.

Saving the best for last, Elizabeth praised the collection of letters from the poet Hart Crane for "the sheer power of mind they reveal," whether he was writing about books, his contemporaries, his own writing, or a landscape. Despite his peripatetic, often dissolute existence, he wrote many lively letters to his parents, "so squeezing in their anxiety and egotism, so screeching in their divorce." In fact, "what the letters amazingly suggest is the disturbing possibility that Crane had a happy life. . . . Contrary to the guilt feelings usually surmised Crane seems to have 'enjoyed'—no other word occurs to me—his homosexuality." Although Elizabeth did not spell out the entire situation behind Crane's apparent suicide in 1932 (his great love affair was over, and he was in a creative slump), it struck her as almost miraculous that shortly before his death he was praising life in Mexico and "detailing his incredibly funny difficulties with a drunken servant." As Elizabeth would do so often, she allowed for the workings of grace. "You cannot easily account for the amount of joy in [the letters]," she concluded, which suggested that "this 'doomed' poet was, after all, under the protection of a charm."[31] The playwright Clifford Odets wrote to her to praise the piece and to ask whether a rumor he had heard that Crane was actually pushed off the boat after propositioning some of the crew might be true.[32]

* * *

After Cal read an article in *Time* magazine that linked throat cancer to smoking,[33] he decided to try giving it up. "Elizabeth started
stopping a month ago," he wrote to Elizabeth Bishop, "and was very
Spartan and undemonstrative about it; I don't think she suffered.
Now after listening to me for a few hours groaning and boasting,
she's ready to quit." He also told Bishop that they wanted to have a
child "as soon as we get to Duxbury. (Really!)"[34] In early December,
when Cal was briefly out of town, Elizabeth wrote to tell him that
his "beloved car" was buried in snow: "It seems to feel very sorry for
itself and makes me feel very sorry for us and our trip"—to Cincinnati in January, for Cal's teaching position.[35] By the first of the year,
she had finished writing *The Simple Truth*. In a letter to Bishop, Cal
wrote that the novel was "the best thing she's done, very stern with
a subdued satirical edge. And everything she didn't say about the
locale is tearing through her."[36] (When Elizabeth was about to give
a local reading from a draft of the novel, he wrote to Allen Tate that
this event was "rather ticklish" because "the victims are really the
Iowa City mind.")[37]

   In February 1954, she wrote to Peter and Eleanor that she was
"bewildered by Cincinnati." It was "an intellectual desert" with
"strange" people, a "dark empty campus," and a university library
that closed at six p.m. and was not open on weekends.[38] For $130 a
month, the Lowells were squeezed into two bedrooms on the second
floor of a private house; the owners lived in the third bedroom and
shared the bathroom. As if that were not sufficiently discouraging,
the Lowells' lives were suddenly upended with the news that Charlotte had had a stroke in Rapallo. Cal flew to see her, but she died
on Valentine's Day after a second stroke, an hour before he arrived.
After receiving the news in his letter, Elizabeth wrote from Lexington, where she was visiting her mother, regretting that he had to

sail back to New York with the body ("that long miserable trip").[39]
Two days later she remarked acidly to Blair and Holly Clark about
her "profound disbelief" in the death of such a formidable woman.
Her bleak mood was due to the dreariness of Cincinnati and Cal's
absence. She planned to arrive in New York a week before his boat
docked: "I expect the great city to buck me up again."[40]

What she didn't know yet was that Cal had reconnected with
Giovanna Madonia—the Italian woman who had caused Elizabeth
so much grief when they were in Italy—who was now unhappily
married.[41] In late February, he sent her a passionate letter. "I'm very
devoted to Elizabeth and don't want to hurt her," he wrote. "But
O my Giovana [sic], I am not alive without you."[42] After Charlotte's
funeral, at which Cal "seemed very much the man of the family, [the
black sheep] at last reclaimed,"[43] the Lowells returned to Cincinnati. He was edging into another manic period, exultant about the
$50,000 he would receive from his mother's estate. Elizabeth knew
he was ill "when he woke up and said, 'Honey, I love you but I think
I want a divorce to marry Giovanna.' . . . After ten days of that I was
forced to leave the small quarters in which we were living."[44]

On March 19, Elizabeth wrote to Blair Clark that she was now
back in New York, at the Algonquin Hotel—"and all indications are
that we won't resume our 'relationship.'"[45] Reminding the Lowells'
mutual friend of "the moral and psychological torture [Cal] can
inflict," she explained that she left him "one afternoon, just before
we were supposed to go to a dinner party." He accompanied her to
the train station, and "the parting was amicable." She wanted Blair
to write to Cal, "urging caution." Elizabeth realized that the situation had "elements of a bad Italian comedy," what with the potential
involvement of Giovanna's circle of friends in Milan. Unlike Cal's
usual passivity in love affairs, which allowed them to peter out, he
seemed likely to urge Giovanna to leave her husband and come to
the United States. If that was the case, "there is no way he can with-

draw." In addition to her extreme anxiety about the state of her marriage, Elizabeth was concerned that the Duxbury house would not
be fixed up in time to make it habitable by June. (Cal would soon
write "insulting letters" to the person hired to supervise the interior
painting and—another twist of the knife—call Elizabeth's family to
tell them he had never loved her.)[46] "I love Cal enormously and know
I will never find his equal," she wrote, "but I have a totally unexpected feeling of immense peace and release. I only hope it isn't some
strange psychological malady and that I'll wake up feeling shattered."

From her new perch in a cheaper hotel on West 51st Street, Elizabeth declared to Blair that the marriage was "all entirely over and
without any possible basis for starting again. . . . It is like coming
out of a cave to be free of all this. . . . I feel fine, a bit bruised now
and then. . . . I want to marry a nice, sleepy old man who snoozes in
front of the fire all day."[47] She had decided to stay in the hotel until
April 5, when she would move to an apartment she rented for two
months on Sullivan Street in Greenwich Village. In May she would
file for divorce. Then she would assemble all her possessions ("in
storage houses from coast to coast") and rent another apartment.
To the Taylors, she wrote that she didn't feel "the slightest humiliation or embarrassment or wounded vanity. The circumstances are so
unique none of the old human reactions occur somehow."[48]   ,

On March 30, Elizabeth wrote to Cal ("Dearest One") with a brisk
summation of details unrelated to the breakup. She was waiting for the
translation they worked on to be returned by the author before sending it to Macmillan, and she was writing an essay about George Eliot.
Elizabeth signed off, "All my affection, darling. A quotation from Mary
Wollstonecraft: 'I like the word affection because it signifies something
habitual.'"[49] Meanwhile, unbeknownst to Elizabeth, Giovanna was
applying for a passport. In a letter to Cal, she had declared, "You are
mine" and expressed her wish to have a child with him.[50]

On April 3, Elizabeth wrote to Cal that she "certainly" wanted to marry again: "It is terrible to be without love and companionship when you've had it." She included a passage from a letter written by Jane Carlyle—unhappy wife of the nineteenth-century essayist Thomas Carlyle—that quoted the eighty-year-old Countess of Essex: "When does a woman have done with love? Ask someone older than me!"[51] But in a letter to Blair two days later, she declared that she did not want to leave her husband after all. Her reasons for this decision must have been hard to fathom. "He simply came back from Europe in a very hostile state," she wrote, "talked about Giovanna all day and night, had nothing to do with me whatsoever and yet would not let me sleep."[52] Elizabeth also received an incoherent phone call from Cal, who was no longer in the hospital. She wrote to the English department at the University of Cincinnati to alert them to his condition. To her frustration, the department chair thought there was nothing wrong with her husband. She realized that because he was "so friendly, so available," people failed to realize that he was ill.

After another long, "very abusive, very mad" phone call from Cal, Elizabeth wrote again to Blair.[53] She was now faced with two problems: how to take care of her husband—she was still writing to the department chair and trying to get a doctor to see Cal—and what would become of their marriage. She was appalled at "the rudeness, the meanness, the stinginess" he displayed, "and on a deeper level he has been of course indescribably cruel." She reviewed the facts: Cal's four collapses during the past four and a half years. Whenever he was released from a hospital, it fell to her to do the "nursing." While she had "always felt the joy of his 'normal' periods," he had now "torn down . . . everything we have built up . . . completely exposed to the world all of our sorrows which should be kept secret." (She had no way of knowing that Cal would expose those griefs in a much larger and more public way decades later.) He was seemingly unable to write letters, and his phone calls disturbed her. She now felt that Giovanna was "simply the excuse to get me to leave so that he could 'go off.'" This woman didn't understand Cal and his illness. "She simply thinks I have him carted off to the hospital everytime he causes me trouble!"

Because Cal refused to see a psychiatrist voluntarily, Elizabeth had to sign the warrant that committed him to a hospital in Cincinnati on April 8 for a twenty-four-hour observation period. She had returned to the city with Cal's Kenyon College friend John Thompson to take control of the situation. By this time, the university faculty realized that what they had seen as genius at work was boiling over into something else; an appreciative lecture Cal gave on Hitler was apparently the turning point. Even so, a group of local busybodies lacking any understanding of mental illness had connected Cal with a lawyer to protect him from his wife, and some had even written to Giovanna to warn her against Elizabeth's supposed vindictiveness and to invite her to visit.[54]

Hunkered down in the Sinton Hotel without even a change of clothes, Elizabeth was feeling overwhelmed. Adding to her torment, she learned that Randall Jarrell had called Cal to congratulate him on the separation. At the hospital, Cal was heavily sedated; the next step would be to give him shock treatments. Her plan was to return to New York and wait until he improved before visiting him. Informed by a doctor that this was likely not Cal's last attack, she wrote, "It is crushing. I can hardly bear to think of it—even looking at it from my own point of view every possibility is grim."[55]

In mid-April, Elizabeth settled into her "divine" Sullivan Street apartment with a garden view, sublet from an architect. The owner of the house was an employee of *Harper's*; a writer for *The New Yorker* lived upstairs with his family. After the barrenness of Cincinnati and the impersonality of hotel rooms, this was a soothing environment for her. As the days passed, she was able to read again and contemplate a return to writing. But she had no illusions. Although she believed Cal loved her "and that we have had an amazingly good marriage which has meant everything to both of us . . . [t]he blow will always fall on me." When he shifted into a manic state, his immediate urge was "to be away from the person who represents reality, responsibility, skepticism, and to make new connections. I cannot have him divorcing me every year!"[56] At least she had the support of Cal's relatives. Cousin Harriet Winslow, who had called Elizabeth's mother to express her sorrow, confided that "Bobby" told her in December that his marriage had made him "happy for the first time in his life."[57] Aunt Sarah Winslow Cotting had written to praise Elizabeth's "dignity and great kindness" in handling the situation and hoped that the couple would reunite.[58] Aunt Alice Winslow Meade told her that "Bobby's" letters always mentioned her "with pride and love."[59] Cousin Alice Winslow Sommaripa informed Elizabeth that mental illness had affected her siblings and daughter, but that they had recovered fully after electroshock treatments.[60]

Seemingly stabilized, Cal called Elizabeth in late April to ask her to return to Cincinnati. But during her visit, he slipped into a hypomanic state, talking all day about Giovanna. Without informing him, Elizabeth wrote to her in an effort to explain his condition, which she herself had imperfectly understood because the doctors would not discuss it with her. Although the plan was to release Cal on May 7—an occasion at which she would need to be present, because she had signed him into the hospital—he was acting in a "murderous" way toward her. "My days have been a torment of accusations," she wrote. "This half-sane, half-mad condition is truly defeating my spirit."[61] Returning from the hospital, she was so worn out that she would fall asleep in the afternoon and not awaken until the following morning.

The specter of Giovanna continued to haunt Elizabeth. While she couldn't see the attraction of a woman who seemed to lack a sense of irony and who had a "marked masculine quality," she realized that the woman "is going to remain in the sky like a fixed star.

She terrifies me."[62] Elizabeth decided that if Cal still insisted on getting together with Giovanna after his hospitalization ended, she would immediately divorce him. Blair assured her that "everyone who knows anything and has sense is rallying behind you, supporting you." In his eyes, she was "heroic."[63] Indeed, she was, at great cost to her own peace of mind. "To spend nearly a whole day talking to a mentally ill person is wearing beyond endurance," she wrote, "the way you go over and over things without coming out anywhere."[64]

In mid-May, Elizabeth and Cal finally returned to New York. He stayed temporarily at a sanatorium in the Bronx before being admitted to Payne Whitney. Her worries continued—about the Duxbury house, about whether Dr. Moore (who had refused to help her deal with the situation in Cincinnati) would take over Cal's care when they left the city, and about whether Cal would even agree to long-term psychotherapy. Then in early June, his mania took hold once again. "People are now urging me to make some kind of move, get a divorce—I don't know," Elizabeth wrote to Blair. "A month is like a day in these matters."[65] She decided to meet with a doctor unconnected with Payne Whitney for an unbiased opinion and was no longer visiting Cal, though he called her every morning. She also had to move yet again, to a small apartment on MacDougal Street in Greenwich Village, where she expected to be able to stay until at least September. The rooms reminded her of the Duxbury house, and she now had a radio on which to listen to the opera music she loved. A visit from Peter and Eleanor Taylor in June also helped raise her spirits.

Released from her state of constant anguish, she realized that she did not want to divorce Cal. He needed her—this would always be an important element in their relationship—and she knew that "it is going to be terribly difficult to restore his confidence, when this false, sick confidence is gone."[66] His new diagnosis for the recent attack was "acute schizophrenia."[67] He would yell at her or threaten to sign himself out of the hospital and calmly phone her the next day to discuss some ordinary activity, like buying a phonograph. The doctor stressed that Cal, now being treated with Thorazine (a new drug), would need to be under medical care for the foreseeable future.

Meanwhile Elizabeth was reading *Individualism Reconsidered*, essays by the sociologist David Riesman, whose earlier study, *The Lonely Crowd*, brilliantly analyzed the behavior of twentieth-century Americans. But in this book, she told Cal, "he goes on forever and has only two or three really good perceptions."[68] Her review, "Riesman Considered," would appear in the September–October 1954 issue of *Partisan Review*. "He is a cheerfully curious and lively observer," she wrote, "as free of 'liberal piety' as one of the teen-agers he is so much interested in." Yet she felt that he "likes to select his 'truth' according to the occasion . . . like a therapist . . . tr[ying] this line and then another, following the patient's moods." She found that Riesman "treats his own opinions as if they were those of a character in a novel he was writing." In her inimitably down-to-earth way, she likened plucking out his ideas from his obfuscating prose to "the difficulty of extracting the meat from [lobster or crab] claws."

Rahv admired the tone of her piece: "just right—not a frontal assault on ideological or political grounds but an all-round characterization that will open people's eyes."[69] Mary McCarthy tartly remarked in a letter to Hannah Arendt that the piece was "utterly demolishing" of Riesman's reputation, "a good thing, even if some of Lizzie's premises àre a little peculiar."[70] Elizabeth Bishop, worried not to have heard from Cal for a long time, wrote a rare letter to Elizabeth, praising her book reviews "for their sudden quite natural remarks, occasional wry and common-sense phrases."[71] Elizabeth explained to a friend seeking writing advice that she would reread each page in her final draft and "look for a line where I might insert a vivid phrase, or change a few adjectives, alter a verb to a more unusual one."[72]

* * *

In the fever-chart existence Elizabeth was leading, doubts continuously assailed her. She wrote, "My heart tells me I should get out of this difficult marriage, that I will only have all these months and months of agony to go over again after a few years, that a mentally disturbed person simply cannot give enough."[73] Giovanna had written to Blair that she had not abandoned her plan to come to America. Still, Elizabeth had decided to wait before making a decision. That July a visit to the house in Duxbury was a bright spot in her troubled life. "It is enchanting," she wrote to Cal. "All fresh, neat & beautiful . . . garage painted & the garden is lovely . . . lawn clean and mowed." Inside, "the kitchen is perfect," and eight hundred dollars remained with which to complete the renovations.[74] At a time when so much was unsettled, the tidily organized house was both a physical and a mental haven.

On July 14, Cal told Elizabeth that he had written to Giovanna to say that he was returning to his wife. Relating this conversation to Blair Clark, Elizabeth noted both her amazement at the declaration (usually, Cal's romances just faded away), and her fear that Giovanna would not take no for an answer, especially since Cal had given her money that she planned to use to come to America.[75] After his release from the hospital, Elizabeth decided they would stay in a rented apartment in Boston for the next two years to keep him near his psychotherapist, spending time in the Duxbury house during the spring and summer. Boston made sense in other ways: they could see friends; Cal might be able to teach a term at Harvard; they both used the library there; and she hoped to find a teaching job of her own. (Unstated was the fact that Charlotte would no longer be hovering, potentially agitating Cal.) Elizabeth cared deeply about making a comfortable home that would allow the two of them to pursue their writing. The prospect of finally reclaiming all their possessions—especially their many books and phonograph records—from five storage places gladdened her heart. Even so, she still believed, as she wrote to Blair, that she would have to get a divorce if Giovanna succeeded in barging into Cal's life again.

A few weeks later Elizabeth happily announced to the Taylors that it was "wonderful to have Cal well."[76] Able to leave the hospital for a few days every week, he joined her for walks, movies, and trips to museums. A "sporting period" followed, with Brooklyn Dodgers games and tennis matches in Forest Hills. In late September, the Lowells would move into his mother's house on Commonwealth Avenue. ("Both of us look forward with real enthusiasm to the winter.") Cal had destroyed Giovanna's letters, and he and Elizabeth agreed not to speak of her again. But her joy was tempered—"My heart nearly stopped beating"—by reading that people with Cal's illness have more frequent and prolonged attacks as they age.[77]

* * *

Harcourt, Brace sent Elizabeth Bishop an advance copy of *The Simple Truth*, which would be published on February 10, 1955.[78] The poet

Elizabeth's author photo,
The Simple Truth *(1955).*

wasn't sure if she was expected to provide a blurb, but just in case, she wrote that it was a "beautiful ~~little~~ job. . . . You've given a marvelous clean, clear picture of Iowa and some of its people."[79] Bishop admired Elizabeth's portrayal of the lawyers "and the maddening banalities of courtroom speeches," concluding that the novel "has all the earmarks, whatever they are, of a 'minor classic,' and should go on selling and selling for years." Bishop wrote to Elizabeth several weeks later to say that the book had stayed in her mind and she felt "surer all the time" of its worth.[80]

The novel is based on the Tuxedo Murder Case, named for the attire of the defendant, Robert E. Bednasek, when he was arrested. A Marine Corps veteran and university student, he showed up at the Iowa City police station at two a.m. on December 11, 1949, and said he had accidentally choked his girlfriend, Margaret Anne Jackson. When the police arrived at the scene, she was dead. At the trial, which drew a huge crowd, a psychologist who had treated Bednasek testified that the young man had told him he was haunted by two impulses—to kill himself and to kill his girlfriend. Jackson's father cried on the stand, and her friends related the couple's quarrels. Among those testifying for the defense were Bednasek's fraternity buddies. Despite the evidence against him, he was acquitted.[81]

Elizabeth described the trial through the eyes of two fictional members of the courtroom audience: Joseph Parks, a college student in his late twenties, and Anita Mitchell, a professor's wife. They both take the defendant's side, though for different reasons. Parks thinks having a wealthy girlfriend dooms him; Mitchell believes he was in the grip of a psychological state that freed him of responsibility for his actions. Yet when the man is acquitted, they are dismayed; they had assumed that the ordinary people on the jury did not share their superior reasoning. This is much the same point Elizabeth made in "Two Recent Travellers," in the voice of the American woman who was so certain she was right about Turkey.

The Simple Truth was reviewed along with several other recent works of fiction in the spring 1955 issue of *Partisan Review*.[82] Although the writer noted the "well-drawn picture of the state of mind" of the two protagonists, he lamented that these characters "never grow much fictional flesh on their skeletons" and that the trial they attend and comment on "is described in a lackadaisical, uncertain manner that is only partially redeemed by a sudden flare of insight or a brilliant impression." The *New York Times* reviewer praised the way Elizabeth marshaled the ideas in her novel but criticized the dialogue for "a textbook woodenness."[83] There was one significant dissenting voice: William Carlos Williams was a fan of the book, praising its "feeling of authenticity"—he "recognized and accepted" her portrayal of a small city in Iowa—and Elizabeth's "detailed knowledge of our lives."[84] The novel also prompted Flannery O'Connor to write to a friend that Elizabeth "is a lot better writer than she gets credit for being."[85] Yet the fact that she did not attempt another novel for two decades says something about her lack of self-confidence in this genre.[86]

* * *

Elizabeth's mother died in a Lexington hospital on January 18, 1955, after which her daughter wrote to the Clarks: "We were shattered by my mother's death, but she was 75 and so even without illness, it wouldn't be entirely unexpected."[87] The matter-of-fact tone in this description reflects Elizabeth's prickly relationship with her mother. In interviews, she always seemed much more interested in talking about her father. Yet Elizabeth had dedicated *The Simple Truth* to her. Returning from the funeral, she received a present from Cal: a new typewriter.

The Lowells experimented with limiting their alcohol intake that winter, which led Elizabeth to remark that this "allowed us to make the discovery that most people drink very little and that we are now . . . at last in step with the civilized world."[88] But while Cal stuck to ginger ale for several weeks, she didn't give up her evening drink. Alcohol was the lubricant at virtually every social event in the 1950s. Elizabeth was among many in the art and literary worlds who overindulged on occasion, leading at times to sharp-tongued remarks she later may have regretted.

Elizabeth and Cal settled into a daily routine; to her amazement, he was even asking to help with the housework. Although he was sometimes briefly clouded by depression, he seemed back to normal, following a daily routine outlined by his doctor. For her part, Elizabeth felt as though she were doing "nothing . . . except have visitors and invite people to dinner" and try her hand at matchmaking between two friends in Cambridge.[89] She was full of praise for Cal's latest project, prose reminiscences of his childhood. Writing to Peter and Eleanor Taylor, she related her "envy" of these pieces "of extraordinary beauty and interest" and her hope that the "strong emotion" of the subject would keep him focused on his work.[90] She now found Boston to be "the most pleasant place in America," what with the Lowells' "great, high-up apartment," their many local acquaintances, and a plethora of classical music concerts.[91] Cultural life also included attending what was supposedly the farewell appearance of the great monologuist Ruth Draper[92] and visiting the Athenaeum (Boston's membership library), using the credentials of a Lowell relative. By late spring, the Lowells hosted several visiting literary figures: Osbert, Sacheverell, and Edith Sitwell; Stephen Spender; John Crowe Ransom; T. S. Eliot; and Lillian Hellman. Other guests were family members. The Virginia-born husband of Cal's first cousin Jackie Winslow-Paine struck Elizabeth as someone she had already known, "perhaps because he seems to have been engaged at one time or another to every girl in Lexington, Kentucky except me."[93]

Her essay "George Eliot's Husband" appeared in the spring 1955 issue of *Partisan Review*. Eliot, she wrote, had "a slow, disciplined, hard-won, aching genius that bore down upon her with a wondrous and exhausting force, like a great love affair in middle age." With those words, Elizabeth introduces us to a strikingly empathetic view of the struggles of a homely woman "at the mercy of her intelligence" who "cared about philosophy, politics, moral issues as other women care about clothes." She describes the philosopher and critic George Henry Lewes, Eliot's "husband"—he had an estranged legal wife—as equally committed to intellectual pursuits, though with a more out-going temperament. He adored her, encouraged her, and served as a buffer against criticism. It is possible to discern a certain wistfulness in Elizabeth's description of Eliot's life with Lewes, who "understood everything pained and precious in her nature [and] saw that striking union of dutifulness and imagination."

In June, Elizabeth published "The Neglected Novels of Christina Stead" in *The New Republic*. This essay opens with the remark that most books that are neither highly praised nor widely attacked tend to be quietly forgotten. Yet in 1940, she wrote, when Stead's novel *The Man Who Loved Children* was published, it received a strongly positive review from Rebecca West on the front page of *The New York Times Book Review*. Elizabeth, who was unable even to dis-cover where Stead was living (her publisher had lost track of her),[94] explained that this book was not the sort of "small, perfect, witty" novel that could retain a loyal following long after it dropped from sight. Rather, it was "a large, sprawling, vigorous work . . . of abso-lute originality" with a "wonderful richness of character." Elizabeth employed characteristically vivid images to describe the inhabitants of Stead's fictional world. The father, a government employee, has "one of those greedy and restless minds that takes in and chews up everything in sight like a disposal unit." The mother is "made up of fantastic odds and ends, leathery grins, stained fingers, squalid lies and brutal hopes." Despite the bleakness of the author's outlook, Elizabeth wrote, the novel was so "magical, abundant, inventive" that it was a pleasure to read.

* * *

The Lowells acquired a new car, a two-tone Ford Tudor sedan, and Elizabeth was finally learning to drive. She practiced with Cal— "We teach each other," he wrote to Elizabeth Bishop[95]—on the road between the Cambridge cemetery and the city dump. After a July visit by two of Elizabeth's sisters, Elizabeth and Cal rented out the Duxbury house and drove to Castine, Maine, where they stayed in a house owned by his cousin Harriet. Perched above the tidal Bagaduce River at the spot where Spring Street bends to become Water Street, the structure was known as the "brickyard house," because it had once served as the men's dormitory of the Castine Brick Company.[96]

Next to it was a barn where Cal worked on his poetry during the day. Castine would become an increasingly welcome refuge for the couple over the next decades. The sleepy twenty-square-mile town, 244 miles from Boston, had been a prosperous fishing center in the early nineteenth century, when merchant families built stately Federal and Greek Revival homes. After the Civil War, tourism took over, with "rusticators"—wealthy urbanites—and literary figures (including Harriet Beecher Stowe and Henry Wadsworth Longfellow) traveling by steamboat to hotels and inns. Although the Depression, the rise of auto travel, and the demise of the local fishing industry took their toll, the establishment of the Marine Maritime Academy in 1941 and a new generation of summer people began to resurrect the town's fortunes. Castine still retains a quiet, austere charm. Main Street is the axis of the town's spare geography, bordered by sober white clapboard houses, the Trinitarian Congregational Parish Church, the post office (built in 1817), and two venerable inns. In the 1950s there was also a village drugstore and Ken's Market.

Cousin Harriet bought her property in the 1930s as a refuge from the summer humidity of Washington, D.C., traveling to Maine and back every year with her cook. A handsome, dignified "maiden lady" with a worldly outlook—she was Cal's favorite relative—Harriet lived elegantly in the Georgetown neighborhood, enjoying her nightly martini and attending classical music concerts. (Elizabeth described her, in "Writing a Novel," as "very tall, old, with her stirring maidenly beauty," playing a record of Alice Raveau in Gluck's opera *Orfeo*.) But in Castine, Cousin Harriet reveled in village gossip. When she became too ill for her annual summer hiatus, Elizabeth's letters supplied detailed updates on the lives of local personalities. She took pleasure in observing how Main Street "slopes down to the harbor, slowly, and houses curve along the waterfront" and how "relations with people are of a gentle and genteel sort."[97] And yet she perceived a strain of morbidity endemic to Maine, reflected in the "old worn-out apple tree" visible from the window at her desk, "extend[ing] a branch with its little wormy green fruits hanging on it like Christmas ornaments."

* * *

The Duxbury house had begun to seem a mistake, both financially and practically. After considering various options, the Lowells sold it that fall and bought a stone house in the Federal style at 239 Marlborough Street in Boston, a block from Cal's boyhood home. His inheritance from Charlotte helped pay for the new house. It would soon be cluttered with inherited furniture ("Bobby won't part with a safety pin, let alone a thing of his family's," Elizabeth wrote to Cousin Harriet), including a highboy emblazoned with a gold eagle and eighteenth-century portraits of ancestors. But she exulted at all the available space: at last, a bedroom and a study for each of them.[98] In a letter to Robert Giroux, her editor at Farrar, Straus and Cudahy, she sounded awestruck at the grandeur of the house—"a mansion, quite splendid"—with four floors that included guest rooms, baths, drawing rooms, and a marble foyer.[99] After William

Carlos Williams visited, he noted "how ideally it suits the life you appear to be living." He was charmed that the house had the convenience of being centrally located, yet the "thick walls" isolated the Lowells from "the mob."[100]

Cal, whose income from the trust obviated the need to earn money, still wanted to teach; he was now at Boston University. Elizabeth, always the one to worry about their finances, vowed to start writing for *The New Yorker*—which paid much more than *Partisan Review*—in order to afford the services of their maid. *The New Yorker* had accepted one of her stories, but she had no idea when it would be published; another one she submitted that autumn had not yet been acknowledged.[101] Two of the stories she sent to the magazine this year—"Portrait of a New York Lady," a character study in the guise of a memoir, and "The Babcock Family"—were rejected. But the fiction editor, Katharine White, reassured Elizabeth that the magazine was "really interested" in her work, enclosing a letter about "Two Recent Travellers" that she had written a year earlier. (It had sat on White's desk because she didn't have Elizabeth's address.)[102] "Portrait of a New York Lady" would find a home in the December issue of *Encounter*, the two-year-old British literary magazine edited by Stephen Spender.[103] This piece, about the last years of a homely Virginia matron living in luxury in New York, is notable mostly for a brief evocation of Elizabeth's own early days in the city. The narrator muses about "how fearful and fabulous the city used to seem" to a young person leaving her home in the South, holding on to "a dream worth any sacrifice." Manhattan—now still rather dreamlike to Elizabeth, marooned in Boston—is described as possessing "splendour and extravagance and discomfort."

Elizabeth's critical acuity continued to sharpen. In "Way Beyond Innocence," her review of Leslie Fiedler's essay collection *An End to Innocence*, published in the fall 1955 issue of *Partisan Review*, she likened the force of his arguments to "the pained enjoyment and partisan excitement of a good sports event." She wittily observed that in his writing, "the erotic and the controversial meet whenever it can be logically arranged." Elizabeth described Fiedler's essay "Come Back to the Raft Ag'in, Huck Honey!"—a daring, homoerotic interpretation of the relationship between the two main characters in Mark Twain's *The Adventures of Huckleberry Finn*—as "fresh and brilliant and extreme" and noted that "it is strangely literal in its understanding of the secretly mythical."

In November, Elizabeth wrote to Mary McCarthy to praise aspects of her novel *A Charmed Life* (in which a woman has a sexual encounter with her former husband), though she found the seduction scene terrifying in its verisimilitude: "Martha's emotions seemed grimly accurate and painful. Perhaps a tired, middle-aged desire to forget is upon me."[104] Elizabeth was only thirty-nine, but the drama she had lived through over the past few years might well have made her feel much older. Although Philip Rahv disliked the novel, which was reviewed negatively by Arthur Mizener in *PR*, he knew she felt differently and urged her to write a letter for publication defending her friend's book. But she did not choose to do this.

Meanwhile the social whirl enveloped the Lowells. Along with Mary and her husband Bowden Broadwater, they were among the guests at a cocktail party given by Arthur Schlesinger, Jr., the historian, and his wife Marian. Dwight Macdonald was in town, along with many of Elizabeth's friends from the past, leading Cal to interrogate her about who these men were and where she met them. The Lowells' avid concertgoing continued in early 1956, with performances by the chamber orchestra I Musici, the soprano Renata Tebaldi, and *Così fan tutti* in a New England Opera Company production. Planning a trip to New York for Cal's meeting with the National Book Award committee, Elizabeth suggested "possible opera nights" to Robert Giroux, who shared her interest in the art form.[105] "I love going to concerts in the evening and could go every night," Elizabeth wrote to Cousin Harriet. "We are usually home by 10:30 and it is both restful and exciting somehow."[106]

Daytime was for writing. Her essay "America and Dylan Thomas" appeared in the spring issue of *Partisan Review*. Rahv was ecstatic: "the best thing that has been written on . . . the entire Thomas experience."[107] The piece was occasioned by the publication of John Malcolm Brinnin's *Dylan Thomas in America*, a detailed chronicle of the author's attempt to shepherd the frequently drunk and always uncontrollable poet during his final American tour in 1953, which ended in his death at age thirty-nine. Elizabeth presciently described the rock star treatment Thomas received in this country as the product of "a longing for the extreme." The adoration of his public included women who believed they had fallen in love with him, believing themselves somehow privileged to nurse this married man during his bouts of delirium and vomiting. Behind her keen analysis of the Thomas phenomenon was her awareness of Cal's own magnetism, his attractiveness to young women as he climbed the heights of his mania. "There was a certain amount of poison in our good will," she wrote about the poet's visit, indicting "the ugly competition for [Thomas's] favors." And yet she suggested that the Thomas spectacle was "a brief reprieve" from "the sober and dreary fact of the decline of our literary life."

Joking to the Clarks that she figured *The New Yorker* had bought her two stories "merely as an income tax deduction," she was pleased that one was about to be published.[108] "A Season's Romance" is about Adele, an earnest and impecunious art history graduate student who is swept off her feet by Matt, a brassy, middle-aged, twice-divorced American ad man who treats her to the luxe life in Europe. Back in New York, she feels disconnected from her friends and unable to continue her studies, but she can't marry her lover because his office is moving him to Texas. Elizabeth mined her own experience as an impoverished graduate student with increasing distaste for her

studies coupled with a desperate need to remain in New York. Once
again the story features a man in a "cheap bachelor apartment," but
no lovemaking takes place there. (In contrast to Mary McCarthy's
graphic stories about young women's involvements with older men,
Elizabeth always avoided describing the mechanics of sex.) "A Season's Romance" is curiously bloodless, more like a sociological case
study than a persuasive narrative. During these years, Elizabeth
seemed wedded to a detached, observational approach. Katharine
White queried her about several aspects of the initial draft, including a certain peculiarity about "the romance itself." It struck her
that Matt "behaves with so much respect and tenderness, as if he
were merely a suitor." While the couple seemed to have been living
together in Europe, they didn't appear to be intimate in New York,
"where only nightclubs and taxis are mentioned."[109] The published
version has Matt telling Adele that he feels uncomfortable having
such a well-bred woman as his mistress: riddle solved. And yet the
reader is hard put to discover a true connection between the couple,
perhaps because we see the affair only from Adele's point of view.

A much larger project Elizabeth had taken on was editing *The
Selected Letters of William James*, part of a series of selections from
"the world's greatest letter writers." It was an honor to be chosen
for this project; the other volumes were edited by leading authors of
the period.[110] Her preface to the book reveals her powers of empathy and close-grained analysis at their highest level. Once again she
addressed the subject of letters: "the nearest things we have to lost
conversations of memorable persons."[111] James's appeal to modern
readers, she wrote, is that "he feared losing touch with the personal,
the subjective, the feelings of real human beings more than he feared
being logically or systematically faulty." This was also his specific
appeal to Elizabeth, a writerly trait she shared. She described William James—brother of the novelist Henry James and best known
as the author of *The Varieties of Religious Experience*—as possessing

"so much wisdom and so much sheer delight." Yet as a young man, he was hounded by depression and physical ailments; trained as a doctor, he did not want to practice. Elizabeth, who had a hard-won knowledge of mental anguish, wrote that these "youthful struggles" probably inspired "his special awareness of merging states of mind, of the blurred flow of consciousness, the involuntary, subconscious mental life." (This subject, too, was of great interest to her, as she would demonstrate in *Sleepless Nights*.) Intriguingly, she explained James's special aptitude as a writer "on the quirks of human nature" as stemming from "a recurring hesitation to commit himself."

Writing about his willingness to accept "mediums and table-rappers" as viable expressions of spiritual belief, Elizabeth likened his tolerance and curiosity to the behavior of "a priest at a jam session." Yet James also had "the most sophisticated knowledge of the way . . . religious experience could be treated as a neurotic symptom by the nonbeliever." She aptly described him as running a race "on both teams"—as "the cleverest skeptic and . . . the wildest man in a state of religious enthusiasm." Elizabeth was predisposed to admire his "preference for the lowly . . . rather than the orthodox and accepted." Praising the "unexpected sympathies" in his writing, she found "a poetical sweetness" in his "spontaneous and casual" correspondence."[112]

Elizabeth wrote to Giroux in November to ask when she would receive her contract and advance, and to request several books she needed, including the first volume of Leon Edel's biography of Henry James. The research involved spending long days at the Houghton Library at Harvard, "coming home at five, utterly exhausted, and beaten down by the fact that I've still got forty years of letters to go."[113] Still, it was a thrill to be handling original correspondence from the historian Henry Adams, who had the "most beautiful handwriting imaginable."[114] Publication of the *Selected Letters*, which she finally submitted in late April 1958, was delayed by the need to wait for the historian Jacques Barzun to finish compiling his volume of James's writings.[115] Elizabeth's book was a labor of love, resulting in "very little housekeeping money"—her advance ($375), which would not be paid until the summer of 1960.[116]

In December, she received a "first reading agreement" from *The New Yorker*; the magazine would have first refusal rights for her submissions, which would be paid by the word, plus an extra 25 percent and an annual cost-of-living increase. Money was always on Elizabeth's mind. Although she regretted having bought a "monstrous" TV on sale—she and Cal were now ignoring it in favor of their classical FM radio station and phonograph records—she felt "a sort of nagging obligation to the beastly tv [sic], merely because I paid money for it."[117] To friends (who would have understood the implicit comparison with radio), she explained that the problem with TV was that "it involved a surrender of one's sight. . . . the total self goes into a tv program; and they are grotesquely bad. . . . Worst of all . . . no matter how big your house is, one tv set ruins its charm, just as if you had a built in odor of some kind."[118]

After a spring 1956 trip to Washington, D.C., to see Cousin Harriet, who was recovering from a stroke, Elizabeth looked forward to taking up her offer of a summer holiday in the Castine house. Then she learned she was pregnant, and her obstetrician told her that having a baby at age forty was a serious matter. Although she and Cal spent a week in New York in May—staying at Lillian Hellman's apartment—there would be no further out-of-town trips. "We lie about on sofas all day eating cornflakes, no-calory [sic] ginger-ale and yogurt," Cal wrote to Elizabeth Bishop. "Elizabeth never moves except to turn the page of an English newspaper or buy a dress."[119] After reading a letter Cal sent to the Taylors, she wrote to them, "I always feel the need to contradict everything he says about me." She agreed that she was "feeling very middleaged and puffy," but she refuted his claim that she thought Eleanor should work at *The New*

Yorker. "It seems to be an office designed to give anyone ulcers within a month," she wrote. "The weight of all those notes and comments alone is too much to bear."[120]

Elizabeth moaned to Mary McCarthy that writing for *The New Yorker* was "just like housework. You wake up in the morning saying, I'll do all these things today and then be free tomorrow. And so, with the money beckoning you, you wake up thinking I'll try a New Yorker story and then . . . I haven't really tried. I'm only on page two this week."[121] Yet Katharine White was warmly supportive. She responded to news of Elizabeth's pregnancy by writing that "all over the world children are competing with short stories." (She had heard from Nadine Gordimer that her three children were keeping her from writing.) "But," White added, "there is hardly a woman who wouldn't think the child more important than the story, including this editor."[122]

Elizabeth's second story accepted by the magazine, "The Oak and the Axe," was published in the May 12, 1956, issue, a year after she received a detailed letter from Katharine White about problems she saw with a character's motivation. Like Elizabeth's previous *New Yorker* story, it concerns relations between a man and a woman, but this time the young woman is a self-assured and well-heeled editor of a women's magazine and the charming, self-deprecating, middle-aged man she falls for is suffering from depression and living on a small trust fund in a dingy hotel room. After persuading Henry to marry her, Clara is dragged down by his anomie to the point of being fired from her job. At the end of the story, he moves back into his old hotel room. White was initially unconvinced by his decision.[123] Was the problem his lack of comfort? Worries that his wife would no longer support him? Having his wife at home all day, quarrelling with him? White felt that this problem was connected with the mystery of why he married her in the first place. Elizabeth briefly clarified these issues in her final version, describing Henry as someone for whom "forward movements, progress, and commitments were slow to be accomplished but retreats were surprisingly rapid." Despite her annoyance with the intensive reworking *The New Yorker* required— Elizabeth never liked being edited—she wrote politely to White that she was "very much impressed and pleased by the kind and amount of interest and the thought you've given to all this."[124] Cal told Elizabeth Bishop that he thought the man in the story "is really *us*, but already several people we never met are having persecution breakdowns because they recognize themselves."[125]

Despite her increasing girth and discomfort, Elizabeth threw a large cocktail party for a Harvard Summer School conference on The Little Magazine, enlisting her cleaning woman and a Harvard student to tend bar. In a letter to Cousin Harriet, she wondered what sort of help she should get after the baby was born. There was enough money for only one full-time person, and she wasn't sure if a nursemaid or a housekeeper was the right choice. Wouldn't it be nice if one person could do both jobs? Harriet advised that a nursemaid was best. Elizabeth hired an expensive baby nurse recommended by another relative for the first month, with the idea that "a young girl" could take over after that, with her own help. On October 24, Cal wrote to Elizabeth Bishop, "Elizabeth is grand, enormous, lovely and sends you her love."[126] But around this time, according to Edmund Wilson, Cal acquired a new casual lover, "a pretty little girl in Cambridge, who wanted to write poetry. . . . She looks like a Renoir." Wilson wrote that at a gathering at the Lowells', "after dinner Elizabeth went upstairs to her room and burst into tears, and the mistress remained with the younger crowd and stupidly tried to play hostess."[127] In a letter to Cousin Harriet, Elizabeth offered only pleasant news, describing "Bobby" as engrossed in his family history project, trying to learn more about musical form, and "playing records and FM [radio] day and night."[128] To Katharine White— who, unlike Cousin Harriet, was herself a mother—Elizabeth wrote about the impending birth: she felt "impossibly doting already and protective apprehensive—everything you're supposed to restrain I guess. But thank heavens not at the beginning. A few years of gushing foolishness."[129]

Harriet Lowell was born on January 4, 1957. *Life* magazine, working on a story about the "Lowells of Boston," sent Alfred Eisenstadt to photograph the baby, shown in the March 18 issue in her elegant bassinet, with her formally dressed parents posing alongside it. Elizabeth peers down at Harriet, while Cal stares grimly at the photographer.[130] (The photo reproduced in this book is a more sympathetic family portrait from this session.) "She is a lovely girl, really, very sweet and good and the nurse we have keeps her starched and perfumed and spotless as a princess," Elizabeth wrote to Cousin Harriet.[131] While she naturally wanted to portray her offspring to her namesake in the most glowing terms, it is telling that the image

Elizabeth and Cal with baby Harriet, 1957.

is so airbrushed. Elizabeth, whose daughter was bottle-fed, was not the kind of mother to revel in the messier aspects of babyhood. Most of the time, she was not even permitted to do so. Cal described the increasingly frosty relationship between Miss Elsemore, the bossy nurse, and his wife: "Poor Lizzie isn't allowed to play with Harriet except . . . between six and six-thirty when she would like to be relaxing over an Old Fashioned."[132] On Miss Elsemore's day off, however, the baby was in Elizabeth's care, rendering her as "paralyzed with fatigue," she wrote to Mary, as if she had ridden a Greyhound bus to California. She hoped her waistline would soon return to its usual size, so that she could fit into the "haute couture clothes bought with sweat and blood at Filene's basement."[133]

Two weeks after Elizabeth gave birth, her story "The Classless Society" was published in *The New Yorker*, marking a new level of psychological insight and a keen ear for the speech patterns of her characters. This was a revised version of "The Babcock Family," which Katharine White had described as "persuasive" until the young woman meets the young man, a florist. He was Elizabeth's "least convincing character." Another problem, White wrote, was that the piece seemed more like "social documentation" than fiction.[134] In the final version, which White called "a wonderfully witty story,"[135] the Nesbitts—Willard, a history professor at the University of Chicago who believes he is destined for greater things, and Henrietta Babcock, his well-born wife, lamenting an opera career that never got off the ground—are entertaining another couple. Dodo Babcock is a vacuous female relative of Henrietta's; Clarence Anderson is an earnest, unmarried, and detested colleague of Willard's. (Elizabeth had turned the florist into an academic, setting the story in Chicago to avoid appearing to be sending up specific New Yorkers.)[136] As the evening wears on, Clarence begins to find Dodo appealing despite the gulf between their political views and economic and intellectual backgrounds. After they leave together, the

Nesbitts bitterly dissect the prospects of their guests, and Willard cringes at Henrietta's familiar aria about academics who "talk about things with such godlike assurance . . . everything out of books and other people's lectures, nothing from actual life!"

In the spring, Elizabeth accompanied Cal to New York on the first leg of his West Coast reading tour, remaining in the city for a few days after he left to see friends. She gave a lecture at Barnard College, "Current American Attitudes on Feminism," as part of a program on American civilization.[137] Parted from her baby for the first time, she missed seeing Harriet's little face. Back in Boston, Elizabeth redoubled her efforts on the James letters, kept up her social life, and mailed Cousin Harriet—who was sending a constant stream of tiny garments—frequent bulletins about her namesake.

On June 22, when the mercury soared to eighty-eight degrees Fahrenheit in Boston, the family left for Castine, with a U-Haul trailer attached to the car. Elizabeth was pleased to discover that during the past two years, small improvements had made a difference—lobsters for sale at the dock, a washing machine and dryer for rent—though the sight of a prefab house plopped onto a lot raised fears of an unsightly new development. Cousin Harriet's Federal-style home at 29 School Street fronted the Town Common. There were eight rooms, two baths, and a high-ceilinged, attached former barn with running water. Elizabeth was enchanted with her surroundings, gazing at "brilliantly green" trees and flowerbeds bright with petunias, nasturtiums, heliotrope, marigolds, lilacs, dahlias, and flowering tobacco plants. "I wake up in delight at 7 every morning," she wrote to Cousin Harriet, "having been fast asleep by ten. That goes for us both, of course."[138]

During the spring, Elizabeth had made her peace with the nurse, a Maine native who came to Castine with the family. But a few days after they arrived, Elizabeth became fed up with Miss Elsemore's bullying tactics. The nurse departed in early July, in a maelstrom of rage like the Wicked Fairy in *Sleeping Beauty*, "blaming everything on Elizabeth . . . saying to the baby . . . Your *Daddy's* one person you'll never forget."[139] The nurse's replacement was the seventeen-year-old granddaughter of Mrs. Gray, a local woman employed by Cousin Harriet to do laundry and house cleaning. Mrs. Gray's misfortunes were legion, including the out-of-wedlock pregnancy of a jilted daughter. Elizabeth found the "languid, unreal, indolent nature of the [daughter's] behavior . . . inexplicable," unless it was a desperate bid for marriage. She observed that "the vanishing fathers" were evidence that these young women doubted their boyfriends would marry them "and perhaps got pregnant in hope to clinch it."[140]

By the end of July, Elizabeth lamented to Cousin Harriet that she had done no work, what with time spent with the baby and outdoor activities.[141] August's interruptions included outings with visitors, who included Fred Dupee and his family, Richard Eberhart, and fellow poet W. S. Merwin, accompanied by his British wife, Dido. As Cal wrote to Elizabeth Bishop, it was "a boy scoutish summer . . . picnics in small outboards [Dupee had attached a motor to a rowboat], sails, a cruise . . . drives to Bar Harbor, Stonington, Camden."[142] He noted with satisfaction that Elizabeth had colored her hair red and was a knockout in her "summer ensembles."[143] Bishop and her lover, Lota de Macedo Soares, arrived for a visit that was cut short after four days when Cal began claiming that he was in love with the poet and was planning a trip to Brazil to see her on his own. Elizabeth also had invited her college friend Susan Turner to visit for the month of August. But according to Cal's letter to Bishop, Elizabeth soured on entertaining a woman who didn't cook and was obsessed with her doctoral dissertation, small-town Kentucky, and her own health.[144] Told (untruthfully) that everyone was leaving in mid-August, Turner departed. Cal also related that, on a boozy cruise with friends, Elizabeth "had drunk a whole water tumbler of the martinis to which she is allergic," which led to an hour and a half of "an amazingly frank and detailed reappraisal of our entire marriage." The upshot, he concluded, was that "we were at last in better agreement than we have been since Harriet's birth." In his long letter, he assured Bishop, "I'm really underneath utterly *in* love and sold on my Elizabeth and it's a great solace to me that you are with Lota."

None of these events were chronicled in Elizabeth's long letters to Cousin Harriet, who had promised to bequeath the "brick house" to the Lowells. Elizabeth subtly angled for the School Street house instead by mentioning that if she and Cal were to buy one of the houses, she would choose the big one "because it is better for a longer season and oh, so beautiful." Of course, she continued, they would never be able to afford it. But they realized this summer how keen they were to keep coming back to Castine. "Little Harriet," she added, in a perfectly calibrated coda, "is already a local character only exceeded in fame and impressiveness by big Harriet."[145]

Back in Boston in September, Cal was working on the poems he began during the last few weeks in Castine. But although Elizabeth hired a young Irish woman to care for Harriet, she was not able to finish editing the James letters or work on other projects.[146] Despite Cal's breezy remark to Bishop, the tension Elizabeth felt in the marriage was not resolved. When someone mentioned an artist who supposedly had been Bishop's "grand passion," Cal wrote, "My Elizabeth answered rather sourly, '*One* of Elizabeth Bishop's grand passions!'"[147] (The inference was that she resented Bishop's closeness to Cal.) In a strikingly candid letter to William Shawn, whom she knew only in his capacity as editor in chief of *The New Yorker*, Elizabeth wrote, "I've had a very low summer with taking care of the baby, family problems, all sorts of things."[148] Now she wondered if he would consider sending her to Lexington, pegging a magazine piece about the city to its new attempt at racial integration. Elizabeth's desperation was painfully raw. "I need this very much," she implored, perhaps referring as much to possibly spending time away from Cal as to demonstrating her ability to write nonfiction for the magazine. Considering herself as "a Southerner of sorts" because of her youth in Kentucky, she wrote, "I know beyond a doubt, that I could do a piece of writing absolutely original and utterly truthful and interesting." The article would, she felt certain, "be the most important thing of my career." No response from Shawn has survived; Elizabeth would have to wait another dozen years to publish the first of several essays about her home city.[149]

In December, the Lowells squeezed in a visit to Cousin Harriet on a trip to Washington, D.C., where Cal spoke at the Phi Beta Kappa convocation at the College of William and Mary. Back in Boston, he speeded up again, inviting a large crowd of people to a cocktail party without telling Elizabeth. Quickly realizing what was happening, she appointed a guest to keep everyone supplied with stiff drinks in hopes that they would not be aware of Cal's increasing mania. At one point, W. S. Merwin was speaking with Elizabeth about a political issue.[150] Cal, who had absented himself upstairs, came down and crashed into the glass coffee table, upsetting people's drinks and setting off a volley of repercussions. Elizabeth burst into tears and was comforted by Arthur Schlesinger, Jr. After the guests left, Cal kept ranting for three days. She finally had to call the police, and he was taken to McLean Hospital. As if the breakdown were not bad enough, he became infatuated with Ann Adden, a Bennington College student who was doing psychiatric fieldwork at the hospital.

Elizabeth said nothing about all this in a letter to the Clarks on New Year's Day 1958. "Boston begins to pall somewhat," she wrote in a wry understatement. She mused about a possible teaching position for Cal in West Berlin, wondering if she had "the energy" to run a household with a baby in a country where she didn't speak the language.[151] She and Cal had planned a week's visit to New York in February. But after his release from the hospital, he rented a room at a motel on Harvard Square where he could meet Adden. Then he abruptly returned to the house, packed a suitcase, and went out of town for a few days. Elizabeth wrote to Cousin Harriet, with whom she now felt a close bond, that she was experiencing "despair in a way I never have before." She felt she was "slowly becoming numb to the whole thing, wanting to be free of the future." She would probably take Cal back, because she still loved him—"or at least I think I do." As always, she was keenly aware of his suffering and knew that it would be her job "to build up his confidence."[152] But she had to make time for herself—by taking walks, dining with friends, and distracting herself with an auction at an old Beacon Street house. (The only items she craved were a couple of flowerpot containers that sold for ten times what she could afford.) In a mid-December letter to Allen Tate, Elizabeth remarked wanly that little Harriet "was flourishing and Mum is declining—the one leading to the other." She criticized Tate for telling the intellectual historian Perry Miller that Cal's recent poems were a reflection of his mania. "He was not sick during the long months that he worked over and over those poems," she wrote.[153] Despite everything, she would always argue for the value of his work.

When Cal returned to Elizabeth, he was still in an excited state, making impossible demands. Although he insisted that he wanted to stay married, he had found yet another young woman, a twenty-year-old mother of two children with mental issues of her own.[154] (Adden was now left in the dark when he refused to answer her calls.) Elizabeth's new strategy was "to keep out of his way for the next ten days" and return to her work.[155] After that period, she would need to decide if she could stand the role of caretaker, and if not, she would "have to get him to leave." As things turned out, there was no ten-day period. Cal began to calm down—likely comforted by the permanence the house represented, crammed with family heirlooms—and resumed his teaching at Boston University. In a letter to Elizabeth Bishop, written the day Cal moved back, Elizabeth poured out her worries.[156] ("He is far from well, alas, and I don't know how I am going to stand it.") She was concerned about the future for herself and Harriet, both in the near and long term, and nervous about the potential results if Cal stopped taking his heavy cocktail of drugs. Yet she was heartened that he was under the care of a "first-rate Freudian analyst" and that he could now return to his work—poetry that was "deeply original, truthful, and immensely interesting, the first thing art must be."

The honeymoon period did not last. In a letter to Katharine White acknowledging her new contract, Elizabeth explained that "intense family troubles" had prevented her from writing more than "drafts and beginnings" that she was unable to finish.[157] Cal was back at McLean in February, and Elizabeth worried about the thirty-dollar daily charge.[158] She called the bank and was informed that the money would be arranged somehow (apparently, from the principal of Cal's trust). The young women were another intractable problem. "They keep me from acting in his best interests often because I don't want to seem pushing or jealous," she wrote to Cousin Harriet.[159] It was no less off-putting to learn that Cal considered baby Harriet "my responsibility, not his!" In a stab at black humor, she realized that she couldn't divorce someone who was not the person she married but rather "some awfully fatuous man I alas happen to be temporarily connected with."

CHAPTER 6

Upheaval

(1958–1960)

In February 1958, Elizabeth spent a few days in New York with the Clarks to see theater and to try to get some sleep. Perhaps as a reflection of her mood, the couple's apartment, which others found charming, struck her as "a tiny, black-holish place."[1] Cal's new position was that divorce and remarriage were necessary. The doctors explained to Elizabeth that by telling himself his marriage was the problem, he avoided having to face the fact of his illness. They urged her not to divorce him, but she wondered if there was a cure for a middle-aged man who had had so many breakdowns. Still, by early March, she was "again full of hope" that Cal could "lighten future attacks and change the symptoms, in so far [sic] as they relate to me."[2] In a letter Cal wrote later that spring to Theodore Roethke about his separation from his wife, he recalled how, "to my grief, I too tried to break away from Elizabeth. It was all part of my mania and nonsense. . . . Then it all passed—again I was home. . . . All that was lost is returned. We even bring back certain treasure from our visits to the bottom."[3]

The publication of his poem "Man and Wife" in the winter issue of *Partisan Review* documented the aftermath of one of these visits. It begins, "Tamed by *Miltown*, we lie on Mother's bed." Later in the poem, the speaker says, "All night I've held your hand, / as if you had / a fourth time faced the kingdom of the mad— / its hackneyed speech, its homicidal eye— / and dragged me home alive." After revisiting his meeting with Elizabeth decades earlier, he returns to the present, when "your old-fashioned tirade— / loving, rapid, merciless— / breaks like the Atlantic Ocean on my head."[4]

The amazing thing is that in the midst of her tumultuous personal life, Elizabeth was writing reviews. Her interest in theater had been sparked years earlier, when she traveled to Cincinnati with a group of college friends to see the Russian actress Alla Nazimova as Mrs. Alving in Ibsen's *Ghosts*—the first time she had seen professional acting.[5] In the spring of 1958, she took over the *Partisan Review* "Theater Chronicle" column previously written by Fred Dupee.[6] Her first review contrasted the emotive qualities of works by two leading American playwrights—William Inge (*The Dark at the Top of the Stairs*) and Tennessee Williams (*Something Unspoken; Suddenly Last Summer*)—with *The Entertainer*, by the British playwright John Osborne. Elizabeth found Inge too preoccupied with "a sort of revelation that passes for action" and Williams, with sexual or outré secrets, whereas Osborne related his characters' miseries to the larger world of the British welfare state. Irritated at the complacency of New York theatergoers, she was delighted that audiences found *The Entertainer* upsetting. In her view, it was "one of the most interesting plays since Shaw."

By invoking the author of *Major Barbara*, *Pygmalion*, and *Heartbreak House*, Elizabeth underlined her preference for the theater of ideas, works that present a sociopolitical argument. This approach aligns with her habitual slighting of acting or stagecraft. (Years later she declared, "I'm not interested at all in production. I'm really interested in the literary side.")[7] Concluding her review with a mention of Beckett's *Endgame*, she remained true to form in praising its "therapeutic beauty and truth." But her most insightful observation in this piece is about the era's underdeveloped roles for young women, characters who "wander about plays of every sort, scattering boredom like dandruff on the stage."

* * *

Elizabeth mused that Cal's multiple breakdowns gave the two of them "a kind of immunity to the 'social' aspects' of his illness," the twin scourges of gossip and shunning. When he was allowed out of the hospital for brief periods, she busied herself in finding suitable films, concerts, and other diversions, "so he won't be too distressed by the lack of real working routine which he isn't quite up to taking on."[8] He would not be released until April. Well aware of the cyclic nature of Cal's illness, Elizabeth and Blair Clark discussed how she could avoid being responsible for committing her husband to a hospital after future episodes; so far there was no solution. After thanking Robert Henderson—her new editor at *The New Yorker*—for her annual contract, she explained that she hadn't been able to do "any sustained work for months, just drafts and beginnings which I don't get back to for long periods because of intense family troubles."[9]

In an effort to return to her writing, she tried to interest *Harper's Bazaar*—which had approached her as a potential contributor—in an impressionistic portrait of Nadia Boulanger, the eminent seventy-year-old French composer, conductor, and music teacher, who would soon be giving a lecture at Radcliffe. But when the young woman who minded Harriet was ill for two weeks, full-time care for the baby prevented Elizabeth from getting back to work. She wrote to Cousin Harriet that she was reminded "of an old Southern saying—I wouldn't take a million dollars for this one, but wouldn't give you a nickel for another one!" It was unimaginable to want a second child.[10] She was hardly alone among her women writer contemporaries in having just one child; others included Susan Sontag, Mary McCarthy, and Joan Didion. Elizabeth looked forward to the time when "one can have [Harriet] milling about in the room and do whatever I was doing before."[11] A child who could entertain herself was clearly the goal. Amusingly, when Harriet was just sixteen months old, Elizabeth claimed to perceive the infant's "sturdy, manly sense of humor that moderates somewhat her common-sense bias."[12]

An April visit to her family in Lexington was a disappointment; Elizabeth found them "unbelievably tedious and charmless."[13] Upon her return, she finally completed the Henry James manuscript and sent it to her publisher. She then turned her thoughts to summer in Castine. Since Cal had to return to Boston for a few days each week to see his doctor and to teach at Harvard Summer School—a position that opened at the last minute, providing much-needed income—she would need to be able to pass the driving test in order to run errands in the village. Not to mention borrowing Cousin Harriet's old Buick and purchasing expensive car insurance. "The mechanics of life in America are exhausting," she concluded.[14]

But she did summon energy for entertaining luminaries of the literary world. Recalling a visit to the Lowells, the playwright and poet William Alfred said, "I'd never talked to people who cared that much about words. It was absolutely electric."[15] Edmund Wilson often dropped by when visiting his dentist in Boston. "A drink seems to dry his tears and his blood," Elizabeth remarked. "He is . . . of inexhaustible interest to us because his interest in things seems inexhaustible." Adrienne Rich often visited on Sundays with her husband and children. Elizabeth would remember her as "so alert, so intelligent, so witty."[16] Sixty-nine-year-old T. S. Eliot, now married to a woman less than half his age, was supposed to be the guest of honor at the Lowells' dinner for eight in May, but a night of dancing with her gave him heart palpitations. He did come to dinner the following autumn, gracing a table of other major literary figures that included Wilson and his wife, Elena, and the critic I. A. Richards—a wearying evening for Elizabeth as hostess.

Sylvia Plath, another visitor, wrote in her diary that Elizabeth was "charming and highstrung, mimicking their subnormal Irish house girl." Plath noted Cal's "half-whisper and sliding glance."[17] She observed him kissing Elizabeth "tenderly before leaving . . . and all the winsome tendernesses of a devoted husband." After inviting them for dinner with another couple, Plath decided to read Elizabeth's stories at the library; what she wanted for herself was "their success without their spirit or work."[18] Months later she decided that Elizabeth's characters were "utterly unlikable in any way," comparing her fiction unfavorably to Jean Stafford's.[19] Years later, Elizabeth would have quite a lot to say about Plath and her poetry.

* * *

After treating themselves to a "farewell dinner" at the Ritz-Carlton, the Lowells left for Castine in late June in a newly purchased Ford station wagon. Cal decided to use Cousin Harriet's car for his trips back and forth, so that Elizabeth could drive the Ford. Getting a learner's permit required lengthy trips north to the town of Ellsworth, which reminded her of "trying to get a legal paper signed in the days of the Austro-Hungarian Empire." A local woman provided driving lessons, stopping for the Lowells' groceries on the way, while making what Elizabeth described as "rather depressing but painfully fascinating efforts at gentility and refinement."[20]

Elizabeth and Cal were pleased to be back in Castine, playing tennis with a visiting clergyman from St. John the Divine in New York, awaiting the arrival of friends who would stay in the brickyard house, and planning a cocktail party "for everyone we know."[21] As she settled in, plucking a leaf from the mint patch for a mint julep, Elizabeth wrote to Cousin Harriet that even without Cal's constant presence, the summer would be just fine. She would have plenty of time for reading and puttering in the garden. (The lack of his presence actually might have seemed a boon, but such thoughts could not be mentioned in a letter to his relative.) With no one to keep her awake—baby Harriet had a nanny—Elizabeth fell asleep by ten p.m. and discovered the beauty of early mornings in the bucolic setting.

Writing to Cousin Harriet about recent changes in town, she mentioned the new yacht club, which offered a tasty boiled lobster dinner, served at tables overlooking the harbor. Friends summering nearby provided amusing gossip, including the unpopularity of one of the two local markets: the new manager was having an affair. Then there were the continuing travails of Mrs. Gray, the house cleaner. Her husband was too ill to work, leaving her to struggle with a huge bank debt—the result of a loan taken to support one of her errant children—and an unpaid oil bill. It was "a tale of folly, false hope, and desolation," Elizabeth wrote. Feeling sorry for the woman, she paid her twenty dollars a week, more than she could afford, despite the slipshod quality of her work.[22] While Mrs. Gray (unlike "Ida," a Castine laundress), does not seem to have a counterpart in *Sleepless Nights*, hers was one of many defeated lives Elizabeth had come to know.

In August several of Cal's relatives arrived, ushering in weeks of cocktail parties, boating, tennis, and trips to nearby towns. "Four o'clock tennis" was the ritual late-afternoon game at the golf club's courts: mixed doubles with players of varying abilities that were followed by drinks and dinner in the Water Street barn. (Despite her love of the game, Elizabeth would claim that "as long as I live, two things will never improve: my typing and my tennis.")[23] After the Lowells returned home, Cal wrote to Bishop that Elizabeth was "much less tense."[24]

The Boston social season was in full swing. At a cocktail party, Elizabeth found herself "getting drunk with Learned Hand," the eighty-six-year-old federal judge. Elderly people had always charmed her; she once remarked that her "great delight in . . . adolescence was the rocking chair with the aged person in it talking away."[25] Van Cliburn's upcoming concert was the big event on the musical calendar—the young American pianist had just won the International Tchaikovsky Competition in Moscow—but Elizabeth disliked a recording of his that Cal had bought for her and didn't want to go. By day, she practiced driving on city streets in readiness for her test, which she likened to getting a Ph.D., and finally received her license in mid-October. She remarked to the Clarks that "a nervous trip alone to the Stop and Shop" made her sorry she had pursued this goal.[26]

In a gossipy letter to Elizabeth Bishop, Cal wrote that Elizabeth and a pregnant Adrienne Rich had a "forty-five minute argument, carried on in [the] dining room, pantry and library about two people neither liked or really knew. We like her very much."[27] He was urging Elizabeth to stop drinking because he had quit, but as she wrote to the Clarks, this directive was annoying because she had cut way down and "to have to stop in the most literal sense is nearly unbearable." The notion of a whole day "of running around the Public Garden with Harriet and nothing but a cup of coffee awaiting me at 7 p.m." was depressing. But if she had a drink, Cal would also have one. "I, then, automatically become responsible for anything that happens of an unpleasant nature during the next year."[28] Something to look forward to was their upcoming trip to Spain in mid-January: "Think of evenings in Spanish restaurants with a Spanish guitar playing!" The drawback was the need to fly there: "I hate the actual being in a plane, and beyond that I want to return to Harriet and flying about in the air seems the last place I should be."

Elizabeth was not fond of Christmas chores, especially shopping for presents, but she enjoyed decorating small trees. After years of using fabric flowers, she delighted at the discovery of Italian-made plastic roses that looked amazingly lifelike. Harriet longed for a rocking horse, but Elizabeth hated the newfangled kind ("glittering, ugly TV things"); the appearance of objects in her home was always of great importance to her. As she tried to focus on her writing and hoped a mysterious pain in her arm was not serious, she regretted that it was too easy to let "petty little details" get in the way of accomplishing anything. She envied Nadia Boulanger, who exemplified the "greatness of the power of concentration upon important matters and those only," allowing the composer "to give more to others rather than less."[29]

The January trip to Spain was initially postponed until May. Answering a question from her *New Yorker* editor about it, Elizabeth wrote, "I have forgotten what was, finally, the most debilitating. Was it Christmas or colds? Perhaps, both. Anyway, exhaustion was too great to provide the energy for a rest."[30] After yet another of Cal's manic episodes in the spring of 1959, vacation plans were postponed indefinitely. "I feel particularly discouraged," Elizabeth wrote to Mary, "because this latest flare-up came after a very happy year for both of us. . . . I miss Cal terribly because he is delightful to be with when he's 'himself.'"[31] He had signed himself into Maclean Hospital in late April; two months later he was in what Elizabeth regarded as "a state of aesthetic loss, doing very poor rewritings of all his early poems."[32] This was especially sad so soon after Faber and Faber had published the British edition of his epic four-part autobiographical poetry cycle, *Life Studies*. (The U.S. edition was published later in the year by Farrar, Straus and Cudahy; it won the National Book Award in 1960.)

Cal's poem "Memories of West Street and Lepke" begins, "I hog a whole house on Boston's / 'Hardly passionate Marlborough Street.'" The quotation is from William James[33]—a link with Elizabeth's project. Another poem in this final section of the book, "To Speak of the Woe That Is in Marriage," written during the dark days of 1957, was a bleak vision of what married life was like for Elizabeth. The title was taken from Chaucer's Prologue to "The Wife of Bath's Tale," in which the woman complains about her drunk, unfaithful husband. In Cal's poem, the husband's "free-lancing" forays for prostitutes suggests a fantasy version of Cal's actual life—his known extramarital experiences were not with call girls—but the "whiskey-blind, swaggering home at five" aspect was sadly familiar to Elizabeth. The wife in the poem has a nightly ritual in which she ties "ten dollars and his car key to my thigh." This was actually a strategy of Gertrude Buckman's, Delmore Schwartz's first wife, not of Elizabeth's.[34] But the final image of the husband—"Gored by the climacteric of his want / he stalls above me like an elephant"—is so appallingly vivid that it is plausible as a rendering of her marital torment.

Cal left the hospital after eight weeks, joining Elizabeth and Harriet in Castine in July; he was apparently "content to be here," she wrote to Blair.[35] In early April, Cal had written to Elizabeth Bishop that he felt "so forlorn" without her. ("There's no one else I can quite talk to with confidence and abandon and delicacy.")[36] Belatedly hearing about his breakdown and sympathizing with the strain it put on Elizabeth, Bishop wrote, "Thank heavens Cal has you."[37] But Elizabeth did not always feel like a tower of strength. She confessed to Allen Tate that "this deranged person does a lot of harm. . . . He is terribly demanding and devouring. I feel a deep loyalty and commitment to him, and yet at the same time I don't know exactly what sort of bearable status quo I can establish with him."[38]

In early September 1959, Elizabeth felt relieved to return to Boston, what with all the domestic emergencies and chores that occupied her in Castine, from a leaky roof and squirrel invaders to a reupholstery project that remained uncompleted. Still, recalling her feeling years earlier about returning to New York from Lexington, she would "no doubt be eager to come back next year."[39] Harriet started nursery school that autumn, and the rules obliged Elizabeth to spend three mornings a week in the classroom. She complained to Cousin Harriet that this new situation was "a big step" for her daughter but "a big retreat for me at my age. I was never so bored in my life as with a room full of tots and their mothers, a fantastic modern idea."[40]

This year Elizabeth's writing was beginning to gather momentum. Her story "The Purchase"—a pitch-perfect depiction of male ego in the personalities of an older, traditional painter ("nostalgic scenes on summer lawns") living on his wife's money and a struggling younger abstract painter with a bullying manner—was published in the May 30 issue of *The New Yorker*. The Lowells had met a group of Abstract Expressionist painters on a trip to New York in early February; witnessing their interactions in a social setting may have inspired this short story.[41] The older artist finds himself captivated yet thrown off-balance by the younger artist's pretty, bohemian wife, to the point that he betrays his better instincts and buys what he views as an awful painting by her husband at a price he cannot afford. While Elizabeth enumerates the types of objects both couples own, complete with brand names, much as Mary would have done, she goes much deeper—probing the personalities and unconscious motives of her characters and evoking them with devastating precision. ("Frazier was not mean-spirited so much as serviceably coarse, like an old army blanket.") In a note on the galleys, William Shawn, the magazine's editor in chief, suggested that the Abstract Expressionist was coming across as "just a little too blunt and rude." But Elizabeth had intuited how crassly direct such a man could be, with "all the bluster of a young beginner."[42]

The spring issue of *Partisan Review* contained her review of Saul Bellow's picaresque novel *Henderson the Rain King*.[43] Wrestling with a way to describe its form—neither realistic fiction nor satire—she proposed that it had to be understood "symbolically" (even though Bellow had playfully warned against this in a recent article).[44] Yet it was still hard to classify. "Perhaps," she suggested, "it is meant as a piece of comic exuberance." While granting its technical mastery ("profuse, splashy, relaxed"), she thought it was inferior to Bellow's earlier work. Yet she realized that *Henderson* was the kind of "large effort" that was a natural undertaking for "an important American novelist."

Elizabeth viewed the writing of men and women differently, but not from a polemical standpoint. "From the men, I demand only excellence" is the way she concluded her essay "I've Been Reading," published in the *Columbia University Forum*. Her relationship to writing by women was more complicated, she candidly admitted: "As a writer, I feel a nearly unaccountable attraction and hostility to the work of other women writers. Envy, competitiveness, scorn infect my judgments at times." Of course, as she well knew from the *Partisan Review* milieu, "competitiveness is the rule of the intellectual world." Although she read "a great many books just because they are written by women," she declared that she was often—she put the word in quotes—"disappointed." In this piece, Elizabeth listed authors she especially admired (Virginia Woolf, Mary McCarthy, Edith Wharton) and discussed novels by Iris Murdoch, Doris Lessing (a favorite), Pamela Hansford Johnson, and two obscure writers (Elizabeth Madox Roberts, a fellow Kentuckian, and Elizabeth Jenkins). Eighteen years later she would help reintroduce "unknown" women writers (and little-known works by famous ones) as series editor of *Rediscovered Fiction by American Women Writers*.

The essay that suddenly made Elizabeth famous was a bombshell article, "The Decline of Book Reviewing," published in October in "Writing in America," a special issue of *Harper's Magazine*.[45] "Sweet, bland commendations fall everywhere upon the scene," she wrote, "a universal, if somewhat lobotomized, accommodation reigns." She lambasted the book review sections of *The New York Times* and *The New York Herald Tribune* for "the absence of involvement, passion, character, eccentricity." In her view, "coverage" had replaced "opinion." Her homespun analogy compares the way the reviews in newspapers and the *Saturday Review* (a weekly magazine) served publishers' needs to the "shredded green paper under the eggs" in an Easter basket.

As evidence, she quoted a study that found that 51 percent of book reviews published in 1956 were favorable, while 44.8 percent were, amazingly, noncommittal. Wouldn't the very nature of a review involve "the production of an opinion"? An array of waffling quotes from five recent *Herald Tribune* reviews of novels clinched her case. Elizabeth contrasted the anemic American scene with the London newspapers and *The Times Literary Supplement*, exemplars of "the seriousness, the independence of mind and temperament" that stem from strong editorial direction. In their absence, book reviews operate simply as another form of publicity, "the great toe of the giant." Cal wrote proudly to Elizabeth Bishop that "injured fans of the Saturday Review and the Times and Herald book-sections . . . pour in letters of protest."[46] Enumerating other outcomes of the essay, he mentioned "an AP news release," a phone call from the media to Elizabeth's sisters in Kentucky, and interest from *Time* magazine, which sent a freelance photographer to Boston.

Without mentioning this article, Elizabeth wrote to Mary to praise her new effort, *The Stones of Florence*: "so fresh, so newly, personally observed." In a more intimate vein, she described her "great, wrenching sadness" as she reached the end of the final chapter. Yet she insisted that this was not nostalgia for her own time in the city. Rather, it was a reflection of "the sadness of all those great and little people who have lived there." She mentioned that she was working on "a long thing about going to jazz nightclubs and 'knowing' people like Billie Holiday and Dizzy Gillespie—in the early forties." Elizabeth also wrote to her *New Yorker* editor about this piece, remarking that she felt "quite enthusiastic" about it.[47] But to Mary, she confessed that she doubted whether she could tell this story. "It all seems weird and I don't know why I spent so much time, half-fascinated, half-frightened, looking at these people in their settings," she wrote. "I'm glad I did, but I am not sure I understand myself at all."[48] In the coming years, the effort to find a way to write about them would take her fiction to a new level, first displayed in 1973 in a quasi-autobiographical story, "Writing a Novel."

During the month of December, Elizabeth spent her evenings reading about Mexico, where the Lowells planned to vacation. "My spirits go up and down, very much as they do once one is in that country," she wrote to her *New Yorker* editor. "You feel the heat and exhaustion of Acapulco and the cool and exhaustion of Mexico City and I go around the house, thinking, 'God, Maximilian!'[49] We are very anxious for our trip, even if it is not Italy." That month she published another controversial article in *Harper's*, "Boston: The Lost Ideal." (She later insisted that the idea for the piece was Cal's.)[50] Elizabeth argued that the city once revered for its intellectual heft had become "a sort of farce of conservative exclusiveness and snobbish humor." While bankers, brokers, doctors, and lawyers could find stimulation in Boston, for anyone engaged in artistic, literary, or intellectual pursuits, its culture had died long ago. Elizabeth anatomized the "wellborn failure"—a Bostonian living aimlessly on a small inheritance, whose speech had become an incomprehensible stew of "hesitations infinitely refined," and whose counterpart was "the nervous, shy, earnest wom[a]n." The young woman in Elizabeth's short story "The Final Conflict," written around this time, reflects another version of suffocating inhibition: a timid fashion design student from a Kentucky coal-mining town, too afraid to move from Boston to New York for her career. Her romance with a hapless former gas station attendant eager for the high life is upended when he leaves to join a speculator in dog races. *The New Yorker* rejected this story "on the grounds that the characters aren't fully convincing."[51]

In her essay about Boston, Elizabeth wrote that it was a city for people "not in a hurry"; it lacked "that wild electric beauty of New York . . . the marvelous excited rush of people in taxicabs at twilight." Her own restlessness with the measured pace of Boston and her yearning to return to New York were not to be denied, though she later said that it was Cal who decided to make the move.[52] Decades later, while professing "love and tenderness" for Boston, Elizabeth told an interviewer that it was "a man's city," lacking professional freedom for women.[53] "If . . . you're clever," she said, "you turn into a faculty wife." For a writer of personal essays about culture, the "academic slant toward experience" was too confining. To another interviewer, she said, "I always take a critical view of things. Who wants to . . . say 'What a beautiful town!'"[54] Then she backtracked and once again claimed that she liked Boston "very much." Perhaps her memories of living with Cal in the city made it impossible for her to maintain her quarrel with it. Yet she still had a bone to pick. Referring to Bostonians' pride in their cultural heritage, she said, "I feel that culture is not an inheritance. It is a life-long cultivation of the intellect."

During the unusually cold, snowy winter of 1960, Elizabeth likened Boston to "a medieval village—garbage stacked up, dirty drifts several feet high, muffled and stunned 'peasants.'"[55] Recalling images of homebound people in winter in Russian novels, Elizabeth wondered how modern-day Russians were able to pursue space exploration in their cold climate. In February, after Harriet's Irish live-in nurse decided to leave, Elizabeth wrote to Cousin Harriet that they hired a "colored woman" to take her place.[56] (Many liberal, educated white people still used the word *colored* to refer to African Americans—even the NAACP had the word in its title—although *Negro* had largely replaced it by then.) In the same letter, she mentioned how exciting it was to see Leontyne Price—the great African American soprano—in Verdi's opera *Il Trovatore*: "She has a wonderful, big voice and is a fine-looking, dignified person on the stage," Elizabeth wrote. She was intrigued to read that "the white family for whom [Price's] mother worked as a maid in the South came up for the first performances."

* * *

Elizabeth mined elements of the Lowells' stay in Italy for her essay "Living in Italy: Reflections on Bernard Berenson," which appeared in the winter 1960 issue of *Partisan Review*. (She had submitted the piece to *The New Yorker* the previous autumn without high hopes, and Henderson had turned it down because it didn't fit into one of the magazine's article categories.)[57] In Italy, she wrote, the American art expert had become "a sort of foreign prince, a character in a fairy tale." In the early 1950s, his villa, I Tatti, struck her as "most memorable for its solidity . . . the reminders of the comfortable Beacon Street standards of Berenson's youth."[58] Berenson, then in his mid-eighties, "lived with the silky regularity and pleasurable concentration of energies that are at once opulent and sacrificial— the prudence of the sensual." Elizabeth segued into a meditation on Americans living abroad, whether they did so as a hermit (Santayana) or as an "innkeeper" (Berenson, so eager to see a new visitor). As she well knew, the longer an American lived abroad—especially in "the dreamlike timelessness of Italy"—the more essential was "the traveler from home . . . bring[ing] knowledge, prejudices, fashions that cannot be acquired from the newspapers." In her exquisite formulation, an American's envy of the Italian way of life "is cut short time and time again by a sudden feeling of sadness in the air, as of something still alive with the joys of an Italian day and yet somehow faintly withered, languishing."

Diana Trilling wrote to Elizabeth to praise "William James: American Hero"—a version of her introduction to *The Selected Letters*, published in the June issue of *Mademoiselle*—as "one of the nicest things you've written."[59] What Diana couldn't understand was how Elizabeth could publish such a high-toned essay in a women's magazine, "unless for the money." Of course, that was precisely why she signed a contract with the magazine, which also ran a piece of hers titled "The Feminine Principle" in 1958. Five years before the publication of Betty Friedan's groundbreaking *The Feminine Mystique*, Elizabeth punctured the myth of "the return of the American woman to that Eden, the American home. . . . once more discovering the joys of a role fixed by nature and custom and . . . happily relieving [herself] of the burden of a personal destiny." She exposed the fallacy of this conception of marriage by referring to the way female movie stars freely exchanged one husband for another, without public censure, while other career women, castigated for the egotism that comes of being clever, could not avail themselves of this special dispensation. In Elizabeth's view, the stars were "a vivid and brilliant example of the difference between theory and practice." (Years later she wrote a piece for *Vogue* in which she noted that film stars' "affability" decreased as their power increased.)[60] Writing at a time when rigid gender roles were the norm, she cautioned that fears of not being "feminine enough or masculine enough" were far more dismaying than "the old bourgeois standards of income and social position." Elizabeth presciently warned that the "boredom, fear, constraint, bullying . . . [that] lie behind the new attitude toward women" would result only in their "hysteria and breakdown." In her final, devastating image, Elizabeth imagines the American woman becoming "as compliant as her dishwasher" in a house in which "all the music of the human drama will die away," replaced by "that great gurgling whirr of domestic efficiency."

* * *

"Exhausted from the pace of 'young marrieds' in Boston and Cambridge & eager for the sloth of Maine"—as Elizabeth wrote to Roger Giroux—the Lowells happily retreated to Castine for the summer.[61] With an unexpectedly large check from *The Atlantic Monthly*, Cal bought two paintings of interiors "with wonderful Vermeer windows" that Elizabeth had admired in a Chinese import shop, never expecting to own them. Now they hung over the fireplace in Cousin Harriet's house. Elizabeth was "trying to get down to fiction again," as she wrote to Henderson at *The New Yorker*.[62] Every day she packed a lunch for Cal so that he could disappear into the sparsely furnished barn (table, chair, typewriter, and cot) next to the brickyard house to work on his poetry. This peaceful routine was interrupted by a visit from Elizabeth's twelve-year-old niece. Cal wrote to Peter Taylor that this girl, who still took a stuffed animal to bed with her, threw into relief the strangeness of the Lowell household: "imperious" three-year-old Harriet, absentminded Cal, and "Lizzie's way of investing small, domestic acts with the splendor of an early Verdi heroine."[63]

Partisan Review's summer 1960 issue contained Elizabeth's piece on Caryl Chessman, whose trial and execution had stirred the moral indignation of world-famous literary and humanitarian figures.[64] In January 1948, as a parolee from Folsom Prison in California, he had committed robberies at gunpoint from couples in parked cars, assaulting two women. After a three-week trial in which he served as his own defense counsel, he was convicted of seventeen counts of robbery and kidnapping—but not the original charge of rape, because the sex had consisted of forcing the women to perform fellatio—and sentenced to death. (An arcane aspect of the law led to the application of the kidnapping charge, which mandated capital punishment for crimes involving bodily harm.)[65] During his years on death row, Chessman presented his side of the story in four books, including a best-selling autobiography, *Cell 2455 Death Row*. He was the sickly only child of devout Baptist parents who loved him and believed his lies. After their lives went off the rails—his father attempted suicide following business failures; a car accident left his mother paralyzed—Chessman spent his teenage years committing petty crimes, beginning with car thefts and escalating to robbery after he joined a gang whose members he met in prison. But it wasn't his troubled past that caused members of the liberal intelligentsia to pursue a stay of execution. Rather, it was the combination of his unswerving declarations of innocence and widespread condemnation of the death penalty, particularly in a case in which no murder (or kidnapping, in the usual sense) was committed.

In describing Chessman's life, with copious quotes from his own writing, Elizabeth applied the probing insight that would illuminate her social justice essays in later decades. "We do not even want to reform the criminal because of our anger that we have sometimes tried and failed," she wrote. "His life represents our defeat, our dread of the clear fact that we do not know how to deal with the senseless violence of the young." Elizabeth found "something almost noble" in Chessman's struggle to use his nocturnal bouts of writing to figure out who he was and to try to save himself. His ability to do this showed "that only through 'art,' through some difficult and utterly personal expression, is reclamation and prevention possible." Prison officials' efforts to keep him from his self-appointed work struck her as "one of the most depressing and telling aspects of this sad case." In her apt metaphor, "Chessman puts himself in the position of a leper who is also a physician."

* * *

In September, when Cal took up his Ford Foundation grant to study opera, the Lowells decisively turned their backs on Boston. At first they traded their home for an apartment at 194 Riverside Drive owned by the theater critic Eric Bentley, who had been appointed to a yearlong lectureship at Harvard. Despite the run-down neighborhood—Elizabeth described the "ulcerated side streets . . . shuddering across the abyss of Harlem and the gully of Amsterdam Avenue"[66]—she and Cal were happy to be in Manhattan and wanted to make it their permanent home. "New York seems so full of people after Boston," Cal wrote to Elizabeth Bishop.[67] The Lowells seemed to be "the only gentiles" at parties, he noted in a letter to Adrienne Rich, adding that Elizabeth "has flatly given up asking people to dinner, because the West side [sic] is so far away and we only have the Bentley's [sic] dishes.[68] (The Lowells' household goods were still in Boston.) He informed Bishop that Elizabeth had bought dresses at Bergdorf Goodman—an exclusive women's shop—"and then accepted two reviews . . . to pay for her dresses."[69]

Elizabeth once said to Mary, "Isn't it awful to be in your forties and still find yourself attacking people? Wouldn't you rather just write nice things about people you enjoy reading?"[70] But both women knew that they were not that kind of writer. As Elizabeth ruefully said a few years later, "I feel I write so much better when I'm attacking than when I'm praising."[71] In December 1960 she delivered one of her all-out attacks in a review of a book of photographs and texts from old *Vanity Fair* magazines.[72] While the contents might have struck another writer simply as harmless nostalgia, she excoriated editor Frank Crowninshield for creating a magazine that ignored its writers' strengths by asking for pieces on trivial topics and "treating the text as if it were another photograph." She had a bone to pick with the way photography sped the reader through a magazine, "leav[ing] a strange, giddy sensation of things large and small, like and unlike . . . brought together without meaning." Elizabeth presciently noted how contemporary photography had turned fashion models into celebrities, celebrities into fashion models, and images of "the poor and the distressed" into "fashion-model faces" of tragedy.

At the end of the year, the Lowells' big news was their decision to sell the Boston house and purchase a spacious top-floor duplex at 15 West 67th Street. The eighteen-story building, known as the Hotel des Artistes—gargoyles of artists adorn the Gothic-style facade—was designed in 1917 by architect George Mort Pollard. "Many interesting people have lived there and still do," Elizabeth wrote to Cousin

Harriet. "It is very well-run, very cozy, very old-fashioned."[73] A tiny "servant's room" under the eaves would become Cal's study. The huge skylit living room had a twenty-foot-high ceiling; visitors would remember the second-floor balcony on which Elizabeth sometimes made an appearance late at night to try to get Cal to come to bed.

CHAPTER 7

New York

(1961–1970)

IN JANUARY 1961, after "all sorts of meetings and inspections" with the nine owners of the duplex on West 67th Street, the Lowells moved in with their heirloom furniture, eighty cartons of books, and a piano—a gift from Cousin Harriet. Traveling to Washington, D.C., later that month for the inauguration of President John F. Kennedy, they were among the 172 invited guests who battled the chaos of snowy streets in the aftermath of a major storm. This was the first presidential inauguration that gave pride of place to poetry. Eighty-six-year-old Robert Frost recited "The Gift Outright" from memory after the strong sunlight prevented him from reading the poem he had composed to mark the occasion. Back in New York, Cal wrote to Elizabeth Bishop that living there "is like discovering there is oxygen in the air—people to talk to, plays, opera. . . . Somehow everything is much merrier, easier and more serious."[1]

As always, the peaceful months eventually came to an end. Another young woman had caught Cal's eye. A few years earlier, accompanied by Elizabeth, he had given a reading at Bennington College, where Sandra Hochman was a student. At a lunch hosted by the college president, Hochman (invited because she was a co-editor of the Bennington literary magazine) observed that Elizabeth was "elegantly dressed" and "had the charm and accent of a Southern belle."[2] Hochman also briefly audited Cal's class at Boston University. In late February 1961, having obtained his phone number from a friend who knew him, she called to request an interview for an *Encounter* magazine article. According to her, he asked what she looked like, liked what he heard ("five foot three . . . green eyes, blonde and brownish hair"),[3] and suggested they meet right away. When he showed up at the Russian Tea Room, he was "dishevelled." Uninterested in talking about his work, he told her that he was leaving his wife and would be renting an apartment on the Upper West Side. Soon after the affair began, Hochman met with Dr. Viola Bernard, Cal's current psychiatrist. Unsympathetic to Elizabeth's struggles with her husband, Dr. Bernard encouraged Cal's liaison, never telling Hochman that he had serious mental problems. On the night of March 3, at a party at Blair Clark's townhouse (she described it as an "engagement party"), Hochman was the terrified witness and victim of his full-blown mania. Calling himself Hitler, he tried to strangle his Jewish girlfriend. An ambulance took him to the Neurological Institute of Columbia-Presbyterian Medical Center, where he spent six weeks in a locked ward.

His infatuation with Hochman still burned brightly. He kept a photograph of her next to his hospital bed. When she visited, he gave her his grandfather's gold watch. But Hochman was unprepared for a lover who required hospitalization for his mental illness.[4] Years later, in an interview, Elizabeth recalled that this episode left her "utterly petrified . . . terribly upset . . . truly depressed."[5] Cal had gone through with his plan of renting a flat, which meant that the Lowells now had four properties—the Boston house (which remained on the market), the West 67th Street apartment, the Riverside Drive apartment (which apparently still had time left on the lease), and

Cal's love nest at 85 East End Avenue. Her impulse was to move back to Boston. "I wanted to take my little girl back up there," she said, "where we had someone to work for us, someone waiting for us." Elizabeth followed through on her plan. Soon after that, Cal left Hochman and told his psychiatrist that he wanted to go home.

On April 3, in a long letter to Mary, Elizabeth wrote that she believed she "finally had the key" to Cal's manic affairs: they were "really a sort of charade so that he won't have to face overwhelming fear . . . of all women."[6] Rather than being "explosions of uncontrollable sexuality," she believed they were "explosions of uncontrollable desire to repress sexuality." Because Cal had a habit of "telling the whole world" about his affairs, he had exposed her "to the most awful sense of sexual humiliation," even though "the failure is his not mine." The prospect of many more years of this turmoil made her seriously doubt the value of staying with him. Yet "the most desolating fact is that Cal and I have, by some strange miracle, a good marriage and great love for each other, except in these manic months and just before they come on."

She wrote that she had decided to bide her time until June, waiting to see "how the cure developes [sic]." While she felt that New York was not "the place for us"—herself and Cal—if she did divorce him, she would need to live in the Manhattan apartment. Rethinking her earlier plan, she felt that "Boston would not be nice for me alone or useful enough in making a living." Yet despite all her anxieties about the marriage, she wrote that she was "so glad" Mary liked Cal's translation of Racine's play *Phèdre*. "I love it," Elizabeth wrote, "and his new book of translations [*Imitations*] is also wonderful."

By the summer, the Lowells had achieved another shaky truce. A buyer had been found for the Boston property, though the sale would not take place until September. Elizabeth wrote to Cal—still in the East End Avenue apartment—that she hoped to leave many books behind, since the only ones worth keeping were nonfiction and "important" fiction.[7] If current novels were needed for her reviews, she could check them out of the public library. She had invited Robert Silvers—the *Harper's* editor who would soon play a major role in her professional life—to spend a weekend in the Boston house. "I wanted to sort of show it off for the last time, or be in it with friends for the last time," she explained, envisioning a convivial interlude. It would include a meal with the Tates and a viewing of the CBS TV documentary "Accent on Pasternak: A Television Essay," to which Cal had contributed.[8] But she had forgotten that the two of them would have only one more weekend in Boston before making their pilgrimage to Castine, so maybe Bob should be told that they had other plans? Thinking about a night they needed to spend in New York, she adamantly refused to stay in his East End Avenue apartment ("I will not go there, ever") and suggested the Plaza or (if that luxurious hotel was "too crazy") the Wellington Hotel, in midtown.

In a long, handwritten letter to Cal from Maine (misdated, likely because of her shaky emotional state),[9] Elizabeth pledged "a superhuman effort to improve as a wife so that your home & daily life won't make you sick again." She wanted him to be happy with his "location." Replaying his words to her—apparently about his need to have more autonomy—she wondered if he might want "a little apartment of [his] own," despite her misgivings about being able to afford it. (The eventual solution was to rent space on the next floor of the New York apartment, with one room for Cal's office and another for overnight guests.) Basking in the calm environment of Castine—"such joy for me, every minute"—as she recovered in bed from a cold, Elizabeth worried about her "disintegration" in New York and "the estrangement in our feelings." Her thoughts in this letter seem torn between her desperate wish to preserve the marriage and her equally desperate need to preserve her sense of self-worth. "I am determined to save myself, somehow, even if I don't know just how," she wrote. In the end, as always, her love for Cal won out. In a postscript the next morning, she told him, "How sweet it will be to have you back with us, dear one." Days later Cal wrote to Elizabeth Bishop from his apartment that he and Elizabeth "are back together, wobbly but reknit, almost."[10]

Cal came up to Castine for a few days in early July before returning to his New York hideaway. Elizabeth wrote to him immediately, telling him that she had finally completed her review of Graham Greene's new novel, *A Burnt-Out Case*[11]—"longer than I had imagined and not bad."[12] That was an understatement. As in her assessment of *The Heart of the Matter* thirteen years earlier, she deftly summed up the quiddity that is the strength of Greene's writing. His characters "are weary and romantic and fascinated by suffering and they look upon themselves and their feelings in a peculiarly intense Catholic-convert way, a sort of intellectual, clannish, delighted sectarianism." (Elizabeth had encountered this behavior in real life, in her husband.) She pointed out that Greene's novels, "dramas of sex and renunciation, belief and defiance," do not involve psychological motivations or aspects of social class, and yet they are "always intellectually exciting."

Writing to Cal, Elizabeth evoked the atmosphere of the house in Castine ("the grass has just been cut and the air is filled with green freshness") and attested to her improved behavior. She wasn't drinking, hard as it was not to have her usual nightly cocktail, which was also keeping her weight down.[13] In another letter three days later—amid a flurry of wifely announcements about mail answered and shirts in his dresser—she let a sigh escape: "I really was tired and confused and unhappy and needed the amount of isolation [Castine] offers to recover my bearings."[14] Anticipating Cal's return to Maine later in July, she was planning a party to celebrate her birthday on the twenty-seventh. Apparently in response to a letter from him, she added, "I don't see how we can celebrate the anniversary of our marriage [July 28] until we are married again and we can't be married until these many separations are over for a while."[15]

In early August, Cal wrote to Elizabeth Bishop that he hadn't had "a drop" to drink; two weeks later, as Elizabeth delightedly informed Cousin Harriet, "this has been the best summer of all."[16] Cal worked every day from 9:30 to 3:30 in the Water Street barn while Elizabeth wrote in the house.[17] After tennis games, dinner, and a couple hours of listening to music or reading, they were asleep by ten o'clock. This may have been the summer a picnic with friends was memorialized in an undated snapshot by photographer Rollie (Rosalie) McKenna. She caught the group at an animated moment: the sculptor Clark Fitz-Gerald, a friend of Cal's and McKenna's, pointing toward Elizabeth (a rare photo of her in slacks and tennis shoes); poet Philip Booth and his wife, Margaret; a smiling Cal; and Fitz-Gerald's then wife, Leah.[18]

At the end of the month, Elizabeth made her debut in *The New York Times Book Review*, identified both as "wife of the poet Robert Lowell" and as "a well-known critic."[19] The book was Oscar Lewis's *The Children of Sánchez*, an account of a family living in a sprawling Mexico City tenement. Told in their own tape-recorded words, their stories had "all the force and drama and seriousness of a large novel." Elizabeth noted approvingly that "like a great film director," Lewis (an anthropologist) had organized his raw material into "a coherent drama." The interwoven lives of the slum residents create "the chief character in this book": poverty itself. She would later decry biographies that largely incorporate tape-recorded interviews; somehow what worked to characterize a mass of poor people was not appropriate in writing about the famous.

The Lowells settled into their new apartment that autumn. "Our place is pleasant," Cal wrote to Elizabeth Bishop, "a big room . . . loaded with our old fashioned Boston furniture rather like a club room."[20] In early November, Elizabeth appeared on a panel about the novel at Vassar, with Paul Goodman and Saul Bellow. An alumni magazine article by the panel moderator described her as "slight, elegant, attractive," speaking "the language of the wearied but still engaged liberal, rich in sophistication and humanity."[21] Although Elizabeth had once believed that the arts replaced religion as a route to personal salvation, she wondered if this belief still held true at a time "when we are torn and splintered about our ideas and values." She doubted whether Shakespeare could "comprehend the world we live in, or feel any assurance about it." Yet after Bellow spoke— agreeing that "the old conceptions of human nature and human action" were no longer valid, but proposing that "existence has a miraculous character, and that art cannot exhaust this miracle"— she said she had changed her mind. The moderator observed that Elizabeth was "visibly encouraged by Mr. Bellow's remarks," to the point of declaring that it *was* possible, after all, to write a serious work today.

The year ended with a visit to New York by Elizabeth Bishop and Lota de Macedo Soares, occasioned by the poet's need to work with Time-Life Books on the final version of a commissioned volume about Brazil. The Lowells invited the women to a dinner party with T. S. Eliot and his wife, Valerie, and promised to visit Brazil in 1962. After spending New Year's Eve with Peter and Eleanor Taylor in Columbus, Elizabeth and Cal entertained some of their literary friends in New York. Allen Tate asked for a kiss from Elizabeth and gave a tipsy lecture to Harriet: "You are a Kentucky Belle because your mother is a Kentucky Belle."

In late January, Diana Trilling sent a long, aggrieved letter to Elizabeth about the second article she had written about David Riesman.[22] As part of a discussion of Riesman's altered view of contemporary life in his recent writing, Elizabeth rather caustically summarized Diana's remarks at the spring 1960 meeting of the Committee for Cultural Freedom as an insistence that American national identity vis-à-vis Russia "should remain . . . a contest between good and evil." Diana wrote that she had no problem about a disagreement on political grounds, but she was outraged that Elizabeth would make public the content of talks given at an "off-the-record occasion."[23] By the time she finished writing her letter, however, Diana seemed willing to believe that Elizabeth didn't know these remarks were not supposed to be published, and she affirmed her desire "to continue [as] friends."

What with social obligations and time spent caring for Harriet, Elizabeth was hard put to get her work done. In March the family tried to relax on a brief visit in Puerto Rico. Cal wrote to Elizabeth Bishop that Harriet and Elizabeth "would retire to their joint bedroom, wrapped in metaphysical argument on some small immediate decision, usually clothes."[24] Elizabeth remarked to Bishop that Old San Juan was "lovely," but that the island was "so strangely, thoroughly Americanized it is like looking in a cracked mirror."[25]

This year's big trip was still to come: a visit to Bishop in Brazil in the antipodean winter month of June. This plan had been in the Lowells' minds since early 1959, when Elizabeth wrote to suggest various ways it could be accomplished—without Harriet, for no more than one month; with Harriet, for longer; with both Lowells giving talks, or only Cal.[26] ("We both feel that it is more gratifying to travel when you have some reason or purpose or job, however slight.") In her lengthy reply, Bishop offered advice about appropriate clothes to bring, medical precautions to take, local doctors and hairdressers, and interesting people to meet. Elizabeth wrote joyously that they "want to do everything" and would arrive by June 1, subsequently revised to June 15.[27] Mentioning that it had been eight years since the Lowells had taken a trip (apparently Puerto Rico didn't count), they hoped to make the most of this costly adventure. Elizabeth let Bishop know that Toni, a "brave, adaptable, interesting" Radcliffe student who played the flute, would be coming to take care of Harriet, so the Lowells would need two rooms at the Copacabana Hotel. What no one seems to have planned for was another of Lowell's bipolar episodes.

The trip began with a stop in Haiti and two weeks in Trinidad, where the thirty-two-year-old poet Derek Walcott, so nervous to meet them, called Elizabeth "Edna St. Vincent Millay." She took him aback by responding, "I'm not that old yet."[28] Working their way down the Brazilian coast, the Lowells finally arrived in Rio de Janeiro. Elizabeth wrote to Cousin Harriet that this was a country where "nothing works and yet it is all beautiful and pleasant." She found the climate much like Maine, the people "sweet and gay." A weekend in São Paulo involved a visit to a coffee heiress living in an old farmhouse that Elizabeth compared, disparagingly, to "a New York nightclub," unlike Bishop's "beautiful home, next to a waterfall."[29] In a letter to Robert Giroux, she praised the "divine" weather and the "huge, perfect suite" that cost only twenty-five dollars a day at the "really first class" hotel."[30] Rio was so pleasant that the Lowells initially planned to spend the entire month of August there before traveling to Argentina, Chile, and Peru.[31]

During the second half of the month, Cal's drinking increased and his mania returned with its usual symptoms. He spent the night of August 24 with a woman he met. (According to Elizabeth Bishop, she was the Brazilian novelist Clarice Lispector.)[32] From ten p.m. to midnight, Elizabeth, who had increasingly absented herself from the hectic, alcohol-fueled social gatherings, poured out her heart to Bishop about Cal's previous bout of mania. When he did not come home that night, it was the last straw. She booked a passage back to New York for herself, Harriet, and Toni; they sailed home on September 1.

The situation in Brazil immediately worsened three days later, when Cal and Keith Botsford (the Congress for Cultural Freedom representative who had helped arrange the trip) traveled to Buenos Aires. On September 9, Botsford returned without Cal—who had continued to act erratically—claiming that unidentified "friends" were now responsible for him. Furious with Botsford, Bishop worried that Cal, who had been ranting about politics (and who didn't speak Spanish), might be attacked or jailed. Her timely intervention resulted in Cal's hospitalization in Buenos Aires.[33] In October, Blair Clark arrived to bring him back to the United States. Elizabeth met the plane together with Cal's psychiatrist, and he spent the next six weeks at the Institute of Living, a residential psychiatric facility in Hartford, Connecticut.

Concealing the worst aspects in a letter to Alfred Kazin (as was her habit when writing to people outside her intimate circle), she described the trip as "amazing" and reported Cal's response to Argentina simply as "'a little unsettling.'"[34] Elizabeth was writing mainly to thank Kazin for his glowing review of her essay collection, *A View of My Own*, published that autumn, with a dedication to Rahv.[35] "The greatest value of this book," Kazin wrote, "is that it re-creates literature as the living experience that it has been for the author." Yet one phrase, even though it was clearly intended to be a compliment, grates on today's sensibilities: "She can be funny and jeering, in the soft slightly cracked voice of Southern ladies." A case perhaps could be made for the "Southernness" of her sly way with a critical assessment, but in this context the reference seems patronizing.

Months earlier Elizabeth had written to Robert Giroux that a piece about Billie Holiday she had hoped to include was still not coming together.[36] (She finally published it in *The New York Review of Books* in 1976; three years later a version of this piece would become a memorable passage in *Sleepless Nights*.) But the book does include seventeen of her deeply considered essays, organized by broad topics: Letters, Lives, and Locations. Her subjects range from Bernard Berenson to the city of Boston, from Eugene O'Neill (whose "strength and weaknesses" are "intrinsic . . . in the American drama as a whole") to Mary McCarthy ("there is something puritanical and perplexing . . . in her utter refusal to give an inch of the ground of her own opinion").

The poet Marianne Moore, who apparently was asked for a blurb, wrote that she found the book to be "an uninhibited 'pinning down' that tells me a great deal I did not know about Christina Stead and adds to my understanding of the 'insulted and injured'" (a reference to Elizabeth's essay about the depiction of poverty in current fiction and nonfiction).[37] Her book even made an appearance in the *Vogue* column "People are talking about . . ."[38] Amusingly, a writer for the *Lexington Leader* registered his disappointment—after reading Elizabeth's excoriation of waffling book reviews in her *Harper's* article— that *A View of My Own* failed to offer the "fearsome blood-letting" he had expected.[39] He failed to see her finely tuned insights. But the miscellaneous nature of the book and a perception of the essays' lack of "topicality" led publishers in London to decide not to issue a British edition.

* * *

From December 8, 1962, to March 31, 1963, *The New York Times* and several other New York papers ceased publication because of a strike by the New York Typographical Union. Weeks without a book review section—as well as the perceived weaknesses of reviews published in the *Times* that Elizabeth had pointed out—sparked the founding of *The New York Review of Books.* She was on the board of the new journal, together with Cal; publisher Whitney Ellsworth; Robert Silvers; Jason Epstein, editorial director at Random House; and his wife, Barbara Zimmerman Epstein. Barbara was a Radcliffe graduate whose editing career included stints at Doubleday (where she gained notice as the editor of Anne Frank's *Diary of a Young Girl*), Dutton, Bobbs-Merrill, Random House, McGraw-Hill, and *Partisan Review.* The plan was hatched at a dinner party at the Epsteins' apartment, near the Lowells' on West 67th Street, when both couples agreed that Silvers would be the ideal editor of the new venture.[40]

Elizabeth later recalled that they "were sort of jokingly saying it would be fun" and viewed it simply "as a one-shot."[41] Cal characterized the start-up in a letter to Elizabeth Bishop as a flurry of "meetings, arguments, telephone calls, and now at the end of two weeks [the promise of] a fairly dazzling first number [that] will come out in the middle of February."[42] He guaranteed a $4,000 bank loan for the new venture, backed by his trust fund, and convinced Blair Clark to invest. ("Our aim was not to have people who would worry about $5,000 or $10,000," Elizabeth said later.)[43] Publishers, desperate to be able to advertise their books, pledged to spend $10,000 on ads, and the Anchor Books distributor (with whom Jason Epstein had worked while at Doubleday) agreed to take on all copies of the first issue.[44]

The list of potential contributors—chosen, according to Jason Epstein, for their "eclectic curiosity and their ability to make difficult subjects accessible to general readers"[45]—included many starry names in literature and criticism. Forty-five of these writers, working for free on a three-week deadline, provided reviews for the February 1 debut issue. It contained two pieces by Elizabeth.[46] One is a reassessment of early twentieth-century short-story writer Ring Lardner ("His is a miserable world made tolerable only by a maniacal flow of wisecracks"). The other piece is a jaundiced view of the lives of writers in New York, from failed middle-aged novelists to a new breed of journalists (Truman Capote, Norman Mailer, William Styron) who presented real life as if it were fiction. In this elliptical essay, about the death of high seriousness in literature and in the culture at large, Elizabeth suggested that even an "eloquent" and "painful" recent memoir (*The Fire Next Time*) by James Baldwin, initially published in *The New Yorker*, had failed to arouse its readers.[47]

The first issue also contained an editorial statement about the aims of the new journal: it would be dedicated to reviews of some of the "more important" books being published while ignoring "trivial" or "venal" efforts, "except occasionally to reduce a temporarily inflated reputation or to call attention to a fraud." Elizabeth informed Mary McCarthy in mid-March that the *Review* "has created a great stir, has sold very well, and [prompted] hundreds of touching letters from all over the country."[48] Silvers had contracted a rare lung disease that temporarily removed him from day-to-day operations, but she and Barbara and a few others were forging ahead. "It is a horrible job, down to the billing of hundreds of little book stores," she wrote. "The first issue was laid out in three mad days in our dining room, with bleary eyed people still there the next morning." Going forward, the plan was to pay contributors ten cents a word and continue with monthly issues until September, when the journal would begin bimonthly publication. Elizabeth wanted Mary to review the first volume of Camus's *Notebooks*, with a deadline of April 12. "Or if you don't want to do Camus, is there anything, even a little note on something you're interested in, that you could give us. Anything!" She requested a "Brazil letter" from Elizabeth Bishop, due by April 6—as little as a thousand words would be fine.[49] ("It seriously might make it easier to imagine you were writing a letter to Cal," Elizabeth suggested.) To the poet Richard Eberhart, eager to review a new book by the elderly poet John Hall Wheelock, Elizabeth wrote in May that the *Review* editors needed to wait until they had "a bit more of an idea of what we will be doing" in the fall before reviews could be assigned.[50]

The Lowells left for Castine at the end of June with a new maid, a widow from Argentina who spoke no English. She was "a compulsive worker" who "cleans and scrubs all the time, washes everything by hand the minute we let it drop, turns down beds. . . . She is learning English and we are learning Spanish, both slowly."[51] Despite Elizabeth's pleasure in the annual visits to the house on School Street, she worried about the increasing dilapidation of the brickyard house and barn, expressing her concerns in a letter to Cousin Harriet and even suggesting that she sell that house to a family that often vacationed in Castine.

Elizabeth in Castine, 1960s.

This summer marked the publication of Mary McCarthy's provocative novel *The Group*, about the lives of a group of Vassar alumnae, modeled on women she had known in college. Cal, who had mixed feelings about it, wrote to Elizabeth Bishop, "Lizzie thinks it's an awful fatuous superficial book."[52] In mid-July he flew to London to attend the Festival of Poetry at the Royal Court Theatre and then visited Mary in Paris before returning to Castine. In a letter to her about how much Cal enjoyed his visit, Elizabeth offered a few polite remarks about *The Group*.[53] The characters were "wonderfully literal," and the book was "very full, very rich." She pointed out a technical problem with the narrative ("Is the writer informing the reader, or is the writer informing the girls, or the girls speaking to the reader?") and concluded noncommittally by expressing her pleasure that the book would "make money" for Mary.

As Lionel Trilling observed—in his review of Elizabeth's essay collection—in writing about Mary, "she plainly gets tied up in the half-truths dictated by friendship." Yet in a 1962 piece published in *Harper's Magazine*, she called out certain deficiencies in her friend's fiction. "Plot and dramatic sense are weak," she noted. "Taste and accuracy are sometimes substitutions. What people eat, wear, and read are of enormous importance."[54] (Elizabeth obviously found this emphasis superficial.) About the graphic contraceptive scene in Mary's story "Dottie Makes an Honest Woman of Herself," she suggested wryly that it might have been meant "as a parody of the excesses of naturalistic fiction."

Elizabeth's distaste for *The Group* led her to write her own parody, published in September 1963 in the *New York Review* under the pseudonym Xavier Prynne. (The name alludes to Hester Prynne, the woman whose illegitimate child causes her to wear a badge of shame in Hawthorne's novel *The Scarlet Letter*, and Xavier Rynne, pseudonym of Francis X. Murphy, who wrote about the Second Vatican Council in *The New Yorker*.)[55] In three paragraphs about the coupling of "Maisie" and her lover, Elizabeth nailed Mary's habit of dropping in the names of famous people (Kierkegaard, Bernard Shaw, Hitler) and brand names (Kraft, Heinz, Macy's), as well as her running commentaries on her characters' taste and her overuse of adjectives. Mary was not amused. Elizabeth tried to make amends in a letter written two months after the parody appeared. "It was meant as simply a little trick, nothing more," she wrote, unpersuasively suggesting that she had been "overwhelmed with home problems" and the assassination of President Kennedy, which occurred after the article was written. "I did not mean to hurt you and I hope you will forgive it."[56]

In November, Elizabeth used her pseudonym again to undermine Norman Mailer's new book, *The Presidential Papers*—a collection of pieces mostly about current politics but also about subjects as diverse as the first Patterson-Liston fight and Jackie Kennedy. The backstory is that Midge Decter had written a review so overwhelmingly enthusiastic that Robert Silvers rejected it. (It was published in the February 1964 issue of *Commentary*.) Elizabeth's devastating parody, "Vice-Presidential Notes: (The 6th Vice-Presidential Note)," took down the increasingly popular and controversial writer in the inflated language of his own swagger. ("Fallout is the orgasm itself, remember, Mr. Vice President.")[57]

The *New York Review* was proving to be a resounding success. Cal wrote to Elizabeth Bishop, "I've never seen anything like Lizzie and the magazine. Instead of her somewhat murky Kentucky Scottish reserve, all is smiles, flutter and superlatives."[58] Praise rolled in, for the *Review* in general and for Elizabeth's writing in particular. The poet and critic Alfred Alvarez wrote to commend her piece on Robert Frost as brilliantly insightful, noting that her discussion of the New England poet as a man with certain limitations was always relevant to his poetry.[59] (One of the characteristics she singled out in this review of a volume of his letters was his "interest in power," of being appreciated as a public spokesman; he was, she wrote, "the most gregarious of lonely men.") However, Alvarez—one of the British writers the *Review* had begun to court—was not thrilled with the hundred-dollar check he received for his own review of two biographies of Keats.[60] Having spent two full weeks working on his essay, he fumed that the *New York Review* paid even less than the *New Statesman*.

Elizabeth, who had hated office work ever since her early jobs in New York, did not want to spend her days at the *Review*'s offices in the Fisk Building on 57th Street. She explained later that she had played "a very negligible editorial role" in the journal.[61] Perhaps that was for the best. As advisory editor, she was given to bouts of impolitic candor, informing Muriel Rukeyser that her submitted poem was too long and "not your best . . . by any means."[62] Although an early editorial assistant remembered Silvers's "long chatty calls" with Elizabeth,[63] she soon withdrew from day-to-day involvement with the

Review while continuing to produce a steady stream of essays. In a letter to Allen Tate, she admitted that she hadn't even read most of the new issues before they were published.[64] Her colleague Barbara Epstein—co-editor, with Silvers—would become renowned for her gracious dealings with contributors and her fierce dedication to good writing. As one author explained, after she praised his prose, "there would be a pause, and she would say something like, 'Now there was just one teeny, weeny little matter I wanted to raise with you.' And by the time she finished . . . you realized . . . that this was a glaring humongous mistake."[65] Edmund Wilson noticed how Barbara, formerly "so quiet," had become "quite a brilliant figure . . . animated and attractive."[66] Silvers's concerns as an editor were primarily with the strength of writers' arguments and the clarity of their prose; his notes to Elizabeth were invariably valentines for her great work.

* * *

In early December 1963, Cal returned to the Institute of Living after another episode of mania, apparently triggered by the horror of President Kennedy's assassination on November 22. Elizabeth wrote to him constantly, relating her exasperation with the maid's inability to learn English ("I do begin to think that it will take at least two years before Theresa can answer the phone") and Harriet's delight at seeing his photo in the *Times* (as a nominee of the Academy of Arts and Letters). Elizabeth also kept him apprised of her work on his behalf to make sure the rehearsal dates and opening of his play *The Old Glory* did not conflict with his lecture schedule. She vented her disappointment with the New York theater scene, which had little substance to offer for her play reviews. And she always reminded him of how much he was missed.[67] By December 20, she was relieved—after a visit to the institute—that he was once again his "dear old self." Yet he wasn't able to come home until mid-January 1964. Elizabeth wrote to thank Bishop for a poem she submitted to the *Review*, updating her on Cal's recovery and his schedule of publications and productions, which included a staged reading of *The Old Glory* in February.[68] She added that the Brazilian trip had influenced the dinner she was cooking that night: black beans and rice.

Elizabeth and Cal were both invited to the 21st Annual Writers Forum in March at the University of North Carolina at Greensboro—a first for them as an author duo. She spoke on "Plot in Fiction," he gave a poetry reading, and they both served on a panel discussing student writing.[69] At some point this year—the date is uncertain—Elizabeth also took part in a symposium, "American Literary Criticism Today," at three-year-old Sonoma State College in California.[70] Her fellow panelists were the critics Susan Sontag, Dwight Macdonald, John Simon, and Robert Adams. Elizabeth invoked T. S. Eliot, R. P. Blackmur, Ivor Winters, and other magisterial twentieth-century critics in order to point out that interest in serious criticism had declined in recent years. The problem, she suggested, was that readers had grown tired of "so much over-explanation of old texts and new texts," and that current literature didn't seem to need the kind of explanation required by a novel like *Ulysses*. When Macdonald claimed that, ultimately, all criticism "is simply opinion," Elizabeth and Sontag both disagreed. Unfortunately, Elizabeth's typically discursive way of working out how best to explain her point of view—that it's a question of whether the critic emphasizes her own response or tries to describe the book in neutral terms—was ill-suited to the ping-pong rhythm of the panel format. Still, although Macdonald constantly interrupted her, she never let him gain the upper hand. Buoyed by the amplitude of her Southern vowels ("ariiiiive at," "feeeeeling," "profouuund"), she insisted on having her say.

* * *

After a chilly summer in Castine, the Lowells returned to New York, where Cal soon plunged into rehearsals for *The Old Glory*—a trilogy of short plays—at the American Place Theater in St. Clement's Church on West 46th Street. During the weeks before the November 1 opening, Elizabeth kept a close watch on rehearsals, suggesting cuts and criticizing the acting. The director was thirty-year-old Jonathan Miller, an English medical doctor fresh from his success as a member of the *Beyond the Fringe* ensemble, which had moved to Broadway two years earlier. The current production was only his second experience in leading the cast of a play. Decades later he told one of Cal's biographers that Elizabeth, in common with other New York intellectuals, struck him as having "a very sharp, *Variety*-reading, Broadway sense of what's going to work and how you're going to make a fool of yourself in front of the critics."[71] (It is not clear whether she agreed with his decision to cut *Endicott and the Red Cross*—the first play in the trilogy, based on a short story by Hawthorne—to avoid making the evening overlong.)

Walter Kerr, the *Herald Tribune* critic, never a friend of experimental theater, panned the highly stylized production. In *The New York Times*, Howard Taubman dismissed the first play, *My Kinsman, Major Molineux*—set on the eve of the American Revolution—as an "arty trifle." He complained about the slow-moving aspects of the second play, *Benito Cereno*, loosely based on a novella by Herman Melville about a revolt on a Spanish slave ship.[72] The *New York Review* critic was the poet W. D. Snodgrass, a former student of Lowell's. He said later that Elizabeth had pressured him to attack the reviewers in the commercial press for their obtuseness—which had been his intent anyway—but that he needed to stake out a position as distinct as possible from her "highly improper" solicitation.[73] His strategy was to describe newspaper critics as men whose job was to "stomp out excellence" while praising Miller's direction, the "ensemble excellence" of the acting, and Lowell's "mastery of language."[74] Despite the mixed reviews, *The Old Glory* won five Obies (Off-Broadway theater awards), including Best American Play.

In December, *Phaedra*—Cal's version of Racine's play *Phèdre*—
was in previews at Wesleyan University with Vera Zorina, a celebrated ballerina turned actress, in the title role. Jean Stafford,
widowed after the death of her third husband, was a fellow of the
Center for Advanced Studies at the university that year. She was upset
to have her cloistered world invaded by Cal but agreed to sit next to
him at the dress rehearsal. When he kept clutching her hand—to her
annoyance—it was a sign that his mania was returning.[75]

After meeting Vija Vetra, a Latvian dancer, at St. Clements, Cal
invited her to the January opening of *Benito Cereno*, which had trans-
ferred to the Theatre de Lys in Greenwich Village. Alert to the signs,
Elizabeth realized that this was a new infatuation; she left the theater
when he invited Vetra backstage. According to Vetra, he threatened
suicide if she didn't let him stay with her.[76] He leased an apartment
at 16 West 16th Street—Vetra was impoverished and needed a place
to live—and began introducing her as his future wife. In a letter
to Blair Clark, Elizabeth poured out her anguish.[77] "I don't feel any
longer that he loves me," she wrote. She would travel to Washington
"to calm down" and work on her writing. At this point, she considered allowing Cal "to set up a new life." She didn't want him "to be
violently treated with drugs" and return in a depressed state "to a
home he probably doesn't want to come to." All she wanted now was
to find some peace.

But the old pattern continued: Cal was immediately committed
to the Institute of Living, and Elizabeth took up her accustomed
activity of sending him concerned letters. On January 30 she wrestled with the great divide in their view of the marriage. If only he
didn't feel that she had "done such a poor job and that all those years
were bad." In her mind, they were "productive" years. "Unlike you,
I have had a wonderful time with you," she wrote, "and I would not
change my mind even [if] I knew what I know now. So there."[78] The
following day she told him that talking to him that morning brought

her joy.[79] In a subsequent letter, responding to a despondent one from him, she wrote, "I would kill myself if it would cure you. But don't give up hope. I never shall."[80] Yet the next day she did seem to have lost all hope for the marriage. She told him where to find his grade lists "when you come to get your things and to leave us."[81] Or was this remark a secret strategy? If so, it worked; almost immediately, he asked to return. Later, she told one of Cal's biographers that the Vetra affair was the only one he was "truly, honestly ashamed of."[82] Vetra was ordered to give up the apartment immediately; she sent her bills to Cal, and Elizabeth uncomplainingly paid them.

In the spring, she published two strong pieces: a damning review of Norman Mailer's novel *An American Dream* and an eye-level view of racism in action—informed by her understanding of the ways of the American South—as it played out in the Selma-to-Montgomery civil rights march. In "Bad Boy," she described Mailer as "a bombed out talent" and his new book as "an uglier, smellier pop-fiction" animated by "a crippling wife-hatred, degrading sexual boasting." It was carelessly written, with an "incoherent mixing of cheap effects." Missing were all the elements she admired in his other novels: humor and his "free, radical spirit, and remarkable literary gifts."

With her essay "Selma, Alabama: The Charms of Goodness," Elizabeth began to address major political issues of the day. The piece opens with a panoramic view of the Deep South that she acknowledges her readers already have in mind. (As she perceptively wrote elsewhere, "Since films and television have staged everything imaginable before it happens, a true event, taking place in the real world, brings to mind the landscape of films.")[83] With a rare blend of moral outrage and a novelist's empathy, she turned her attention to the "joyless" middle-aged sheriff's volunteers, with their "burning incoherence," and "savage superstition." Confronted with "the moral justice of the Civil Rights Movement"—the "exuberant and communal" mood of the marchers led by Martin Luther King, Jr.—the vigilantes finally had an event that would gave their lives meaning: the murder of a Black Protestant minister.

Three years later, in "The Apotheosis of Martin Luther King," Elizabeth would write about Memphis in the days after King's murder, when the streets were empty except for the "monstrous glut" of the National Guard.[84] The atmosphere just before the march to honor King—with its expected turnout of as many as sixty thousand people—elicited one of her singularly keen observations: "Perhaps there was fear, but in civic crises, there is always something exciting and even a sort of humidity of smugness seemed to hang over the town." The march marked a watershed; with the rise of Black militancy, "the pastoral period of the Civil Rights Movement had gone by." King had admitted in his recent book that the "dream" in his famous speech had turned into a "nightmare." Elizabeth would have been aware that the previous summer the New York Review ran a piece by Andrew Kopkind alleging that the Black leader had become irrelevant to his cause, "shuffling"—a loaded word in this context— "between Chicago and Cleveland."[85] Kopkind, who argued for the power of "tough black street leaders" who "make noise and trouble," wrote that King's "morality" did not reflect "where his followers are." Elizabeth took a different tack. Writing for a sophisticated urban readership that was largely scornful of evangelical religion, she pointed out that King's religiosity harked back to "a previous and more spiritual evangelism, to a time of solitude and refined simplicity," and that he possessed "an impenetrability and solidity often seen in those who have given their entire lives to ideas and causes."

During the 1960s, official rhetoric often gave Elizabeth a toehold from which to observe the political scene. Her essay "After Watts" was a reaction to the period of civil unrest in the Los Angeles neighborhood of Watts sparked by an altercation between an African American motorist and police. She described how the "hot night and the hatred and deprivation burst into a revolutionary ecstasy." In contrast, the official report was "an extreme example of the distance a debased rhetoric puts between word and deed." Two years later, in "Chicago," she wrote about the 1968 Democratic Convention. Elizabeth viewed the party's presidential candidate, Hubert Humphrey ("a wound-up toy"), as similar to Richard Nixon: both of them "blind and deaf but still wholesomely smiling." Standing apart from both the rage of the demonstrators and the banality of the leading candidate, Eugene McCarthy—liberals' great white hope—offered only "a flat recital" of his views; a "radical . . . refusal to make the expected gestures." For Elizabeth, this was "a hint that many of the acts in our political repertoire aren't worth putting on your makeup for."

* * *

A brouhaha erupted in early June 1965 over Cal's letter to President Johnson—a copy of it, sent to *The New York Times*, was signed by twenty writers and artists—stating his refusal to take part in the White House Festival of Arts because of the "dismay and distrust" with which he viewed the administration's foreign policy.[86] But by mid-July, ensconced in Castine, he wrote to Elizabeth Bishop that he felt "at peace. . . . How much I love my little, not very well treated and indomitable family!"[87] Elizabeth and Cal were both invited to meet Ted Kennedy that summer, but she declined, uninterested in "those jet-set Kennedy women in their tight pants."[88] (The following year Jacqueline Kennedy was a guest of honor at a dinner given by the Lowells. After listening to the former first lady's anecdotes related in her whispery voice, Cal thought Elizabeth disliked her, but it turned out that she was "charmed.")[89]

In the autumn, Elizabeth began teaching writing at Barnard College. She regarded this adjunct position as a source of needed income if Cal ever chose to leave the marriage. Likely unaware of this aspect of her new job, he reported to Bishop that Elizabeth's "first comment was, 'the students aren't very good, but I am.'"[90] Her low opinion of them was based on her sense that they lacked intellectual and literary sophistication. Where was the intense dedication to great literature that had inspired her at the University of Kentucky? What she stressed was "creative reading . . . reading as a writer reads."[91] By asking what prospective members of her class had read, she ascertained their worthiness. Anyone who was not interested in doing "a lot of reading" would not be accepted. Fortunately, her class did have one student "who reads everything" and "a little coterie" who were familiar with classic literature as well as with the *New York Review*, the Polish short story writer Bruno Schulz—a particular favorite of Elizabeth's—and Susan Sontag's first novel, *The Benefactor*.[92]

Elizabeth's essay "Reading" criticizes a tendency she witnessed among her students: describing characters in great literature as if "gossip[ing] about one's friends."[93] Students reading *Madame Bovary* called Emma Bovary "too romantic," Charles Bovary "a clod," and Rodolphe "selfish." She found the tone of these remarks "too intimate, too cosy . . . a sort of present tense of judgment that establishes a feeling of equity between author and reader." Elizabeth felt strongly that this equity did not exist when the author was a great writer. She castigated students unable to give themselves over to a narrative at a remove from their everyday lives: "There is too much self-esteem and too little surrender."[94] More controversially, Elizabeth wrote that a similar lack of nuanced understanding afflicts feminist interpretations that take issue with classic fiction: "nothing is to be accepted as given, created, composed in accordance to the truth and imagination of its own terms."

During her twenty-year teaching career, Elizabeth discovered that her students also tended to blur the difference between speaking and writing. "There are two things on the page, words and thoughts behind the words," she wrote in notes for a talk about writing.[95]

Thinking was the hard part: "The thoughts develop . . . by contrast, pauses, revision, which is the writing itself." Beginning writers are always told to write about what they know. But the hard part is "*getting at* what you know"—finding the words that will lead you to "a truer knowledge of the visual or root psychological picture that is in your mind." Too often, she found, students would employ a metaphor or simile only in passing, "when actually the pursuit of it could lead to a richer & deeper psychological portrait."

Elizabeth stressed the immense difficulty of writing well. You start out "as a cripple, an invalid, and gradually by revision, with a sort of intense concentration, something that was not there [before] appears." And yet "you are always confronted with the limits of yourself, your knowledge, your ear, your character. . . . And for that reason, writing is a very daunting activity and it will not make you happy." That last clause is a provocative statement. Should we take it to mean that writing did not make Elizabeth happy? More likely, this remark was meant to reflect the struggle involved in writing a piece that met her high standards; happiness did not come until the battle was won.

Promoted from instructor to adjunct associate professor in 1966, with a salary increase in the $7,500 to $8,500 range, Elizabeth was interviewed by the *Barnard Bulletin* about the current state of literature.[96] Troubled by the difficulty that unknown short story writers had in getting their work published, she suggested that one solution—itself not easy to achieve—was to seek a publisher for a book of collected stories. Of course, she added, the main challenge was having something to say and writing well. Asked whether the real test of good writing was the best-seller list or "the quiet admiration of fellow writers," she noted that when an accomplished writer makes the best-seller list with a less-than-stellar book, he is sometimes puzzled when fellow writers fail to praise him. It's likely that she had someone in particular in mind, but the student interviewer did not press her on this matter.

* * *

October 1965 brought the sad news of Randall Jarrell's death; he was run over by a car in what was almost certainly a suicidal act. Weeks later Cal's mania flared up again. On December 7, at an opera performance the Lowells attended with literary friends, he declaimed loudly about "brilliant women" before falling asleep during the first act. When he awakened, his unruly behavior continued—he tried to conduct the orchestra from his seat, according to some witnesses. Cal was hospitalized that night. On December 22, Elizabeth sent him a postcard with a Renoir painting of a dancing couple. "This is not us," she wrote, "except in dreams, some dreams."[97]

Cal ended the year at McLean. Upon his release in February, he and Elizabeth celebrated their reunion with a trip—this time to Guadeloupe. For his fiftieth birthday, on March 1, she invited fifty guests to a celebration at the New York apartment. Eleven days later he left for London, where Miller's production of *Benito Cereno* was opening.[98] Elizabeth opted instead for a ten-day holiday in Barbados with Harriet.

That winter she was the first woman to receive the George Jean Nathan Award for Dramatic Criticism, for "a distinguished series of reviews of plays and discussions of the situation in the American theater." In April she was a member of a panel of University of Kentucky graduates—including the actor Donald Galloway, beginning his eight-year stint as Detective Sergeant Ed Brown in the TV series *Ironside*—discussing the value of theater in America. Elizabeth's comments, as recorded by the *Lexington Leader*, were scathing. "I don't think we have a theater so I don't want to encourage students to go into it," she said. "The American theater is not in repute anywhere in the world."[99]

The *Leader* subsequently sent a reporter to New York, presumably to interview her, although the piece is mostly a description of

Elizabeth in the Lowells' New York Apartment, 1967.

her apartment, with some quotes appended at the end.[100] The anonymous interviewer noted the "half-read magazine" on a chaise near the fireplace, the red plush Victorian sofa, the needlepoint cushions, the upright piano, and the floor-to-ceiling bookshelves on which Elizabeth had trouble locating copies of her own books. A 150-year-old Abyssinian painting, purchased for twenty dollars, hung from the balcony, and flowers bloomed along "the sunny wall of windows." Elizabeth's remarks were about the lack of progress in theater ("No playwrights have come along . . . that are any better than Aeschylus"), critics ("A critic should have some interest in going to see a particular play"), playwrights (Sam Shepard was the best young one), and the vitality of theater outside the financially driven world of Broadway ("Perhaps off-off Broadway can become like the independent movies").

Unlike most mainstream critics, Elizabeth often disparaged

famous plays and supported avant-garde ones, and her reviews appeared on an irregular basis. (A dozen were published in the *New York Review* from 1964 to 1967; during the next seven years she contributed only occasional reviews.)[101] Her first piece for the *Review*, "The Disaster at Lincoln Center," was a ferocious attack on the new Repertory Theatre of Lincoln Center, a short-lived experiment in presenting classic and new plays with a resident company.[102] "Heartless banality . . . flaccid acting . . . appalling scripts"—she had nothing positive to say about the production of the first three plays, by S. N. Behrman, Arthur Miller, and Eugene O'Neill. Her primary complaint was that American producers and directors seemed not to know that "drama is first and last an act of literary composition." This was a peculiar view. Few knowledgeable people would disagree that plays achieve their full expression when their words are spoken and embodied by actors on a stage. Yet even the narrator in *Sleepless Nights* describes herself as "one who dislikes the theater and would instead stay at home reading the texts out of which spring the actors in boots, the letters on trays."[103] (Note the deliberate references to details predating the modern era.)

During the next few years, Elizabeth would roundly criticize plays by Edward Albee, Tennessee Williams, and William Inge—her distaste for the latter two playwrights dated from her *Partisan Review* days—arguing that they seemed overly concerned with personal obsessions.[104] She disparaged the middlebrow taste of the powerful critic Walter Kerr (now at *The New York Times*), whose "impatience with experimental art is radical [and whose] forbearance in the case of light comedies . . . is excessive." Writing about Peter Weiss's Auschwitz play, *The Investigation*, she faulted the production for its "didactic naturalism," when what was needed was "stylization . . . the work of a free imagination" willing to create a new vision based on "some ruling design or idea." Samuel Beckett's *Endgame*—which she had reviewed years earlier for *Partisan Review*—was just such a play, created, she wrote approvingly, by "a mind free of the obsessions of conventional forms."[105]

The following year, Elizabeth was a member of the small audience for *La Turista*, a play by twenty-three-year-old Sam Shepard, at American Place Theater. Eviscerated by newspaper critics, this symbolic drama features two sunburned Americans in a hotel room, a young Mexican man, and a witch doctor and his son (replaced in act two by an American country doctor and his son, wearing Civil War costumes). Elizabeth rightly described the play as an "episodic . . . obscurely related . . . collection of images [and] moods"—a play with the resonance of a poem.[106] What she failed to mention in the review was the political consciousness underlying its characters and actions; produced at the height of the Vietnam War, this was clearly a play about the American Way versus the Third World. But when a letter writer mentioned this subtext, complaining that the review was mystifying, Elizabeth refused to be pinned down. "Literal 'understanding' is not always the whole aim of an author," she maintained.[107] With this sentence, she summed up the animating spirit of her fiction, most perfectly realized in the dreamlike quality of *Sleepless Nights*.

In an interview a few years later, Elizabeth lambasted the way American theater had become "buried in the marble of liberal cliches."[108] By expecting characters to have "reasonable explanations" for their actions, playwrights were ignoring the complex and mysterious ways people really behaved, with their "unexpected explosions" and "tragic misunderstandings." She maintained that "it is art's purpose to find some way of recording the peculiarities of the society."

Elizabeth had pursued this thread in a brilliant essay about Leonardo da Vinci, published in *Art in America* in 1966. After viewing an exhibition of models built from Leonardo's sketches, it occurred to her that what "awes us" today is not the science behind his inventions but "the prophetic nature" of his art. While Leonardo believed technology to be "a liberation for mankind," it now inspires both fear and "a hint of surrender to its gorgeous power. Fear and love of technology . . . seem to have replaced the fear and love of political power, of totalitarianism." Elizabeth was captivated by the vulnerability of a dangling figure in Leonardo's drawing of a parachute: "there we are, all of us."

* * *

On the cover of the June 2, 1967, issue of *Time* magazine, an artist's rendering of Cal included a laurel wreath that made him look weirdly demonic. (Adrienne Rich had given him a real laurel wreath at the party to celebrate his fiftieth birthday.) The accompanying profile announced that he was "by rare critical consensus, the best American poet of his generation." While Jean Stafford is described as "intense, beautiful, a gifted writer," Elizabeth is dealt with curtly as a "Kentuckian" and "another writer . . . who is now an editor of *The New York Review of Books*."[109] In keeping with the magazine's practice at the time, the article is unsigned, but it's hard not to wonder if the author had a personal grudge against Elizabeth. The accompanying photo showing her with Cal and Harriet on a bench in Central Park almost seems calculated to make her appear unattractive. She looks away from them, unsmiling, her hair hidden under a scarf, her figure looking oddly bulky in an unflattering jacket.

That summer Elizabeth signed the first of several political and cultural petitions published in the *New York Review* on behalf of Régis Debray, a French philosophy scholar and journalist, and Andrew Roth, a British freelance photographer, both of whom had been held incommunicado since April by Bolivian military authorities and threatened with the death sentence. According to the petition, these men had been arrested without any proof that they were active in the guerrilla movement.[110] In later years Elizabeth would also append her name to a protest against the imprisonment of members of the Black Panthers charged with intent to murder a police officer (1968); a condemnation of the U.S. invasion of Cambodia (1970); a demand for the end of military involvement in Indochina (1972); a plea that the curriculum of the School of the Arts at Columbia University be maintained despite the university's deficit (1971); a request for information on the status of poet, novelist, and SUNY professor Kofi Awoonor, arrested in Ghana (1976); a protest of the illegal takeover of *Excelsior*, the leading Mexican daily newspaper, by "a small group of conservative employees" who were supporters of President Luis Echeverría (1976); a boycott of the new American Book Awards, replacing the National Book Awards (1979); and a call for more humane treatment of Moscow writer and archivist Alexandr Bogoslovski, arrested for disseminating anti-Soviet literature (1984).

* * *

When Mary hinted that she was thinking of buying a house in Castine, Elizabeth warned her that the town was "very slow and quiet" and "the swimming isn't good," but "most people like it after they dig in."[111] She explained that "real estate prices were still low," especially for the stately residences on Main Street, because the "new people" wanted to live right on the water. She advised Mary about appropriate clothes for the chancy weather (some summers were hot; others were cold) and offered a word of warning about household help: "You can get farm ladies to clean up a day or so a week, but independence is the word for the Maine native!"[112] The early-nineteenth-century Federal-style house at 90 Main Street that Mary bought—and painted yellow, to the consternation of other residents—was conveniently situated right behind 29 School Street. Cousin Harriet's house now belonged to Elizabeth, who had inherited it on the older woman's death in 1964. Joining forces, Elizabeth and Mary would organize picnics at Smith Cove, on the opposite shore from Castine.

The poet Philip Booth recalled one of these outings, attended by more than twenty people talking about subjects ranging from Pasternak to Poland.[113]

A few years later Elizabeth began writing essays about her adopted state. "In Maine," published in the *New York Review* in 1971, is the most deeply considered of these pieces, filled with poignant observations about the cold climate that "makes everyone poor" and the visible evidence of financial and ecological distress: "Lost people, lost mills, lost fish in the sea . . . unpredictable potatoes, bereft farms, stony and slighted fields, patchy pastures."[114] As always, Elizabeth is alert to the condition of struggling people whose "truth is found in the rusting, immovable car . . . that has come to rest in the front yard," along with all the other household items scattered on the land. ("What is an old appliance except a tomb of sorrow, a slab of disappointment . . . a reminder of life's puzzling lack of accommodation?") Unlike residents of the South, where bigotry is "standardized, packaged, predicable," Mainers live "solitary lives with solitary ideas." And yet the American flags that decorated even the most humble shack seemed to indicate that residents felt "a part of something very old, a sense of living in an ancient land."

Two years after this essay was published, Elizabeth heard from Elizabeth Bishop, who was upset at the mention in this piece of an unnamed Brazilian whom she knew to be her now-deceased lover, Lota de Macedo Soares. After being taken to visit an old, formerly grand house without electricity on an island off the Maine coast, the woman in the essay was unimpressed. Her complaint ("not one bit amusing!") was "lisped in fury." Elizabeth promised Bishop not to include this piece in her new essay collection, agreeing about the unpleasantness of having "yourself or someone you have really loved and deeply known suddenly lighted up in a way that seems so far from the real, the true."[115] Of course, she had no idea that this kind of false illumination would one day confront her and Harriet.

In later years, Elizabeth continued to write about her adopted state. Her gorgeous prose poem "Accepting the Dare: Maine" describes it as a place of "loveless severity and aloofness," where white hawthorn bushes symbolize "the melancholy, piercing beauty of the region itself." The sudden advent of a summer heat wave resembled "the roar of motorcycles on a Sunday." Her final thoughts about the state appeared in "Puritanical Pleasures: Summer in Maine." She proposed that "difficulty inhabits Maine like the great spruce trees. . . . The weather is not convenient, the water is not convenient, the isolation is not convenient. . . . Maine is humbling to ambition and therefore hospitable to thrift and endurance."[116] In a letter to a friend, however, Elizabeth was more candid about summer visitors' image of Maine as "an isolated, old-fashioned precinct of trust [and] economy." As she had discovered, there was also "a sly, deceitful world of native artisans, 'spoiled' by the scarcity of their kind and by a bold notion that the summer people can't count"—a reference to the high prices she was paying for work on the Castine house.[117]

* * *

In July 1967, Elizabeth Bishop visited New York, following her psychoanalyst's directive to keep some distance from Lota, whose urge to control her lover had become intolerable. At first, Bishop stayed in the apartment of painter Loren MacIver and her husband, poet Lloyd Frankenberg, who were out of town. After sending Bishop a barrage of letters, Lota—now visibly unwell—joined her in New York in September. On their first night together, Lota took an overdose of the sedative Nembutal. Following five days in a coma, she died— whether due to the suicide attempt or to her cardiac problems, or both, was uncertain. Although Bishop had other lovers by this time, the loss of Lota and battles over her will plunged her into depression. One night, after moving to the Lowells' apartment, she found the vodka Elizabeth had hidden. A drunken fall caused Bishop to break her left arm and shoulder, sending her to Lenox Hill Hospital. She returned to the Lowells', apologizing for her behavior, before flying back to Rio in mid-November.

In December, Elizabeth published a coruscating review of a widely praised revival of Lillian Hellman's *The Little Foxes*, directed by Mike Nichols.[118] She described the play as "a melodrama, mechanically put together, but redeemed . . . by the energy of Regina"—the Southern matriarch whose banker husband Horace refuses to invest in her brothers' cotton mill—"and the brutal yet enjoyable piracy of the brothers," one of whom forces his son to steal Horace's railroad bonds. But Horace, she wrote, is simply "a puppet in the service of an idea," because he never acknowledges "the seductive power of the investment in the mill." Elizabeth asked readers to imagine "what Ibsen could have done" with this character. She also found fault with the play's sentimental approach to "a lost Southern agricultural life" and with the Black characters' moral commentaries, "addressed as much to [Hellman's] conscience as to that of the audience." Elizabeth generally disliked the way the South was depicted in plays and fiction; even when the authors were natives, she would find something exaggerated or false in their conception of the region. At the end of this review, criticizing what she saw as Nichols's overly worshipful approach to the script, Elizabeth wrote that she recalled the daughter carrying a suitcase at the end of the play. Where, she scoffed, could this character possibly be going at night, other than offstage? In fact, as a letter writer noted, there was no suitcase in this production.[119]

In addition to the published letters that took umbrage at Elizabeth's takedown of such a revered literary figure, she received a frosty note from her dear friend Blair Clark.[120] He claimed to be angry not at her literary judgment but rather "on personal and moral [grounds], all of which I think are venomously bad, not to say evil." He wrote to sever their friendship, intending never to see her again. It was clear that Hellman had called on her friends to defend her. "I don't [know] when she'll call the posse off," Elizabeth wrote sadly to Mary. "There are some sociological lessons to be drawn I suppos [sic] but not many others."[121] Cal, who felt obliged to give the letter writers the cold shoulder, wrote to Elizabeth Bishop that the review was "ill-judged . . . on personal grounds, not critical [grounds]."[122] Claiming that she "wholly admired" the review, Mary nevertheless spared no details in recounting the way it was received at a February dinner party given by Stephen Spender and his wife.[123] The guests included the British theater critic Kenneth Tynan. He read the review aloud in an affected accent—he was a friend of Hellman's—before reverting to his normal voice. When he finished, the guests applauded—but were they pleased by the review or by his performance?

The following month Mary asked Elizabeth to be the coexecutor of her will with her fourth husband, James West. In her gracious response, she wrote that she would never have to serve because Mary's death was unthinkable.[124] Mary believed, as she wrote to Hannah Arendt, that Elizabeth "would be excellent in handling publications problems."[125] (However, she inexplicably changed her mind again the following year and appointed Arendt in Elizabeth's place.)[126] Elizabeth had praised Mary's article about her trip to Hanoi as "very affecting"[127]—a rather low-key remark perhaps made in the spirit more of friendship than of honest criticism. Speaking of politics, she found the Senate Foreign Relations Committee hearings on the war "extraordinarily moving" in a theatrical sense—"the physical beauty of the old, dovish Senators [with] their 'distinguished' profiles" versus "the villains . . . thin-lipped, pudgy, [with] bad diction." She exulted at Eugene McCarthy's "astonishing showing" in the New Hampshire primary (Blair Clark was his campaign manager) and pondered the way television had "changed the scene," boosting Robert Kennedy's appeal: "The main thing is that this is a new country—the hopeful things are new and the terrifying are also."

Cal, she reported to Mary, was immersed in rehearsals for a

revised version of *Endicott and the Red Cross*. This play, about a Massachusetts governor's desecration of the British flag when a royal governor was appointed in 1634, had a timely resonance during stepped-up protests against the Vietnam War and sit-ins at Columbia University. With a cast that included a young Spalding Gray, *Endicott* would open in April at American Place Theater for a six-week run, directed by John Hancock. In an undated letter to Cal, Elizabeth assured him that the play was "absolutely brilliant and moving and important in every respect," and that she was "elated, nervous, sleepless with joy."[128] But she added that several people she respected—Jonathan Miller, Robert Silvers, Kenneth Tynan—thought the governor's "dream speech" should be excised, because "he's up there too long and loses the audience." In a burst of self-congratulation, she added, "Now, I know why I am a theatre critic. There is no one to know how good this is—except me. What a play it is now, so complex, so original—and the last speech is as beautiful as anything in English dramatic literature."

Before the opening, Harriet and Elizabeth vacationed in Miami, which she found inferior to the Caribbean, "awfully sort of middle class."[129] Relaxing on the sand, she was immersed in James Watson's *The Double Helix*, an account of the discovery of DNA that few would consider a beach read. "The water, the sun, the rest are truly useful for all of us," she wrote to Cal, suggesting that he join them next year in Jamaica. Whether it would make much difference in his outlook was a question she did not pursue. His drinking had escalated, and his pursuit of women seemed unstoppable.

In January 1969, Cal wrote to her from Canada, where he was booked for a reading. Admitting that he had been "hard going the last couple of years," he swore that he loved her.[130] But the virtues he mentioned—her "varied interests," "refreshing teaching," "neat clothes," "capacity for keen conversation and argument," and their "lovely child"—are not the endearments of a man in love. Elizabeth seems not to have been daunted by this message. On March 1, when he was traveling abroad, she wrote to wish him a happy birthday: "These last years of your work on your wonderful book [*Notebook, 1967–1968*] are really over and I am happy that you did the work and happy to have it done with."[131] In June she wrote to Mary from Castine that she and Cal would be traveling to Aspen, Colorado, for a weeklong conference and then to Santa Fe. July marked the twentieth year of their marriage. Cal's two-part poem, "The Twentieth Wedding Anniversary," published nine years later, presents an unblinking view of the status quo: the couple who, like the leaves growing on a window, have "weathered the wet of twenty years"; Elizabeth as the "unsteady swallow / who will uproot the truth that cannot change."[132]

That autumn the focus was on Cal's impending eight-week fellowship at Oxford University's All Souls College. The philosopher Isaiah Berlin had written the previous year to mention various lodging possibilities. ("I have a feeling that it is best to take what, by our standards, is a modern apartment, near shops. . . . This prevents gloom.")[133] Meanwhile Cal had begun another affair, with a twenty-one-year-old college student who was writing her thesis on the *Notebook*. By now, Elizabeth was grimly accustomed to these infatuations.

In a February 1970 letter to Mary, Elizabeth's description of her daily life thrums with a sense of powerlessness and nervous despair: "The phone rings all day with meetings one could attend, plays one is urged to go to in the freezing night."[134] There were "malignant growths of mail, bills, anxiety about the cost of things, the look of things, clothes, weight, hair, hems." She described "the depressing quiet in the midst of so much rush and anxiousness. You feel as if you'd been in a play running for years and then it closed and you went uptown and no one called." This feeling was at least in part due to the malaise liberals felt after President Nixon's speech in November asking Americans to support a protracted war with North Vietnam. Elizabeth admitted that she had not kept her bargain with Cal "to talk less," but he was staying away from hard liquor, "and so we've been cheerful."

Another source of cheer was the Lowells' mid-March trip to Florence, Venice, and Rome—a holiday interlude before Cal took up his All Souls fellowship. More good news was on the horizon. Courted that spring by the University of Essex, he accepted a teaching position that would start in the autumn. Elizabeth began happily planning for the family's relocation to England. She would request a leave from her teaching at Barnard, rent the apartment to the author Carlos Fuentes and his family, find renters for the two studio apartments in the building the couple used as offices, and enroll Harriet in an English school. Writing to Bishop in late May, she found it amusing that Cal was thinking of spending three years in England rather than just one, a degree of optimism that she attributed to "the sweet green springtime."[135] While dealing with the details of the move and looking for a university archive to house Cal's papers—Elizabeth worried that a fire could destroy these valuable documents—she awaited news of the apartment or house Cal was supposedly locating for the family in London. Once again the future seemed promising.

CHAPTER 8

The Rift

(1970–1973)

IN LATE APRIL 1970, Lady Caroline Blackwood attended a dinner party for Cal at the office of his publisher, Faber and Faber. They had met in New York in 1966 during one of his manic states, when she was in the midst of an affair with *New York Review* editor Robert Silvers, and he brought her to dinner at the Lowells'. At thirty-eight, she was on her second marriage, to composer Israel Citkowitz, with whom she had two daughters;[1] her first husband had been the painter Lucian Freud. As his portraits of her reveal, Blackwood was a blond, waiflike beauty with strikingly large eyes. She was also an aristocrat—the daughter of an heiress to the Guinness brewery and a titled father who had a political career as a member of the Conservative Party. Blackwood had fallen in with a bohemian crowd in London and made a name for herself as a witty freelance journalist. Cal was smitten. He spent the night of the dinner at her house and subsequently took off with her on trips to Ireland and England's Lake District. The trajectory of his courtship eerily resembles that of his relationship with Elizabeth—previous meetings and then (when they were both at Yaddo) the sudden kindling of an affair.

He was slow to respond to Elizabeth's letters, and she was increasingly impatient to find out what sort of housing he had found for the family in London before his expected return to New York in the summer. In early June she wrote to Blair Clark that she planned to travel to England later that month to investigate, as soon as she delivered Harriet to summer camp.[2] Then on June 20, Elizabeth received a telegram: PERSONAL DIFFICULTIES MAKE TRIP TO NEW YORK IMPOSSIBLE RIGHT AWAY LOVE CAL.[3] What did that mean? Five days later, after a transatlantic phone call, the truth came out: the new woman in Cal's life was Caroline.

"I knew Cal had a girl and had been distressed for some time," Elizabeth wrote to Mary, "but it was just this afternoon that I knew it was Caroline. I felt such relief and burst out laughing!" When she phoned him, he was "laughing and joking and saying you are spending all your alimony on this call."[4] Elizabeth initially felt that she couldn't take this new infatuation seriously. But Silvers, who adored Caroline (she had refused to marry him), was "crushed" and failed to see the humor in the situation. He told Elizabeth that Caroline's life in England was so delightful that Cal likely would never leave her.

The trip to England was now out of the question, but the following months would bring more serious problems. In a furious letter to Cal, she expressed her "utter contempt for both of you for the misery you have brought to two people who had never hurt you knows no bounds" and told him she was unable to get her Barnard job back.[5] She urged him to give up his teaching position and come home. "Harriet is destroyed, deeply distressed," she wrote. Compounding Elizabeth's pressures, Harriet had left Dalton because of the impending move to London, and it was too late in the year for an admissions interview at another private school. Later, Elizabeth would discover that she and Harriet no longer had medical insurance through Harvard.

Six days after the phone call, Elizabeth told Mary that she had "cooled down" and realized that "pain can't be avoided. . . . Cal is still, in a certain sense, right here in the house, all his things, his books, his mail, his business, his taxes, his clothes."[6] She supposed that what they were going through was "just that strange thing that happens to you when you know you don't want it any longer." Worried about Caroline's "passion for having babies she can't take care of," Elizabeth nonetheless insisted that she "would not take Cal back unless this is over in a month or so." Mary proposed her own peculiar theory about the Lowells in a letter to her close friend Hannah Arendt: Cal had "bored" Elizabeth in recent years "to the point of excruciation," though perhaps neither of them had realized it.[7]

With the fresh memory of a disappointing visit in June to a friend in the Hamptons, on Long Island ("I hated the 100,000 dollar shacks on the beach, the publishers, the people"),[8] Elizabeth was especially looking forward to returning to Maine. Her hectic summer of driving involved taking Harriet to her camp in Connecticut, picking her up for a private school interview in New York, bringing her back to the camp, and returning to the New York apartment to ready it for renters before the long drive to Castine on July 12.

In early July, Cal's manic state returned, and he was admitted to Greenways Nursing Home in London. After Blackwood left London—claiming that she was in the throes of her own breakdown—Blair began fielding constant calls from Cal. Meanwhile Elizabeth had heard scurrilous rumors about his behavior. Once again frantic with worry, she decided to fly to London and see for herself. Her companion on this trip was William Alfred, an English professor at Harvard who was a good friend of Cal's. She found Cal in bad shape physically and thought a thyroid disorder might be the reason. Although he displayed no signs of mania, he seemed unresponsive. People close to him—Caroline, Citkowitz, Gowrie Gray, and his wife, Bingo (Alexandra Bingley)—did not seem to grasp the enormity of the problem. Elizabeth worried that she was unable to stay in London long enough to see Cal through the worst of his illness. "I feel [Caroline] will be an awful disaster for him with her deep unbalance," she wrote to Mary. "Cal seemed so helpless, so needing love & openness & wifely care."[9] With Alfred's help, Elizabeth cut his hair, sent out his shirts to be washed and his trousers to be cleaned, and maneuvered him to a nearby pub. Two days later she wrote that he was improving: "the hospital is charming & right for him, the doctor is good." She also realized that she did want "to start over again."[10]

Enchanted by the leafy, intellectual neighborhood of Hampstead, and urged by Cal's doctor to remain in London as long as possible, she nonetheless was impatient to fly home. On August 7, five days after she arrived in London, Elizabeth returned to New York. She had left Cal a note saying she would "always be there" if he needed her. He immediately wrote to tell her that she "couldn't have been more loyal and witty" and that he couldn't give her "anything of equal value."[11] When he was released, in mid-August, Caroline wouldn't let him come to the house because Citkowitz didn't want him near the children, so Cal rented an apartment. In September he informed Elizabeth Bishop that he and Elizabeth had "more or less separated, though as good-naturedly as such things can be. I have someone else."[12] He enlarged on this topic the following month with a description of Caroline designed to flatter ("she reads you with great admiration and thinks you much brighter than Mary").[13] Now, he admitted, "though things [with Elizabeth] are not embattled, nothing is settled." Bizarrely, he added, "I could be happy either way, if things could be settled."

Barely two weeks later, in October, Cal wrote to Elizabeth that he felt "torn apart," but that state was preferable to being obliged to make a decision.[14] "After all I have done, can I go back to you and Harriet?" He didn't think so. He could not "weigh the dear, troubled past . . . in which you saved everything" against a future with Caroline. And yet, he wrote, "allow me this short space before I arrive in New York to wobble in my mind." He planned to visit New York at Christmas with his new love, comparing his feeling for her to his feeling for Elizabeth when they were at Yaddo. She wrote to Blair that she didn't believe Caroline would come with him ("This is his fantasy"), and that he was probably afraid to leave without her, because "she might not be there when he got back."[15] He did not seem to realize that he would never see Elizabeth again after this visit, when he needed to "settle up things, make arrangements and then leave forever." (In a phone conversation, Elizabeth had told Blair that if Caroline accompanied Cal on this trip, she planned to leave town.) But maybe he wouldn't come after all. "In all the months he has been gone," she confided, "I've heard from him a lot and he has never answered one question that I have put to him, or discussed really anything . . . except himself." What especially irritated her, she told Mary, was "that terrible breeziness and casualness about the deepest feelings of your own life, and also of his own."[16] She described him as "such a childish torturer—that little side look of malice he gives you—and so spooky, more and more."[17]

Elizabeth added that she was thinking about the next book she wanted to write, "about Kentucky, myself in college, a little, and coming to New York, etc." She would "try to be as removed from myself as possible and try to get the feeling of the thing." Jason Epstein, who was now at Random House, had called her to talk about "the possible themes that might make it a book of interest right now," which gave her hope that he would publish what she wrote.

Her essay about Zelda Fitzgerald, the troubled writer married to F. Scott, appeared in the *New York Review* that autumn.[18] It struck Elizabeth that, while the interest in Zelda's life was once focused on "the grandeur and glamour of her love story," Nancy Milford's new biography had brought out "the heroism of her efforts and the bitterness of her defeats." Unmentioned in the essay is the second-wave feminism that compelled attention to those issues.

Worried about her tenuous financial situation, Elizabeth had begun writing for *Vogue*, which paid well. "It makes me very nervous to feel my whole future riding on writing," she confided to Mary a few months later, "but it is also pleasant and good."[19] Elizabeth's first piece for *Vogue* was a review of Doris Lessing's novel *The Four-Gated City*, published in the July 1969 issue. Her articles for the magazine during the next decade would range from reviews of books and the performing arts to essays about women's issues and politics. During the months before the 1972 presidential election, she wrote a six-part series, "One Woman's Vote." *Vogue*'s interest in exposing its readers to writing of this caliber was due to the magazine's new direction under editor-in-chief Grace Mirabella.

The essay Elizabeth published in *Vogue* in the summer of 1971 was unusually personal. "The Ties Women Cannot Shake and Have," begins with a confession about her ever-present anxieties and tendency to worry about all sorts of things.[20] As a young woman, she wrote, her worries were centered on "disgrace," the potential results of her involvements with men (at a time—as she did not feel the need to explain here—when the taint of promiscuity or an out-of-wedlock pregnancy could destroy a woman's good name). Even marriage to the wrong man could mean not living "the life you wanted." Then, as a married woman, the birth of her child temporarily made her reluctant to travel. Working on her writing involved "an almost puritanical pressure," but it was important to pay attention to housework as well, "if that makes someone else happier." (In reality, as soon as Elizabeth could afford it, she hired other women to do the cleaning.) This shadowy "someone" takes on a greater presence in succeeding paragraphs, where she invokes a poem by Sylvia Plath about children whom "an educated, sophisticated man" has left behind "when he changed his mind." The woman doesn't become accustomed to the absence of this man. She is forced into self-reliance, but not by women's liberation. "The brevity of love must be acknowledged," Elizabeth concluded. Her self-revelation is heartbreaking.

She was able to disengage sufficiently from the morass of her personal life to write a short story—her first in more than a decade. Elizabeth sent it to The New Yorker, telling Robert Henderson that she was "trembling with the thoughts of writing fiction again. How hard it is!"[21] He returned "Toward the Equator" to her a week later, writing that there were "many fine things in it," but that the magazine was "considerably overloaded with material . . . to the point where we are taking only what seems irresistible." The problem with this piece was that "after a fine beginning," it seemed more like "analysis as opposed to emotionally involved fiction."[22] While this quality had dogged Elizabeth's short stories in the past, The New Yorker was also responding to the post-1960s watershed in literary styles by rejecting work that might have passed muster in earlier years. She worked on her story and sent it out again, but Henderson—while admitting that the editors had "more division of opinion" about this version—once again rejected it.[23]

Essays were now Elizabeth's primary genre. In "Militant Nudes," one of several pieces the New York Review would publish the following year, she discussed the way sexuality "is suddenly political." Ranging over content as diverse as Gimme Shelter, the documentary of the Rolling Stones' doomed concert at Altamont; a film about Huey Newton; a novel by Marge Piercy; and Andy Warhol's film Trash, she decried the "pitiless and pathological" that "has seeped into youth's love of itself, its body, its politics." She was repelled by "the moral numbness" of these works, "the loss of pity for the poor body, of respect for its life, its suffering."

* * *

By early November, Cal was rethinking his decision. He wrote to Peter Taylor, "I think Lizzie and [I] will come back together. If that can be done."[24] The next day he confessed to Mary McCarthy, "I have done great harm to everyone. . . . To go on seriously toward marriage with Caroline against the grain, the circumstances, our characters, etc. is more than can be got away with."[25] Five days later he finally wrote to the one person who most needed to know his thoughts: "I wonder if we couldn't make it up?" Then again, "Maybe now . . . you will quite rightly draw back, happily rid of your weary burden."[26] He mentioned that his new book (*Notebook 1967–68*) had been published in England to "gratifying" reviews, but he didn't let on that some of the poems in it were about their marriage. On the same day, in a less abject mood, he informed Bishop that his return to Elizabeth was likely.[27]

His new state of mind did not last. In a November 21 letter to Blair, Cal argued that he was "perfectly happy with Caroline," and "not being married somehow loosens the bond, man and woman's mutual self-killing desire to master the other."[28] At the end of the month, he wrote to Elizabeth, "I do nothing much but bury my indecisions in many many poems."[29] A subsequent letter to her mentioned that a reviewer who wrote negatively about his book "seems to think" that the subject was "the breaking and final break up of our marriage. That's not in the text."[30] But it was clear to anyone who read it. He admitted that he had "vers[ed]" one of her letters "in my poems on you in *Notebook*."[31] There would be worse to come.

Cal arrived in New York by himself, but Elizabeth saw that he was wearing Caroline's ring. He had decided to stay with Blair rather than return to the apartment. From her point of view, the three-week visit was sadly underwhelming. "The person I had been missing so painfully was the rare, glorious person of at least a decade ago and when I saw him at the airport, disheveled, that darting wild look in his eye, heard the eternal jokes, it was just so pitiful."[32] Back in London in early January, Cal seemed to have no awareness of her disappointment. Enumerating the various "kind charming things" about her and his visit, he wrote, "Above all you stand out at the airport with your curled hair and beautiful smile that survived the long dull wait. Then the blue washcloths, the buttermilk, the calm Christmas day, and the wonderful wit and good spirits of Harriet, surely rather owing to you—I mean your old undeviating loyalty."[33] Yet it wasn't as if Elizabeth had hardened her heart. Stepping into Cal's studio that winter, she told Mary that she felt "more than a little triste because dear old Cal seemed to be in the very woodwork writing poems, the air still alive with his cigarettes."[34] Three months later Mary wrote to Hannah Arendt that she hadn't heard from either Elizabeth or Cal recently, which was unusual. "One can't remain a friend of both, that seems clear," she noted, "and perhaps, trying to, I've become the friend of neither."[35]

Elizabeth wrote to Cal in early January 1971 that her "financial situation is desperate and is going to be for the rest of my life."[36] Fortunately she was able to return to her teaching position at Barnard, which she now found "terribly pleasant and easy."[37] Although the pay was low, she was determined to find other positions to augment her salary, beginning with three lectures for the Christian Gauss Seminar in Criticism at Princeton that she was invited to give the following year.[38] This appointment was serendipitous: the content of these lectures provided the basis for her essays on the Brontës, Dorothy Wordsworth, and Jane Carlyle, published in the New York Review and subsequently in Seduction and Betrayal. Elizabeth was also working on an essay for the Review about Ibsen's play A Doll's House, the first of her four analyses of the playwright's psychologically acute understanding of his women characters.[39]

Yet her life was still continuously disrupted by her dealings with Cal. After Caroline became pregnant with his child, due in the autumn,[40] Blair informed him that any goodwill Elizabeth might have had toward him had disappeared. Still, she tried valiantly to foster a good relationship between him and Harriet, although she decided against sending their daughter to visit him in the summer.[41] Months later Adrienne Rich expressed her view of Cal's behavior in a blunt letter to him: "My affection and admiration for Elizabeth make it difficult to be debonair about something which—however good for her it may ultimately be—has made her suffer."[42] He responded that Rich did not understand his situation, claiming "the only important thing wrong with marriage with Lizzie was our unending nervous strife."[43]

After a disappointing vacation in South Carolina with Harriet, Elizabeth joined the massive Vietnam War protest march in April in Washington, D.C., with her daughter and several friends. She found it "tiring" and "not especially interesting, merely necessary."[44] It is likely that her personal worries kept her from fully entering into the spirit of the event. Still, many would have agreed with her "hopeless" feeling about the U.S. government. Mary's own political musings appeared in her new novel, *Birds of America*, a satire about a male college student who goes abroad in the 1960s and his much-married mother, a musician, who has many of the novelist's own traits. Elizabeth contributed a brief profile of her friend to the Literary Guild book club newsletter. Writing privately to Mary, she followed an enthusiastic "I love it" with somewhat guarded praise: "a work utterly your own—your own ideas, your peculiar, valuable obsessions, and very sweetly, touchingly sad, rather than angry." The ending—in which the hospitalized son has a vision of Immanuel Kant—was "wonderful." But Elizabeth said nothing about stylistic matters.[45]

* * *

For the spring 1971 issue of a short-lived journal, Philip Rahv interviewed Elizabeth on a range of topics, including the women's movement.[46] Echoing her *Vogue* article, she said its roots were in "the breakdown of marriage." Rather than being a choice, self-reliance was "a necessity growing out of genuine instability and altered expectations." As a result, she had "come to think of the old waitresses and store clerks as heroines." In response to a question about whether the counterculture was fading, she remarked, "Here in America, every decade is like a century. That is the fascination and fatigue of our lives."

In June, Elizabeth was sufficiently riled by the publication of excerpts from Edmund Wilson's diary in *The New Yorker*—pages of praise for an attractive young Hungarian woman who typed his manuscripts followed by the curt mention of a quarrel with his wife, Elena—that she came up with a new idea for a women's lib button: "Good wives finish last!"[47] Elizabeth was not an unqualified fan of the movement. Two months later she wrote to Cal that its only positive aspect "is that women seem more able to lean on each other. . . . The rest is bad writing, bald simplicity and simple-mindedness, usually."[48] Yet her own newfound empowerment enabled her to confront Cal about several issues: the money she needed; his and Caroline's treatment of Harriet; the contents of the papers to be sold to Harvard; and his lack of appreciation for all the work she had done to find a home for them.[49]

Elizabeth spent most of this summer in Castine, polishing a trenchant essay for the *New York Review* about the late Sylvia Plath. "Her work is brutal, like the smash of a fist," Elizabeth wrote. "Perhaps being born a woman is part of the exceptional rasp"—a strikingly apt choice of word—"of her nature, a woman whose stack of duties was laid over the ground of genius, ambition, and grave mental instability."[50] Elizabeth knew a thing or two about the latter: "Persons suffering in this way simply do not have room in their heads for the anguish of others—and later many seem to survive their own torments only by an erasing detachment."

Cal found her article on Plath to be "dazzling as usual"[51] and described her *Vogue* essay as "a tirade in the best sense, every feeling every cadence alive."[52] Writing the night before his play *Prometheus*

Bound opened in London, Cal also praised her emendations to this work as "a hailstorm of gifts."[53] She had suggested more elevated diction or more clarity in certain speeches as well as passages that he needed to cut. For example, Cal had Prometheus say, "Zeus had to make nothing of me, because I had made him everything." Elizabeth changed the last phrase to "so that he might himself be everything." Another character says, "Zeus knows well from experience how power refreshes the subservient. He gave Hesione an island to rule."[54] Elizabeth, likely drawing on her own experience, changed the first sentence to "Zeus knows well from experience how possessions refresh the grief-stricken."[55]

It is tempting to see Cal offering his abundance of praise at least partially out of guilt for the cruelty he was inflicting on his wife in his new book, *The Dolphin*, dedicated to Caroline. Some of the poems—which Elizabeth would not read until months later— included verbatim remarks from her frantic, sometimes bitter letters and phone conversations. (Sample passage: "I wait for your letters, tremble when I get none, / more when I do.")[56] Elizabeth would object even more strenuously to lines he attributed to her that she never wrote or uttered, such as, *"Don't you dare mail us the love your lie denies; / do you really* know *what you have done?"*[57]

By late September 1971, she had learned secondhand what the book was about and became aware of "the shocked reaction of our mutual friends."[58] Cal had made an awkward and cavalier bid to head off her fury while keeping her from reading the poems before they were published. He insisted that poetry did not reveal "the literal or ultimate truth" and that she wouldn't "feel betrayed or exploited," but he couldn't "imagine [she] would want to scrape through the sadness and breakage now."[59] On October 1 he reiterated his earlier remark about possibly not publishing his book, while making a case for it as "my best (last) work maybe." He tried to compare *The Dolphin* to her "Notebook," suggesting that "in calmer times" they could "publish the two books in one volume."[60] (Using a leather-bound blank book received as a gift, Elizabeth had been working in a desultory way on a memoir, jokingly titled "Smiling Through," but it struck her as "sentimental and unreal," and she eventually destroyed it.)[61]

News of the birth of Cal's and Caroline's son, on September 28, came in a second October 1 letter—provokingly addressed not to Elizabeth but to Harriet. The enormity of the whole Cal-and-Caroline situation was apparently too devastating for Elizabeth to mention in a late September letter to Mary, in which she claimed to be "fine, very busy, quite happy."[62] Mary and her husband, traveling in England, spent Christmas Eve with Cal and Caroline, a seemingly disloyal visit that she blithely related to Elizabeth before the trip, hoping this news "won't give you pain."[63] Elizabeth buried her response to this news ("it will be nice for Cal and so that pleases me") at the end of a note on a Christmas card in which she described a visit to the Cleveland Museum with Robert Silvers and his new companion, Lady Grace Dudley. ("I must say Bob is having real fun.")[64] In her New Year's Day letter to Mary, she reported that the tiredness she had felt weeks earlier had lifted, she had "an unusually good time" during the holidays, and she was now immersed in "a long piece on the Brontes."[65]

* * *

Attempting to preserve a shred of privacy apart from the ongoing saga of the end of her marriage, Elizabeth wrote to Peter and Eleanor Taylor that the winter had been "happy" and she felt "lucky."[66] The elements of her good fortune, as she enumerated them, were her apartment, her friends, and her work. Another letter to Peter complained about what she thought was his attempt to help her secure a speedy divorce. How could he think that Cal, whose "brutality knows no bounds where his own wishes are concerned," had the slightest reticence about discussing this matter with her?[67] Of course they would divorce, but it couldn't happen without "more active cooperation on his part." Meanwhile she had "caused Cal absolutely no trouble" about anything while continuing to "take care of all his affairs," although he was not giving her the information she needed to file his taxes. Elizabeth worried about sending fifteen-year-old Harriet to visit Cal, as he had requested, because of the chaotic nature of his household. But she finally set off for London in late March 1972. Cal groused that Elizabeth's detailed notes about caring for their daughter reminded him of Napoleon's Italian campaign, but the visit went well, and Harriet would return to see him the following spring.

Remarks by Elizabeth were published that month in *Time* magazine's special issue, *The American Woman*.[68] In her view, the women's movement "has the profoundly native ethical themes of self-reliance, personal responsibility, and equality." She added a wry coda about Sophia Hawthorne's reaction to her husband's paradoxically liberated yet socially constrained character Hester Prynne: "Mrs. Hawthorne . . . said she liked it but 'it gave her a headache.' In a sense, that is where we are still."

Writing to Elizabeth Bishop about his forthcoming book of poetry, *The Dolphin* (Cal had sent her an excerpt), he called Elizabeth "the poignance of the book, tho [sic] that hardly makes it kinder to her."[69] He admitted, "I attribute things to Lizzie I made up, or that were said by someone else," while omitting the worst things she said about him, "so as not to give myself a case of seeming self-pitying." He rationalized that the letters "make Lizzie real beyond my invention." But he had nothing to say about how Elizabeth might feel about them. A few weeks later, as if none of this drama had been swirling around the book, Cal let Elizabeth know that he missed having her "to joke with, reason with, unreason with."[70] For her part, Elizabeth claimed in a letter to Mary that Cal's book struck her as having an "awful silliness about it," that "the whole thing is a sort of half-manic caper," and that she felt "indifferent to it."[71] Apparently unaware that *The Dolphin* was to be released the following year, she referred to the book as something Cal would publish "someday." Still in the dark about the specific wording of the poems, she wrote to him to affirm her belief that his poetry could not harm her.[72]

Both before and after the publication of *The Dolphin*, several poets weighed in about Cal's use of Elizabeth's letters. Bishop, whose own words had been quoted in a poem he dedicated to her[73]—to her dismay—couched a warning in a letter to him about the poems' formal qualities. She wrote, "It is not being 'gentle' to use personal, tragic, anguished letters that way—it's cruel."[74] He had wreaked "infinite mischief" by changing Elizabeth's words. "Art just isn't worth that much." While Cal admitted to the poet Frank Bidart (a former student) that Bishop's letter was "a kind of masterpiece of criticism," he criticized her "extreme paranoia about revelations."[75] But as the poet Thom Gunn astutely noted, "Bishop found two betrayals"—of Elizabeth and of the reader, "who had no control over the text . . . to check for the distortions and omissions and changes of emphasis that he made."[76]

Cal adjusted the original version of his poem "Voices" in response to Bishop's criticism, but only to make Elizabeth's rage at his "clowning" sound less visceral. Bidart, whom Cal had consulted about *The Dolphin* as late as August 1972, told Ian Hamilton, Cal's first biographer, that Elizabeth's letters were "the all too raw material for Lowell's lightly fictionalized drama of *his* indecision."[77] Decades later he remarked that he prefers the original version of the book, in which he believes Elizabeth is shown as "a strong, powerful woman who owns her anger," whereas in the published version, "she is a voice overheard in another room."[78] Having listened to the couple's quarrels, he said that Elizabeth "could be incredibly difficult," to the point that a joke Cal made "would drive her crazy." But Elizabeth was surely fed up with the undertone of self-righteous mockery that much of Cal's humor had taken over the years.

In *American Poetry Review*, Adrienne Rich dismissed Cal's work as "bullshit eloquence, a poor excuse for a cruel and shallow book. . . . The inclusion of the letter poems stands as one of the most vindictive and mean-spirited acts in the history of poetry."[79] (the poet Richard Tillinghast would later suggest that Cal's action was more likely "a colossal thoughtlessness.")[80] Rich also wrote to Elizabeth: "When 2 people have had something together, however difficult & powerful, it is not the right of one to choose to 'use' it in this fashion. I think people are ultimately more important than poems. (I know you do too!)"[81] Stanley Kunitz deplored "details which seem to me monstrously heartless. . . . some passages I can scarcely bear to read: they are . . . too intimately cruel."[82] In response, Cal wrote that the ensnared eel in the poem "Dolphin" was Elizabeth, and that he realized she would "feel bruised by the intimacy."[83] W. H. Auden was so distressed to hear about the poems that he refused to speak to Cal again.

In *The New York Times*, Anatole Broyard called the book "so much blabbed biography."[84] But the novelist Jonathan Raban thought the book ought to stand as written, "for literature's sake," rather than be changed "out of fear of what Lizzie was going to say."[85] In his view, the poems in question were "some of the best poems in the book." The Pulitzer Prize jury also believed in the overriding literary importance of *The Dolphin*, which won the poetry prize in 1974. Elizabeth, who felt that the poems that used her voice were of poor quality, attempted to put a brave face on the betrayal. "Well, you can't be dishonored by bad work," she said to Gore Vidal. He responded, "Don't you believe it!"[86]

Her crisis was made even more intense by the fact that Cal had simultaneously published another book of poetry about his marriage. Coinciding with *The Dolphin*, poems from Cal's *Notebook* (originally published in 1969, revised and expanded in the 1970 edition) were revised again and reissued in two separate books. While *History* consisted of poems on public topics, *For Lizzie and Harriet* documented his perceptions of family life, the trajectory of the marriage, and his affair with the woman he was involved with before Caroline. In "No Hearing I. The Dialogue," Cal couched his embattled view of the marriage in terms of a bullfight. "We meet face to face in the 6 p.m. hour / nursing two inches of family Bourbon," he wrote, the object being "not . . . victory but survival."[87]

Cal was not the only poet who had written about the end of a marriage, nor was he the only one who had used excerpts from the personal writings of someone close to him. However, this practice seems to have been a predominantly male form of entitlement. Wordsworth borrowed phrases from his sister Dorothy's journal for his poetry. William Carlos Williams incorporated letters by a lover, poet Marcia Nardi (whom he refers to as "Miss Cress"), in book two of *Paterson*.[88] He offered several explanations for his behavior, including his sense that Nardi's prose was "a strong reply . . . to many of my male pretentions." Responding to Cal's positive review of Williams's book two in 1948, Elizabeth Bishop argued that his use of the letters "seems mean," adding that he "has always had a streak of insensitivity."[89] While Cal had incorporated the words of others in much of his own writing, quoting passages from poet friends' letters is hardly on the same scale as exposing the pain of the woman who had shared his life for more than two decades. The biographer Hazel Rowley pointed out that women in *The Dolphin* "have three roles: the abandoned woman, 'woman loving,' and woman as mother."[90] As the abandoned woman, Rowley wrote, Elizabeth is in the humiliating position of having her anguish observed and dramatized by the man who abandoned her. "More cruel (and controversial) . . . was his colonization of her voice."

* * *

With "Working Girls: The Brontës," published in the *New York Review* in May 1972, Elizabeth began a memorable series of reconsiderations of classic literature by and about women.[91] Together with her writing about depictions of women by Ibsen, Hawthorne, Dreiser, Hardy, Tolstoy, Samuel Richardson, and Mozart's librettist Lorenzo da Ponte, these essays would form the spine of her most celebrated nonfiction collection, *Seduction and Betrayal*. The title essay, based on a talk Elizabeth gave at Vassar, discusses the psychology of seducers in opera and literature (including Don Giovanni and Reverend Dimmesdale in *The Scarlet Letter*) and the fate of female protagonists (Hester Prynne, Richardson's Clarissa, Hetty Sorel in George Eliot's *Adam Bede*, Roberta in Dreiser's *An American Tragedy*, Hardy's Tess). "The men do not really believe in consequences for themselves," she wrote. "Women, wronged in one way or another, are given the overwhelming beauty of endurance . . . for violent feeling absorbed, finally tranquilized, for the radiance of humility, for silence, secrecy, impressive acceptance. Heroines are, then, heroic." *Endurance* was a quality she herself had come to embody.

In June, Elizabeth wrote to Peter Taylor about the "inertia" that accompanies the end of a long marriage. "Everything comes at once, grief, financial worry, extra work; it is a long time before you have the spirit for climbing ladders and dusting heavy books that haven't been touched for twelve years."[92] By now, she felt that she had been "able to adjust to the grief," despite continuing to love Cal, "a rare, beautiful man." She was happy to be free, "even though there is always something lacking in that as in not being free." And she hoped to have another relationship "if I liked him, had a good time with him and he liked me." In fact, Elizabeth admitted that, she had had "'a gratifying relationship' with an extraordinary friend" the previous winter, but it was not a serious affair.[93]

The Lowells signed their divorce papers in early October, when Cal and Caroline arrived in New York. (Afterward the couple flew to Santo Domingo to divorce each other's spouse and remarry—on the same day.) Elizabeth and Harriet would receive $20,000 annually from Cal's trust fund, and Elizabeth would retain the New York apartment and its contents, including thousands of books, artwork, and Lowell family silverware. She would also receive a $10,000 share in Cal's papers, which he sold to Harvard for $140,000 the following year. (She had requested $5,000 for correspondence addressed to her and to both of them.)[94] Harriet was provided for through her postgraduate education, with Elizabeth in sole charge of those funds. A quirk in state law made it mandatory for the house in Maine to be included in the divorce settlement, even though Harriet Winslow had deeded it solely to Elizabeth. She had a hard time convincing Cal that he had no rights to it.

In November Elizabeth received a letter from Adrienne Rich that praised both her writerly brilliance ("a style like yours with its apparent simplicity and tensility") and her independence: "you . . . remained your own woman, so that in making many things possible for Cal you were never limited to that dedication, or limited by it. This must be the most difficult thing in the world; not many women have actually managed it, certainly not women writers."[95]

* * *

In January 1973, Elizabeth met the effervescent art lecturer Rosamund Bernier—just back from a trip to India with the jeweler Kenneth Jay Lane—at a dinner given by the pianist couple Arthur Gold and Robert Fizdale. Elizabeth told the group that she had suggested to two "well-preserved" women in their fifties that they needed to find "a seasoned widower."[96] Both of them replied, "But I like younger men." Recounting this conversation to Mary, Elizabeth wrote that "a gasp went around the table," and it turned out that Bernier (who was Elizabeth's age) was involved with a "very attractive" younger man— a situation applauded by Gold. The exchange seemed to give Elizabeth a lift: "Having set my sights ahead"—meaning, to a relationship with an older man—"I immediately moved them back, encouraged to hope." Later that month she spoke about Sylvia Plath at the Poetry Center of the 92nd Street Y. Daphne Merkin, then a student at Barnard, reported on the event in the college newspaper, writing that Elizabeth "seemed to be the only one there who had an interest in Plath's poems as poetry."[97]

Elizabeth was in a good mood that spring. She was getting ready to sell Cousin Harriet's large, damp house in Castine and turn the barn on the waterfront into a compact, livable home. In a letter to Cal, she enumerated the ways she currently believed herself to be lucky: "I am closer to more people, care more for them, feel more happiness somehow."[98] But this feeling lasted only until early July, when her fury at Cal's continual peevish objections to the sale[99] and at an early review of *The Dolphin*[100] caused her to write to him that their marriage "has been a complete mistake." She was "paranoid and frightened" that her letter might wind up in a future poem.[101] On the same day, Elizabeth wrote to Robert Giroux, Cal's editor, to inform him of her distress. She emphasized that her permission had never been sought "for the prodigal use of my letters, for the use in the most intimate way of my name and that of my daughter."[102] After pointing out that reviewers of the book had criticized her personally, she wrote that she knew "of no other instance in literature where a person is exploited in a supposedly creative act, under his own name, in his own lifetime." Although the manuscript had been shown to many people prior to publication, she was not among them. When she received the book, "the reality was disturbing far beyond anything I could have imagined." Elizabeth enumerated some of the "wrong impressions" readers would have, including the notion that she had been unwilling to divorce her husband.

Cal's response was to send her a cable: THE REVIEWS FRIENDLY OR UNFRIENDLY ARE MORE OR LESS ONLY CRUEL PUBLICITY POSTERS GOD HELP US AND SPARE US.[103] At an earlier period, when he was working on a poem in a complicated style about another subject, Elizabeth had suggested, "Why not say what really happened?"[104] She never could have imagined how this remark might boomerang.

In the review that Elizabeth mentioned in her letter, poetry critic Marjorie Perloff described Harriet, as portrayed in the poems, as "one of the most unpleasant child figures in history."[105] She and her mother "seem to get no more than they deserve," according to Perloff. Discussing the two of them as though they were identical with the characters in the poems was the last straw. To Elizabeth Bishop, Cal described Elizabeth as so upset that "friends had to drop in and telephone to see that she didn't take too many pills."[106] (Bishop wrote to her, sending "all the sympathy I can.")[107] To Giroux, Cal insisted that "the portrait [of Elizabeth] is very careful and affectionate," and he hoped "this will blow off without a lawsuit."[108] Giroux wondered if a case could be made that Cal had used letters from someone else in his previous published poems. "I can't understand why it came to her as such a surprise," he wrote, obtusely ignoring the source of her pain.[109]

A photo of Cal's new family accompanied Walter Clemons's review of the trio of poetry books in *Newsweek*. In the caption, Caroline's bedraggled-looking daughter, Ivana, is called "Harriet."[110] For Elizabeth, this was just one more dagger in the heart. She looks severe and every bit as old as her fifty-six years in her own small photo. The caption, "Heart's Ease," is from a poem in which Cal evoked the two of them at age fifty. Clemons characterized Elizabeth's presence in *The Dolphin* as an "accusing, regretful, forgiving voice" and quoted a passage taken from one of her letters.

As if the agony of having her private life opened for public inspection were not a sufficient burden, Elizabeth was also on the receiving end of Cal's complaints about the settlement. "It's a desolate thought that all I have from the past is grandpa's gold watch and some fifteen books," he griped.[111] What Cal failed to say in so many words was that all his life, for better or worse, he had felt the weight of the Lowell family history, and now he no longer had the tangible objects that reminded him of it. He also mourned photos of Elizabeth that he had tucked into a lost wallet.[112]

A long article Elizabeth wrote during this fraught period offers a window into her state of mind. In "When to Cast Out, Give Up, Let Go," she likens the "pinching shoe, the single glove" that women often hang on to despite their uselessness to "the longings, the clingings" of women's inner lives.[113] She writes of "painful memories . . . enshrining resentments and long, futile angers" that only forgiveness would allow women to relive "without desperation." In her view, "the inclination to repeat our grievances, to insist that payment is always due us . . . is an indulgence that everyone must sooner or later give up." Elizabeth concludes that by throwing away "one-sided love," women can attain "a true condition of 'loving' someone who has long ago treated us badly. Then affection is not a weird, ambivalent manipulation of the death of love, but a sort of salute to its happier beginning." This extraordinary essay suggests an answer to those who wonder how she could have loved and stayed with Cal all those years: "To think about a troubled person is to ask . . . where does he hurt and how can it be changed? . . . Sympathy is a gift, sometimes almost an occupation." Elizabeth's ultimate loyalty was to an ethical ideal: "Always what is most important in one's personal life is to forgive the unforgivable."

Despite the high-mindedness expressed in that essay, Elizabeth wrote to Cal that she never wanted to hear from him again. On July 27, 1973, unable to bear the continual assault on herself and her child, she left Castine for a month's rest in Italy. On that day, she wrote to Elizabeth Bishop to thank her for her support and to tell her of the great agony the poems, "so inane, empty, unnecessary," had caused her.[114] In Rome, Elizabeth enjoyed the company of Barbara Epstein and Gore Vidal, who invited her to his villa in Ravello for the weekend. Reading, swimming, and walking "among the pines and views and sunsets" made her temporarily feel less troubled.[115] But her subsequent stay at the Rockefeller Foundation in Bellagio was a source of irritation. She found that the "aging academics" had "as much intellectual vivacity as a woodchuck," and their wives "have not made one single demand upon themselves, whether of mind or body."

Back home that autumn, she confessed to Bishop that she had "the feeling of being out of breath" and was having trouble managing the everyday aspects of her life "with any special efficiency."[116] Two days later she wrote again to the poet, with heavy foreboding: "I can't tell you how I dread the future with biographies. . . . Fortunately I'll be dead when most of them come out."[117] To Mary, she wrote that she was "sunk in housekeeping, going to the market, cooking, going downstairs to the washing machines."[118] But she was well, the skies were clear, and "the Nixon affair"—the fallout from Watergate—"keeps one almost literally breathless." By the end of her letter, she seemed to have cheered up somewhat, writing that she had been "going to the opera, buying and playing records" and that her house was "always crowded with people coming and going."

In October, Elizabeth's story "Writing a Novel" was published in the *New York Review*. Her way of responding to Cal's perfidy is oblique, but he is undeniably present—not only as a "genius" with "stooped shoulders" and rumpled clothes but also as the invisible memoirist who "accuses others of real faults and oneself of charming infidelities, unusual follies . . . excesses, vanities, and sensualities that are the envy of all."[119] The narrator says that she is "an amputee. . . . in my heart I do believe I am more damaged than most." (These remarks would be omitted in *Sleepless Nights*.) Another autobiographical piece Elizabeth published this year hints at her terrified state of mind. This reminiscence about her experience of the squalid aspect of New York life in the 1940s concludes on an ominous note: "I know some new form of the Hotel Schuyler lies in wait for me."[120]

* * *

Philip Rahv died on December 22 at age sixty-five, disillusioned after having lost his influence on the literary scene and weary of the financial demands of his last wife, who was divorcing him after a brief marriage. In a letter to Mary, Elizabeth mourned his late-life disintegration, his "awful aloneness at the end."[121] Reliant on alcohol and sleeping pills to deal with his depression, he had asked her to spend New Year's Eve with him; she had agreed despite being put off by his "bullying" tone on the phone. Elizabeth was also thinking sadly about Elizabeth Bishop, prey to alcoholism, depressed and alone in her apartment while her current lover was away. Rahv lacked a "gift for happiness," Elizabeth wrote, but "he had power and a certain amount of discipline and clarity at times." Mary—who had heard from the writer Frances Fitzgerald that he seemed "very much the old Philip" on his last night—was not buying Elizabeth's assessment of a broken man. In her view, her friend was projecting her feelings about her own life onto her old colleague.[122] But Elizabeth's life would soon be on an upswing, propelled by the power of her writing.

CHAPTER 9

Literary Splash

(1974–1979)

ON MAY 5, 1974, Random House published Elizabeth's book *Seduction and Betrayal*, versions of ten essays she had written for *The New York Review of Books*. It was dedicated to *Review* editor Barbara Epstein, who with her husband, Jason, executive editor at the publishing house, hosted a dinner to celebrate.[1] Elizabeth had written to Roger Straus that she wanted to leave Farrar, Straus and Giroux (as it was now known) because "of Cal and all of that." She assured Straus—whose normal reaction to author defections was rage at their unfaithfulness—that she was "extremely fond of you and Bob [Giroux], just as much as ever."[2] But she never returned to FSG, whether due to Straus's (unrecorded) response or to her friendship with Epstein. Susan Sontag wrote to him to offer her praise: "Elizabeth Hardwick knows virtually all there is to know about adjectives, desperate feelings, the literary vocation and the sweet vertigo of domesticity. *Seduction and Betrayal* is the most subtle of feminist books."[3] Sontag described it as the contemporary equivalent of Lytton Strachey's groundbreaking biography *Eminent Victorians*.

Reviews were mostly positive, lauding Elizabeth's independent point of view. The best essays were judged to be those about the women in Ibsen's plays, Jane Carlyle, Zelda Fitzgerald, Sylvia Plath, and the Brontës. The *New York Times* reviewer lauded "the high order of [her] sensibility . . . and her subtle style, . . . a rare gift to the reader," despite finding her writing "at times . . . too subjective and hermetic in her approach to real women."[4] (As Elizabeth told an interviewer, her self-described "hallucinatory state" while reading certain works led to allusive passages—"undercurrents and light in dark places about the imagined emotions and actions"—reflecting what she felt were often "quite mysterious discoveries.")[5] One of the most thoughtful reviews came from Daphne Merkin, writing in her student paper, the *Barnard Bulletin*: "One can read the book with pleasure and ease, without quite realizing the quality of its observations, which ripple the pages like waves on a calm sea."[6] Merkin praised the way Elizabeth's "insights well up from life's experience as well as from its observation," noting that her "criticism is intuitive rather than conceptual, of the heart at least as much as of the mind." In Merkin's view, Elizabeth "possesses a genuine liberality of spirit, a lack of elitism that stains so many literati."

Although *Seduction and Betrayal* was published at the height of the second wave of feminism, Elizabeth's tacit refusal to take a doctrinaire position inevitably led to accusations that she was mired in the judgmental standards of the bad old days. In the title essay, she explores fictional women who were "seduced and betrayed" and anoints those who can be taken seriously because of their moral nobility as silent sufferers. This personal characteristic, she writes, is no longer considered desirable in contemporary fiction, and for that reason the theme has lost its validity. She was lamenting a loss to literature that somehow struck her as more serious than the gain in women's assertiveness. (Predictably, the reviewer for *Ms.* magazine offered an unsympathetic view of Elizabeth's opinion.)[7] Then again, literature was always Elizabeth's lodestar. She was also a writer of minute distinctions and fine-grained opinions—often misunderstood or slighted by reviewers looking for bold strokes—and her view of men was colored by her personal experience. When she writes, "Scarcely anyone would wish [sexual activity] to define, enclose, imprison a man's being," she may seem to be canceling out the censure implicit in her remark that men won't "confess to adultery when their success or their comfort hangs in the balance." Yet she constantly faced a version of this conflict in her life with Cal. Writing about witty Jane Carlyle, browbeaten by her literary husband, Elizabeth criticized her for looking to servants to provide the attention she craved and for not sufficiently appreciating Thomas's "raging productivity." In Elizabeth's view, genius is not to be gainsaid by the needs of others. This stance is an attribute of the noble woman whose stoic silence transcends the pull of ordinary passions. It is a romantic ethical standard, in thrall to the power of literature and the unassailable stature of a character who embodies a self-sufficient valor.

Because the essays are concerned with the treatment of women in literature, an interviewer asked Elizabeth if she "specialized in women."[8] Explaining that she wrote "about ideas," she replied that the real question was "Is there a feminine sensibility?" She denied that such a thing existed (though she admitted that her writing style was "rather feminine" in a way she failed to define). Elizabeth shifted the conversation to the shared experiences of men and women. "Men do just what we do: they sit behind a desk and pick up the phone and drive the car. I'm leaving out whether they do the housework; I'm talking about their working life." Asked for her views of feminism, she replied airily, "Well, I'm very much for everything we can get that's just, of course." But Elizabeth did have trenchant things to say about women's political power. To get it, as she wrote in a *Vogue* essay, "women will have to take it from the present holders—men. . . . Chivalry will not play a part. . . . It will not come as a gift."[9]

In another *Vogue* essay, "Is the 'Equal' Woman More Vulnerable?" she once again located the impetus for the women's movement in "the breakdown of marriage."[10] She wrote that "liberation, self-knowledge, self-reliance . . . are a sort of private investment, a savings account that acknowledges the shakiness of marriage." Noting that the lack of equity in divorce is often a result of "the hidden, brutal fact" that "young women are often fond of men older than themselves," Elizabeth was acknowledging a truth about her own marriage—though without placing any blame on those older men.

Toward the end of her life, replying to a question about the possible connection between *Seduction and Betrayal* and her life with Cal, she replied evasively that the origin of the book lay in the lectures she had given at Princeton University.[11] But her concern with "the betrayal of love between a man and a woman" must have been influenced by the drama of her married life. Her own experience surely lies behind the remark, in her 1970 essay about Zelda Fitzgerald,[12] that "the will to blame [mentally ill people], to hold them to account, soon appears futile to those closest. Instead the mad entwine their relations in an unresolved, lingering, chafing connection [of] guilt, exasperation, and grief." When she writes about "moral dignity," she is celebrating the same qualities of "fortitude" and "endurance" that she herself exemplified. Yet one observation in this essay seems off-key. Elizabeth—who had yet to experience the appropriation of her own letters in *The Dolphin*—wrote, "It does not seem of such importance that [Zelda's] diaries and letters were appropriated [by F. Scott], the stories wrongly attributed for an extra $500." She failed to credit the pain this caused, and the brutality of the deed for someone with such a fragile sense of self. She insisted that only one member of the couple was "real as an artist, as a person with a special claim upon the world." That person was not Zelda.

In "Bloomsbury and Virginia Woolf," another essay reprinted in *Seduction and Betrayal*, Elizabeth seems to be feeling her way toward a view of Woolf as "a theorist of fiction. . . . testing and confronting the very structure of the novel itself." She writes that Woolf's "novels are beautiful, the language is rich and pure, and you are always, with her, aware of genius, of gifts extraordinary and original. . . . And yet in a sense her novels aren't interesting." (As we've seen, Elizabeth endowed this colorless word with a special power, akin to "enthralling" or "absorbing.") While praising Woolf as a feminist, she believes that the androgynous climate of Bloomsbury (a description recently popularized by several literary critics) "imprisons her in femininity." In Woolf's novels, the male world is "almost erased by the powers of the domestic and the social." From this narrow view of life comes Woolf's overwhelming sense of nostalgia—the "mist of loveliness [that] covers everything, even sorrow and regret" and "the inner life of feeling, the shifting, never recovered, never completely to be known flow of existence." Elizabeth perceives Woolf's mental illness in "the endless, stretching sense we have of her life as a soliloquy." Again drawing on her own experience, she has sympathy for Leonard Woolf, and she sees Virginia's suicide as "heroic"—the highest praise in Elizabeth's lexicon—determined as she was not to be a burden any longer. *Heroic* was also her word for the Brontë sisters, who managed to triumph over the multiple impediments of poverty, gender, and the disruptions of their troubled brother, Branwell.

* * *

The 1974 Pulitzer winners were announced in May. Elizabeth had been a member of the jury that unanimously recommended *Gravity's Rainbow*, Thomas Pynchon's complex, experimental, and highly regarded novel, but the fourteen-member Pulitzer board refused to honor this choice.[13] Although there was no official comment, some board members described the book as "unreadable" and partly "obscene."[14] Yet they apparently had no moral scruples about giving Cal the poetry prize for *The Dolphin*.

In June, Elizabeth published "Sad Brazil" in the *New York Review.* She had returned to the country in late March for a few days to soak up local color. Twelve years had passed since her visit with Cal to Elizabeth Bishop, who was now living in Boston. The earlier trip had flavored her recent essay about her years at the Hotel Schuyler: a hotel maid had "the inexplicable, spendthrift manic energy that built Brasilia and which, like the spirit of her people, would suddenly subside into languors and torpors."[15] Now, to illustrate the aggressive newness of the country, Elizabeth evoked a scene of cars in São Paulo, "with their attractive, volatile occupants," streaming past a beggar leaning on a wall. Her ironic verdict was that the city must have been "conceived in order to be dramatically photographed from an airplane." Decades later Elizabeth's experience of the "beautiful megalomaniac natural phenomenon" of the "vast, dominating" landscape would illuminate her foreword to an English-language edition of a novel by the Brazilian author Machado de Assis, who had turned his back on this natural splendor to dwell on the "interiors of Victorian houses and the interiors of the minds of his memory-bound, compulsive narrators."[16]

* * *

Elizabeth's Bloomsbury essay in *Seduction and Betrayal* had elicited an angry letter from Paul Levy, editor of previously unpublished work by Lytton Strachey that was the target of Elizabeth's distaste ("an indiscretion") for its sexually tinged anecdotes.[17] She responded with an apology, he said later, "a cross between a sort of love letter and a command" to visit her in Castine.[18] Levy turned up in early August and came along to a party at the home of Mary McCarthy and her husband. Everyone was clustered around the rented television set—summer people didn't own TVs in those days—to watch President Nixon's resignation speech.

Elizabeth was now summering in the refurbished barn at the

waterfront. ("Will the barn consent to become what I have decided to make of it?" she would write in *Sleepless Nights*. "The claims and cries of Lightolier, Design Research, colored rugs on the painted wood.")[19] The new two-story wing added two baths and three bedrooms, one of which she used as her office. She loved the way the windows in her bedroom made the water at high tide look as though it lapped at the foot of her bed. Glass doors in the living room provided a view of the Bagaduce River and the tiny town of Brooksville on the far shore.

This may have been the summer someone took a snapshot of Elizabeth and Mary sitting together in a boat—Elizabeth beaming in her trademark headscarf, Mary in a huge straw hat.[20] A few months earlier Mary had called *Seduction and Betrayal* "seductive" and "very Southern . . . intensely feminine," in a letter to Jason Epstein.[21] It's not clear what she meant by applying the *Southern* label; perhaps she associated it with what she described as Elizabeth's ability to combine "passages of the purest literary insight" with "practical, common-sensical speculations . . . as if all these people, dead or imaginary, were real and living a few blocks down the street."

Back in "violent and expensive" New York that autumn, Elizabeth slipped and broke a bone in her foot, obliging her to hobble around with a cast for ten days, feeling tired and irritated. She described herself as "hopelessly overworked" but "cheerfully anxious" in a late November letter to Cal.[22] He and Elizabeth had been on a friendly footing since the spring, when she expressed her concern about his hospitalization for lithium intoxication during a visit to New York. In December, when *Seduction and Betrayal* made a year's best list in the *Observer*, he praised the essays as having "the passion of fiction."[23]

To usher in the new year, Elizabeth stayed with Mary in snowy Castine, marveling at a "landscape startling in its grandeur and strangeness, almost lunar."[24] Despite this invitation and other aspects of their friendship, Mary—assuming her role of Superior Woman—

had a habit of gossiping about Elizabeth behind her back. Whether in jealous response to the success of this book, or simply because she couldn't help herself, Mary wrote to Hannah Arendt that Elizabeth was one of "a whole collection of neurotically afflicted friends . . . almost abnormally rational [and yet] they fall apart when outside their own controlled environment."[25] Considering what Elizabeth had been through as Cal's wife, this judgment seems both shockingly hard-hearted and inaccurate. In another letter, Mary offered a barbed description of Elizabeth's conversational style in Castine: "Lizzie's tongue rattles, like a child's toy, sometimes making amusing sounds."[26] A contentious property tax issue that summer elicited Mary's remark that Elizabeth "has most of her facts insistently wrong."[27] It appears that she was simply trying to square her belief in an assessment that would raise taxes for schools in poorer areas of Maine with the inequity of judging Nelson Rockefeller's 14.5-acre estate on Mount Desert Island and the home of a mill worker in Portland according to the same standard. Elizabeth remained fond of Mary ("I love her more and more") but felt lonely in Castine, where social life was completely centered on couples "with their gardens . . . their perfect cooking, their dinners for eight (that is four couples)."[28] This was literally and figuratively miles away from what she was used to—"the anarchic life of the city."[29]

Along with Maya Angelou and the poet Nikki Giovanni, Elizabeth received an honorary doctor of letters degree from Smith College that winter. According to the account in the local paper, she delivered her talk, "Necessity and the Romantic Will in Creative Women," in "a somewhat disorganized manner and with a pronounced Southern accent."[30] Discussing the lives and works of George Sand, Mary Wollstonecraft, and Margaret Fuller, Elizabeth stressed that a writer's greatness was a matter not only of personal experience but also of a connection to "common life." All three women supported themselves by writing, and through their writing came to define "their essential nature." Elizabeth reminded her audience—as she often did in her lectures—that society is indifferent to artistic creation; the arts are "a self-propelled activity."

Not that it was easy to propel oneself. In September she began a three-month appointment as Elizabeth Drew Professor of English Literature at Smith. Before leaving town to teach, she tried to reassure herself that she would be able to write her novel. As she explained to Mary, "It is very important for me to have a project that stands there like the good friends I leave when I have to go away alone. . . . I think I found the key that will make it possible to write it, and then at other times I am not sure."[31] Elizabeth stayed on campus from Monday to Wednesday, returning with relief to her books and records at the New York apartment. Her Northampton apartment was depressing in its starkness, with "nothing but the faithful phone to break the sense of loneliness."[32] But she did appreciate the New England landscape ("our Disneyland of autumn foliage") and the "beautiful, serene" college library, open until midnight. Ensconced there, she found herself "transported by Spinoza's Ethics."[33] On days when she had a "settled feeling," she worked on her novel. As she wrote to Cal in early 1976, progress amounted to "one trembling paragraph per day," but she was determined "to persevere," describing a frame of mind that made "the life of literature beautiful and thrilling."[34]

Elizabeth also continued to teach at Barnard and lead a graduate writing workshop at Columbia University School of the Arts. The writer Elizabeth Benedict, who had a senior tutorial with Elizabeth, described her "languid Kentucky drawl, her easy laughter, and her unvarnished criticism, delivered with a disarming originality that took away some of the sting."[35] Sometimes there was just a sting: returning a story by a student who has since become a much-lauded novelist, Elizabeth said she had wanted to read it, "but I couldn't finish it, it was just so bad."[36] In a similar vein, the novelist Susan

Elizabeth at Columbia School of the Arts, ca. 1982.

Minot recalled that after reading the first line of another student's story "in a tremulous Southern accent, Elizabeth said it was like the curtain rising on an unpromising play."[37] Cue tears in the eyes of the young woman who had written the piece. "She didn't sugar-coat things," Minot said. "One time I heard her say, 'I don't want to encourage someone to work at this when it's not good work.'" At times—prompted by her exasperation with poorly written stories—she proposed rules for writing, urging her students to be "selective about details" and not show a character walking across the room.[38] Minot remembered Elizabeth declaring that she did not want to read another mention of *socks*.[39]

Elizabeth "loomed large . . . almost as though she was a char-acter in a novel," the novelist Anna Quindlen said. "That combina-tion of charm and brilliance, and manners, and steel-trap mind."[40] Students felt there was something formidable about Elizabeth. "You didn't feel like you were going to be pals with her," Minot said. In a class full of young people in casual attire, her presence was memorable: a chain-smoker with curled hair, wearing eyeliner and bright lipstick. Her skirts were full, her blouses were neatly pressed, and her shoes were low heels or elegant flats. The novelist Mona Simpson thought Elizabeth's style gave the impression that she was "too busy to care how she looked but just happened to look great."[41] While some students were put off by her Southern-ness and her critical edge, others found her fascinating. Frances Connell fondly recalled the way Elizabeth would gesture "as if there were an imaginary audience over her shoulder."[42] Sigrid Nunez was surely not alone in being curious about "how she lived, what she ate, and what she did when she wasn't with us."[43] Because of the fracas around *The Dolphin*, Elizabeth's private life had become all too public. In Benedict's view, this "taught us about the messiness of adulthood and the consolations of literature in the midst of it."[44]

Mary Gordon had been writing only poetry at Barnard. "You're a prose writer, honey," Elizabeth told her.[45] When Gordon showed her the manuscript for *Final Payments*, Elizabeth asked why she had written a first-person narrative in the third person. "She sat down with me and did two pages," Gordon recalled. The revised novel received a contract with Random House and became a best-seller that was adapted for a film. "Her praise was difficult to achieve," Gordon said, "and when you got it, you felt anointed."[46] But this student-teacher relationship was ultimately fraught. Although Elizabeth threw Gordon a publication party, she had refused to blurb the book. "One day she might write something we'll be proud of," she told Gordon's editor.[47] Elizabeth was not interested in the kind of narrative-driven fiction Gordon wrote. Years later, at a dinner at a writers' conference in Sicily, Gordon disagreed with Elizabeth's praise of a particular writer. "What would you know about it," she snapped, fueled by several drinks. "You've never written an interesting sentence in your life." After that, the two women did not speak for more than two decades. During Elizabeth's last year, there was a rapprochement: Elizabeth asked Gordon about her family and complimented the younger writer on her hair and complexion. But the subject of writing did not come up. After Elizabeth's death, Gordon said she "mourned the loss of her brilliance" but also "the pain that she had caused by her appetite for malice."

Others were more accepting of Elizabeth's sharp pronouncements. "You did brace yourself," Minot said. "I could say something wrong and she could comment on it not in a mean way but in a sharp way, with a smile. Her brain couldn't help but point out something."[48] It was not a style particularly suited to nurturing a promising talent. "I wouldn't say that was her goal," Minot said. "It was to uphold literary standards. She truly loved literature. When she would talk about other writers and work that she loved, it was fascinating." Elizabeth's apartment, with its double-story bookshelves, "really was like a temple devoted to books and book reading," Minot said. "Books open on chairs, the dent on the sofa where she had been sitting. I think she just read for hours."

Elizabeth Benedict described Elizabeth's writing classes as "inhaling the vapors of Hardwick. . . . It was just sort of being in the room with her. . . . It wasn't about how many pages you wrote. . . . She wasn't there to pick apart sentences. I just remember a general chatting about this and that and about her life and not having any money."[49] Benedict described Elizabeth as "rare and exotic," because of her accent, with a "languid and eccentric" affect, "just saying what was on her mind." Although her mild encouragement of Benedict's writing was of a different degree than her early praise of Gordon, she was "as generous as I asked her to be. She would say that the only thing she could do for a student is tell you what to read."

Daphne Merkin, who had so insightfully reviewed *Seduction and*

Betrayal as a Barnard student, singled out Elizabeth's "elusive quality" as a teacher. "I was always interested in the way she said things . . . it was almost like an aside that you were free to take up."[50] Merkin recalled Elizabeth's "Southern, feminine presentation of self," with "a kind of laugh somewhere between delighted and conspiratorial." With her "almost turquoise blue eyes always rimmed with liner," she was invested in "remaining seductive," viewing the world with "a flirtatious mind." Although Elizabeth clearly believed Merkin had talent, "there was something about her that I kept a slight distance from," Merkin said. "I didn't want to be her acolyte or protégé." There was, it seemed, a level of untrustworthiness: "She'd say one thing *to* you and another *about* you." They did stay in touch over the years. But when Elizabeth offered to read the manuscript of Merkin's first novel, *Enchantment*, chapters from which had already been published in *The New Yorker* and *Partisan Review*, she didn't think she wanted additional input.

On Elizabeth's tenth anniversary at Barnard, she merited a lengthy interview in the college newspaper.[51] She said she was trying to return to fiction and would prefer not to write more criticism, though she would probably have to continue for financial reasons. Literary criticism, she explained, is "not a question of having the right opinion. It's a question of establishing a certain authority. . . . It's a question of keeping up, on a high level, a sort of literary dialogue." (In her *Paris Review* interview, she also stressed "the authority of the voice . . . the quality of [the critic's] mind.")[52] Speaking of fiction, Elizabeth noted that people no longer expected that something you had done in your youth would "come back and haunt you"—a common theme in novels of the past. "In the mid-twentieth-century, we don't believe in this long moral causality." (She could not have predicted the return of public shaming in the era of social media.) The result, she said, has been a deemphasis on plot in favor of "catch[ing] little moments of experience." To pull this off successfully, she said, writers needed an "ironic spirit" like the one that animates stories by Renata Adler, Guy Davenport, Donald Barthelme, and Kurt Vonnegut.

Turning to the teaching of writing, Elizabeth said that rather than help students revise their work, she preferred "to stimulate a whole questioning of the process, how you go about it, and what's worth writing, and what's being written." She looked for students who read all the time, discussed books, and thought about literature "as a philosophical and moral question." She lacked sympathy with students who "think short stories are written out of sensation and feelings," which are, she said, among "the most difficult things to make real in literature."

In 1978, after a campus lecture by John Cheever, whose controversial novel *Falconer* had just been published, Elizabeth was irritated at the trivial questions students asked. "There was nothing about the inspiration," she told an interviewer.[53] "People who don't really have the gift or who don't have the discipline of an artist always think there's some little mechanical thing: 'If I do it every day I'll be all right.' . . . First of all, you have to have something to say and then you do have to have a gift for language. You have to be *interesting*." Elizabeth once again leaned on this bland adjective, endowing it with an aura of mental acuity and glittering promise. But she thought *Falconer*, with its prison setting, drug use, and homosexual encounters, was "a very disagreeable, peculiar book"; elsewhere she admitted that she had "no attraction to dissipation and disorder" in fiction.[54] And yet, she read this book twice. Perhaps that was because, in a dark corner of life, Cheever had found a vein of spiritual redemption—the very aspect she believed was no longer a valid theme for fiction. (He had written earlier to the *New York Review* to dispute her opinion that an appeal to the sense of original sin was no longer valid in fiction.)[55] A few years later she praised "the great imaginative force" of his evocation of prison life."[56]

* * *

When Elizabeth saw promise in a student, especially one with whom she identified in some way, she would go to great lengths to help. Nancy Lemann, who grew up in New Orleans, remembered her teacher as "such a pivotal person in my life."[57] Elizabeth would say, "Honey, come over" to the apartment, so that they could work on Lemann's manuscript, spread out on the floor. She promised to write a supportive letter to the publisher of her student's choice. Bowled over by a lecture given by Knopf editor Gordon Lish (a fan of Elizabeth's writing, as it happened), Lemann chose him, so Elizabeth wrote her letter, and that's how Lemann came to publish her first novel, *Lives of the Saints*. Although many of Elizabeth's suggestions involved "little elegant touches" that changed a clunky phrase to a smooth one, even a protégé could receive the blast of Elizabeth's negative opinion. Once in reviewing a draft of *Lives*, she said, "Honey, when I looked at this, this is hideous, girl!" In class, Lemann said, Elizabeth could be "scary . . . her comments were withering for the most part." Even in later years, when she sent her new book to Elizabeth, "it was still scary when you got the letter." Lemann was put off by the intellectualism of the *New York Review*, baffled by the praise for *Sleepless Nights*, and regretful that Elizabeth did not care for the fiction of fellow Southerner Walker Percy. But she admired the flesh-and-blood Elizabeth, with her "unpretentious" remarks ("Honey, it's adorable!").

Elizabeth was Mona Simpson's thesis adviser in the early 1980s. "Everything she did for me was overwhelmingly positive," Simpson recalled, speaking of Elizabeth's help with the manuscript of her first novel, *Anywhere But Here* (1986).[58] "She had nice hands, and they would sort of hover over a few paragraphs, and she would say, 'Here, here, here' . . . to identify areas of heat and thinness." Once when Simpson showed her a story with "some suggestion of sexual inappropriateness" that she herself felt embarrassed about, Elizabeth "had her oval, filed fingernail exactly on the place. 'Mona,' she said, 'this is a wonderful story, but nobody wants to read *this*.'" Simpson also took a literature class from Elizabeth, which involved reading a book a week—a book Elizabeth would reread the night before, as she told an interviewer, in order to freshen her memory of it.[59] "She would conduct [the class] like an adult book club," Simpson said, "accepting of [students'] alternate interpretations. . . . She was a wonderful teacher, very very wry and funny and subtle. And very patient."

Frances Connell, who grew up in St. Louis, said she had felt a kinship with Elizabeth because they came from large, economically straitened families with stay-at-home mothers who "suppressed their own history." They both had a "Flannery O'Connor attraction to this Southern Protestant stern spiritual core" and "saw politics as the way to make the world right."[60] For her senior thesis, Connell was working on a novel about a large family with generations of mental illness.[61] Rather than discussing that topic, Elizabeth suggested that she simplify the narrative by removing some of the characters and read Christina Stead's novel *The Man Who Loved Children*. Elizabeth urged her to give up her graduate scholarship to the University of British Columbia in favor of the University of Virginia, where she could study with Peter Taylor. In a letter introducing her to Taylor, Elizabeth called Connell "a fantastic writer" who "has read everything, takes criticism very well."[62] After Connell spent several years teaching in Afghanistan and was writing about her experience of living there, Elizabeth invited her for lunch at the apartment. "We were eating quiche and a mushroom soup which she had made herself, and the table was beautifully set," Connell recalled. "She said, 'You don't want to become a writer who can only write about Afghanistan; you need to write about your own society.'"[63] Connell appreciated Elizabeth for "inspiring us with her excitement about good writing" and for her interest in "the particular weirdness of human-kind. . . . She spent a lot of time observing people and listening and fine-tuning that into something larger than one conversation."

Another young writer Elizabeth helped—by arranging a university scholarship for her—was Gayl Jones, an African American student at Henry Clay High School in Lexington. She published her acclaimed first novel, *Corregidora*, in 1975. A brief, graphic account of a 1940s blues singer's attempt to come to terms with the sexual oppression that was the legacy of slavery—a slave owner had sired generations of her family—it was widely praised.[64] More books followed, while Jones became increasingly reclusive. In 1998 her husband committed suicide after a standoff with Lexington police. A troubled man with a police record, he had sent angry letters to Jones's former editor at Random House, the novelist Toni Morrison. When the local paper called Elizabeth for comment, she dismissed the notion that she was Jones's mentor. "We never corresponded," she said. "She came to my apartment once."[65] Now the two women are linked in the Hardwick/Jones Reading Series, inaugurated in 2004 at the Kentucky Women Writers Conference.

* * *

Elizabeth took on a new project in 1976, serving as advisory editor for the eighteen-book Arno Press series *Rediscovered Fiction by American Women: A Personal Selection*. Her brief introduction to the series explains that the novels were "chosen for merit, whole or partial"— she was not one to overpraise—as examples of early work by major authors (e.g., *Work*, by Louisa May Alcott), books that were once popular (Octave Thanet's *The Anglomaniacs*), or "brilliant works of literature more or less unknown."[66] Among the later were novels by Ruth Suckow, Evelyn Scott, and Josephine Herbst.

In January, Elizabeth served on another jury—for the PEN translation prize—despite her desire to give up this work, "because I never have a winner, always somehow ending up intimidated."[67] So much for complaints from certain quarters that *she* was the intimidating one. (After her death, Joel Conarroe, president of the Guggenheim Foundation, said that Elizabeth "sometimes made fellow jurors feel as if they had no literary judgment whatsoever.")[68]

Her intensely sympathetic memoir of Billie Holiday was published in the *New York Review* in March.[69] In this piece, she recalls her first view of the singer—"large, brilliantly beautiful," with "the lascivious gardenia . . . the heavy laugh, marvelous teeth"—as well as later encounters, when she intuited "the deepest melancholy in her black eyes." Thoughts about the past, never far from Elizabeth's mind, surfaced again in April, when Cal spent time with her while he visited New York for a performance of *Old Glory*. Back in England, he wrote that he missed "having you to talk to. I feel deeply all you had to put up with me for so many years."[70] His new poem "Central Park" contained the lines " 'After so much suffering,' you said, / 'I realize we couldn't have lasted / more than another year or two anyway.' "[71] Whether he was quoting her accurately this time is unknown.

In June, Elizabeth gave a ten-day criticism seminar at the Graduate Center of City University, which cut into her precious time in Castine. But repairs at the house had been costly, and she welcomed opportunities to make money by guest lecturing—much as these occasions often bored her, with their "dull, perfunctory dinners and cocktail parties."[72] Summer marked a pleasant change from routine: she was now able to take advantage of regularly scheduled New York–to-Bangor flights to avoid the long drive to Maine. Yet the season was shadowed by Cal's recently published *Selected Poems*, which included excerpts from *The Dolphin*. Elizabeth experienced "a pounding of feelings," as she once again encountered "images . . . like knives, slicing through the block of experience."[73] Cal responded that he regretted believing that he needed to include some of the letter-based poems.[74]

In late August both Lowells appeared on a panel at the PEN International Conference in London. Afterward Cal wrote to Elizabeth that it had been "comforting and enjoyable" to see her, and that seeing her and Caroline "easily (?) together" was "so strange . . . that I almost feel I shouldn't refer to it."[75] After reading Elizabeth's Billie Holiday essay, he had intuited that the novel she was working on would be "something close to autobiography," yet "artfully angled and chosen, so that the form might seem startlingly experimental." He suggested that she could incorporate "anything about me . . . even what you haven't shown me."[76] As Saskia Hamilton points out in her introduction to *The Dolphin Letters*, the burning issue in their correspondence during these years and in their published work was "a debate about the limits of art."[77] In this letter, Cal addressed both the public use of private material and the need to create new ways of expressing it.

His own life was hurtling into a period of enormous chaos. Another manic episode sent him back to Greenways Nursing Home until late October. Caroline chose to leave on her own for Cambridge, Massachusetts, where the family would live while Cal taught at Harvard. In November, soon after he arrived at their rented apartment, a blowup with Caroline led him to stay with Frank Bidart for ten days. After her suicide attempt, she returned to England. Elizabeth wrote to Mary McCarthy that she had spent several hours with Cal, who was "weeping and saying he would do anything he could to make the marriage work."[78] He returned to England for Christmas.

* * *

That autumn Elizabeth published a wide-ranging, if somewhat disjointed, essay about why "the private and serious drama of guilt" was no longer meaningful in contemporary fiction.[79] She wrote that *Speedboat*, Renata Adler's elliptical new novel, offered an alternative in which there was "a sense of the way experience seizes and lets go, leaving incongruities." The voice is that of a young woman "gaz-ing out from a center of a complicated privilege, looking about with a coolness that transforms itself into style and also into meaning." Elizabeth contrasts the shaping intelligence of *Speedboat* with current American novels that were (in her view) mostly concerned with sex and yet were "the most traditional in form and imagination," often concluding with "accidents, illness, or death."

Another book she cited was Francine du Plessix Gray's sexu-ally graphic semi-autobiographical novel *Lovers and Tyrants*, about a woman's life in pursuit of personal liberation. Discussing the way contemporary novelists are still "reluctant . . . to leave so much of life morally unaccounted for," she assumed the hysterectomy Gray's heroine undergoes is a "rebuke to her promiscuity." Gray wrote to her months later to disagree with this interpretation. She admired Elizabeth as "the greatest craftsman of English language in the coun-try," but she disliked the way the erotic freedom of men's writing was criticized when it occurred in novels by women.[80] Yet Elizabeth was invariably hostile to feminist-themed novels that failed to meet her standards for stylistic brilliance.

* * *

Elizabeth's social life was in full swing during the 1970s ("going about in my black dresses and high heels"),[81] to the point where she would complain about "deadly parties," as contrasted with "telephone therapy with friends," which "keeps the spirit almost together."[82] She described a cocktail party for forty-five guests that she gave for Ste-phen Spender as "the most unrewarding expenditure."[83] But smaller gatherings could be immensely satisfying. "In the long run," she wrote, "I think I would rather have my literary friends than any-thing, any family; they are what count, and I feel they know about love." In February 1976, Arthur Schlesinger, Jr., wrote in his journal about the "uncommonly pleasant evening" he spent at her house the previous night, with Mary McCarthy, Bob Silvers, and Susan Sontag, who was undergoing chemotherapy for breast cancer.[84]

Elizabeth had grown close to Sontag, now that "her ideas are a good deal less chic and narrow than they used to be and the beautiful energy is very special."[85] She struck Elizabeth as having "a sort of orphan quality" that made her dependence on Silvers, Barbara Epstein, and herself especially vital.

Seventeen years younger than Hardwick, Sontag had begun writing for the fledgling *New York Review of Books* in 1963, the year she published *The Benefactor*. Asked by Farrar, Straus and Giroux to provide a blurb for this novel of ideas, Elizabeth offered stiffly cautious praise: Sontag was "strikingly able to write about serious subjects in a felicitous manner."[86] But by the early 1970s, the women had become close friends, at least as far as Elizabeth was concerned. In December 1975 she wrote to Sontag that she was "very happily" looking forward to Christmas, in part because she felt "free" and was "starting to write again with a great deal of pleasure."[87] Elizabeth's state of mind might have been influenced by her affair with "Ben"— Ben O'Sullivan, an international tax and literary estate lawyer who would later represent Mary in the defamation suit brought by Lillian Hellman—a romance that apparently fizzled out by June. "How odd it is in these things that are not quite the deepest and truest, but are still very near and important to us," she wrote to Sontag that month. "When the time comes to go the suffering is real and yet it is also from the first a relief. I am happy and of course full of problems and anxieties and jokes—that is the way it is."[88] (Another man in her life was Corliss Lamont, a philanthropist and former director of the American Civil Liberties Union. She told a close friend that she dropped him because he was cheap, counting out nickels for tips at restaurants.)[89]

Now, she told Sontag, she was working every day on her novel and feeling that she would be able to pull it off. Meanwhile, having promised to write a piece about Thomas Mann, she had galloped through *The Magic Mountain, Buddenbrooks*, and *Doctor Faustus*, "most of the stories, the new and old letters, the little books coming out now"—all in just a few days. Mann's novels alone would have been an enormous amount of reading, well over two thousand pages, even granted that Elizabeth had probably read most of them years earlier. She confessed to Sontag that she felt she had "nothing to say." In fact, of course, her long essay, "Thomas Mann at 100," contained many well-considered ideas. While times had changed, and "Mann's elaborate heroes . . . already cast in their own bronze" were no longer in fashion, "what ties them to our time is their demonism, their hidden passions," and their inability to attain the balanced state of mind of ordinary people "because of their violent consciousness and vulnerability." (A few years later Elizabeth would write about another dauntingly magisterial literary figure, William Faulkner, whose "magical, unique texts . . . with their passions that ask everything of the receiving mind, ask that the sensibility submit to a profound saturation.")[90]

Elizabeth had urged Sontag to hurry and finish her current book (*On Photography*) so that she could finish her next novel.[91] That summer Sontag wrote to tell Elizabeth that she was having "immense difficulty" completing the last two essays in the book "because of you."[92] *Seduction and Betrayal* "made it impossible for me to be satisfied with my essay writing. Belatedly, and largely through your example, I've understood something about prose I never really grasped." After asking whether Elizabeth had completed her Mann piece, she wrote, "I would love to see it." And then—touchingly, as if she were either expressing too much emotion, or sounding trite—she replaced the crossed-out words "would love" with "want."

Despite their vastly different essay styles—Elizabeth offered an elliptical series of acute perceptions; Sontag proceeded from a conceptual, theoretical standpoint—Elizabeth became an ardent fan.

In her introduction to *A Susan Sontag Reader*, she invoked Sontag's "large and coherent sensibility," "the urbanism of her spirit," and her "speculative, studious, and yet undogmatic" writing.[93] As if under the spell of her formidable subject, Elizabeth's piece only rarely gives free rein to her own idiosyncratic voice—the one that pinpoints Sontag's "rather anxious and tender authority—the reward of passion." In the pages of *Vogue*, Elizabeth offered a more personal view, describing Sontag as "a romantic of the intellectual life" and comparing her "dramatic entrance" on the scene to that of Mary McCarthy. Yet the two women's "thought and temperament" are essentially different. Lauding Sontag's "obsessive concern with form . . . a fascination with the extreme," Elizabeth bestowed the ultimate Hardwickian praise: "the most *interesting* American woman of her generation."[94] Years later Sontag would celebrate Elizabeth's "beautiful sentences, more beautiful sentences than any living American writer."[95]

* * *

Cal returned to Cambridge for the spring 1977 semester—a plan initially postponed by his hospitalization for congestive heart failure. In March a quick visit to Caroline, now living in Ireland, made him feel that his new marriage was doomed. Now he was constantly calling Elizabeth. She agreed that he could return to his studio at the apartment if he lacked a place to stay when the semester ended. Caroline flew to New York in May to attend his award ceremony at the American Academy of Arts and Letters, a stormy visit that resolved nothing. Told that Caroline should not be left alone in her depressed condition, he anxiously stayed with her until he needed to return to Boston for a week, whereupon she returned to Ireland.

In the summer, Cal accompanied Elizabeth to Castine, where he worked on essays about Franklin, Emerson, Hawthorne, Thoreau, and other eminent Americans, in a rented boathouse on the beach, a short stroll from Elizabeth's home. Life with Cal was "no great

Elizabeth and Cal in Mary McCarthy's garden,
Castine, August 1977 (detail).

renewed romance," she wrote to Mary, "but a kind of friendship, and listening to his grief. There is no thought of getting a divorce, but there is a general peacefulness (except when there isn't) and a great preoccupation with Caroline, her future, the children."[96] Elizabeth had felt "quite lonely much of the time and worried about the future." Much as she liked being on her own in New York, it was comforting to have Cal with her in Castine: "We are trying to work out a sort of survival for both of us."

Elizabeth wrote to Robert Silvers that she was working every day on her novel, making fixes "that gleam out like flares."[97] Revision was what she liked best about writing: "You're up against your mind, you're up against your experience, you're up against the quality of your insights, you're up against your command of language, up against your knowledge, you're up against your moral vision."[98] Cal was still trying to stay in touch with Caroline, writing to her and calling her for hours-long conversations in the early afternoons. Elizabeth paid the bills.

Rilla Bray, who was a teenager when she worked for Elizabeth that summer as a house cleaner, recalled her as "kind, thoughtful, generous" and "very interested in who I was. She wanted to know about my life."[99] The Lowells would invite her to sit and have coffee before the vacuuming began. Elizabeth was sorting through possessions she was ready to part with, telling Bray a story about each one; she gave the girl bags of clothing and other items to share with her family. Bray remembered Elizabeth saying, several times, "I am so in love with my husband"—a revealing expression of her feelings couched in a white lie about her marital status that she may have thought appropriate for a teenager. Bray said she confided her own romantic problems to Elizabeth and Cal, who "talked about love with me."

The Maine interlude was interrupted in July by a ten-day visit to Russia, where Cal and Elizabeth were both part of an all-expenses-paid cultural exchange sponsored by the Charles E. Kettering Foundation, a nonpartisan research entity, and the Soviet Writers Union. Other American literary eminences on the trip included Edward Albee, William Styron, and Norman Cousins, editor of the *Saturday Review*. Styron recalled that although a seating error had placed the Lowells in the nonsmoking section, Cal insisted on smoking anyway.[100] During a stopover in Frankfurt, he "led a revolt" in a restaurant—ordering bottles of expensive wine—despite warnings by the group's officious minder to economize. At the hotel in Moscow, while several members of the group waited impatiently for food they had ordered, Cal left and was gone so long that Elizabeth went to his room to investigate. He had fallen asleep, a sign of the fatigue that led the Lowells to leave for the United States before the event was over. After Cal's death months later, Styron said that he had seemed melancholy; speaking of a hoped-for visit to Pasternak's grave, Cal had said, "We all have one foot in the grave."

Perhaps partly inspired by this trip, Elizabeth responded to a query from *The New York Times Book Review*—"Who is the living author you most admire?"—by choosing Aleksandr Solzhenitsyn, whose "claim upon the spirit is immense."[101] She decided to read two of his works, "Matronya's House" and *Cancer Ward*, before responding. None of the other authors who answered the question offered such deeply considered and richly wrought prose to explain their choices, and the only other living non-Anglophone authors proposed were Heinrich Böll (Muriel Spark) and Gabriel García Márquez (Norman Mailer, Anne Tyler).

In early August, Elizabeth wrote to Robert Silvers to empathize with his parting from a lover. She knew that it would be ideal if "the moment of the end" would come at the same time for both parties.[102] "But, of course, it can't be; whoever utters the first goodbye is inevitably because of that 'ahead.' And so anger, resentment, the whole thing." But her life with Cal had changed: "I don't feel vulnerable, don't feel sent out on approval, as it were. . . . We are just going along, having a very agreeable time." On July 28 she and Cal had realized that, had he not left, they would have been married for twenty-eight years. "I cannot say that such a record would have been a certain glory," she wrote. "So, don't worry, darling. It is not all up to <u>him</u>." Elizabeth was reading *Eugene Onegin* "in the odd Nabokov translation" and worried about her upcoming guest teaching position at the University of Connecticut, thinking that she would "try to slide by on the grease of <u>personality</u>." Frank Bidart, who visited in late August, recalled that the Lowells were "quite nice to each other—extremely warm and comfortable—but at the same time he seemed, emotionally, in a kind of suspended animation."[103] That month Cal inscribed a copy of *Day by Day*: "For Lizzie / Who snatched me out of chaos, / With all my love."[104]

Back in Caroline's house in Ireland in early September, he became increasingly upset with her. Although he had planned to return to Boston on September 15, he decided instead to fly to New York on the twelfth. Elizabeth, worried about both his physical and mental health, agreed to let him stay with her, telling Harriet that he was "worthy of care."[105] He took a taxi from Kennedy Airport to the apartment on West 67th Street, holding a package that contained a portrait of Caroline by Lucien Freud. (She had asked him to have it appraised.)[106] Among the items in his briefcase were testaments to his divided affections: a photograph from the 1960s of himself, Elizabeth, and young Harriet in a small boat, and a more recent one of a smiling Elizabeth at the doorway of the barn in Castine.

When the taxi reached Elizabeth's building, the elevator operator called up to her. She came down and peered into the taxi. Cal was slumped in the backseat. The two of them rode the eight blocks to Roosevelt Hospital. As she said later, she knew he was already dead. When she discovered that she didn't have a dime for the pay phone to call Harriet, she had to pay someone ten dollars for the ten-cent piece. In the space on the death certificate for "informant," she listed herself simply as Lowell's "friend"—a word that perhaps best summed up her nearly thirty-year relationship with this brilliant, troubled man.[107]

The funeral was held four days later, at the Church of the Advent in Boston, with six hundred mourners in attendance. Elizabeth, who had taken Caroline to buy suitable clothes, watched as she shook with grief during the service; at one point, she walked out with her children. Mary had butted in, as she was prone to do, writing to Caroline to express her sympathy about the unraveling of the marriage and letting her know that Cal had been visiting Elizabeth in Maine. This enraged the widow, who talked nonstop about Mary's letter at the funeral and on the way to the family graveyard, which Elizabeth described as lying "under a mist of rain, [with] great trees and a few autumn leaves on the ground."[108] Afterward Caroline stayed with Elizabeth for eight days to organize the memorial service, pushing her almost beyond endurance with "her poor drunken theatricality hour after hour."

Finally, Elizabeth fled to a furnished room she had rented in Storrs, Connecticut, for her upcoming teaching stint. "Only then could I burst into sobs and realize that Cal was truly gone forever," she wrote.[109] Living alone "had been much more painful than I thought it reasonable to show, much more lonely and sometimes frightening." The time she had spent with Cal the previous summer and part of the spring "was a wonderful break of lightness and brightness for me." In December she was grieving "more and more," as she sorted through "boxes of letters and things of the past." She wrote sadly that she knew Cal "would like to be stumbling about in his carpet slippers or Bucksport crepe-soles, smoking, drinking vodka, writing."[110] Elizabeth received more than one hundred condolence letters and telegrams from people in the literary world and beyond, many of whom recalled memorable times with Cal—in Iowa City, in New York, in Berkeley, in Boston, in Castine, in Washington, in Europe, in Rio, in Russia. Adrienne Rich wrote movingly of her concern and wondered if her friendship could "be of any solace."[111] Even Lillian Hellman conveyed her sympathies in a brief note.

Back in Castine the following June, Elizabeth found it "very sad to see the dear old warrior's clothes about everywhere: the red shirt, the red socks, the strange green striped trousers—and a box of hundreds of work sheets [of his writing] from the effort of just those two months."[112] Passing the boathouse, which he had rented again for this summer, she felt "a terrible pang." Yet despite all the reminders of Cal in Castine, Elizabeth treasured the time she spent there. She wrote to Elizabeth Bishop about how she had "never loved Maine more, the place itself, my house, and the changing islands which you describe with such perfection."[113] As she later told an interviewer, "Maine has taken the place of Kentucky in my life."[114] On the phone, Frank Bidart had read aloud Bishop's poem "North Haven," in memory of Cal, named for one of the small islands in Penobscot Bay. Alluding to his habit of constant revision, "North Haven" ends by noting that his words are now fixed in perpetuity: "Sad friend, you cannot change." In her letter to Bishop, Elizabeth told her, "This poem moves me unbearably."

During the next few years, she would deal with Caroline's lies and demands. Before his death, Caroline had told people that he was not coming back to her. But afterward she put out the word that she and Cal had mended their rift and that she was going to join him in New York. She complained that the estate had reimbursed Elizabeth for "bills," without bothering to find out that they were for matters to do with his funeral, not for his transatlantic phone calls to his wife. She claimed erroneously that Elizabeth had made Cal see a lawyer that summer in order to leave money for her in his will. It turned out that Caroline was referring to the Lowells' original divorce settlement of 1972. "You see," Elizabeth wrote to Mary, "I don't think she really wanted him, and that had long ago broken his heart, but she could not allow him to wish to leave, to survive."[115] It was Elizabeth's belief that "Cal was terrified of Caroline" during his last summer, "deeply worried about what she might do." And yet this experience "had made Cal a better person, more in touch with the terror of this kind of turmoil than he had ever been before." She had written earlier that the "passion and grief" he experienced made him "more like the rest of us."[116] He had finally experienced the kind of agony she herself had long felt.

More than three years after Cal died, his briefcase was still in her study, along with his cigarettes, cigarette lighter, nail file, and glasses. "Somehow I can't take the other things out," she wrote. "The death is unacceptable and yet I know he has gone and it is very difficult to bring the two together ever."[117] When an interviewer suggested that Lowell had been a burden, she responded that during their years as a couple, "he supported us and was enormously productive. . . . And we had a tremendous interest in common. Every conversation was absolutely original and special."[118]At the end of the sheaf of single-spaced pages of notes she sent to Cal's first biographer after reading his draft of his book, she wrote that even in her husband's last years, "the work he was writing stunned me by its brilliance. . . . his beautiful, free, independent intelligence, still hourly, daily there for him to call upon."[119]

* * *

In 1978 Elizabeth published "Domestic Manners," an ambitious piece about the so-called sexual revolution of the 1960s, and "Wives and Mistresses," which continued aspects of her arguments in the *Seduction and Betrayal* essays. Some of these women were muses of famous men; others served as "the inspiration of poems" or found themselves "expropriated" for fiction. Elizabeth did not take a specifically feminist tack in looking at the lives of these six women—Sophia Tolstoy; Annabella Byron and her daughter, Ada; Anna Dostoevsky; Nadezhda Mandelstam; and Olga Ivinskaya.[120] Instead, she offered a clear-eyed scrutiny of the women's delusions and obsessions. Despite briefly crediting "the great weight of patriarchal baggage" in her opening sentence, she does not see these women as victims of oppression. Rather, they were feisty combatants in their struggles with the men in their lives, battles revealed in a generally self-serving way in their memoirs.

The conflicts involved in living with a hugely difficult man who was also a genius—a version of the life Elizabeth herself knew—led Sophia to be "devoted one minute, embattled the next." Annabella, whose marriage with Byron lasted only a year but who devoted her life to investigating his incestuous relationship with his sister, suffered from "outlandish pride." Ada's mathematical gift was doomed by "maneuver, manipulation, and her own marked self-satisfaction." Most of the essay is devoted to Olga Ivinskaya, Pasternak's mistress.

Elizabeth believes her to have treated his career compassionately in her memoir, yet her "florid" style was "a disaster," and her "hallucinated folly" was to treat his life and its place in history as an aspect of their relationship. Only Anna Dostoevsky and Nadezhda Mandelstam avoided the pettiness of the others—Anna in her plainspoken diary and Nadezhda in her two books, *Hope Against Hope* and *Hope Abandoned*, which constitute "a battle against tyranny and death." In this complex essay, Elizabeth's geopolitical awareness—sharpened during the past decade—joined her novelistic and personal interest in the psychology of couples.

* * *

During Elizabeth's early period in New York, summers back home in Lexington offered rent-free writing time. Now a summer in Maine lent itself to a concentrated focus on *The Cost of Living*, the novel she had begun a few years earlier based on her semiautobiographical story from 1948, "Evenings at Home."[121] (The publication of Marge Piercy's novel *The High Cost of Living* caused her to change the title to *Sleepless Nights*.)[122] Working every day in the summer of 1978 as she combined finished drafts with new thoughts, Elizabeth figured out how to assemble the scenes that made up the novel. It was difficult "to keep up the tone," she told an interviewer. "I would write twenty pages and start doing something else. Because I couldn't figure out where it was going."[123] While the speaker is herself, the scenes are composites of real and imagined events. "What holds it together," she explained, is "the sensibility of the person who has observed these incidents." As she revised the novel, she took pleasure in "working toward the final sentence of a little scene, the crux of sensibility and observation."[124]

The problem of the contemporary novel—what form it could take, at a time when "world horrors have stepped into the bloody shoes of domestic cruelty and private revenge"—was one she had wrestled with a decade earlier in her essay "Reflections on Fiction." The classic novel, she wrote, depended on "tranquility, slow hours and days, the need to discover through the imagination what the world contained. . . . You entered a life, as if you were walking through a door." But the contemporary novelist must contend with a "feeling of borrowed, shortened time and relationships subject to cancellation" as well as with "the very openness of our life, particularly of sexual life, [which] makes the discoveries of fiction far less striking." Already in 1969, Elizabeth was also conscious of the way imaginative writing often seemed less exciting, less "real" than images in the media. She admired the contemporary strategy of presenting "the broken, the episodic, the ironical" as authorial interventions, "whispered from the wings, reminding us not to be swept away, someone is in charge." As she remarked a few years later in her *Paris Review* interview, "there is always the problem of who is seeing, who is thinking. I am excited when I feel the author is trying to cope with this dilemma."[125] The problems involved in translating life to art had taken on a new urgency after *The Dolphin*; it has been suggested that the reticence of *Sleepless Nights*—in which Cal's existence is only hinted at—is at least in part a response to his approach.

In an interview on the front page of *The New York Times Book Review* after the novel was published in 1979, Elizabeth said that although she "was not writing an autobiography," she realized she had "an unconscious identification with damaged, desperate people on the streets, cleaning women, rotters in midtown hotels, failed persons of all kinds. *C'est moi*, in some sense."[126] (She had recently observed a far deeper level of human misery on a three-week lecture trip to India for the U.S. Information Agency. "Nothing in my life has ever struck me with the same degree of profound, unending sadness," she wrote to Mary. "The suffering . . . is as dense, thick, hard as a rock and immovable.")[127] Questioned about the near-invisibility of the narrator's husband, Elizabeth replied that she had discovered the value of using *we* and *ours* as "a way of disposing with marriage." Demonstrating her need to separate herself from Cal's looming posthumous image, she said she "hated the idea" that just because a couple lived together, "they are somehow collaborators in the struggle to create something." She compared her frequent identification as "wife of Robert Lowell" to "putting a little ruffle on a housedress." Although she used her married name in daily life, "the name Lowell has nothing to do with my writing."

She told another interviewer, "I did not want to put my husband in it . . . [because he had] written so fully about marriage and all that. I feel that would be gilding the lily."[128] Yet he *is* in it, namelessly, as "the Mister" (the appellation given by a cleaning woman)—the man who "often [has] the preoccupied look of a secret agent," the man who "reads and writes all day, here in this house on the top floor, drinks quarts of milk, smokes cigarettes."[129] Asked in a more general way whether her closeness to poets and her reading of poetry had influenced her style, Elizabeth genuflected to Cal's "immense learning and love of literature" as "a constant magic" for her.[130] His library may have led her to read "the prose written by poets." What she treasured were "the off-hand flashes . . . the quickness, the deftness, confidence, and even the relief from spelling everything out." To illustrate this, she quoted a sentence in Boris Pasternak's autobiography, *Safe Conduct,* that juxtaposes the beauty of early spring in Moscow with the suicide of the thirty-six-year-old poet Vladimir Mayakovsky.

* * *

"Writing a Novel," the short story Elizabeth published in the *New York Review* in 1973, opens the same way the novel does: "It is June. This is what I am going to do with my life." Among the many fascinations of this piece is her notion of "a short-wave autobiography, one that fades in and out, local voices mixing with the mysterious cadence of a stranger. Truth should be heightened and falsity adorned, dressed up to look like sociable fact." She quotes Pasternak: "To live a life is not to cross a field"—life is no easy stroll.[131] Memoirs were beset by "troubles large and small," as a result of writers' "defamed and libeled" self-portrayal. There was also the problem of a *woman's* memoir, "because there isn't enough sex, not even enough longing for consummation." (She was apparently referring to potential negative opinions of the book she would write.) "In love," she wrote, what really matters "is to discover whether we have experienced conquest or surrender—or neither. Courage under ill-treatment is a woman's theme." Of course, it is very much her theme.

At one point, Elizabeth asks the reader, "Should I choose the events interesting today, or try . . . to remain true to what I felt and thought at the time?" She answers this question by including four letters to "M"—the first one about winter in Boston in 1954; the second (1962), about her move to New York; the third (1972), about her plans to renovate the barn in Maine; the fourth (undated), about her life of "events, upheavals, destructions that caused me to weep like a child." These imaginary letters—also part of the narrative in *Sleepless Nights*—allow Elizabeth to capture the immediacy of aspects of her life and the lives of others and present them in a seemingly intimate manner. At the same time, these missives have a presentational quality, filtered through an awareness of what her friend "M" (Mary McCarthy) would understand and want to hear.[132] In the last sentence of "Writing a Novel," Elizabeth wrote that she "cannot decide whether to call myself 'I' or 'she.'" This metafictional twist had intrigued Gore Vidal and Susan Sontag, who were both surprised that she was going to leave it out in the novel. But she felt that it just didn't make sense.

Elizabeth folded portions of her memoir about Billie Holiday into *Sleepless Nights*, which includes more about the Hotel Schuyler, Greer Johnson, and the down-at-the-heels musicians who stayed in the hotel. Holiday, Elizabeth told an interviewer, "is the only historical character in the book." There are also echoes of "The Faithful," a short story based on her time in Amsterdam.[133] Some scenes in the novel "are rather close to people" she knew in Kentucky, she admitted, including her mother and father.[134] Speaking before the book was published, she worried about her family's response: "I've written very little about myself and about home for that reason." Elizabeth joked that she would need "to write a strong letter . . . saying I do not want any flack from home." In her view, the passages about her family were "completely friendly and loving," and the book as a whole was "deeply tolerant and full of feeling." Having "given her whole life to literature," she felt that her family should acknowledge that she knew what she was doing.

Yet she understood why people who didn't read experimental literature would be shocked to see themselves depicted in her novel. She realized that people generally tended to prefer "a kind of *exterior* sugaring of things," while her portraits were touched by sadness. Elizabeth saw her novel as being "really . . . about poor people." While most of them were deceased, the laundress ("Ida") was still living in Maine. Elizabeth was concerned that the description of this "very bizarre looking" woman made her recognizable. Yet surely, she argued, this passage was a tribute: "I can't believe in her whole life she has ever been as honored as she is through this. This deep looking at her, this lifetime of washing and ironing and cooking and pots on the stove."[135] Although Elizabeth did not mention her mother in this context, her life was likely also "honored" in this way. In a letter to Alfred Kazin, she remarked that "the gap" between the writer's ideas and someone else's is "the problem, aesthetic, always of writing, especially writing that draws on one's life as all of it does and must."[136]

Because her own life was so deeply rooted in literature, Elizabeth said, her narrator needed to have the same background; she didn't want to "have the burden of pretending that I was this person who hadn't read all these books."[137] But the book was not a memoir; Elizabeth was adamant on this point. "Most of the scenes never took place," she insisted. "I don't even know such people. They are types and composites of memory." One of the latter is the scene in which Dr. Z. holds the arm of his lover, Simone, at night as they walk along the canal and he sings "In questa tomba oscura," Beethoven's setting of a poem by Giuseppe Carpani in which a dead man recalls an unfaithful lover. When Elizabeth and Cal had met the poet Eugenio Montale in Florence in 1950, they were unable to communicate—the Lowells didn't speak Italian and he had no English—so he sang that song as they walked on the banks of the Arno River.[138] Elizabeth also claimed that the narrator's affair with "a sort of composite New York intellectual type" ("Alex") never happened.[139] She did admit that her portrait of Greer Johnson was "pretty accurate," but that was possible only because he had died; otherwise she would have worried that his mother might see it.[140] Mary thought she recognized a couple of Castine people, and wondered if "Louisa" was partly based on Caroline Blackwood and Natasha Spender.[141]

Sleepless Nights is dedicated to Harriet and "my friend Mary McCarthy." Elizabeth had given Mary a heads-up about this and the "Dear M." letters in the book, "although of course M. is never identified or described or anything of that sort."[142] Mary astutely observed that the book's "random, almost fugitive reminiscences are held together by a magic centripetal force—the force of suffering, refined to purity."[143] By leaving out Cal, Elizabeth made him "a sort of black hole in outer space . . . which is poetic justice." Mary was somewhat concerned that "the effect . . . of [Elizabeth's] mounting pain will worry some of [her] friends." But she realized that it was just one of many truths about Elizabeth, "as though a secret part spoke suddenly for the whole."

Before the publication of the novel that Elizabeth once thought "wasn't publishable . . . because it was so strange,"[144] she was nervous about its reception and surprised that it merited a first printing of twenty thousand. (The Book of the Month Club offered *Sleepless Nights* as an "alternate" selection, boosting the novel's sales.) Aware that other authors were writing novels with hostile portrayals of former wives and husbands, she told an interviewer, "I don't know why I'm so shy about what I consider the loving reticent portraits."[145] Then again, she said, perhaps the people she wrote about would mind more than the cast-off spouses evoked in other novels. "Some people will hate it and just say it's so vague and it's so allusive and what's it all about," she fretted. But she needn't have worried; the major voices were ecstatic.

Susan Sontag's blurb was a fond tribute: "Nobody writing prose now gives me as much pleasure as Elizabeth Hardwick. She honors our language and enlivens our woe. . . . *Sleepless Nights* is elegant, wise, tasty—a truly wonderful book." On the front page of *The New York Times Book Review,* Joan Didion called the book "subtle and beautiful . . . extraordinary and haunting."[146] She suggested that Elizabeth's "great subject" in her novels and essays was "the mysterious and somnambulistic 'difference' of being a woman." (Months later *Sleepless Nights* was singled out as a *New York Times* Book of the Year.) Novelists expressed a fascination with the book's restrained style as well as its subject.[147] Edmund White wrote that Elizabeth's portraits of the characters were "etched on glass by a diamond, and then the glass has been held up to the full light of a splendid intelligence."[148] He praised the "wisdom" of the novel, with its "melancholy, humorous worldliness, an unsentimental affection for the poor and a cool appraisal of the rich." In the *New York Review,* Diane Johnson called the novel "virtuous and liberated," because of "the charity and empathy with which the author experiences others in the world."[149] With a mastery of both "the startling adjective, the amazing simile," and "the ordinary discursive properties of language," Elizabeth "makes the invisible visible" in the lives she writes about.

The *Village Voice* critic wrote that "by saying just enough, and never too much, she has perfected the art of making private meaning public."[150] In *New York Magazine*, poet and art critic Carter Ratcliff observed that Elizabeth was "a not altogether reluctant captive of memories whose epic complexity she has stilled into a vapor of nuance and regret."[151] Walter Clemons, *Newsweek*'s reviewer, admitted that the lack of suspense "narrows the novel's appeal," but he found it "extraordinary . . . graceful, laconic and wise."[152] *Time* lauded the way Elizabeth "has turned the crutch of feminine sensibility into a dangerous weapon."[153] H. van Galen Last, the Lowells' old friend in the Netherlands, described the novel's main theme as "loss—the loss of relatives, loved ones, and friends, through death or separation. . . . The sleepless nights are the result of the Orpheus feeling—the sense that . . . a look over one's shoulder is enough to see [them] again."[154] Reviewing the novel in *The New Republic*, Daphne Merkin offered an elegant tribute. Writing that "the spirit of melancholy haunts its pages," she identified "the pain that shimmers around the edges of [the novel's] symmetry—the bewilderment and sorrow that has been fashioned, with consummate artistry, into gravures of dark beauty."[155]

Francine du Plessix Gray interviewed Elizabeth for *Vogue*. Evidently still smarting from her review of *Lovers and Tyrants*, Gray included a dig at her "frequently savage sarcasm toward colleagues who fail to meet her criteria" and her lack of support for "women writers who do not meet her demands for 'high style.'"[156] Pressed to answer a question that seemed to come out of the blue—what qualities she "values most in her friends"—Elizabeth returned the volley by singling out "women who are flawed and to whom things don't come easily, like yourself." Gray noted that despite Elizabeth's adherence to elegance—in her furnishings, her clothing, the meals she cooked—she did not like to spend money on personal items, even on stockings, which she wore until her toes stuck through them. But the younger woman failed to make the connection between Elizabeth's frugality and her earlier life, which connected her to the disadvantaged people she wrote about. "I myself am poor people," she said.

In Britain, where the novel became a best-seller, the response was equally positive.[157] Writing in *The Guardian*, novelist Angela Carter found the novel "most moving in its stoical reticence," yet permeated with "a cool, lucid, infinitely haunting anguish."[158] In *The Observer*, literary critic Lorna Sage wrote that all of Elizabeth's "critic's experience and discrimination, all her scepticism about making life over into stories and people into characters . . . has been turned on herself. And the result is an impressively personal book that manages to fit none of the formulas."[159] She found the novel's "sense of strain . . . of tight-strung, nervous energy" to be "essential to its effect of individuality and honesty."

The Observer also published a long interview with Elizabeth, described as "a slim woman who looks younger than her 62 years," whose hair was "tied with a yellow scarf, flapper style," and whose clothes suggested "more Paris than Lexington."[160] Asked whether she had ever written anything for money, Elizabeth said no, choosing to ignore the book reviews and essays she once relied on for income. Her hope for *Sleepless Nights* was that it would have some lasting merit, but the time span she suggested was a mere three months. During the interview, she lit a succession of cigarettes "and put them out before they are half smoked, like a good Southerner." The phone rang constantly, often with women writers calling for advice; to one of them, Elizabeth offered an invitation to visit and bring her manuscript. Writing to a friend, she was less charitable about these "strange and unsettling telephone calls that come as if you . . . could find the time for someone who just happened to think that although they don't know you very well they would like to have a meeting."[161]

Foreign rights for the novel were also sold to France, Sweden, Germany, and Denmark.[162] In France, a gushing magazine article written after Elizabeth attended a conference in Paris imagined this "star of the New York Review of Books" entering "the castle of stone and Vermont marble"—her description of the New York Public Library in her short story "Back Issues"—"much as an ecclesiastical dignitary enters his basilica."[163]

Inevitably, some critics were unsure what to make of a novel that seemed to lack a plot. (About the scarcity of plot in her work, Elizabeth's memorable response was "If I want a plot, I'll watch *Dallas*.")[164] Others, depending on their perspective, took the book to task for being too downbeat, too precious, too reticent, or lacking in political or feminist consciousness. Some insisted that it was autobiography or memoir, not really a novel. Yet even when flaws were spotted, praise was usually forthcoming. While the *Esquire* reviewer tut-tutted that "Hardwick seems to commit herself excessively to the soft emotions of lamentation and regret," she nevertheless acknowledged the novel's "subtlety and power."[165]

CHAPTER 10

Literary Lion

(1980–2007)

Elizabeth enjoyed being a member of New York's cultural A-list, populated with lively, clever people. On the last night of 1979, she was a guest at Woody Allen's New Year's Eve party, along with the playwright Arthur Miller, actors Tammy Grimes and Tony Randall, *Paris Review* editor George Plimpton, historian Arthur Schlesinger, Jr., and other arts elite who filled the four floors of the Rebekah Harkness School of Dance. But the crush of social invitations eventually became overwhelming. She was not above pretending to have the flu to avoid cocktail parties she had promised to attend.

The many nights she spent at home were devoted to reading or watching TV, which she viewed as "soaking in the irrational and the cruel."[1] The presidential campaign between incumbent Jimmy Carter and Ronald Reagan had been dispiriting, like "a lot of huge, fresh zucchini from overstocked gardens, turning up on your doorstep." During the day, Elizabeth found it easier to carve out time to write now that she was living on her own. If an essay was due, she could wake up at six a.m. and work on final changes until the early afternoon. But the pressure of writing all the articles and lectures she had agreed to—"which have suddenly, gloomily, loomed"—was keeping her from making a good start on a new book.

Elizabeth was sympathetic to Mary's bitter quarrel with Lillian Hellman, who had sued Mary for saying (on *The Dick Cavett Show*) that "every word [Hellman] writes is a lie, including 'and' and 'the.'" Having waged her own battle with Hellman over *The Little Foxes*, she wrote that Lillian "will always find a personal, even a political[,] if forced, reason for criticism, anything . . . that will avoid a negative judgment about the quality of her work."[2] It struck Elizabeth, looking back, "how mild, how short, how inadequately written and thought out my 'famous' review actually is. And her response to it: violent, manipulating friends to write letters, 'blacklisting' as it were."[3] Elizabeth's irritation lingered; in 1982 she uncharitably described seventy-seven-year-old Hellman at the American Academy of Arts and Letters award ceremony as "a pitiful wraith in a hat" whose sight was too poor to recognize an enemy.[4] (Elizabeth was the same age as Hellman when she won the academy's Gold Medal for criticism eleven years later.)[5]

Mary wondered what Elizabeth thought of *Robert Lowell: A Life Study*, David Cheshire's 1980 film for BBC Two.[6] She replied that there was "too much about Cal's madness . . . at the expense of . . . his great courage . . . in going on, and the long periods of sanity that made him able to write as he did."[7] (Elizabeth apparently had declined to participate in the filming.)[8] She would have similar complaints in 1982 about the first major biography written about him. This year she was outraged by C. David Heymann's *American Aristocracy: The Lives and Times of James Russell, Amy, and Robert Lowell*, which had prompted a lawsuit from Harvard over Heymann's unauthorized use of Cal's letters. Elizabeth wrote to the poet Richard Eberhart, one of Cal's former teachers at St. Mark's School, to request that he withdraw his long, enthusiastic blurb ("a vital guide to all sorts of subtleties").[9] In a letter to Robert Silvers, accompanied by a long list of errors in the book, she denounced its "scandal language," undocumented mentions of violence, and ignorant treatment of intellectual topics—the work of "a curious, resentful thug."[10] She also wrote to Cal's trustee, Frank Bidart, to enumerate outrages that included the author's thanks, in his acknowledgment, for interviews with her.[11] In fact, he had asked her no questions about Cal's life when he visited, and Elizabeth had not answered subsequent questions he mailed to her. Worst of all, she wrote, was the "spurious air of intimacy" achieved by "rephrasing things put into art as the very flow of life."

During a spring visit to Lexington, Elizabeth was initiated into Phi Beta Kappa at the University of Kentucky ("I'm benefiting from grade inflation," she joked) and spoke at a class on women's literature. Her demeanor and appearance—"be-ringed fingers waving a cigarette, the ladylike laughter . . . the tossing of still-blond curls"—reminded a local newspaper writer of "a Tennessee Williams character."[12] This, of course, was her deceptive facade. Speaking about recent women's fiction, Elizabeth decried the emphasis on sex. "Subject matter is not what counts," she said. "It's the radicalization of view and style that matters." As a feminist, she was not about to toe the party line when it conflicted with her own sensibility: "Of all the problems writers have, being a woman is the least grave." (It was her belief, as she told an interviewer, that literary and artistic women "have an enormous amount of energy," some of which naturally was exerted in keeping an orderly home and cooking dinner for guests.[13] "Usually," she said, "it turns out that people that can do one thing really can do practically anything.")

She told the class that her "greatest inspirations" were Susan Sontag, Hannah Arendt, and Simone Weil. (On another occasion, Elizabeth said she was "floored" by "the vastness of the learning, the intellectual confidence" of Arendt's *The Origins of Totalitarianism*.)[14] Her interest in Weil was sparked by reading Mary's translation of an essay by the Frenchwoman that had appeared in the magazine *Politics*.[15] In 1977 Elizabeth wrote an impassioned piece about Weil's "willed deprivation"—pushing her frail self "to honor the sufferings" of mankind and writing with unusual clarity and originality about "oppression, exploitation, liberty . . . force, dignity, history, faith."[16] In this review of a biography of Weil, Elizabeth criticized the way biographers' "scrupulous accounting" of their subjects' activities from year to year "makes a long life of a short one." She maintained that the accumulation of banal facts weakens biographies of short-lived individuals like Weil or Sylvia Plath, who "burn themselves up in final explosions of work and action." This piece—in which Elizabeth employs an ecclesiastical metaphor, perceiving Weil's life as if "in panels of stained glass"—is a worthy companion to Sontag's seminal 1963 essay about the French author.[17] Honoring her for her "scathing originality" and "personal authority," Sontag wrote that Weil also wrestled with what it meant to acknowledge "the presence of mystery in the world."

* * *

At nine a.m. one day in early August, Elizabeth sat at her typewriter in Castine, admiring the "luminist" view of calm water under a hazy morning sky. She wrote that she was "longing" to see Sontag and to read her final essay for *On Photography*. Knowing that her recipient would sympathize, she added the writerly lament, "Every pain is one of <u>structure</u>, demonic twin of each happy inspiration."[18] Later that month she responded to the initial queries of her *New Yorker* editor, Frances Kiernan, about "The Bookseller." This short story, a time capsule of a fast-disappearing aspect of Manhattan, offers a loving portrait of the rumpled proprietor of an imaginary shop on Columbus Avenue who is writing his fourteenth unpublishable novel. She assured Kiernan that the story "was not remotely based upon anyone."[19]

Back at her apartment in the autumn, Elizabeth wrote to her friend Sally—whom she had visited briefly in St. Louis—that a party they attended there reminded her of the life led by "normal people."[20] She was feeling overwhelmed by anxiety about a mysterious illness of Harriet's (which turned out to be pneumonia), the pileup of bills, and annoying phone calls from people she hardly knew who wanted to meet with her. Meanwhile correspondence with her editor about "The Bookseller" continued. After thanking Kiernan for her "careful work," Elizabeth suggested that a passage about the Hungarian cleaning woman "could be better in the present tense." Also, she preferred "fat jackets" to "fat down jackets," though she wasn't sure why.[21] A month later, making her way through detailed fact-checking queries, she admitted having "mucked up [the] galleys with indecision."[22] To Mary, Elizabeth confessed worries about her finances ("a nightmare"), adding sarcastically, "Of course, we will all be saved by Reagan!" She was astounded at the level of trust people had in the president-elect. After a busy autumn of teaching, travel, and "the constant threat to sanity of the mail and the telephone"—which had reached a crescendo after the publication of her novel—she was returning to her writing "with some pleasure and hope."[23]

In February 1981 Elizabeth joined William Gass and Tim O'Brien on the jury for the inaugural PEN/Faulkner Award for "the most distinguished work of fiction published by an American writer." The award was founded after an uproar over the decision by the Association of American Publishers to replace the distinguished National Book Awards with a new prize, the American Book Awards, which would honor popular books and increase sales. In addition to writers and critics, the judges would include editors, librarians, and booksellers. Forty-four former winners and judges of the NBA—including Elizabeth, Saul Bellow, William Styron, Alison Lurie, and Wallace Stegner—signed a petition accusing the American Book Awards of being too commercially oriented. Members of PEN America (the nonprofit organization dedicated to defending writers' creative expression) voted overwhelmingly not to participate; three months later the novelist Mary Lee Settle founded the PEN/Faulkner Award. Elizabeth's preference for serious European fiction was borne out in the jurors' choice. At a ceremony in May at the University of Virginia, the award went to Walter Abish, an Austrian émigré, for *How German Is It*, a novel about a young man's struggle to reconcile modern-day Germany with its bitter past.[24]

The following March Elizabeth complained to Mary about "the horror of a photograph" of her on the front page of *The Village Voice*, accompanying an article about women writers. It was "a dreadful feminist slam, not very interesting or telling and very long. . . . Yet, such is 'fame' in the city that I have been congratulated several dozen times."[25] Elizabeth moaned that half the money she made with *Sleepless Nights* had to be paid in income tax, wiping out her savings. "It is the most sickening feeling. . . . I don't see how I can possibly keep Maine and this exorbitant life here going." Although she continued to give paid talks at universities, she worried that the two lectures she had written for her appearance at UCLA in April could not be published, as she had hoped. "The subject just didn't turn out to be the proper one for me," she wrote, "even though I chose it."[26]

One of these talks may have been "Contemporary Women Fiction Writers," which exists as a draft in Elizabeth's papers.[27] There are significant ideas here, but as she realized, the writing is too diffuse to do justice to the topic. In the draft, she describes the poetry of Marianne Moore and Elizabeth Bishop as "a sort of magnifying glass trained on objects . . . and finding . . . extraordinary details." Turning to fiction, she explains that contemporary women writers attempt to capture "the fluid, ever-changing rhythms of American speech, the echoes from films and television." Characters are no longer fixed types, as in traditional fiction, because people can change their image, remarry, move away, and alter their lives in other ways.

However, Elizabeth had to admit that her observations pertained equally to current fiction by men. Toward the end of the draft, she veers into a discussion of essay writing, introducing Susan Sontag's "sensibility of modernism—a reach of attitude and feeling that includes . . . the modern disturbance of the sense of self." Bestowing high praise, she adds that although Sontag is thoroughly American, "you might in a sense call her a good European," because "there is a particular urbanism in her spirit." Elizabeth's mental compass needle always pointed toward city life, where the greatest excitement derived from the clash of ideas.

In a lecture she gave that year at the Creative Women Conference at Washington University in St. Louis, Elizabeth suggested that having "the materials of [daily] life close at hand" might have helped give women of past centuries "the confidence" to write.[28] This was "the confidence of knowing," which Elizabeth distinguished from the male "confidence of the ego." Speaking about the great flowering of Russian literature in the nineteenth century—all of it written by men—she mentioned the impassioned letters of Countess Tolstoy to her husband, sometimes cited as proof that she had the makings of a novelist or short story writer. Elizabeth disagreed. Scholars had "no right to go back into history and create little lost artistic figures," she declared. Her chief observation about women novelists of the past was that the impetus to write was often "a rather sudden and serious economic upheaval." Among the examples she gave were the Brontës, George Sand, Mary Wollstonecraft, and George Eliot.

One of the fascinating byways of her talk is her focus on the calumny heaped on prominent women writers by their male peers. Margaret Fuller was a prime example: a difficult but brilliant woman who died tragically in a shipwreck at the age of forty, she suffered posthumous cruelty from Emerson's pen. He wrote that she was "defective and evil," and that it was providential that she had died in that manner. Elizabeth concluded with a final caution: "Women in the arts who excel are at least in one way stripped of their womanhood." She had looked up the word *master* in the dictionary and found that it referred to "a man having control or authority."

* * *

During the summer of 1981, a bacterial illness spread throughout Castine; Elizabeth caught it twice. She wrote to Sontag that people were exaggerating its effects, as they did in New York with muggings. Despite the quiet, she hadn't been doing much writing and felt unsure of her direction. "And who is out there, Susan, to read what one has in mind," she asked, despairing of the contemporary literary scene. "Don't you feel that? I mean the emptiness out there, that emptiness so stuffed with all the 500 page retreads."[29]

Published in December, her essay "Back Issues" reflects the emptiness she was feeling, but with the darting linkages and acutely observed details of her best fiction. She begins by noting the way women dress (stylish winter clothes on pedestrians, "the impatient appearance of resort clothes" in shop windows) on a January day in 1981 as she walks to the public library on 42nd Street. The neighborhood is caught in one of the city's constant cycles of change, in which "the honorable suicide of old buildings" and a cryptlike excavation are replacing familiar shops. Thoughts about loss continue to prick at her in the library, where an elderly widow researches her Revolutionary War ancestors and a foreign-looking man reads about nervous diseases. In the course of the story, Elizabeth learns that he has left his native Greece and his teaching position only to be obliged to work as a waiter. She has come to do research in the back issues of old literary magazines, which evoke another kind of loss. While the authors spent more time writing book reviews "than on lovemaking or even on making a living," their judgments were often negated by the passage of time. Famous authors derided by reviewers regained their reputation; budding novelists heralded as brilliant were long since forgotten.

In early 1982 Elizabeth was "swamped with work," she wrote to

Mary.[30] An honorary Doctor of Letters degree, awarded by Skidmore College in April, required her to deliver the annual Frances Steloff Lecture.[31] By late May, she was complaining of "merciless meetings and obligations."[32] That summer she discovered that her usual trip to Castine via Bangor was bedeviled by the rerouting of the Delta flight to leave from Newark Airport, which would have made it impossible to bring the "ten duffle bags" of items she needed at the house. Booked instead to Bar Harbor on a small airline, she fretted that they would not mail the ticket and had few seats available.

Elizabeth's book reviews from this period included a devastating takedown of Joan Givner's biography of Katherine Anne Porter for failing to separate the self-made myth from the work. "Each character and each scene of Miss Porter's fiction is looked upon as a factuality honored by its provenance as autobiography," Elizabeth wrote with heavy irony.[33] She described Porter as a woman who "never lost her inclination to romance," pursuing "a conscious and careful make-believe."[34] (Porter fantasized about a nonexistent lineage and indulged in expensive jewels.) But as a writer, "the most useful condition for her . . . sense of things came from the part of her . . . who knew about poverty and rooming houses and bad marriages and standing alone."[35] Although Elizabeth does not seem to have written any earlier pieces about Porter, the novelist nonetheless held a longtime grudge against her. In an interview, speaking of the *New York Review*, Porter called its writers "hatchet men," a phrase that included Elizabeth: "Hatchet woman sounds too gentle for her."[36]

In a lighter mode, "Eye-Witness ARTnews," Elizabeth's spoof of the absurdities of the contemporary art scene and its hype, appeared in the *Review* in December 1982. The piece consists of separate "reports" about fictitious artists like "Fred Waring," whose work is composed of "the black spaces he finds when the ads are being changed" in the subway. He is deliciously quoted as saying, "Commerce stops to take a leak and art moves in."

* * *

The following spring Elizabeth, who always favored stylish shoes, had foot surgery "to correct the tormenting middle toes."[37] As she told Alfred Kazin, "minor is a word that has always only to do with the surgeon and not the patient."[38] The two days of recovery she was told to expect stretched into two weeks. Then came a three-week siege of painters at the apartment, who turned all the rooms except the living room (too large for an affordable makeover) into a "very expensive whiteness." She wrote to Mary that she felt "as if I moved to California when I go to my kitchen."[39] Trying to figure out what to say in a lecture she had to give at Harvard in May, she hoped to "float for awhile" afterward.

Castine was the perfect place for floating. She told a journalist who interviewed her on a chilly day in July that Maine had become a sort of "second Kentucky" to her.[40] Dismayed that he had never heard of current authors she admired—Jayne Anne Phillips, Raymond Carver, Bobbie Ann Mason—she gave him a copy of *The Atlantic* with a story by Mason. Elizabeth was somewhat defensive about the clutter, explaining that the piles of literary, political, and general-interest journals and magazines in both her homes were her way of keeping in touch with the world. (The New York apartment also consisted of "a lifetime accumulation of furniture, objects, paintings, posters, photographs, records, heirlooms, and countless books"—by now Elizabeth had amassed about seven thousand volumes—as well as scattered notebooks and pads of paper on which she wrote ideas and questions to herself.)[41]

Elizabeth's essay collection *Bartleby in Manhattan and Other Essays* was published earlier that year, dedicated to Robert Silvers. She confided to the interviewer that she had spent months revising the title piece. (A note in the book explains that several of her other essays, first published in magazines, also had involved substantial alteration and expansion.) Her writing method, she said, was "to go right through and get it all down and then go back over it." But once she completed the arduous task of revising and the article or book was published, she never reread it. In another interview, she explained that it could take her six months to write a fifteen-page essay. "I don't have that flow you really need, that fictional flow," she said. "Because whatever gift I have is for condensation and for putting things in images."[42]

Bartleby in Manhattan had a mixed reception, mostly because the range of topics covered lacked cohesion, and because Elizabeth typically expressed her opinions by means of a series of discrete observations and unusual metaphors—the opposite of lawyerly prose that builds a case by marshaling increasingly weighty arguments. As Wendy Lesser wrote in *The Hudson Review*, the essays "drop their most telling comments under their breath, as it were."[43] British biographer Hermione Lee pinpointed the "idiosyncratic" quality of Elizabeth's voice: it was "at once austere and impassioned"—the latter stemming from the "morally strenuous" quality of her writing.[44] In Lee's view, it shares certain traits—"a fierce, intelligent, disciplined, Southern Catholic distaste for sentimentality, lies, Northern liberalism and decadence"—with the letters of Flannery O'Connor. But "Catholic" applies only to O'Connor, and Elizabeth's moral stance was hardly the enemy of "Northern liberalism." Also, despite the singular brilliance of O'Connor's fiction—Elizabeth greatly admired its "severe humor" and "harsh acceptance of life"[45]—her letters, with their cloying folksiness, have little in common with the cool authority of Elizabeth's published writing. If Lee hadn't known that Elizabeth grew up in the American South, would she have made this connection? Yet Lee aptly noted that Elizabeth's heroes and heroines are "all solitary, intrepid, self-determining figures."

In the title essay, "Bartleby in Manhattan," she discusses Herman Melville's short story about a tight-lipped clerk whose invariable response to his boss's requests is "I would prefer not to."[46] (His oddly passive negativity eventually lands him in prison, where he refuses food and dies of starvation.) Rather than choosing to probe the psychology of this character, Elizabeth focuses on the "expressiveness" of the "strange, bone-thin dialogue . . . that encloses his past, present, and future." In a memorably apt image, she likens the mind of this singularly unknowable man to "the interior of a small square box containing a pair of cufflinks." She ponders the relevance of Melville's subtitle, "A Story of Wall Street," finding "something of Manhattan in Bartleby . . . especially in his resistance to amelioration." In one of her vaporous linkages of a mood with an object, the "sulky" twin towers of the World Trade Center are "great sightless Brahmins brooding upon the absolute."

The other essays in the collection—originally published in *The New York Times Book Review, Daedalus,* and *The New York Review of Books*—range from "The Apotheosis of Martin Luther King" to appraisals of theater productions in New York. Whatever her subject, Elizabeth treated it in a distinctively allusive manner, described by one reviewer as "diffuse, open observations about the world" and by another as "so exactly right, that they strike the reader as inevitable."[47] Elizabeth's essay "A Bunch of Reds," ostensibly about Warren Beatty's film *Reds* (a "good-natured . . . representation of a bloody, suffering, unbearably complex historical period"), has nothing in common with a standard film review. Her real interest was in the lives of John Reed and his lover, Louise Bryant, based on two biographies newly released in paperback.[48] It's a good bet that Elizabeth was the only commentator on the film who invoked her own memories of the "twilight gathering" of a small group of socialists in the 1940s in lower Manhattan, marking the anniversary of the assassination of an Italian radical gunned down in front of his office.

As Anne Tyler pointed out in her review of *Bartleby,* Elizabeth "catches odd quirks that most people miss"—such as the unconscious way biographers "obscure and blur" in order to favor "memories and moments of the normal and natural" when writing about people "of spectacular and in many ways exemplary abnormality."[49] Even in "Domestic Manners," an essay that rambles over too much territory to be effective, a sentence can leap out, powered by her ability to locate significance in the most banal sights. In the 1970s, she wrote, people still tended to think of the poor in America as sharecroppers, miners, laid-off factory workers. "One thing that distorts our comprehension of the life of the poor is that on the street . . . the marvelous disguise of the mass-produced American clothes give a plausible surface, almost a shine, to what is really implausible and dark."[50] Once again it is the poor who are on her mind.

Elizabeth's thoughts about essay writing would receive an airing when she edited the inaugural volume of *The Best American Essays*. In her introduction, she noted that readers of essays "consent to watch a mind at work . . . only for pleasure."[51] Intriguingly, she observed, "to proceed from musing to writing is to feel a robbery has taken place." Setting down her thoughts on paper meant letting go of "the smiles and ramblings and discussions." (We can imagine her entertaining friends in her living room, cigarette in hand, teasing out a thought with gestures and pauses.) Even so, in her view, the essay is not the place for "absolute true assertion." Rather, "it rests on singularity rather than consensus," the unique expression of "a free and unbound intelligence and sensibility." Complicating this practice, she believed (as we've seen) that the essayist should not explain any references in her text, because of the assumed "equity . . . between the writer and the reader." Unfortunately, as the years go by, fewer readers will be able to claim that equity.

Her essay about Elizabeth Bishop as a prose writer—occasioned by Farrar, Straus and Giroux's publication of *The Collected Prose*—appeared in *The New Republic* in the spring of 1984. Elizabeth noted "the characteristic curiosity . . . muted, as in her poems, by a respect and tolerance for what the curiosity discovers."[52] She wrote that Bishop's best short stories—like "The Sea and Its Shore," about a man employed to pick up bits of paper from the beach who begins to see everything as made of print—are "aesthetically radical, rich, and new in conception and tone." Bishop's autobiographical piece, "In the Village," evoked "a sort of sonata of sounds filled with emotion," transmuting lived experience into another realm. Although this volume did not include Bishop's letters (they were published later), Elizabeth described the ones the poet wrote to Cal, which he had passed on to her "as an offering of pleasure for the morning." The subject of poets writing prose prompted a brief rant about "certain [unnamed] slothful and not very intelligent poets" whose "distraction about word and idea" when they wrote reviews was "more suitable to the shooing away of the family dog." Yet when it came to the "casual prose" of the masters—Coleridge, Mayakovsky, Baudelaire—she was enthralled by "its quick and dashing informality, its mastery of the sudden and offhand." Unsurprisingly, these were qualities she shared.

Elizabeth also remained at the top of her game as a short story writer. "On the Eve" presents a day in the life of a neoconservative writer named Ackermann (seemingly loosely based on Norman Podhoretz) who is "living in the gold of his middle age." Despite his politics, he treats his disorganized left-wing sister with forbearance. He taxis to Penn Station to "rescue a homeless lady," in the forlorn hope that a former lover serious about humanitarian causes will be there to help. Elizabeth vividly evokes the city's tarnished glory in the early 1980s: "in the gutters, a litter of appeals for fortunetelling, massage, keep missiles out of Europe, hands off Nicaragua"; "very young girls in fedoras and tarnished belt buckles"; "a human bundle surrounded by unfathomable lumps of treasure"; "shaved heads of dummies in Macy's window"; "a transvestite in a muskrat coat, hobbling home on sequined heels."

* * *

As a member of the selection committee for the Edward MacDowell Medal for outstanding contributions to American culture, Elizabeth presented the 1984 award to Mary in August at the MacDowell artists' colony in New Hampshire.[53] Noting that her friend's writing was always "in the service of striking ideas," Elizabeth singled out Mary's "optimistic" view of humanity—which notably diverged from Elizabeth's own skeptical understanding of the world. But optimism did not characterize Mary's remarks on this occasion. The seventy-two-year-old author railed against the deteriorated state of the world, on which, she said, "as a person and as a writer, I seem to have had little effect."[54] In her twenty-minute speech, even "Cusinarts, word processors and credit cards" were targets of her ire, because she believed "the more labor, the better."

In December 1984 Elizabeth published "Cheever and the Ambiguities" in the *New York Review*. Her genius for making unexpected historical connections led her to link the "shadowy and troubled undergrowth" in the short stories of John Cheever, who had died two years earlier, to the works of Hawthorne and Melville. In Cheever, she wrote, "the nostalgia is curiously, and with great originality, combined with a contemporary and rootless compulsion to destroy, even to crash [sic] by repetition, the essence of nostalgia." Discussing his daughter Susan's memoir, *Home Before Dark*, Elizabeth remarked that "displacement . . . first from New England and then again in the literary landscape of his time . . . is at the center of his view." (It was a period when Southerners and Jews dominated literary life, whereas he was the inheritor of a crumbling WASP lineage.) While praising the "limpid fluency and eloquence" of the diary passages Susan Cheever chose to include, Elizabeth takes her to task for emphasizing "striking revelations" about her father while failing to attend to his life as an author. In this piece, Elizabeth also remarks that alcoholic writers often feature the "stage business" of characters fixing themselves another drink.

She returned to Castine to usher in the new year. "It was great fun, every minute," she wrote to Mary.[55] "Sun-filled, blue sky days," attractive views, and the familiar village, "just busy enough to be alive," added to the charm of this visit. With friends, she cooked "a turkey, lamb leg, beef stew and lobsters from the Brewer foundry." There was "a little cocktail party, of course" and gossip about the doings of local people. One member of the group was sliding into dementia; bluntly truthful, Elizabeth confessed that it was "annoying" to wait for this woman to lapse into unawareness of her surroundings, "in order to be more forgiving."

When cable TV came to Castine, Elizabeth had followed the cable installers in her car, calling out, "Don't forget me! I signed up early!"[56] An ardent fan of televised tennis matches, keeping up with ratings and scores, she also enjoyed the cultural programming. While visiting a friend in Virginia in early January, she watched a broadcast of the movie based on Peter Taylor's short story "The Old Forest" and wrote to him to express her pleasure at hearing his voice on the soundtrack of this "beautiful film about the lovely, moving story."[57] (It is about a young society woman in Memphis in the 1930s, engaged to a young man who is secretly involved with a working-class woman, and an event that touches all their lives.)

She also mentioned to Taylor that she had heard about a forthcoming biography of Jean Stafford. The author was Ann Hulbert, whom she had met and thought well of, so she planned to give her names of people to interview. That may have been the most positive remark about biography Elizabeth ever made. Yet she added, "Why would anyone want to write a biography? There are no standards and, as I see it, for the most part the thing is just the hunger for a project." (To an interviewer, she called biography "a scrofulous cottage industry" pursued by academics no one had ever heard of, propped up by grants. What the genre needed was "some equity between the subject and the author. And serious, incomparable reflection.")[58] That autumn, having heard that other writers were attempting biographies of Stafford, her tart response was, "Now we have a new reason to understand that it doesn't pay to die."[59]

These words echo Elizabeth's disparaging comments on the genre in her review of Carlos Baker's *Ernest Hemingway: A Life Story.* "It is a form of book-making that rests upon only one major claim of the author: his access to the raw material," she wrote. "Nothing is weighed or judged or pondered." In her wry analogy, "A catalog does not gossip about its entries." Quoting the adage that no man is a hero to his valet, Elizabeth wrote that Baker "makes valets of us all [as] we adjust to his new wives, endure his friends, accept his hangovers." But the biographer failed to include material that would reveal "the real joy of the man, his charm, his uniqueness, his deeply puzzling inner life."[60] Elizabeth once amusingly compared tedious, overstuffed examples of biography to "the sense of being on a long trip with the subject in the family car."[61] Yet she realized that honoring the unique aspects of a creative person did not mean sanding off the bumpy bits. In a letter to Taylor, she criticized the efforts of Mary Jarrell, who was assembling an annotated volume of Randall's letters, for trying to turn "this queer, unaccountable fellow into a family man like many another."[62]

A decade later Elizabeth's review of a new biography of Edmund Wilson in *The New Yorker* would offer another occasion to brandish the antibiography knives that had been part of her arsenal for decades.[63] Biographers, she wrote, produce books that are time-consuming to complete and rarely receive large advances. Yet these authors plug on, because the reader they are really writing for is "the subsequent biographer." Along the way, Elizabeth gets in a dig at Mary McCarthy, likening her repeated unconvincing attempts in her fiction at disguising Wilson (her former husband) to giving him sunglasses. In this review, Elizabeth criticized Wilson-the-critic for his "lack of interest in richly metaphoric prose." But his personality was another matter. She took his biographer to task for failing, in this detailed chronicle of the life and work, to "recreate . . . his subject's brilliant mind and spirit."

* * *

Back in New York in the autumn, she pledged herself to "a fast and a wind-down" while the phone kept ringing and solicitations kept arriving in the mail. Mary had heard from a friend that Elizabeth was seeing specialists about problems with her hearing.[64] She explained that she was finally getting used to wearing a new, more power-ful hearing aid, "in spite of a few problems."[65] Like many hearing-impaired people, she failed to realize that she was now speaking in a louder-than-necessary voice.

This year marked the twentieth anniversary of her teaching career at Barnard, which may have been the impetus for her decision to retire. Asked how she felt about growing older, she responded that it was "just another piece of rotten luck. . . . Its only value is that it spares you the opposite, not growing older."[66] As often happens to famous aging authors, her honors continued to pile up. In January 1986 she was one of seven people who received the Mayor's Award for Art and Culture.[67] The citation noted "her reputation as a tough-minded critic and innovative novelist."

Elizabeth's talk on this occasion was about reading and readers—specifically, "the readers a writer has in mind when he writes."[68] Many of her observations are still timely. She distinguished between readers who understood the difference between "the wish to write a book, which every citizen seems to have, and the wish to make a contribution to literature." She noted that, although reading appears to be passive, it is actually "violently active" because of the imaginative work involved "to create in [the reader's] own mind a sort of moving pageant of action . . . and emotion." She rued the fact that the time-saving aspects of modern life did not result in an accumulation of time for reading; on the contrary, "people with time on their hands are an object of pity." Information overload was to blame for novels that no longer served to inform readers about life in other places and other times. The current vogue for first-person fiction seemed to be based on the premise that the author was unable to say "anything new about the larger world."

A few weeks later Elizabeth was among the novelists, poets, editors, and translators who signed a statement protesting PEN president Norman Mailer's invitation to Secretary of State George P. Shultz to attend the organization's international congress. The letter accused Shultz of representing an administration that "has done nothing to further freedom of expression, either at home or abroad." The conference itself was "deeply depressing" to Elizabeth, because of the "oh so big male writers," with their "bad books, a sort of sterile, spurious energy, nothing to say."[69] Still, she noted the presence of "some extraordinary people . . . most of them, if not all, from outside the US."

That winter, she worked on an essay about Margaret Fuller, the short-lived New England intellectual, author of *Woman in the Nineteenth Century*.[70] Mary, who read the piece in advance of publication, thought it was one of Elizabeth's "best things" and wondered if it could be filmed, with Vanessa Redgrave in the title role.[71] It's possible that Mary was so keen on this portrait of Fuller because it reflected an aspect of herself. (In a 1961 essay, Elizabeth had imagined Fuller as Mary's "ancestor," linked by their "will power, confidence, and a subversive soul sustained by exceptional energy.")[72] Despite the empathetic recounting of a life of "strained nerves, fantastical exertions, discomforts large and small," Elizabeth's gift for pointed observation is less in evidence in this piece. But she wittily captures a key trait of Fuller's: "the trait of all conversationalists: an immense avail-

Elizabeth in her Castine home, 1980.

ability. . . . Soul mates appeared—or so it seemed—but her soul was too soon declarative and consuming."

Summer in Maine was rainy and foggy that year, which meant that visitors were "just sitting in the house looking at the gray sky and tossing waves."[73] To Elizabeth, this was annoying. (In New York, her visitors would go out all day, and her "only distress" was the many telephone calls they received.) One visitor to Castine described the serene living room of the former barn in detail, with its "free-standing, bittersweet-colored steel fireplace, open rafters, pumpkin-colored painted floor, scatter rugs; goldenrod in jugs, hanging baskets of flowers; Japanese pictures, furniture of cane and bamboo, slipcovered in opaque motifs; a Winthrop desk; [and] a pewter bowl . . . full of smooth black stones."[74]

Elizabeth had been working with Robert Giroux on a collection of Cal's prose.[75] In October she wrote to praise his editing and "the tone and charm" of his introduction."[76] On rereading the book, she appreciated the qualities of Cal's writing anew: "his generosity, the quick, casual brilliance of the way he tosses off an opinion, a portrait, a line." She wondered if *The New Yorker* or the *New York Review* would want to publish an excerpt. As she wrote to Peter Taylor the following spring, it was important for Cal's "greatness to be alive once more" after what she viewed as his "diminishment" by Ian Hamilton's biography.[77]

After reading Hamilton's manuscript, Elizabeth had sent the British poet and literary critic many pages of typed, single-spaced information about Cal's family background and work habits, and corrections of various kinds.[78] One aspect she was unhappy about was the amount of material he included about Vija Vetra. Passages about the couple's European trip in the early 1950s also prompted a raft of corrections. Yet while it may be true that she "came to love Holland" and believed that Cal's decision to live there was "excellent," her letters from this period reveal the depths of her misery—which was not just about housekeeping problems, as she now claimed. (These remarks recall the passage in *Sleepless Nights* where the narrator offers a contradictory assessment of her time in Holland: "I wrote many complaining letters. . . . and this is one of the happiest periods of my life.")[79] In a rare flash of self-promotion, Elizabeth asked for the inclusion of a quote from a "portrait" she wrote about Berenson, "because it will give me a little more presence as a writer in the book if something 'stunning' is quoted."

Most crucially, she took pains to stress that Cal was "'well' more of his life than he was not," and that after a manic cycle had run its course, "the old gifts of person and art were still there, as if they had been stored in some serene, safe box somewhere." She wanted his diligence to be known ("the discipline, the dedication, the endless revision") and also his "sociable" side, and the "happiness" he experienced "when he was fortunately for such long creative and private periods 'himself.'" Hamilton had sent a cordial letter in reply, promising to revise his manuscript according to her guidelines.[80] But certain details were not altered in the published version. Elizabeth wrote that Hamilton's decision not to introduce his own judgments about Cal's life produced a manuscript of "elegance and fineness," yet it also led to the inclusion of too much negative information that was allowed to stand without comment. She also had hoped for a more thoughtful evaluation of Cal's work.

* * *

January 1987 brought news of the *New Yorker* affair—the outcry after longtime editor William Shawn was forced out and replaced by Robert Gottlieb, editor in chief at Knopf. Elizabeth disagreed with Mary that Gottlieb should step down. She couldn't see that being able to appoint a successor was "always a moral necessity."[81] In her view, the magazine had "more thick underbrush . . . than greenery." Still, she worried about changes in the direction of "lightness and so-called readability."

In February, Elizabeth traveled to Berkeley, California, to give a lecture on Gertrude Stein that was later published in *The Threepenny Review*.[82] She wrote to Mary that she viewed the experimental author as "rather amusing, large and harmless, with a few little pieces of wit and outlandishness."[83] In the essay, she called Stein "as sturdy as a turnip," likening her penchant for "wring[ing] the neck of words [and] sentences" to "a peasant assaulting the chicken for Sunday dinner." The erudition that allowed Elizabeth to see patterns invisible to others led her to compare Gertrude and Leo Stein as art patrons to the Adams and James families "in the history of American taste." She noted that Gertrude's "amused chauvinism" illuminates *The Making of Americans*, and that in the "moving portraits" of *Three Lives*, "nothing is sentimental." Elizabeth offered her highest praise for the declamatory speech of the Black woman in "Melanctha," because of its musicality and its lack of the condescension typical of white writers rendering Black speech. In Elizabeth's forgiving view, Stein was "unworldly in her self-isolation"—not exactly a valid reason to let her off the hook for her admiration for Vichy leader Philippe Pétain as she placidly hunkered down in the countryside under the French Occupation.

While serving on a panel that winter at the University of Alabama, Elizabeth met Ada Long, a professor of English. "We ended up spending a lot of time together," Long recalled.[84] "She was endlessly exciting to be with and always surprising—who would have guessed that she liked country music?" The women remained friends throughout her life, with many visits from Long to the New York apartment and the Castine house. "She loved asking questions and probing and probing and probing," Long said. "She would find some detail you hadn't quite thought about and just rattle it over and over again—she never stopped at the surface level." As in Elizabeth's writing, Long said, "She's not interested in straight answers. It's not about a statement that will make sense of things. It's about all of the statements that question the truth of things."

That spring Elizabeth was "outraged" and "bewildered" when Taylor's novel *A Summons to Memphis*—a gravely paced chronicle of family wreckage, friendship, and forgiveness that would win the Pulitzer Prize—failed to receive the National Book Critics Circle Award.[85] Although ill health had kept her from voting—she was a member of the jury—she had felt confident about the prospects of his book. (Elizabeth would win the NBCC Lifetime Achievement Award in 1995.) She also enjoyed Mary's new memoir, *How I Grew*, which reminded her of aspects of her own life. "Even though we were in different places, we lived through the same time," she wrote. "Being in school . . . meeting various girls and of course boys, struggling to make sense of things, reading, thinking."[86]

In late April, Elizabeth gave a paper on "The Fictions of America" at the Wheatland Conference on Literature, in Washington, D.C.

This event, closed to the public, drew more than fifty major international literary figures, including John Updike, Mario Vargas Llosa, William Gass, Octavio Paz, Derek Walcott, Margaret Drabble, and Joseph Brodsky. Translators allowed everyone to listen in the language of his or her choice. Toward the end of Elizabeth's talk, she turned from views of America in the fiction of Kafka, Melville, and Dickens to a critique of contemporary American writing. American fiction was "parochial," she said, reduced to "the shadowy scenery of domestic drama." Novels lacked "a large intention, an intellectual structure making its demands upon language, ideas, originality." The state of publishing, which she had been deploring for years, also came in for her censure, in its "devaluation" of writing, now that "almost anybody can be a writer."[87] While Gass blamed university writing programs for producing the kind of short stories Elizabeth disapproved of, Updike disagreed that there was something wrong with the "small" effort.[88] Vargas Llosa took a different tack: "real literature has never told the truth," he said. Novels were about "a profoundly distorted manifestation of reality."

"The Fictions of America" was published in the *New York Review* two months later. Oddly, it was listed only as an also-ran "notable" piece in *The Best American Essays 1988*. Instead, editor Annie Dillard chose "The Heart of the Seasons," which Elizabeth wrote for *House and Garden*, inspired by a catalog of American Impressionist paintings at the Terra Museum of American Art in Chicago.[89] Observing tartly that "there was a time when girls did not lie about the beach in pieces of string, offering an intimidating revelation," she evoked the aspect of summer depicted in the paintings as "a luxurious pause, an inattention except for the concentration on pleasure." After offering glimpses of paintings by Winslow Homer, Charles Curran, and John Singer Sargent, she drifted away to reminisce about summers past in the "upper South." Turning to summer romance with help of a line from one of Cal's poems—a strange choice, because the "girls of summer" were the ones who caused him to stray from the marriage—she evoked works by Edith Wharton, Thomas Hardy, and Anton Chekhov before finally circling back to the world of the paintings: "the gardens, the terraces, the flowers in vases." Charming in its airy digressions, this is far from her most focused writing.

With William Gass and Susan Sontag, Elizabeth participated in the PEN symposium on Henry James in November 1987. Her discussion of his writing presented an intimately biographical and practical point of view that contrasted with the theoretical approach of her fellow panelists. Elizabeth once teasingly called James "the greatest American *female* novelist," later claiming that this remark was meant simply to "lighten the gloom" of the discussion.[90] On this occasion, she spoke about *The Awkward Age*, an unsuccessful novel James published in 1899.[91] His habit of putting the wrong words in quotes or italics in this book struck her as a function of his "vocalizing"—hearing the words in his own voice as he wrote them—as well as a result of his fear that the reader would not properly understand "the delicate shape" of the conversation. Noting that the book was written after the dismal failure of his plays, she explained that the dialogue ("so bewildering, and so mysterious," despite its simplicity) would never work on the stage "because it doesn't give the kind of information" that actors need to create a believable character. Behind this insight stood her years of theater reviewing and editing of Cal's plays.

James was one of Elizabeth's fascinations. The *New York Review* later published her essay "On Washington Square," about the novel of that title. "In this perfect novel of immense refinement," she wrote, the wealthy but dull and plain Catherine Sloper "is as alone as an animal in a field." This image, so alien to the book's New York setting, characterizes this young woman with startling brilliance.[92] While Elizabeth also observed that "money in exchange for love is the dilemma of many of the heroines of James's novels," her gift is less for the overarching statement that other commentators might make than for her devastating grasp of the inner lives of those heroines.

* * *

At some point during the final decades of the twentieth century (the date is unknown), Elizabeth wrote a filmscript for a version of Kate Chopin's novel *The Awakening* (1899), which was to have been directed by Barbara Karp.[93] Chopin's heroine, Edna Pontellier—a twenty-eight-year-old Presbyterian from Kentucky—is a married woman living in the Creole high society of New Orleans. She falls in love with Robert Lebrun, a young clerk. Eventually, she abandons the grand house her husband built for a cottage of her own and has a brief liaison with Alcée, an older man-about-town. Rejecting nineteenth-century propriety that deemed sexual behavior unmentionable, Chopin reveals her character's sensual blossoming with Lebrun and its consummation with Alcée—this is her "awakening" but also the source of her emotional distress. Edna, who always has been drawn to the sea, ends her life by drowning. In Elizabeth's introduction to the filmscript, she describes the novel as "perfectly balanced in intention and execution," lacking "the sentimentality and provincialism that defaced so much of the American fiction of the 1890s." She makes special mention of the distinction between the worldly pragmatism of French-Creole society and Edna's "American, Protestant, impulsive romanticism of individual fulfillment." That was something she knew quite a lot about.

It seems curious that Elizabeth decided to write a screenplay, given her remarks in "Fiction and Film: Problems of Translation," a lecture she gave under the auspices of the American Film Institute.[94] In her view, films based on classic nineteenth-century novels necessarily fall short of their originals. That's because it is not possible to show the multiple forces in play ("chance, extraordinary desire and impulse, coincidence, suspicion, longings, memory"), and the fate of the characters depends on a social framework that can only be hinted at onscreen. A filmscript, she said, is necessarily "a curious-looking prose artifact of violent verbal condensation." At the end of her talk, Elizabeth compared the mesmerizing power of cinema in bygone eras—when walking out of the theater with its "world of dreams" gave viewers a "mistrust of [their] grasp of the real world"—to the current "bleached-out sensibilities of the audience" that have led to "a frantic escalation of violence, more and more noise, and the inevitable sex scenes."

Another departure for Elizabeth was *Ruth Benedict: A Biographical Essay for Television*, the script for a Ken Burns–style documentary about the anthropologist, influenced by the photographic style of Michael Lesy's 1973 book, *Wisconsin Death Trip*. Based on Benedict's papers at Vassar College, this biography was to be presented with vintage and staged photographs, classical music excerpts, voice-overs, and film footage of cultural practices Benedict observed. Elizabeth also specified reenactments in which "we do not see people's faces—the camera angles are from the sides of heads, over shoulders—the focus and lighting is soft."[95]

This script begins promisingly, with Benedict recalling how repelled she was at her mother's grief over her father's death. We see her trying to teach bored students at a girls' school—shades of Elizabeth's own unhappy experience in New York—and lamenting that her feelings of loneliness and futility stem from being a woman. Married to a biochemist, she writes poetry and a book about three women, including Mary Wollstonecraft, who has fascinated her since childhood. The marriage fails ("we grow more and more strangers to each other, united only by gusts of feeling"). But when Benedict escapes from rural New York to the New School for Social Research, discovers anthropology, and studies at Columbia under Franz Boas, the vivid biographical aspect drops out. Elizabeth's stiff phrase about the failure of Benedict's "academic advancement" doesn't clarify the fact that she was not chosen as department head after Boas's retirement, and her relationship with her student Margaret Mead never comes alive. Perhaps Elizabeth intended to add more connective tissue at a later date; in any case, the program was not produced.

* * *

Elizabeth wrote to Alfred Kazin to praise his appearance in *Ezra Pound: American Odyssey*, a PBS television program that aired in early 1988.[96] She added that she had never wanted to meet Pound and did not do so until he visited the Lowells during his "silent period." It occurred to her now that his willed silence was really "an example of depression . . . after a lifetime of manic exhibitionism." She mused that his main folly was "an unreal idea of the worldly power of art." Clearly, her years with Cal had alerted her to the complexities of mental illness.

In August, Elizabeth published "Church Going" in the *New York Review*. Nominally a review of books about ecclesiastics of past eras—Jonathan Edwards, Henry Ward Beecher, and early nineteenth-century English pastors—the piece gave her the opportunity to evoke "the great roar" of current-day evangelicals. Pat Robertson ("maintainer of his marbelized, polished, imperturbable fatuity") and Jimmy Swaggart ("scratching and clawing up the Family Worship trail") are just two of her zestfully pursued targets. She remarked on the existence of "ever-increasing number of Evangels, way way beyond the discrete settlement on The Twelve [apostles] . . . each with his style of stagecraft . . . and all competing to be heard and placated and supported unto old age." Their ministries, she wrote, had no truck with the notion of the "hallowed poor" and nothing in common with "the dense and . . . morally painful studies and disputes of centuries past." Elizabeth likened the televangelists' fitful appeal to the Gospel of Saint John to "a gull skimming and diving in and out in a relentless search for food." In a wide-ranging interview at the Institute of Contemporary Arts in London two years earlier, she had labeled this spurious form of religion as "a kind of primitivism" that was playing an increasing role in American politics.[97]

The following spring, Robert Silvers wrote to Elizabeth that the *New York Review* "had compliments from all over on the terrific Updike piece."[98] While giving the novelist his due for his "shimmering knowledge of the way things look, how they deface or illuminate the towns" and for "his almost effortless command of . . . the speech of America," she criticized "the humbly repetitive Pandemonium" of sexual activity in his books and deftly unpacked his curious reasoning for defending the Vietnam War.

Elizabeth received another official recognition in 1989, an honorary Doctor of Letters degree from Bard College. The citation praised Elizabeth for her "elegance of style and clarity of logic" and for "us[ing] writing to discover the truth and to hold that truth unflinchingly and candidly before the eyes of your readers."[99] At a Whiting Foundation event in New York, she spoke about reading and readers. Once again invoking the notion that reading appeared to be a passive occupation, she said that engaging with "a challenging work of the imagination" required work on the part of the reader: a payment "for the pains, inspiration, and daring of the author."[100] In a more lighthearted spirit, she assembled an amusing compendium of bad English translations of Zola, Balzac, Dumas, and de Maupassant ("Basic Englishing") for the *New York Review.*[101] Most of the transgressors display a surfeit of English slang. French characters expostulate with "Blimey!" "Crikey!" and "Dash it!" when they are not calling people buggers, toffs, ninnies, or "boob's [sic]."

The *New York Review* nominated Elizabeth for the 1990 Jefferson Lecture of the National Endowment of the Humanities, but that honor went to the historian Bernard Lewis. Two years later Silvers would recommend her for the NEH's Charles Frankel Prize ("for outstanding contributions to the public's understanding of the humanities"), writing that she was "one of the most valuable and instructive commentators on literature today . . . distinguished by original insight into the American temper and a subtle sense of changing values." Unfortunately, this effort also went nowhere. Yet Elizabeth was still writing extraordinary essays.

In the spring of 1990 her visceral evocation of her adopted city, "New York City: Crash Course," appeared in *Granta*. Describing it as "a spectacular warehouse" of "folks from anywhere," she gets under the skin of its denizens, past and present, from the xenophobic crowd pelting English actor William Macready at the Astor Place Opera House in 1849 to the current-day homeless person addressing the "f---ing little rat-faced volunteer on vacation from the country club of Wellesley College." A meditation on the plight of delivery boys segues to the slave insurrection of 1712 and then to the men who "run the elevators" and guard the "flaking, tedious columns" of the Temple of Dendur at the Metropolitan Museum before returning to their homes in outer boroughs. In today's Manhattan, Elizabeth found the same impulses of greed, fear, and deep-seated prejudice that existed centuries earlier. Her skeptical view discerns "the sacrificial athleticism of the joggers," the financiers, "trim from the rigours of the conference call" and the "turbulent campaigns of consumption in the imperial mode." People who settle in the "ever promising and ever withholding" city "fill the streets with complaints and whines." Yet she acknowledges, they wouldn't have it any other way.

A visit to Moscow in November for a conference with the Soviet Writers' Union fascinated Elizabeth, as she wrote to Alfred Kazin.[102] She was "pleased to find the room-key girls prettier and often off-duty when not looking at the tele," and she enjoyed tasty food at pleasant restaurants—a far cry from the dreary meals of 1977. Yet despite glasnost, "the cost of Communist rule" was "suffering . . . with no relief in sight." She imagined that, had there been no Russian Revolution, Moscow and St. Petersburg "might have been . . . two very agreeable Stockholms."

The following year Elizabeth wrote to a friend to lament the "duties" in her immediate future: "Baltimore this month, Ohio in May followed by the Academy meeting where I have to deliver a citation, then Middlebury, a dreadful duty, then Ireland."[103] As things turned out, the latter trip was canceled because she needed to deal with "too many foot and tooth problems."[104]

* * *

Mary died of lung cancer in late October 1989, after years of living with serious ailments and illnesses. Elizabeth sat at her bedside in New York Hospital "nearly every night, after the other visitors had left."[105] At Mary's memorial service in November at the Morgan Library, attended by two hundred people, she was one of the six speakers.[106] Much of what she said was recycled from the speech she gave five years earlier at the MacDowell Colony. In her eyes, Mary was a romantic with "a charming touch of the Jesuitical," an "impractical and romantic intransigence on behalf of what she saw as moral," especially in her devoted friendship with Hannah Arendt.[107] Bucking the common view of Mary as a "forbidding satirist," Elizabeth said that her writing was actually "very cheerful, light-hearted, and oddly optimistic." Despite her liberal views, Mary "practice[d] a sort of eccentric conservatism in matters of daily life"—a reference to her avoidance of labor-saving devices—and seemed to be "searching for some lost American ideal." Praising Mary's legendary hospitality, Elizabeth also remarked on her friend's attempts at reengaging friendships with people whose personalities she had skewered in her fiction: "I would think, 'Oh, we're going to have to see them for dinner the rest of our lives because Mary has made fun of them in a book.'" The audience laughed.

Elizabeth's foreword to Mary's last book, *Intellectual Memoirs: New York 1936–1938*, published posthumously, noted that she had "a somewhat obsessional concern for the integrity of sheer fact, in matters both trivial and striking."[108] With the fond tolerance of a close friend, she remarked on how Mary's "enduring crankiness" and rejection of convenience kept her working on a manual typewriter to the end of her days and carrying rolls of bills because she refused to get a charge card. Elizabeth summed up Mary's existence by bundling together "her wit, great learning, her gardening, her blueberry pancakes, beautiful houses." Decades earlier, despite reservations about much of Mary's fiction, Elizabeth had praised her essays, observing that she had "gradually sloughed off the need for novelty" and joined the ranks of "writers of great intelligence" by "learn[ing] to trust a greater plainness."[109] Now Elizabeth stealthily resisted the ultimate encomium, noting only that Mary "worked as a master of the art of writing every day of her life. How it was done, I do not know."

After Mary's death, Elizabeth became "the queen bee of parties" in Castine, according to her friend Ginny Foote.[110] She raised money for the local historical society with the parties she threw and with a reading she gave at the Unitarian church that attracted a standing-room-only crowd. Knowing that her writing time was in the morning, people often dropped in during the afternoon. The filmmaker and author Peter Davis, whom Elizabeth welcomed "every time I went to her house, bidden or unbidden," recalled how devastating she could be to anyone she viewed as pretentious. A remark "would start out as if she was going to make a compliment," he said, "and by the time the sentence was finished you know that she had very little regard for that person."[111] Alison West, Mary McCarthy's stepdaughter—who had known Elizabeth since childhood—described her as "the perfect concoction of this wonderful welcoming warmth . . . but you just knew the minute you left the room [she would say], 'Well now, isn't it too bad . . .' "[112]

* * *

In September 1993, Elizabeth's assessment of Willie Morris's *New York Days*, a bittersweet memoir of the Mississippi native's editorship of *Harper's Magazine*, was published on the front page of *The New York Times Book Review*.[113] While praising Morris's "fluent affection" for his adopted city and "acute rendering of the turmoil" of the 1960s, she concluded that the book reveals "a fragility of temperament, beneath the sunny sociability," a mix of "nostalgia and hurting regret." Elizabeth's name appears only glancingly in this book, as the author of a *Harper's* memoir about returning to her Kentucky home. Morris didn't mention that the two of them were part of a literary group—including William Styron and Gloria Jones, widow of the novelist James Jones—who vacationed on the island of Salt Cay in Turks and Caicos in early 1978. But in his earlier memoir, *North Toward Home*, he refers to an unnamed "well-known lady writer, one of the more caustic critics for one of the famous reviews just then getting started"—surely the *New York Review*—who was a guest at the first fancy New York cocktail party he attended after arriving in the city in 1963. He recalls that she acknowledged his greeting by recalling his origins: "Mississippi . . . Texas . . . am I right?" Then she said, "*Harper's*, isn't it? And how do you like it *there*?" He sensed "a curt edge on the word *there*" and was clearly miffed that she turned away to continue her conversation with someone else.[114]

Despite being fellow Southerners, Elizabeth and Morris had markedly different feelings about New York. As an attractive, beguiling woman who enjoyed sharp-elbowed literary shop talk, she seemed to fit in from the very beginning. Morris had to overcome a temperament rooted in the slow rhythms and unique blend of earthiness and gentility that typified life in small-town Mississippi. He wrote unforgivingly of "the callousness, the senseless violence, the lack of simple courtesy," and the "harsh, cliquish, nervous" literary world, with its "extravagant claims and exaggerated dismissals"—a world that prized ideas above "a regard for individual people with their flaws and weaknesses."[115]

Elizabeth returned to *The New Yorker* in October with a keenly observed work of fiction, "Shot: A New York Story," about a Black woman working as a cleaner on the Upper East Side and the efforts of her nephew to collect money from her well-to-do clients for the funeral after her murder. Packed with incident and vivid description, this story—which completely avoids the taint of caricature—is formally ingenious, with a suspension of time that creates a haunting cinematic quality. Elizabeth received a call from the magazine on a Saturday, two days before the issue was finalized: the fact-checking department objected to dialogue about an unclaimed body that was to be cremated, because such corpses were still buried in Potters Field. Elizabeth understandably found it "nerve-wracking" to have to make up new dialogue on the spot.[116]

On New Year's Day, Elizabeth wrote to her friend Sally that she was "older than anyone I sometimes think," but otherwise fine.[117] Catching her up on a year's worth of news, Elizabeth mentioned a summer visit in Maine from the writer Elizabeth Kendall. (Years later Kendall recalled "the Southern seductiveness in the way she presented herself and the way she spoke, the accent very charming. It was a shock when she said something bitchy about someone.")[118] Calling Harriet "the best thing I ever did," Elizabeth hoped that her daughter might marry the chemical engineer she was dating: "She's educated him in the Humanities and he gave her a very expensive book about maps for Christmas—if you see what I mean." That spring renovations on the New York apartment created "a nightmare of dust and dirt," as Elizabeth wrote to another friend.[119] She apologized for all the typos in the letter, but "even the typing room is such a mess I can hardly see the page."

In October 1994, Elizabeth inaugurated a new lecture series, "Places in the Mind," at the Folger Shakespeare Library in Washington, DC. Her subject was New York City. She had told a *Washington Post* reporter that, although Manhattan had become much harder to live in for young people than it was when she arrived, it remained "a visionary place."[120] In her talk, Elizabeth described a metropolis that seeks "to overthrow the future before it arrives, always creating a new stasis rather than resting on an achieved one."

Brushing aside her blond curls as she peered at pages of notes, she observed that New York's "destruction of the more-or-less new in favor of the newer" is not seen "as a defect in its municipal nervous system, but as a sort of celebration of new cells or new growth." Presenting a view informed by history and literature as well as by personal observation, she touched lightly on subjects ranging from immigrants in tenements ("their emblem was the clothesline") to the consumption habits of the wealthy (the acquisition of "furniture collections, art, and wives"). If her conclusions were not particularly new, her turns of phrase remained freshly minted. Criticizing portraits of the nouveau riche as hicks in novels by Edith Wharton and William Dean Howells, she declared, "Nothing is easier to acquire than the prevailing taste."[121]

* * *

In these years, whether in New York or Castine, Elizabeth was always nattily turned out, often in a silk dress. "Even going to the dump, she'd put her lipstick on," Ginny Foote said, "a silk scarf on her head to go downtown." In Foote's fond memory, "nobody was more entertaining or witty or sharp or gossipy. . . . She was very inquisitive, like a dog with a bone if she wanted to know more and more" about the life of "a fisherman or a grocery clerk." Deborah Joy Corey, a young writer who met Elizabeth in the early 1990s, thought of her as "an instant girlfriend" despite the vast difference in their ages. "Everyone interested her," Corey said. "I think that was what made her such an excellent writer."[122] Jon Jewett, another friend in Castine, said that Elizabeth was particularly interested in the husbands and wives who both had blue-collar jobs—gardener and gas station attendant, handyman and cook, the couple at Ken's Market who took orders and delivered them.[123] She had great sympathy for the hard work of Sylvia Pratt, sole proprietor of a landmark general-store-cum-diner at the corner of Main and Water streets that kept long hours. Sylvia's, later known as Castine Variety, served as the community's prime gathering place. When Janis and Ernie Fitch took over in the early 1990s, Elizabeth wondered aloud, "There can't be enough profit in a cup of coffee and the *Bangor Daily* to keep that place going."

Jewett had met Elizabeth in Castine years earlier when he saw her fumbling with the gate to the Water Street house and offered to help. She enlisted him to tote her bags from the rental car, and a friendship was born.[124] He recalled how she loved to "scoot around town" in her car.[125] "She used to say, 'Sweetheart, let's drive around and see where we weren't invited.'" Spotting a long line of cars one evening, Jewett suggested that there might have been an accident. "No no no, sweetheart," she said. "Wednesday night is prayer meeting." Much as Elizabeth enjoyed driving, even simple mechanical aspects baffled her. One night she rushed into Jewett's house, unsure about how to turn off the car lights. After a cataract operation in her mid-sixties, the prospect of taking an eye test to renew her license made Elizabeth very nervous. At the motor vehicles office, when asked what shapes she saw when looking through the ophthalmic testing device, she said, "Those shapes have nothing to do with my driving!" The man suggested they take a break, during which Jewett explained that she really had to answer the question. Her Maine license was renewed, much to her joy—and skepticism: "Sweetheart, they'd give a license to a blind man!"

* * *

At the opening of the Republican convention in August 1996, Elizabeth published a tongue-in-cheek op-ed piece, "On Behalf of the Unborn: A Celibacy Amendment." It proposed a waggish constitutional amendment: that young men be required to remain celibate until marriage. Politicians, she wrote, don't learn from "the wisdom of fiction"—Hardy's *Tess of the d'Urbervilles*, Tolstoy's *Resurrection*.[126] The middle-aged and elderly male antiabortion zealots apparently believed that women become pregnant all by themselves, "out of reprehensible indulgence or folly or criminal impulse."

That autumn, in her review of Joan Didion's novel *The Last Thing She Wanted*,[127] Elizabeth took a long look at the celebrated author's publishing history. (Writing about a body of work by an author, rather than a single book, made sense because a work "isn't published in a vacuum; it's part of a greater whole.")[128] She pinpointed the key elements of Didion's style as "abrupt closures rather like hanging up the phone without notice . . . a remarkable ear for the rhythms . . . of current speech" and "a strong sense of willful obfuscation, a purposeful blackout of what was promised or not promised." By these means, Didion "expressed a peculiar restlessness and unease" characteristic of "the extreme fluidity" of the world she writes about. By employing a "dogged concreteness of detail," Didion allowed readers to accept "an often capricious mode of presentation."[129] Four years later, in her introduction to a new edition of *Slouching Toward Bethlehem*, Elizabeth wrote that Didion "seems to enter her work as a stranger in a foreign land. . . . The ordinary movements of life . . . are rich in idiosyncrasy, bafflement, confusion of intent."[130]

Elizabeth closed out 1996 with an affectionate tribute to the grits soufflé, a dish of the Deep South. This *New Yorker* piece also included sidelong glimpses of baked cheese grits, red-eye gravy, and lettuce dressed with cooked bacon and bacon grease—a favorite, she explained, of the urbane composer Virgil Thomson.[131]

During this decade, Robert Silvers tried to coax Elizabeth to write more essays for the *New York Review*. Suggesting a new book that might interest her, he added his unvarying query, "Might there be something to be done?" Beginning in 1997, he also dropped a dollar figure (usually $4,000) into these notes, to sweeten the deal. Elizabeth's contributions were now increasingly about current events. Her longtime fascination with murder trials took a new form in an essay about the trials of Lyle and Erik Menendez, charged with first-degree murder of their parents in 1989, and O. J. Simpson, who was ultimately judged not guilty in the 1994 murders of his former wife, Nicole Brown, and her friend Ron Goldman.[132] Inundated with court documents compiled by the *Review*, Elizabeth wrote a thoughtful piece that dwells largely on her cuttingly ironic assessments of the players, especially the Menendez brothers, who found it "necessary to re-load and shoot the mother twice before she expired . . . when the father's murder might alone have achieved the change desired." The nature of celebrity murder trials, with their "LA 'mansion' scripts," was a world apart from "the austere and informative trials on Court TV." Once again she invoked the vastly different way life works for ordinary people.

Elizabeth also continued to write reviews—of books that included Philip Roth's novel *American Pastoral* and George Plimpton's biography of Truman Capote—and one-off pieces, like her capsule memory of Christmas in Kentucky ("dusty whiffs . . . of soft coal burning in the grate").[133] The novels of Roth, she wrote, "are prickled like a sea urchin with the spines and fuzz of many indecencies." Rather than basing his fiction on "actions and counter-actions," he wrote "tirades of perfervid brilliance . . . a promotion of self, often as if on the stage." Unlike most of her reviews, her treatment of Roth is thick with plot summaries and quotations that (deliberately?) leave little room for her own thoughts. As if exhausted by the effort of explaining the plot of *American Pastoral*, she concludes that this saga of the fictional Levov family, which she compares to the work of Dreiser, is not only "a touching creative act" but also "can be rated PG, suitable for family viewing—more or less."

In 1998 Random House published *Sight-Readings: American Fic-*

tions, a collection of eighteen of Elizabeth's essays from the 1980s and '90s. It had been fifteen years since *Bartleby in Manhattan and Other Essays*, and she was gratified that her old friend Jason Epstein—to whom the book is dedicated—saw fit to gather her more recent work between covers. As Joyce Carol Oates wrote in her review, the title really should have been "Depth-Readings," because of the wide-ranging quality of these essays, the expression of "a sensibility that 'judges' in such a way as to expand the significance of the subject."[134]

"Head Over Heels," published in the April 22, 1999, issue of the *New York Review*, presents Elizabeth's thoughts about the sexual scandal that rocked the Clinton presidency. Brainstorming the piece with Ginny Foote, Elizabeth remarked that what seemed to be different about the adulterous behavior of men in high places was that "the women talk."[135] A few months from her eighty-third birthday, she was looking back at a time when women "were somewhat restrained by self-protection, by not wanting mother, family, children, or job supervisor to know what was going on in the back seat of the car, in the after-hours office. Now there is the book, the lawsuit, the settlement." But only for the privileged: "For the working class, there is nothing to be gained by going public. . . . The truck-stop waitress who has caught the attention of the tired trucker . . . can overstep, call his home. . . . Shut up, bitch, the wife says, and returns to the patio where he is putting a match to the charcoal." With these words, Elizabeth inserted a vivid short story into the tiresomely long one played out in the media. A miasma of disgust permeates her essay ("the wanton licentiousness of the questioning of Monica Lewinsky by the Independent Counsel's Office"), lightened here and there with a Hardwick-ism: President Clinton denying that sexual relations took place struck her as a figure "solemn as a rogue in a Molière comedy."

That year Modern Library published the paperback *American Fictions*, a compilation of most of *Sight Readings* plus selected pieces from

Seduction and Betrayal, Bartleby in Manhattan, and *A View of My Own*. As Elizabeth explained in the preface, these essays usually stemmed from the publication of a novel or a biography of an author. She also provided an introduction, "Locations." Saluting authors as distinct and distinctive as Edith Wharton, F. Scott Fitzgerald, Richard Ford, Henry James, and William Faulkner, she wrote that "the landscapes of fiction" are the places where "the seven deadly sins do battle with probity and reality or outrageous demand and vanity."

* * *

Elizabeth was keen to read Susan Sontag's new novel, *In America* (1999), aware of the author's struggles to write it while dealing with cancer. After finishing it, Elizabeth wrote to her to exclaim over "the number of aesthetic and structural decisions you had to make to write this book!"[136] While her favorite among Sontag's novels remained *The Volcano Lover*, she was fascinated with the commonplace American "oddities" the book revealed, as seen through the eyes of a Polish actress modeled after real-life tragedienne Helena Modjeska. A decade earlier Elizabeth had called Sontag one of her three "close friends" (along with Mary and Barbara Epstein).[137] Although her letter congratulating Sontag on the National Book Award for *In America* suggests that the two women had drifted apart, Elizabeth was the dedicatee of Sontag's last essay collection, *Where the Stress Falls* (2001). In her letter of thanks, she wrote, "Susan your gallantry is in your work and your life is an astonishment—going on in defiance."[138] The closeness Elizabeth felt for her seems to have been of a different quality—more intense, more yearning—than her long friendship with Mary. (When a friend asked Elizabeth what she thought of a quote from Isaiah Berlin in Frances Kiernan's new biography of Mary McCarthy, *Seeing Mary Plain*—"Elizabeth Hardwick has a feminine mind, much more bitchy than Mary's but sharper and more original"—she laughed and said she loved it.)[139]

Elizabeth's last book, *Herman Melville*, was published in 2000 as part of the short-form Penguin Lives series edited by James Atlas. It may seem surprising that someone so critical of biographers' premises and methods wrote one herself. But Melville had been stalking through Elizabeth's writings for decades. She had helped shape *Benito Cereno*, Cal's play based on Melville's novella, and in 1992 she wrote an essay for *Opera News* on *Billy Budd*, Benjamin Britten's opera based on Melville's posthumously published novel.[140]

Atlas had a gift for inspired matchups of author and subject. Years earlier Elizabeth had praised his biography of the poet Delmore Schwartz as "careful and fair-minded."[141] Now he suggested that she could write about Melville.[142] "She said, 'Oh dear, I could never write a biography! I wouldn't know how!'" Atlas recalled. He reassured her that the books in the series were not standard biographies but rather "biographical essays that had to do with point of view and voice." She said she would think about it and finally agreed after Atlas paid a visit to what he remembered as a somewhat shabby, book-crammed apartment, over which she presided "in a kind of grande dame manner." (Another visitor during this period remembered the apartment as "tidy and elegant . . . a huge space just right for an oversized personality.")[143]

But the manuscript she completed was not what Atlas expected. "Even by the standard of Penguin Lives, the book she wrote was very idiosyncratic," he said. "Just Lizzie riffing on whatever she felt like riffing on. The book is bizarre." True to form, she resisted his efforts at editing. ("I'm very against editors," she had told an interviewer in 1978. "Lots of books are really quite transformed by editors, but in my work nobody ever has anything to say. They can't do it any differently than I do it. You have to take it or not.")[144] The reviews were mixed—not surprising for a biography that is largely a literary analysis with topical chapters rather than a conscientious chronicle of the life. The *New York Times* critic found fault with Elizabeth's "repeti-

Elizabeth in her New York apartment, 1978.

tive superlatives," despite her "stylistic elegance."[145] In *The Observer*, David Michaelis rejoiced at Elizabeth's "exquisite fidelity to the spirit of Melville."[146] A writer for *Salon* described the book as "a dead-on, if highly abstract, portrait." By emphasizing the author's "unknowability," the book suggested "an argument against the very practice of biography."[147] John Leonard's verdict, in the *New York Review*, was unabashedly positive: Elizabeth "always had the shaman's gift of disappearing into writers she loves, speaking their voices, seeing through their eyes. . . . She makes us *need* to read the books she has chosen to care about."[148]

Excerpted in the *New York Review* ("Melville in Love"), this slender biography offers freshly conceived readings of the author's works, attentive to their homoerotic aspects as well as to the events in his life that made the novels possible. "He is elusive," Elizabeth wrote, "the facts of his life only a frame," but all the more inviting for someone whose method of analysis floats on currents of elusiveness. Family status that another biographer would have dropped into the narrative without elaboration receives the following gloss: "Genteel poverty, an ambiguous condition, each contradiction feeding upon the other." Calling his early novel *Redburn* "the most appealing and certainly the most personal of his works," Elizabeth describes its reflection of the author's "early sense of the ambiguity, the chaos of life." She writes that Melville's subsequent move—signing on to a whaling ship— was likely due to "a nagging irresolution about his future, a melancholy assessment of the present, guilt for not being able to assist" his family. The experience of that voyage yielded *Moby-Dick*, "an unexpected masterpiece," with an "innocent or unquestioning erotic lyricism [that] takes a turn of fantastical brilliance, a wild, sunlit flow of adjective; an active, sonorous explosion of sheer sensation arising from the affluent sperm of the great sea creature." Elizabeth devoted a chapter to Melville's wife, Elizabeth Shaw, who "changed him from an unanchored wanderer into an obsessive writer." His "frenzy, his bad temper with too much to drink at night," drove her to consider a separation, but she desisted; they stayed together for forty-four years. It is impossible to read Elizabeth's thoughts about a long marriage to a genius with personal problems and not sense her awareness of exactly what this meant.

Two years later she returned to *Redburn* when she wrote the introduction to a new Modern Library edition. She explained that the novel reflects Melville's experience as a well-bred nineteen-year-old with "a heart heavy with family sorrow and emotional despair" who signed on to a merchant ship in Liverpool—a city evoked with "the crowded brilliance" of Dickens's London—and found himself in a closed society of shocking depravity. Writing in 1849, he described this world with "a freedom from tribal superstition, a rejection of superiority of race or nation."

Elizabeth also wrote introductions for other Modern Library editions. She described V. S. Naipaul's masterpiece, *A Bend in the River*, as "a haunting creation, rich with incident and human bafflement, played out in an immense detail of landscape rendered with a poignant brilliance."[149] Introducing Henry James's *Washington Square*, she called it "perfectly balanced . . . narrow in its focus, rather claustrophobic, yet moving along with a speed suitable to the importunate demands of Morris Townsend," Catherine Sloper's calculating would-be suitor.[150] She wrote that in *The House of Mirth*, Edith Wharton "is not always clear what the moral might be and thereby creates a stunning tragedy in which the best and the richest society of New York reveals an inner coarseness like pimps cruising in Cadillacs."[151]

In "Mrs. Wharton in New York," a 1988 essay, Elizabeth had noted that while the novelist was "free of lush sentiments and moralizing tears," she did not spurn "contrivance" if it furthered the plot. With her penchant for homespun, ironic metaphors, Elizabeth wrote that the mother-in-law's French chateau in *The Reef*, a Wharton novel about an American family, "somehow appears as naturally as if it were a deed to a woodlot." She is an excellent guide to individual characters, like Lily in *The House of Mirth*, who was "never unaware of her own motives." Writing about Wharton also allowed her to offer a final characterization of New York itself, which "lives in a continuous present, making it difficult to recall the shape of the loss deplored."

During Elizabeth's last years, her introductions also graced Knopf's edition of the William Weaver translation of Italo Svevo's *Zeno's Conscience* ("a novel of money and an idle, introspective man's way of hanging on to it . . . a brilliant psychological document about procrastination")[152] and new editions of rediscovered works published by New York Review Books. J. F. Powers's 1962 novel *Morte d'Urban* follows the trials of a worldly priest in Chicago, demoted to a community in small-town Minnesota. In her introduction, Elizabeth put her finger on the novel's essence ("a comedy of manners— clerical manners—has turned into a morality drama") and described

Powers as "forever down-home alert to the plodding demands made on an ancient church in a new, go-go country."[153]

Her introduction to the 2002 edition of Tess Schlesinger's 1934 novel *The Unpossessed* salutes "a daring, unique fiction, a wild, crowded comedy set in New York City in the 1930s."[154] It seems fitting that Elizabeth would celebrate a book by a young New Yorker with "a sensibility formed by the period and yet almost helplessly alert to the follies of a programmatic 'free love' and the knots and tangles of parlor radicalism." From the first pages, in which a woman comes home from an office feeling "sorrow for the departing year curling smaller and smaller until it was dead" and observes a house "again squatting smug on its rump like an injured woman," we are in the presence of an original sensibility who knew her way around a metaphor much as Elizabeth did. Schlesinger, who died at thirty-nine of cancer, was the mother of her friend Peter Davis. "Lizzie, with no prompting from me, decided to write the introduction," he said. "It was so endearing to me that she felt it was good enough to be published again."[155]

One introduction she had declined to write, back in the late 1970s, was for a volume of *Paris Review Interviews*. "I said I don't like the interview form myself," she explained. "I don't get anything out of it." Although in 1985 she had been the subject of a *Paris Review* interview conducted by her former student and good friend Darryl Pinckney, she claimed not to like talking about herself. "In general, I'd rather talk about other people," she said. "Gossip, or as we gossips like to say, character analysis."[156]

* * *

In the spring of 2000 Elizabeth wrote that she was now using a cane to get around New York, "a wonderful invention, but of course full of imperfections. Hard to shop or to hold things, trundling in and out of cabs."[157] Toward the end of the year, she told Susan Sontag that she was "more frail every year & don't go out much except for my work when that calls here and there."[158] In a 1972 review of Simone de Beauvoir's *The Coming of Age*, she had described old age as "a sort of natural injustice" in which "good luck, good health, certain prosperities of temperament and situation play a part—with the need for money looming over them all."[159] Asked in 2004 about why writers stopped writing, Elizabeth noted that aging was a major reason. "Writing is so hard," she said. "It's the only time in your life when you have to think."[160] The previous summer a young admirer who spotted her as she left a doctor's office on the Upper East Side attempted to tell her how extraordinary her writing was. "She said nothing," Linda Hall recalled. "Her eyes were clear and merry, her face pale in the August sun. She took both my hands in hers and held them for what seemed a very long time. Then she dropped my left hand, and gave my right a kiss."[161]

After a pacemaker implant, Elizabeth used a wheelchair. Jon Jewett, who became her personal assistant in New York, would push her chair to museums and once a week to Central Park. "Lizzie was not an outdoor girl," he said. "After fifty years of living next to the park, she finally visited it."[162] She would suggest getting a hotdog from a vendor, and she enjoyed watching the street artists. Once she said, "I never thought there were so many different colors of green."

While many of her friends had died before the end of the twentieth century, Barbara Epstein (who had divorced Jason in 1980) continued to edit until a few weeks before she died of lung cancer in 2006. In the last piece she wrote for the *New York Review*, Elizabeth described her good friend as "petite, pretty, elegant, and learned, especially in literary culture" as well as "a benign observer of human folly."[163] Silvers would carry on at the *Review* until his death in 2017 at eighty-seven. This time Elizabeth was not available for a comment; she had died on December 2, 2007, at Roosevelt Hospital. According to the *New York Times* obituary, she had been admitted for "a minor infection"—likely a polite fiction concocted by Silvers. In fact, she had been feeling poorly, with severe stomach pain.

A few weeks before her death, Ginny Foote and Alison West had visited Elizabeth, finding her forgetful but still mentally sharp. In late November 2007, she had had one last outing with Jewett at P. J. Clarke's, a restaurant across the street from Lincoln Center, where the Christmas tree had just been lighted. "She was extremely frail, but her wits were about her," Jewett recalled. "She started singing 'Hark the Herald Angels Sing' as she looked at the Christmas tree." As usual, she and Jewett each had a glass of white wine and a half-dozen oysters. "I tried to help her with the oysters," he said. And she said, 'No, sweetheart, let Mother try her oysters one more time.'" She had a way of grabbing a person on the wrist and patting his hand with her other hand, until she had teased out every bit of information she sought. Now she seized his wrist and said, "Sweetheart, I'm dying, and it's really not so bad"—the beginning of a soliloquy on this subject.

A photograph taken at Thanksgiving shows a smiling Harriet standing behind Elizabeth in her chair. She is stylishly dressed in a red print dress and black houndstooth shawl, her hair bound in one of her trademark scarves, gamely trying to smile. Five days later, in the hospital, Jewett said, she was perspiring and breathing heavily, irritated that the nurse wouldn't give her a glass of water. After he brought her ice cubes to slake her thirst and was ushered out of the room, she died.

Elizabeth was the last survivor of her circle of women who were notable twentieth-century cultural critics, including Mary McCarthy, Susan Sontag (who had died in 2004), and Hannah Arendt (1975). At her memorial service, Derek Walcott's remarks—read by Hilton Als—described Elizabeth's merry side. She was, he said, "more fun than any American writer I have known. She preferred gaiety to malice and had the laugh to go with it."[164] Joan Didion said, "every line she wrote suggested that moral courage required trusting one's own experience in the world, one's own intuitions about how it worked." She had "a way of putting words together that could make the most subtle connection seem at once thrilling and matter-of-fact. . . . She never took for granted what is often presented as a given." Elizabeth's former student Darryl Pinckney recalled how she told the class that "there are really only two reasons to write: desperation or revenge" and that "the only way to learn to write is to read."[165] The December 16 memorial, held at the Lincoln Center Library for the Performing Arts, was an intimate affair befitting Elizabeth's under-the-radar existence at the time of her death. After the service, a group of her friends gathered for dinner at Café des Artistes in her building to celebrate her long and extraordinary life.[166]

In 2015 Elizabeth was one of four authors posthumously inducted into the Kentucky Writers Hall of Fame at the Carnegie Center for Literacy and Learning in Lexington. Her photo hangs in the reading room with those of other Kentucky writers: Hunter S. Thompson, Guy Davenport, Wendell Berry, Effie Waller Smith, and Jim Wayne Miller. Elizabeth, never reticent about voicing a literary opinion, might have protested being lumped in with Berry, a prominent defender of agrarian values. As a member of the jury when Berry was proposed as a potential honoree for the 1988 Edward MacDowell Medal, she had called him "the most sentimental man in America." The jury chose William Styron instead.[167]

* * *

When the New York Review was founded, Elizabeth wrote about "the great difficulty" of being an intellectual: "making a point, making a difference—with words."[168] In her view, "An author's unexpected marriage to his subject is in many ways the essence of each new plot." By presenting real life "as if it were fiction," the novelist makes "the concreteness of fact . . . suggestive, shadowy, symbolical." Although she was writing about other authors (William Styron, Truman Capote, James Baldwin), her remarks apply equally to her own complex working out of the themes and insights that illuminate her prose. Spinning large and small observations out of inventive allusion and gossamer subtlety, she always required the reader to keep thinking along with her.

ACKNOWLEDGMENTS

I am deeply grateful to the staffs of libraries and archives without whose patient assistance this biography could not have been written: Boston University, Howard Gotlieb Archival Research Center; British Library Sound Archive; Castine Historical Society: Paige Lilly, curator; Columbia University Rare Book and Manuscript Library: Tara Craig, head of public services; Folger Shakespeare Library: Sara Butterfass Schiep, project archivist and cataloguer; Glendale [California] Central Library: Bryan Griest, interlibrary loan; University of Texas at Austin, Harry Ransom Center, Reference & Research Services: Mariah Wahl, graduate research associate; Harvard University, Houghton Library; Lexington [Kentucky] Central Library, Kentucky Room: Wayne Johnson, librarian; New York Public Library, Astor, Lenox, and Tilden Foundations, Berg Collection and Manuscripts and Archives Division: Meredith Mann, librarian; Princeton University: Brianna Cregle, Special Collections assistant; Skidmore College, Scribner Library, Special Collections: Jane Kjaer, curator; Smith College Library: Roxanne Daniel, reference assistant; Sonoma State University Library: Laura Krier, systems and metadata librarian; University of Kentucky Libraries, Louis B. Nunn Center for Oral History and Special Collections Research Center; University of California Los Angeles, Charles E. Young Research Library, Special Collections; University of Minnesota Libraries: Kathryn Hujda, assistant curator, Upper Midwest Literary Archives, Archives and Special Collections; University of Wisconsin–Madison Memorial Library, Department of Special Collections: Lisa Wettleson, public services coordinator; Vanderbilt University, Jean and Alexander Heard Library, Special Collections and University Archives: Teresa Gray, public services archivist; Washington University in St. Louis, Olin Library, Modern Literature Collection /Manuscripts, Special Collections: Joel Minor, curator; Vassar College, Archives and Special Collections Library: Ronald Patkus, associate director of libraries, and Dean Rogers, Special Collections assistant.

A much-appreciated grant from Vassar College Special Collections enabled me to receive copies of McCarthy's correspondence. Among the various rights holders who granted permission to quote from unpublished materials, I especially would like to thank Harriet Lowell, Sophia Wilson Niehaus, the Adrienne Rich Estate, and Farrar, Straus and Giroux. Special thanks go to Leslie Jean-Bart for allowing me to publish his lovely photo of Elizabeth without charging a fee.

Most of Elizabeth Hardwick's closest friends during the prime of her life were no longer alive when I began researching this book, though they do make an appearance in these pages via correspondence and published writing. But I would like to thank the writers, academics, and others who spoke or wrote to me, providing invaluable information, pointing me toward further sources, or offering encouragement and advice. They include (in alphabetical order): the late James Atlas, Steven Axelrod, Ann Beattie, Elizabeth Benedict, Michael Blumenthal, Rilla Bray, Frances Connell, Peter Davis, Terence Diggory, Helen Epstein, Barbara Fisher, Stephen Fitz-Gerald, Ginny Foote, Linda Hall, Saskia Hamilton, Kay Redfield Jamison, Jon R. Jewett, Elizabeth Kendall, David Laskin, Nancy Lemann, Paul Levy, Ada Long, Daphne Merkin, Susan Minot, Mona Simpson, Alison West, and someone who provided invaluable guidance in Lexington, Kentucky, but wishes to be anonymous.

I am also indebted to my patient, steadfast agent, Emily Forland, at Brandt & Hochman; to my editor, Jill Bialosky, who saw the promise in my proposal; to Jill's assistant, Drew Elizabeth Weitman, for help with procedural details; and to my expert copyeditor, Janet Biehl. Finally, my heartfelt thanks go to T.R.M. for many thoughtful comments and suggestions as I wrote and rewrote this book.

NOTES

List of Archives

Bishop Papers: Elizabeth Bishop Papers, Vassar College Archives and Special Collections Library

FSG Records: Farrar, Straus and Giroux Records, Manuscripts and Archives Division, NYPL

Hardwick Letters: Elizabeth Hardwick Letters, Special Collections Research Center, University of Kentucky

Hardwick Papers: Elizabeth Hardwick Papers, Henry Ransom Center, University of Texas at Austin

Jewett Collection: Jon R. Jewett Collection, Henry Ransom Center, University of Texas at Austin

Knight Papers: Grant C. Knight Papers, University of Kentucky Libraries

Lowell Papers: Robert Lowell Papers, Houghton Library, Harvard University

McCarthy Papers: Mary McCarthy Papers, Vassar College Archives and Special Collections Library

New Yorker Records: New Yorker Records, Manuscripts and Archives Division, NYPL

NYPL: New York Public Library

Silvers Papers: Robert Silvers Papers, New York Review of Books Records, Manuscripts and Archives Division, NYPL

Sontag Papers: Susan Sontag Papers, UCLA Library Special Collections

Tate Papers: Allen Tate Papers, Princeton University Library Special Collections

Taylor Papers: Peter Taylor Papers, Special Collections, Jean and Alexander
    Heard Library, Vanderbilt University
Yaddo Records: Yaddo Records, Manuscripts and Archives Division, NYPL

Prologue
1   EH to Robert Giroux, July 3, 1973, FSG Records.

Chapter 1: Lexington
1   Neither house number exists today; Rand Avenue peters out into an empty
     lot owned by Shiloh Baptist Church, on the next block.
2   EH, "Going Home in America," 78. Quotes in this section not otherwise
     attributed are from this essay.
3   EH, "Funny as a Crutch."
4   Eugene Hardwick was listed with this occupation in the 1930 U.S. Cen-
     sus, when he was twenty-four years old. The Kentucky Association Race
     Track closed in 1933 and was torn down two years later. The U.S. Housing
     Authority built a housing project on the site that intrigued Elizabeth as an
     example of good planning for a worthy cause. The present-day Keeneland
     Association racetrack opened in 1936, six miles outside the city.
5   EH, "Going Home in America," 80. Elizabeth also used this phrase in *Sleep-
     less Nights*. But I have not been able to find any information about a fire at
     the racetrack in the 1920s or '30s.
6   Quotes are from the New York Review Books edition (2001) of EH, *Sleepless
     Nights*. In "Elections: Renewal or Just Replacement?" Elizabeth compared
     "the struggle for what we are newly to become, through our political lead-
     ers and through ourselves" to "the last race of a day," when "we feel the
     apotheosis of the sacrificial power of the horse and its Faustian contract
     with the jockey."
7   EH, "Celebrities." This is a review of Laura Hillenbrand's *Seabiscuit: An
     American Legend* and Ann Hagedorn Auerbach's *Wild Ride: The Rise and
     Tragic Fall of Calumet Farm, Inc., America's Premier Racing Dynasty*.
8   "Facts About Lexington," *Polk's Lexington City Directory* 14 (1928). Burley is
     the plant variety commonly used in cigarette production.
9   EH, "Going Home in America," 79.
10   Information about Mary Ramsay from U.S. Delayed Birth Records (for the
     children born before the Hardwicks moved to Lexington; see note 20). In
     EH, *Sleepless Nights*, the narrator's mother lives in several North Carolina
     towns and was raised "by brothers and sisters." Some sources cite Raleigh
     as Mary's birthplace.
11   Ramsey is the author of *The Annals of Tennessee to the End of the Eighteenth
     Century* (1853) and a pamphlet, *Battle of Kings Mountain* (1867). His auto-
     biography, written in the 1870s, was published in 1954 by the Tennes-
     see Historical Commission. A newer edition also contains letters he wrote
     before and after the Civil War that demonstrate his support of slavery. *Dr.
     J. G. M. Ramsey: Autobiography and Letters* (Knoxville: University of Tennes-
     see Press, 2002).

12   Unless otherwise specified, all information about Elizabeth's parents and quotes in this chapter are from EH, Oral History, May 8, 1978. In *Sleepless Nights*, the narrator mentions that one of her mother's brothers, a particularly intelligent man, was institutionalized for unexplained reasons. If true, his fate must have suggested parallels with Lowell's mental illness.

13   EH, *Sleepless Nights*, 5–6.

14   EH to Harriet Winslow, July 11, 1958, Lowell Papers.

15   Curiously, one observer observed that Lowell was so accustomed to his mother's quarrelsome nature that he believed such behavior was "the nature of affection." Snodgrass, "Liberal Education," 452.

16   EH, *Ghostly Lover* (1989 ed.), 7.

17   EH, *Sleepless Nights*, 13.

18   EH, notes answering questions from Hilton Als for his "A Singular Woman," n.d., Hardwick Papers.

19   EH, notation on back of torn photograph, Jewett Collection.

20   Decades later these Hardwick siblings received "Delayed Birth Records" with dates based on baptismal certificates and notations in the family Bible: Margaret Allen (1903), William Randolph (1905), Eugene Thomas (1906), Mary Annette, known as Annette (1907), James Frederick (1909), Florence Ramsey (1910), and Mary Nell (1913).

21   Eugene and Mary Hardwick were not listed in the 1914–15 Lexington city directory, but if they came to town in 1915, the publication would already have been printed. Their names do appear in the 1916 directory, suggesting that they were able to secure the listing the year before.

22   The narrator in *Sleepless Nights* says that her father was also "something in the health department at the courthouse." This may have been a red herring Elizabeth added to separate fact from fiction, but if her father ever claimed such a position, he was likely making it up; no documentation exists.

23   According to his obituary, he was also a member of the International Order of Odd Fellows, Merrick Lodge no. 31. "E. A. Hardwick Dies From Heart Attack," *Lexington Leader,* May 29, 1944.

24   According to the 1930 U.S. Census, Addie Moore, age sixty, was part of the household, as a "roomer"—a source of income for the family. William and James, then in their twenties, were not living at home, freeing up a bedroom. James, who worked as an auditor for a retail automotive supply company, is listed in the 1940 census as living at the house; his job likely served as a primary source of support for the family.

25   EH, Oral History Interview, October 8–9, 1977.

26   Ibid.

27   "Master Plumbers Say Men Out on Strike," *Lexington Leader,* June 23, 1925.

28   EH, Oral History Interview, October 8–9, 1977. Quotes not otherwise attributed are also from this interview.

29   "Party at Duncan Park," *Lexington Leader,* January 11, 1925.

30   "Social Events: Progressive Dinner," *Lexington Leader,* December 11, 1932.

31   Today this building houses the Carnegie Literacy Center.

32   In Robert Lowell's poem "The Graduate," published in *For Lizzie and Harriet*

(1978), he puts into Elizabeth's mouth a description of Margaret as a college basketball player, who "came home / crying each night because of 'Happy' Chandler, / the coach, and later Governor of Kentucky." Albert Benjamin Chandler was the girls' basketball coach at Transylvania University.

33   "William R. Hardwick," *Lexington Leader,* March 25, 1982.

34   On page ix of his introduction to EH, *New York Stories,* Darryl Pinckney writes that this brother's gambling winnings at the track paid for Elizabeth's graduate school tuition. I have not found any information about this, but it fits with her statements about being supported by family members.

35   "Hardwick Sisters Will Meet Today at Duncan Park to Decide Junior Tennis Title of Lexington Parks," *Lexington Herald,* July 31, 1925.

36   Beauty salon advertisement, *Lexington Leader,* March 25, 1954.

37   Patrick Lee Lucas, "Lexington's Wolf Wile Department Store: A Mid-Century Achievement in Urban Architecture." *Kentucky Review* 15, no. 1 (2000), https://uknowledge.uky.edu/cgi/viewcontent.cgi?article=1003&context=kentucky-review.

38   Federal Writers' Project, *Lexington and Bluegrass Country,* 44.

39   The population in 1920 was 41,534. Ten years later it had grown by just over 4,000.

40   James Duane Bolin, *Bossism and Reform in a Southern City: Lexington, Kentucky 1880–1940* (Lexington: University Press of Kentucky, 2000), 66–67.

41   EH, "Life and Death of Chessman."

42   EH, "Billie Holiday."

43   EH, "Heart of the Seasons" (1988 ed.). All quotes in this paragraph are from pages 186–87.

44   EH, "Art of Fiction 87," 32.

45   EH to Elizabeth Bishop, May 10, 1950, Bishop Papers.

46   EH, "Billie Holiday."

47   To understand what a novelty this was, consider that Lexington was almost entirely inhabited by native-born whites and African Americans; in 1930, it had only 612 foreign-born residents.

48   EH, Oral History interview, November 5, 1978.

49   *Graduate School Bulletin, 1938–1939,* University of Kentucky Archives.

50   This is the equivalent to about $538 in today's dollars.

51   EH, Oral History interview, November 5, 1978.

52   EH, Oral History interview, October 8–9, 1977.

53   Ibid. The Moscow Trials, ordered by Joseph Stalin, were held between 1936 and 1938. Defendants were supporters of Leon Trotsky—the so-called Old Bolsheviks, party members before the Russian Revolution. The charge was that these men had conspired with Western leaders to assassinate Stalin, with the overriding aim of restoring capitalism.

54   Andrew Eckdahl, "Miss Hardwick's Novel Should Intrigue Lexingtonians," *Lexington Herald,* June 11, 1979.

55   Ibid.

56   EH, Oral History interview, October 8–9, 1977. The *Sleepless Nights* narra-

tor recalls "a woeful night on the sofa in a fraternity house," but Elizabeth seems to have steered clear of such places.

57   EH, Oral History interview, October 8–9, 1977.
58   Ibid.
59   EH, "Art of Fiction," 33.

Chapter 2: Discovering New York
1   In his introduction to EH, *New York Stories,* Darryl Pinckney confused this earlier trip to New York, when she stayed at the Hotel Taft, with the one she made in 1939.
2   EH, "Insulted and Injured," in EH, *View of My Own,* 183–84.
3   EH, Oral History interview, October 8–9, 1977. All quotes in this chapter not otherwise attributed are from this interview.
4   Morton White (1917–2016) later taught at Princeton; Richard Volney Chase (1914–62) wrote a classic study of the American novel; Robert Snyder (1916–2004) married Allegra Fuller, daughter of Buckminster, and made films about him, Henry Miller, Pablo Casals, and Michelangelo.
5   "Book Review Is Given at Altrusa Gathering," *Lexington Leader,* June 13, 1940.
6   "Columbia Scholarship Goes to Lexington," *Lexington Herald-Leader,* April 7, 1940.
7   EH to Sally Alexander, n.d. [December 1940], Hardwick Papers.
8   He may have been the boyfriend whose doctor father received opera tickets from a patient—tickets that enabled Elizabeth and the boyfriend to attend the opera frequently, as she recalled in her Oral History interview, May 8, 1978.
9   EH to Sally Alexander, [n.d.], Hardwick Papers.
10   EH, Oral History interview, May 8, 1978.
11   EH, preface to a new edition of *The Ghostly Lover* (typescript), 1985, Hardwick Papers.
12   EH, Oral History interview, May 8, 1978.
13   EH to Sally Alexander, [n.d.], Hardwick Papers. Quotes in the following paragraph are also from this letter.
14   EH, *Sleepless Nights* (2001 ed.), 27.
15   EH, *Sleepless Nights* (2001 ed.), 121.
16   EH, Oral History interview, October 9, 1977.
17   EH to Sally Alexander, "summer" [1940s], Hardwick Papers
18   EH to Sally Alexander, May 22, 1941, Hardwick Papers.
19   All the temperature-controlled cars—sleeping, dining, and salon (seats with no Pullman berths)—were named for aspects of the first president's life.
20   EH, "Going Home in America," 70.
21   EH to Sally Alexander, n.d. [1940s], Hardwick Papers.
22   EH, "Evenings at Home," 448.
23   EH, "Cross-Town."
24   Meyers, *Lowell in Love,* 87.

25   EH, "Scene from an Autobiography."

26   Hotel Schuyler postcard, ca. 1930–45, Tichnor Brothers Collection, Boston Public Library, https://www.digitalcommonwealth.org/search/commonwealth:kp78gk81x.

27   EH, "Billie Holiday." However, she later said she didn't meet him until they were both in New York. EH, Oral History interview, September 20, 1979.

28   EH, "Billie Holiday." In an interview a decade later, she criticized the singer's 1958 autobiography, *Lady Sings the Blues*, as "ghastly"—full of lies that Holiday had told her collaborator (William Dufty)—and said that her dislike of this book led her to set down her own memories of Holiday. EH and Lorna Sage in Conversation.

29   EH, "Scene from an Autobiography," 61.

30   Those disgraceful actions likely consisted of his entire career in the theater, which the Puritans viewed as a cesspool of sin. *The Dyer's Hand and Other Essays* is also the title of a book by W. H. Auden, published in 1962.

31   EH to Alfred A. Knopf, March 8, 1943 (following up on her submission months earlier); Mrs. Alfred A. Knopf to EH, April 8, 1943 (rejecting the manuscript). Knopf Papers, Manuscript Division, NYPL.

32   EH to Sally Alexander, May 2 and 7, 1944, Hardwick Papers.

33   Founded by Julius Rosenwald, president and chairman of Sears Roebuck and Company, the Rosenwald Fellowship was primarily intended for African Americans in scientific, academic, and cultural fields, but white Southerners were also apparently considered for aid. https://pqdtopen.proquest.com/doc/1095708693.html?FMT=ABS. However, she seems to have been awarded the fellowship the following year: the *Lexington Herald* announced on page one that Elizabeth won "one of 46 Rosenwald Fund Fellowships for 1945" (May 18, 1945). She would list this fellowship on her Yaddo application in 1948.

34   Elizabeth told an interviewer that she finished it "back home," which—given the context—I feel is more likely to be correct than her claim, in the introduction to *New York Stories* (page x), that she finished it at her sister's home on Staten Island.

35   EH to Grant C. Knight, September 20, 1944, Knight Papers.

36   EH to Grant C. Knight, August 8, 1946, Knight Papers.

37   Other authors published in *O. Henry Memorial Prize Stories* (New York: Doubleday, 1945) included Mary Lavin, Irwin Shaw, and Jessamyn West.

38   EH, Oral History interview, November 5, 1978.

39   EH to Sally Alexander, "I have a character named Bruce—but no relation, of course." May 2 and 7, 1944, Hardwick Papers.

40   EH, preface to new edition of *The Ghostly Lover* (typescript), 1985, Hardwick Papers.

41   *Kirkus Review,* April 18, 1945.

42   Henry Hornsby, "Miss Hardwick's Novel Is to Literature as Surrealism Is to Art—But It's Good," *Lexington Herald-Leader,* April 29, 1945. This long piece was surrounded by ads for the book placed by three local bookstores. The *Lexington Herald* had published an announcement on November 12, 1944,

when Elizabeth received her contract from Harcourt, Brace for the still-untitled novel. On March 18, 1945, the *Lexington Leader* followed *Publishers' Weekly*'s lead in announcing the publication date, adding that Elizabeth's short stories would be appearing soon in *Yale Review, Harper's Bazaar, PR,* and *New Mexico Quarterly.*

43   Rosenfeld, "In and Out of the War."

44   Buckman, "Wandering Parents."

45   EH to Grant C. Knight, August 8, 1946, Knight Papers.

46   EH, Oral History interview, November 5, 1978.

47   Philip Rahv to EH, February 6, 1945, Lowell Papers.

48   Phillips and Rahv, *New Partisan Reader,* vi.

49   EH, Oral History interview, May 8, 1978. All quotes from Elizabeth in this section, unless otherwise identified, are from this interview.

50   Mary McCarthy was certain that Elizabeth had been involved with Rahv, as she told her biographer Carol Brightman, warning her that if Elizabeth denied this, she should not be believed. Brightman, *Writing Dangerously,* 301. Mary claimed that Elizabeth and Rahv had separately confided to her that the lovemaking fell short. However, Elizabeth told her good friend Darryl Pinckney that she had *not* had an affair with Rahv. Pinckney, "Ethics of Admiration." I think the truth lies in between, as shown in Elizabeth's remark to her oral history interviewer. "A brief encounter" suggests exactly that—a brief dalliance, maybe no more than a night or two, rather than something she would have considered a full-blown affair.

51   An earlier version of *PR* was published by the Communist Party's John Reed Club.

52   "American Literary Criticism Today" (symposium), Sonoma State College, 1964.

53   Phillips, *Partisan View,* 113.

54   EH, foreword to McCarthy, *Intellectual Memoirs.*

55   By law, bourbon, the drink dear to Kentuckians, must be produced from a mash that contains at least 51 percent corn and cannot be blended with other whiskeys or neutral grain spirits or additives.

56   Quoted in Kiernan, *Seeing Mary Plain,* 268–69.

57   Heller, *Hannah Arendt,* 8.

58   EH, interview by Helen McNeil, *Writing Lives,* 74.

59   Trilling, "Fiction in Review."

60   Trilling, *Beginning of the Journey,* 350.

61   Decades later Harriet Lowell mentioned the abortions in her introduction to a reprint of a piece her mother wrote in 1996 ("On Behalf of the Unborn: A Celibacy Amendment"), published as "A Solution to the Abortion War: The Celibacy Amendment" in *New York Review Daily,* June 17, 2019. Elizabeth wrote about an abortion in part three of *Sleepless Nights.* If this fictionalized account is accurate, after fleeing other under-the-radar abortionists, Elizabeth had her procedure done by a Black man who also ran a funeral home.

62   Quoted in Disney, "Heaven Without God."

63   EH, *Sleepless Nights* (2001 ed.), 55.
64   Allen Tate to EH, October 21, 1947, Lowell Papers.
65   EH, Oral History interview, September 20, 1979.
66   EH, "Mysteries of Eleusis," 207–13. The Eleusinian mysteries were secret religious rites of ancient Greece. In October 1946, the *Lexington Herald* announced, "Miss Elizabeth Hardwick, daughter of Mrs. E. A. Hardwick, 264 Rand Avenue, has had two of her short stories accepted for publication in new anthologies." The other story was probably "The Golden Stallion."
67   EH, "Artist and Spokesman" and "Poor Little Rich Girls."
68   EH, "Ten Years' Experiment."
69   EH, "Fiction Chronicle" (June 1948).
70   McAlexander, *Conversations with Taylor,* 125.
71   Anaïs Nin, *Under a Glass Bell and Other Stories* (Athens: Ohio University Press, 1948). In April, Edmund Wilson had offered qualified praise for this book in *The New Yorker,* but his opinion was likely colored by the fact that he was smitten by Nin and attempting to kindle an affair.
72   Philip Rahv to Mary McCarthy, August 1, 1947, McCarthy Papers.
73   EH to Mary McCarthy, August 20, 1947, McCarthy Papers.

Chapter 3: Love and Torment
1   EH to Sally Alexander, January 27, 1948, Hardwick Papers.
2   In his preface to Elizabeth's *New York Stories,* Darryl Pinckney relates a story told to him by her daughter, Harriet Lowell, who heard it from her father (p. xii). Elizabeth meets Lowell in 1945 at a midtown hotel where she is grilled by "literary wives" about her relationship with Allen Tate. This story seems apocryphal. It does not appear in the Lowell biographies, and I have not encountered any information—in Elizabeth's writings, letters, or interviews—that would lead me to believe it is true. Lowell was still married to Jean Stafford in 1945; the couple was living in Connecticut and, beginning that summer, in Maine. Pinckney does not mention the couple's actual meeting, at the Rahvs' in 1947.
3   Robert Lowell, "Man and Wife," *Life Studies* (1959), reprinted in Lowell, *Collected Poems,* 189.
4   EH, Oral History interview, September 20, 1979. In this interview, Elizabeth called the description in the poem "hyperbole."
5   Jamison, *Setting the River on Fire,* 42–46.
6   EH to Ian Hamilton, n.d., Hardwick Papers.
7   EH to Elizabeth Ames, May 9, 1949, Yaddo Records. John Woodburn, her editor at Harcourt, Brace, had written to Ames on February 18, 1946, to propose Elizabeth as a candidate. He wrote that she was "working on a second novel under contract to us which she expects to have finished sometime in the Fall of 1946." Likely because her progress on the novel was not going well, she did not follow up until the following year. Yaddo sent an application to her on February 5, 1947, but she put off applying until two years later. Yaddo Records.
8   Yaddo Report for Committee on Admissions, Yaddo Records.

9   Mary Townsend, secretary to Elizabeth Ames, to EH, May 12, 1948, Yaddo Records.

10   Travisano, *Love Unknown*, 201–2.

11   The divorce was finalized in March 1948.

12   EH to Mary McCarthy and Bowden Broadwater, January 12, 1949, McCarthy Papers. Flannery O'Connor stayed in Elizabeth's apartment for a few days in late February, while she was visiting her editor. O'Connor to Elizabeth McKee, February 18, 1949, in O'Connor, *Habit of Being*, 10.

13   Elizabeth Ames to EH, November 23, 1948, Yaddo Records.

14   Quoted in RL to Elizabeth Bishop, "Christmas Eve" (1948), in Lowell, *Letters*, 121.

15   RL to Peter Taylor, n.d. [January 1949], Taylor Papers.

16   RL to George Santayana, January 5 [1949], in Lowell, *Letters*, 126.

17   Philip Rahv to EH, February 13, 1949, Hardwick Papers.

18   EH to Richard Volney Chase, January 22, 1949, Richard Volney Chase Papers, Rare Book & Manuscript Library, Columbia University.

19   Dwight Macdonald to Elizabeth Ames, March 3, 1949; EH to Michael Wreszin, July 21, 1990, quoted in Wreszin, *Rebel in Defense of Tradition*, 223n18.

20   Alfred Kazin, *New York Jew* (New York: Alfred A. Knopf, 1978), 204.

21   Ibid., 205.

22   Allen Tate to EH, March 3, 1949, Lowell Papers.

23   Allen Tate to EH, March 8, 1949, Lowell Papers.

24   Members of the panel included W.E.B. Du Bois, Norman Mailer, and Dimitri Shostakovich. Notwithstanding the assurances of a Soviet government representative, five of the six writers Macdonald asked about were either imprisoned or dead; Boris Pasternak was the lone exception.

25   Allen Tate to EH, March 31, 1949, Lowell Papers.

26   Allen Tate to EH, April 4, 1949, Lowell Papers.

27   Allen Tate to EH, April 11, 1949, Lowell Papers.

28   EH to RL, April 13, 1949, Lowell Papers.

29   EH to RL, April 19, 1949, Lowell Papers.

30   EH to RL, June 14, 1949, Lowell Papers.

31   EH to Mary McCarthy, June 28, 1949, McCarthy Papers.

32   EH to RL, July 2, 1949, Lowell Papers.

33   EH to John Berryman, June 22, 1949, John Berryman Papers, University of Minnesota.

34   EH to RL, July 6–7, 1949, Lowell Papers.

35   EH to Mary McCarthy, June 28, 1949, McCarthy Papers.

36   To remarry within the Catholic Church, it is necessary to secure an annulment voiding the previous marriage, in addition to a secular divorce. (This is different from a civil annulment.)

37   RL to Peter Taylor, April 27, 1949, in Lowell, *Letters*, 138.

38   RL to EH, July 1, 1949, ibid., 141.

39   RL to EH, July 4–5, 1949, ibid., 141–42.

40   EH to Mary McCarthy, July 16, 1949, McCarthy Papers.

41　EH to Mary McCarthy, August 8, 1949, McCarthy Papers.

42　Hamilton, *Lowell: A Biography,* 162.

43　EH to Mr. and Mrs. Lowell, August 15, 1949, Lowell Papers.

44　EH to Sally Alexander, August 18, 1949, Hardwick Papers.

45　EH, interview by *Observer,* 1969, Hardwick Papers.

46　EH to Mary McCarthy, September 4, 1949, McCarthy Papers.

47　RL to EH, n.d. [September 1949], in Lowell, *Letters,* 147.

48　EH to Mary McCarthy, September 14, 1949, McCarthy Papers.

49　EH to RL, September 20, 1949, Lowell Papers.

50　EH to RL, "Tuesday" [September 1949], Lowell Papers.

51　EH to Charlotte Winslow Lowell, September 15, 1949, Lowell Papers.

52　Merrill Moore to EH, October 5, 1949, Lowell Papers. Moore earned his medical degree at Vanderbilt University, where he turned out reams of bad verse and attempted to align himself with the so-called Fugitive poets. Even as a doctor—his specialty was the treatment of alcoholism and syphilis—he appears to have been thoroughly unprofessional. Moore took on the role of psychotherapist without having appropriate training. After sessions with Charlotte, he had told Cal that he was an unwanted child. His unprofessional behavior included revealing to Charlotte what her grown son had said during sessions with him. Meyers, *Lowell in Love,* 25–26.

53　About $211 in 2018 dollars.

54　EH to Mary McCarthy, September 30, 1949, McCarthy Papers. In the 1940s, the median rent for a New York apartment was fifty dollars, rising to seventy-five to ninety dollars by the mid-1950s. Jessica Dailey, "What Would $50 in 1940 Rent a New Yorker Today?" *Curbed,* November 21, 2013.

55　EH to Mary McCarthy, December 13, 1949, McCarthy Papers.

56　EH to Mary McCarthy, October 21, 1949, McCarthy Papers.

57　Charlotte Winslow Lowell to EH, October 22, 1949, Lowell Papers.

58　RL to Charlotte Winslow Lowell, November 5 [1949], in Lowell, *Letters,* 149.

59　The check is still in the December 13, 1949, letter from Mary McCarthy to EH, which does not mention the enclosure. Lowell Papers.

60　The amount of this check is unknown. After Lowell knew he would be teaching at the University of Iowa, he wrote to Tate to say that he would not cash it until Tate let him know if the money should instead go to "two still poorer people." RL to Allen Tate, December 29 [1949], in Lowell, *Letters,* 152.

61　Sarah Winslow Cotting to EH, "Wednesday" [late December 1949], Lowell Papers.

62　EH to Allen Tate, December 28 1949, Tate Papers.

63　EH to Charlotte Winslow Lowell, February 5, 1949 (actually 1950), Lowell Papers.

64　EH to Eleanor Taylor, February 14, 1950, Lowell Papers.

65　EH to Elizabeth Bishop, May 10, 1950, Bishop Papers.

66　Snodgrass, "Liberal Education."

67　Philip Rahv to EH, February 9, 1950, Lowell Papers.

68   EH, "Fiction Chronicle," *PR* 27 (January 1950), 87–91. She had also written a commissioned piece for *Harper's Bazaar* "on American women" that I have not been able to locate.

69   RL to George Santayana, January 8 [1950], in Lowell, *Letters,* 153.

70   RL to Peter Taylor, March 30 [1950], ibid., 155.

71   EH to Sally Alexander, April 12, 1950, Hardwick Papers.

72   EH to Elizabeth Bishop, May 10, 1950, Bishop Papers.

73   EH to Robie and Anne Macauley, June 21, 1950, Hardwick Letters.

74   RL to Peter Taylor, July 29 [1950], in Lowell, *Letters,* 156.

75   EH to Mary McCarthy, September 7, 1950, McCarthy Papers.

76   Ibid.

77   EH quoted in Hamilton, *Lowell: A Biography,* 169.

78   EH to Mary McCarthy, September 7, 1950, McCarthy Papers.

79   Mary Hardwick to RL, September 6, 1950, Lowell Papers.

Chapter 4: European Immersion

1   RL to George Santayana, September 18, 1950, in Lowell, *Letters,* 160.

2   EH to Mary McCarthy, November 11, 1950, McCarthy Papers.

3   Ibid.

4   Caffery was a nephew of the American ambassador to Paris. Herbert, the second son of the elder son of the fifteenth Earl of Pembroke, was a friend of the photographer Cecil Beaton's and was known, tongue-in-cheek, as the "Uncrowned Queen" of Tangier. "David Alexander Reginald Herbert," http://andrejkoymasky.com/liv/fam/bioh2/herber02.html

5   EH, Oral History interview, October 8–9, 1977.

6   RL to Elizabeth Bishop, December 6, 1950, in Bishop and Lowell, *Works in Air,* 114.

7   EH to Mary McCarthy, November 11, 1950, McCarthy Papers. Seventy-five dollars in 1950 is the equivalent of $763 in today's currency.

8   EH to Robie Macauley, November 12, 1950, Hardwick Letters.

9   EH to Robie Macauley, March 18, 1950, Hardwick Letters.

10   EH to Mary McCarthy, November 11, 1950, McCarthy Papers. The following spring, on March 18, 1951, Elizabeth wrote to Robie and Anne Macauley, who hoped to come to Europe, that "it is possible to eat, stay in a hotel, etc. for about $10 a day for the two of you." Hardwick Letters.

11   RL to Elizabeth Bishop, December 6, 1950, in Bishop and Lowell, *Works in Air,* 114.

12   EH to Peter Taylor (postcard), n.d., postmarked October, Taylor Papers.

13   EH to Robie Macauley, November 12, 1950. One hundred sixty dollars is the equivalent of $1,630 in today's dollars.

14   EH to Mary McCarthy, November 11, 1950, McCarthy Papers. The American Academy is housed in the massive Villa Aurelia.

15   Elizabeth later wrote to Cal's biographer Ian Hamilton that there were "wonderful ceremonies in all the basilicas, the Pope on the balcony," but for some reason she had nothing to say about the Holy Year events in her letters of the period.

16   EH to Robie Macauley, November 12, 1950, Hardwick Letters..
17   EH to Eleanor Taylor, November 25, 1950, Taylor Papers.
18   RL to Peter Taylor, January 13, 1951, Taylor Papers.
19   EH to Eleanor Taylor, November 25, 1950, Taylor Papers.
20   EH to Mary McCarthy, December 12, 1950, McCarthy Papers.
21   Ibid.
22   EH, "Florentine Conference." In a typically Harwickian touch, an old, illiterate Italian servant has the last word.
23   EH quoted in Mariani, *Lost Puritan*, 199.
24   EH to Mary McCarthy, January 18, 1951, McCarthy Papers.
25   EH to Mary McCarthy, December 12, 1950, McCarthy Papers.
26   EH to Robie and Anne Macauley, March 3, 1951, Hardwick Letters. The Harmsworths were in Florence because one of their daughters was keeping company there with a man known to her mother as "the Hebrew." Susan Turner to EH, February 15, 1951, Lowell Papers.
27   RL to Peter Taylor, [no date] 1951, in Lowell, *Letters*, 166.
28   EH to Mary McCarthy, January 18, 1951, McCarthy Papers.
29   RL to Elizabeth Bishop, January 22, 1951, in Bishop and Lowell, *Words in Air*, 116.
30   RL to EH, ca. January 5, 1951, in Lowell, *Letters*, 166.
31   EH to Mary McCarthy, May 7, 1951, McCarthy Papers.
32   RL to Robie Macauley, [late November], quoted in Hamilton, *Lowell: A Biography*, 192.
33   EH to Mary McCarthy, February 9, 1951, McCarthy Papers.
34   EH to Mary McCarthy, January 18, 1951, McCarthy Papers.
35   EH to Mary McCarthy, February 9, 1951, McCarthy Papers.
36   EH to Robie and Anne Macauley, March 18, 1951, Hardwick Letters.
37   She was married to Roffredo Caetani, a composer and prince of the municipality of Bassiano. *Botteghe Oscure* published significant poetry and prose in five languages. The biannual journal took its name from Via delle Botteghe Oscure (Street of the Dark Shops), the location of the Palazzo Caetani, where the couple lived.
38   EH to Charlotte Winslow, April 9, 1951, Lowell Papers.
39   EH to Mary McCarthy, August 4, 1951, McCarthy Papers.
40   EH, "Two Recent Travellers," 436. Mustafa Kemal Atatürk (1881–1938) was the founder of the Republic of Turkey; he instituted political, economic, and cultural reforms to bring Turkey into the twentieth century.
41   John Crowe Ransom to EH, December 16, 1952, Lowell Papers; EH, "Two Recent Travellers," 436–54.
42   EH to Charlotte Winslow, June 1, 1951, Lowell Papers. The stress on frugality may also have been meant to counterbalance the list of American-made items—nylon stockings, slip, pajamas, and socks for Cal—that Elizabeth asked Charlotte to purchase and bring on her upcoming trip to Europe.
43   EH to Mary McCarthy, August 4, 1951, McCarthy Papers. The "Fulbrights" were people who had won a Fulbright Fellowship for travel abroad. In Paris, one of the people Elizabeth encountered was Patricia Blake Nabokov, a for-

mer model (and former lover of novelist Albert Camus) who was the American second wife of composer and writer Nicholas Nabokov, first cousin of the author Vladimir Nabokov. Elizabeth was bemused by the way she "talks about the parts of the body all the time. . . . tits . . . being an especial favorite."

44   EH to Mary McCarthy (postcard), postmarked July 21, 1951, McCarthy Papers. Months later Cal would enumerate all the places they had visited thus far, luxuriating in the roll-call of exotic names: Naples, Bari, Lecci, Brindisi, Athens, Istanbul, Bursa, Smyrna, Athens, Delphi, Corinth, Sunnium, Naples, Genoa, Paris, Versailles, Chartres, Mont Saint Michel, the Loire country, Fontainebleau, the Basque country, Lourdes, Pau, Brussels, Antwerp, The Hague, Haarlem, Amsterdam, London, Eton. RL to Elizabeth Bishop, November 6, 1951, in Bishop and Lowell, *Words in Air*, 126.

45   RL to EH, [late July or early August] 1951, in Lowell, *Letters*, 172.

46   RL to EH, [late July or early August] 1951, ibid., 173.

47   RL to Flannery O'Connor, [late May or early June 1952], ibid., 188.

48   EH to Mary McCarthy, August 4, 1951, McCarthy Papers.

49   RL to EH, ca. September 18, 1951, in Lowell, *Letters*, 174.

50   EH to RL, September 15, 1951, Lowell Papers.

51   EH to RL, September 20, 1951 ("Thursday night"), Lowell Papers. Elizabeth's solution for luggage transport was to have most of it shipped.

52   EH to Mary McCarthy, October 5, 1951, McCarthy Papers.

53   EH to RL, September 21, 1951, Lowell Papers.

54   EH to Robie and Anne Macauley, November 4, 1951, Hardwick Letters.

55   EH to Mary McCarthy, October 5, 1951, McCarthy Papers.

56   EH to the Macauleys, November 29, 1951, Hardwick Letters.

57   EH to Mary McCarthy, October 5, 1951, McCarthy Papers.

58   They were military tribunals held by Allied forces after World War II.

59   EH to Mary McCarthy, October 28, 1951, McCarthy Papers.

60   RL to Charlotte Winslow Lowell, ca. October 1, 1951, in Lowell, *Letters*, 175.

61   RL to Peter Taylor, n.d. [spring 1952], Taylor Papers.

62   RL to Elizabeth Bishop, February 26, 1952, in Bishop and Lowell, *Words in Air*, 132.

63   RL to Elizabeth Bishop, April 24, 1952, ibid., 137.

64   EH, Oral History interview, May 8, 1978. Elizabeth likened a return to Kentucky to "exile to Siberia."

65   EH to Macauleys, November 29, 1951, Hardwick Letters.

66   Philip Rahv to EH, November 27, 1951, Lowell Papers.

67   "The American Woman as Snow-Queen: Our Self-Contemptuous Acceptance of Europe's Myth," *Commentary* 12 (December 1951), 546–50. Elizabeth wrote that this archetype of a "tall, beautiful, appallingly splendid [woman], all cleanliness and whiteness, living in her empty, silent, frigid palace" was actually not a realistic reflection of American women. Mary McCarthy to EH, February 25, 1952, Lowell Papers.

68   Mary McCarthy to EH, February 25, 1952, Lowell Papers.

69   EH to Peter and Eleanor Taylor, January 3, 1951 (actually 1952), Taylor Papers.
70   RL to Elizabeth Bishop, November 6, 1951, in Bishop and Lowell, *Words in Air,* 125.
71   EH to Mary McCarthy, October 5, 1951, McCarthy Papers.
72   RL to Peter Taylor, October 6, 1951, in Lowell, *Letters,* 178.
73   RL to Elizabeth Bishop, November 6, 1951, in Bishop and Lowell, *Words in Air,* 126.
74   EH to Mary McCarthy, December 13, 1951, McCarthy Papers.
75   EH to Mary McCarthy, October 28, 1951, McCarthy Papers. All quotes in this paragraph are from this letter, unless otherwise noted.
76   RL to Randall Jarrell, February 24, 1952, in Lowell, *Letters,* 182.
77   The New Criticism, named after the title of a 1941 book by John Crowe Ransom, asserted the primacy of analyzing works of literature as self-referential aesthetic objects.
78   RL to Elizabeth Bishop, April 24, [1952], in Bishop and Lowell, *Words in Air,* 136.
79   EH to the Macauleys, November 29, 1951, Hardwick Letters.
80   van Galen Last, "Hardwick on Human Comedy."
81   EH to Mary McCarthy, December 13, 1951, McCarthy Papers.
82   Ibid.
83   Elizabeth published no further short stories in *PR* after the May–June 1951 issue. I have not been able to find out anything about the publication history of this story.
84   RL to Elizabeth Bishop, April 24, 1952, in Bishop and Lowell, *Words in Air,* 137.
85   EH to Mary McCarthy, April 15, 1952, McCarthy Papers.
86   EH to Mary McCarthy, February 7, 1952, McCarthy Papers. It's not clear when Elizabeth visited California with Clark, a writer friend of Mary's.
87   EH to Robie and Anne Macauley, February 22, 1952, Hardwick Letters.
88   RL to Randall Jarrell, February 24 [1952], in Lowell, *Letters,* 181.
89   EH to Robie and Anne Macauley, February 22, 1952.
90   RL to Elizabeth Bishop, February 26, 1952, in Bishop and Lowell, *Words in Air,* 132.
91   EH to Peter and Eleanor Taylor, February 21, 1952, Taylor Papers.
92   EH to Robie and Anne Macauley, February 22, 1952, Hardwick Letters.
93   Quoted in Meyers, *Lowell in Love,* 100. In the early 1970s, Huyck van Leeuwen left his wife for a younger woman, a fate Elizabeth knew to be especially difficult in Holland, because of its close-knit intellectual world.
94   EH to Mary McCarthy, March 3, 1952, McCarthy Papers.
95   EH to Robie Macauley, April 10, 1952, Hardwick Letters.
96   EH to Mary McCarthy, April 15, 1952, McCarthy Papers.
97   EH to Mary McCarthy, March 25, 1952. Five dollars was the equivalent of about forty-six dollars in 2019.
98   RL to Elizabeth Bishop, April 24, 1951, in Lowell, *Letters,* 186.
99   Founded in 1950, the Congress for Cultural Freedom, which represented

intellectuals united against Communism, was later discovered to have been funded by the CIA.

100   RL to George Santayana, March 19, 1952, in Lowell, *Letters,* 185.

101   EH to Mary McCarthy, May 27, 1952, McCarthy Papers. She also reported that, in a meeting with Cal at the Deux Magots café—apparently Elizabeth was either not invited or didn't feel like going—Auden delivered some nuggets of wisdom, including his belief that "drinking interferes with the quality of American writing."

102   EH to Mary McCarthy, May 27, 1952, McCarthy Papers.

103   RL to Peter Taylor, n.d. [June? 1952], in Lowell, *Letters,* 189.

104   EH to Mary McCarthy, May 27, 1952, McCarthy Papers.

105   EH to Mary McCarthy, March 25, 1952, McCarthy Papers.

106   EH to Mary McCarthy, April 15, 1952, McCarthy Papers.

107   RL to Elizabeth Bishop, April 24, 1952, in Bishop and Lowell, *Words in Air,* 137.

108   This gathering is now known as the Salzburg Global Seminar.

109   EH to Charlotte Lowell, August 25, 1952, Lowell Papers.

110   EH to Robie and Anne Macauley, August 24, 1952, Hardwick Letters. Elizabeth had sent a telegram earlier telling the Macauleys that Cal was well. In this letter she explains that it was "an exaggeration, which I did for his sake."

111   EH to Robie and Anne Macauley, August 25, 1952, Hardwick Letters.

112   EH to Robie Macauley, September 5, 1952, Hardwick Letters.

113   According to Kay Redfield Jamison, Cal received "a course of five or six electroshock treatments in the U.S. Army hospital in Munich," which "stopped his mania." Jamison, *Setting the River on Fire,* 116. This was his second experience of electroshock, also known as electroconvulsive therapy (ECT); three years earlier he had undergone six treatments at Baldpate Hospital in Georgetown, Pennsylvania. The procedure involves sending small electrical currents into the brain in order to induce a seizure, thereby rewiring the brain chemistry and regulating stress hormones.

114   EH to Robie and Anne Macauley, August 24, 1952, Hardwick Letters.

115   EH to John McCormack, [August 27, 1952] ("Wednesday night"), Hardwick Papers.

116   This figure seems exaggerated. In 1955, TWA was advertising flights from New York to Rome for $360.

117   EH to Robie and Anne Macauley, September 5, 1952, Hardwick Letters.

118   RL to Charlotte Winslow Lowell, October 19, 1952, in Lowell, *Letters,* 192. In this letter, however, Cal significantly downplayed the seriousness of his attack.

119   EH to John McCormack, August 31, 1952, Hardwick Papers.

120   EH to Blair and Holly Clark, September 7, 1952, Hardwick Papers.

121   The conference ran from September 22 to 28, 1952. Speakers included artists Georges Rouault, Henry Moore, and Jacques Villon; Brazilian architect Lúcio Costa; composer Arthur Honegger; Italian film director and screenwriter Alessandro Blasetti; and playwrights Ashley Dukes, Marc Connelly, and Thornton Wilder. Under the circumstances, it was fortunate

that poetry was not among the offerings of the conference, so Cal was not tempted to make a public statement.

122 EH to Robie and Anne Macauley, October 19, 1952, Hardwick Letters.
123 EH to Blair and Holly Clark, September 7, 1952, Hardwick Papers.
124 EH to Blair and Holly Clark (postcard), n.d., Hardwick Papers.
125 RL to Charlotte Winslow Lowell, October 19, 1952, in Lowell, *Letters,* 191.
126 EH to Robie and Anne Macauley, October 19, 1952, Hardwick Letters.
127 EH to John McCormack, October 26, 1952, Hardwick Papers.
128 RL to Allen Tate, November 5, 1952, in Lowell, *Letters,* 193–94. This was the story published in the summer 1953 issue of *Kenyon Review* as "Two Recent Travellers."
129 EH to the Clarks, November 16, 1952, Hardwick Papers.
130 RL to Robie Macauley, December 2, 1952, quoted in Mariani, *Lost Puritan,* 220.
131 RL to Allen Tate, November 5, 1952, in Lowell, *Letters,* 193–94.
132 EH to Blair Clark, November 27, 1952, Hardwick Papers.
133 EH to John McCormack, December 8, 1952, Hardwick Papers.
134 EH to the Clarks, December 10, 1952, Hardwick Papers.
135 EH to Blair and Holly Clark, February 3, 1953, Hardwick Papers.

Chapter 5: Boston

1   EH to the Clarks, February 3, 1953, Lowell Papers.
2   EH to Charlotte Lowell, February 5, 1953, Lowell Papers.
3   Charles Shields, *And So It Goes: Kurt Vonnegut, a Life* (New York: St. Martin's, 2011), 191.
4   Flannery O'Connor to EH and Robert Lowell, March 17, 1953, in O'Connor, *Habit of Being,* 57.
5   The reference is to *Sewanee Review.*
6   EH to Mary McCarthy, February 5, 1953, McCarthy Papers. After sounding indecisive the year before, John Crowe Ransom, editor of *Kenyon Review,* wrote to Elizabeth to accept "Two Recent Travellers," her story set in Turkey, noting that it had "a lot of style, & very special atmosphere, and the people are not underdone or overplotted."
7   EH, "Subjugation of Women."
8   Robert Giroux to EH, June 19, 1953, Lowell Papers.
9   RL to Peter Taylor, March 25, 1953, Taylor Papers. Elizabeth quoted Cal's words in a letter to the Clarks on April 17, Lowell Papers.
10 Robie Macauley to EH, March 8, 1953, Hardwick Papers.
11 EH, "Art of Fiction 87," 42.
12 The School of Letters had moved from Kenyon College to Indiana University in 1951, retaining its faculty of prominent literary men.
13 EH to the Clarks, April 17, 1953, Lowell Papers.
14 EH to Charlotte Lowell, April 25, 1953, Lowell Papers.
15 Oddly, the new car was the same make as the one in which he had the accident.
16 EH to Blair Clark, September 6, 1953, Lowell Papers.
17 EH to Charlotte Lowell, June 3, 1953, Lowell Papers.

18   EH to RL, September 6, 1953, Lowell Papers.

19   EH to Blair Clark, September 6, 1953.

20   EH to RL, September 10, 1953, Lowell Papers.

21   EH to RL, September 12, 1953, Lowell Papers.

22   Ibid.

23   The poet and playwright Robert Browning married Elizabeth Barrett in 1846, when she was forty years old; in poor health throughout her life, she died in 1861.

24   Elizabeth's college friend Susan Turner, now teaching at Vassar, knew someone in Duxbury with a house for sale. It is not clear whether the Lowells bought that one.

25   Blair Clark to EH, September 29, 1953, Lowell Papers.

26   EH to Blair Clark, November 13, 1953, Hardwick Papers.

27   EH to Blair Clark, October 16, 1953, Hardwick Papers.

28   Phillips and Rahv, *More Stories,* was the slimmer sequel to *Stories in the Modern Manner: A Collection of Stories from Partisan Review* (New York: Avon, 1954), in which Hardwick's writing did not appear.

29   Hardwick's "Faulkner and the South Today" ran in the October 1948 issue of *PR.*

30   Philip Rahv to EH, November 12 and 20, 1953, Lowell Papers.

31   This review elicited a mixed response from Elizabeth Bishop; she agreed that Edna St. Vincent Millay suffered greatly, but she wasn't willing to credit Elizabeth's enthusiasm for Hart Crane. Elizabeth Bishop to RL, December 5, 1953, in Bishop and Lowell, *Words in Air,* 147–48.

32   Clifford Odets to EH, December 14, 1953, Lowell Papers.

33   "Beyond Any Doubt," *Time,* November 30, 1953, was based on an experiment showing that painting cigarette smoke tars on mice could generate tumors.

34   RL to Elizabeth Bishop, November 29, 1953, in Bishop and Lowell, *Words in Air,* 145.

35   EH to RL, December 9, 1953, Lowell Papers.

36   RL to Elizabeth Bishop, January 1, 1954, in Bishop and Lowell, *Words in Air,* 150.

37   RL to Allen Tate, December 2, 1953, in Lowell, *Letters,* 202.

38   EH to Eleanor and Peter Taylor, February 8, 1954, Taylor Papers.

39   EH to RL, February 18, 1954, Lowell Papers.

40   EH to Blair and Holly Clark, February 20, 1954, Lowell Papers.

41   Giovanna Madonia (1927–2008) was now working at the music publisher Ricordi. Her husband was Luciano Erba, a poet, literary critic, and translator.

42   RL to Giovanna Madonia Erba, February 22, [1954], in Lowell, *Letters,* 211.

43   EH to Peter and Eleanor Taylor, April 20, 1954, Taylor Papers.

44   EH to Blair and Holly Clark, April 16, 1954, Lowell Papers.

45   EH to Blair Clark, March 19, 1954, Lowell Papers.

46   EH to Blair Clark, April 4, 1954, and EH to Blair and Holly Clark, April 10, 1954, Lowell Papers.

47   EH to Blair Clark, March 27, 1954, Lowell Papers.

48   EH to Eleanor and Peter Taylor, March 28, 1954, Taylor Papers.

49   EH to RL, March 30, 1954, Lowell Papers.

50   Giovanna Madonia Erba to RL, March 21, 1954, quoted in Hamilton, *Lowell: A Biography,* 207.

51   EH to RL, April 3, 1954, Lowell Papers.

52   EH to Blair Clark, April 1, 1954, Hardwick Papers.

53   EH to Blair Clark, April 4, 1954, Lowell Papers.

54   Robert Giroux told Flannery O'Connor that Cal had apparently "convinced everyone that it was Elizabeth that was going crazy." O'Connor to Sally Fitzgerald, December 26, 1954, in O'Connor, *Habit of Being,* 74.

55   EH to Peter and Eleanor Taylor, "Monday" [April 12, 1954], Taylor Papers.

56   EH to Blair and Holly Clark, April 16, 1954, Lowell Papers.

57   Harriet Winslow to EH, July 15, 1954, Lowell Papers.

58   Sarah Winslow Cotting to EH, "Monday" [probably April 12, 1954], Lowell Papers.

59   Alice Meade to EH, May 4, 1954, Lowell Papers.

60   Alice [Winslow] Sommaripa to EH, April 17, 1954, Lowell Papers.

61   EH to Blair and Holly Clark, May 1, 1954, Lowell Papers.

62   EH to Blair and Holly Clark, May 4, 1954, Lowell Papers.

63   Blair Clark to EH, May 5, 1954, Lowell Papers.

64   EH to Blair and Holly Clark, May 14, 1954, Lowell Papers.

65   EH to Blair Clark, June 9, 1954, Lowell Papers.

66   EH to Blair Clark, June 15, 1954, Lowell Papers.

67   In July, he would be rediagnosed with manic-depressive psychosis.

68   EH to RL, June 14, 1954, Lowell Papers.

69   Philip Rahv to EH, August 5, 1954, Hardwick Papers.

70   Mary McCarthy to Hannah Arendt, September 16, 1954, in Arendt and McCarthy, *Between Friends,* 28.

71   Elizabeth Bishop to EH, November 6, 1954, Hardwick Papers.

72   EH to Susan Turner, July 7, 1953, Hardwick Papers.

73   Ibid.

74   EH to RL, "Saturday morning" [probably July 10, 1954], Lowell Papers.

75   EH to Blair Clark, July 15, 1954, Lowell Papers

76   EH to Peter and Eleanor Taylor, August 2, 1954, Taylor Papers.

77   EH to Blair Clark, August 31, 1954, Lowell Papers.

78   Elizabeth was miffed that the publication day was such a nonevent: she hadn't heard from the publisher for a month. EH to Peter and Eleanor Taylor, February 10, 1955, Taylor Papers.

79   Elizabeth Bishop to EH, November 6, 1954, Lowell Papers.

80   Elizabeth Bishop to EH, November 30, 1954, Hardwick Papers.

81   See Laura James, "The Tuxedo Murder Case," CLEWS Your Home for Historic True Crime, https://laurajames.typepad.com/clews/2006/06/the_tuxedo_murd.html, and *Iowa City Press-Citizen,* March 17–April 6, 1950.

82   William S. Poster, "Fiction Chronicle," *PR* 22 (Spring 1955), 275–82. Poster, also known as William Shakespeare Bernstein (1916–60) was a poet, film critic, and essayist who also wrote for *The Nation, Commentary, The New*

Republic, and *The American Mercury* in the 1940s and '50s. His death was a suicide.

83   John Brooks, "The Trial Watchers," *New York Times,* February 13, 1955, 267, 286.

84   William Carlos Williams to EH, February 7, 1956, Lowell Papers.

85   Flannery O'Connor to "A," January 12, 1957, in O'Connor, *Habit of Being,* 196.

86   When *The Simple Truth* was reprinted in 1982, she is said to have "remained unhappy with it." Darryl Pinkney, introduction to EH, *New York Stories,* xiv.

87   EH to Blair and Holly Clark, January 26, 1955, Lowell Papers..

88   EH to Peter and Eleanor Taylor, February 10, 1955, Taylor Papers.

89   EH to Blair and Holly Clark, November 29, 1954, Lowell Papers.

90   EH to Peter and Eleanor Taylor, February 10, 1955, Taylor Papers. The prose reminiscences of Cal's childhood would be published as "91 Revere Street" in *Life Studies* (1959).

91   EH to Peter and Eleanor Taylor, December 26, 1954, Taylor Papers.

92   Ruth Draper died onstage the following year.

93   EH to Harriet Winslow, April 22, 1955, Lowell Papers.

94   The Australian-born author Christina Stead (1902–83) lived in Europe from 1928 to the early 1940s and subsequently in New York and California. She returned to Australia in 1968. A decade after Elizabeth's review appeared, Simon & Schuster issued a new edition of the novel, with an introduction by Randall Jarrell.

95   RL to Elizabeth Bishop, May 5, 1955, in Bishop and Lowell, *Words in Air,* 157. Lowell also told Bishop that reviewers of *The Simple Truth* were "baffled" that it was about the spectators of the trial rather than about the defendant.

96   The Castine Brick Company operated the brickyard from 1866 to 1881.

97   EH, "In Maine."

98   EH to Harriet Winslow, September 19, 1955, Lowell Papers.

99   EH to Robert Giroux, November 8, 1955, FSG.

100 William Carlos Williams to EH, January 18, 1956, Lowell Papers.

101 The two stories, both published in the magazine in 1956, were "A Season's Romance" and "The Oak and the Ax."

102 Katharine White to EH, April 1, 1955, *New Yorker* Records.

103 At the time, she and Spender were unaware that the magazine was receiving covert funding from the CIA.

104 EH to Mary McCarthy, November 1, 1955, McCarthy Papers.

105 EH to Robert Giroux, November 21, 1955, FSG Records.

106 EH to Harriet Winslow, October 21, 1955, Hardwick Papers.

107 Philip Rahv to EH, February 11, 1956, Lowell Papers.

108 EH to Blair and Holly Clark, February 22, 1956, Lowell Papers.

109 Katharine S. White to EH, December 29, 1955, *New Yorker* Records.

110 Editors of these books included Jacques Barzun (Byron), Lillian Hellman (Chekhov), Francis Steegmuller (Flaubert), Leon Edel (Henry James), Lionel Trilling (Keats), and Diana Trilling (D. H. Lawrence). Quote is from the

back cover of *The Selected Letters of William James* (New York: Farrar, Straus and Cudahy, 1951).

111   The preface was reprinted as "William James: An American Hero" in *View of My Own* and in *Collected Essays*.

112   Elizabeth seemed unaware of the psychological subcurrents at work in the James family. Far from being simply a doting father, Henry James, Sr., played emotional games with his children; William James had a superficially loving but manipulative relationship with his sister, Alice. See Jean Strouse, *Alice James: A Biography* (Boston: Houghton Mifflin, 1980).

113   EH to Blair and Holly Clark, February 22, 1956, Lowell Papers.

114   EH to Harriet Winslow, February 18, 1956, Lowell Papers. On November 22, 1957, Elizabeth wrote to Cousin Harriet that she still hadn't finished her editing work, because the baby was too much of a distraction.

115   Farrar, Straus and Cudahy initially decided to wait for the publication of Barzun's volume, because the Mid-Century Book Club (where Barzun was a managing editor) wanted to promote it and Elizabeth's book as a pair. Robert Giroux to Rupert Hart-David, September 24, 1959, FSG Records. On May 14, 1960, Elizabeth wrote to Giroux to urge publication of her book: she had heard that the two-volume edition of James's letters "from which half or more of my selection comes" was likely to be reprinted. Roger Straus, Jr., chairman of the press, replied that he hoped February 1961 would be "D Day" and that Giroux was "needling" Barzun. Roger Straus, Jr., to EH, May 16, 1960, FSG Records. *The Selected Letters of William James* was published in the spring of 1961. Although the revised book club deal involved having FSG postpone the paperback edition of *Selected Letters* until the following spring, instead of releasing it concurrently with the hardback edition, Barzun still had not completed his manuscript by the summer 1960 deadline. His book, *A Stroll with William James*, was finally published (by University of Chicago Press) in 1983.

116   Farrar, Straus and Cudahy, Inc., check request, FSG Records. This sum is equal to about $3,180 in 2018 dollars.

117   EH to Harriet Winslow, February 18, 1956, Lowell Papers.

118   EH to Blair and Holly Clark. February 22, 1956, Lowell Papers.

119   RL to Elizabeth Bishop, June 18, 1956, in Bishop and Lowell, *Words in Air,* 179.

120   EH to Peter and Eleanor Taylor, June 16, 1956, Taylor Papers.

121   EH to Mary McCarthy, April 12, 1956, McCarthy Papers.

122   Katharine S. White to EH, June 27, 1956, *New Yorker* Records.

123   Katharine S. White to EH, May 13, 1955, *New Yorker* Records.

124   EH to Mrs. [Katharine S.] White, May 20, 1955, *New Yorker* Records.

125   RL to Elizabeth Bishop, June 18, 1956, in Bishop and Lowell, *Words in Air,* 179.

126   RL to Elizabeth Bishop, October 24, 1956, ibid., 188.

127   Wilson, *Fifties*, 452–53.

128   EH to Harriet Winslow, November 25, 1956, Lowell Papers.

129 EH to Katharine White, December 22, 1956, *New Yorker* Records.
130 "The Lowells of Massachusetts," *Life,* March 18, 1957. The caption credits Robert Lowell as a Pulitzer Prize winner and member of the National Institute of Arts and Letters; Elizabeth is identified simply as "wife."
131 EH to Harriet Winslow, January 22, 1957, Lowell Papers.
132 RL to Elizabeth Bishop, February 7, 1957, in Bishop and Lowell, *Words in Air,* 195. An Old Fashioned is a whiskey cocktail, served in a special flat-bottomed glass named after the drink.
133 EH to Mary McCarthy, February 24, 1957, McCarthy Papers. Her reference is to the effort of choosing and snatching up clothes that other women in this crowded basement emporium had their eye on.
134 Katharine S. White to EH, November 1, 1955, *New Yorker* Records. A December 29, 1955, letter from White to Elizabeth suggests that she is waiting to receive a revised version of "The Babcock Family."
135 Katharine S. White to EH, December 5, 1956, *New Yorker* Records.
136 However, the magazine initially had (apparently unwarranted) libel concerns that people by the same name might be on the faculty at the University of Chicago, and White also worried about the potential identifiability of a portrait hanging in the Babcock's dining room. Katharine S. White to EH, December 18, 1956, *New Yorker* Records.
137 According to the *Barnard Bulletin,* May 2, 1957, Elizabeth gave this talk on May 1. Unfortunately, the text is not available.
138 EH to Harriet Winslow, July 2, 1957, Lowell Papers.
139 RL to Elizabeth Bishop, July 3, 1957, in Bishop and Lowell, *Words in Air,* 207.
140 EH to Harriet Winslow, July 27, 1957, Lowell Papers.
141 EH to Harriet Winslow, July 30, 1957, Lowell Papers.
142 RL to Elizabeth Bishop, July 19, 1957, in Bishop and Lowell, *Words in Air,* 211.
143 RL to Robie Macauley, July 27, 1957, quoted in Mariani, *Lost Puritan,* 252.
144 RL to Elizabeth Bishop, August 15, 1957, in Bishop and Lowell, *Words in Air,* 224.
145 EH to Harriet Winslow, August 28, 1957, Lowell Papers.
146 A few years later Elizabeth became extremely dependent on a Spanish woman who cared for Harriet and did housework; when she was recuperating from surgery Elizabeth felt her absence keenly.
147 RL to Elizabeth Bishop, October 25, 1957, in Bishop and Lowell, *Words in Air,* 235.
148 EH to William Shawn, October 2, 1957, *New Yorker* Records.
149 EH, "Going Home in America."
150 In 1948 Alger Hiss, a government official, was accused of being a Soviet spy. Convicted and imprisoned for perjury—the statute of limitations for espionage had run out—he always maintained his innocence. Despite a recent article in *The Nation* claiming that Hess was framed, Elizabeth believed he was guilty.
151 EH to Blair and Holly Clark, January 1, 1958, Lowell Papers.

152   EH to Harriet Winslow, "Friday" [January 17, 1958], Lowell Papers.
153   EH to Allen Tate, December 16, 1957, Tate Papers. In his reply, Tate acknowledged "the great strain you are under." But his opinion of the poems remained unchanged. "You are too deeply in love with Cal and are involved too deeply in his chronic illness to take any other position than one which looks to his immediate welfare," he wrote. Tate to EH, December 18, 1957, Tate Papers.
154   Davison, *Fading Smile*, 277.
155   EH to Harriet Winslow, January 20, 1958, Lowell Papers.
156   EH to Elizabeth Bishop, January 20, 1958, Bishop Papers.
157   EH to Katharine White, February 15, 1958, *New Yorker* Records.
158   Thirty dollars in 1958 is the equivalent of about $254 in 2017 dollars.
159   EH to Harriet Winslow, February 2, 1958, Lowell Papers. Mariani erroneously wrote in *Lost Puritan* (p. 267) that the last quote is from a "January 2" letter to Winslow.

Chapter 6: Upheaval
1   EH to Elizabeth Bishop, February 11, 1959, Bishop Papers.
2   EH to Harriet Winslow, March 2, 1958, Lowell Papers.
3   RL to Theodore Roethke, April 18, 1958, in Lowell, *Letters,* 321.
4   Robert Lowell, "Five Poems," *PR* 25 (Winter 1958), 25–30. Another poem included in this group was "To Speak of the Woe That Is in Marriage," which will be discussed later in this chapter. Miltown was the first anti-anxiety drug.
5   Pauline Kael and Tennessee Williams are both said to have called Nazimova's portrayal the greatest performance they had ever seen on the American stage.
6   EH, "Theater Chronicle: Disgust and Disenchantment." Elizabeth wrote only one of these omnibus reviews; in 1959, the Chronicle was in the hands of Mary McCarthy, and in subsequent years, the feature was abandoned for unknown reasons.
7   EH, Oral History interview, October 8–9, 1977. However, in a rare remark about acting, she complained about the "dismaying lack of style and technique" in performances of classic plays and mourned the fact that Marlon Brando—"the only great stage performer," who was able to play classic roles in an "American" style—had deserted the stage for film. EH, "Editor Interviews."
8   EH to Blair and Holly Clark, March 7, 1958, Lowell Papers.
9   EH to Robert Henderson, February 15, 1959, *New Yorker* Records. The magazine's longtime fiction editor, Katharine White, had just retired. After a lunch with Elizabeth at which he discovered her interest in opera, Henderson wrote that he thought of her on the night she was to see *Don Giovanni*, "hoping [it] was as good as it had seemed to me a couple weeks before." Robert Henderson to EH, February 19, 1959, *New Yorker* Records.
10   EH to Harriet Winslow, March 31, 1958, Lowell Papers.
11   EH to Harriet Winslow, May 7, 1958, Lowell Papers.

12   Ibid.

13   EH to Harriet Winslow, April 19, 1958, Lowell Papers.

14   EH to Harriet Winslow, May 7, 1958, Lowell Papers.

15   Quoted in Davison, *Fading Smile,* 255.

16   Quoted ibid., 203.

17   Plath, *Journals,* 292.

18   Ibid., 294.

19   Ibid., 310.

20   EH to Harriet Winslow, July 15, 1958, Lowell Papers.

21   EH to Harriet Winslow, July 1, 1958, Lowell Papers.

22   EH to Harriet Winslow, July 6, 1958, Lowell Papers. Twenty dollars in 1958 are equal to $174 in 2019.

23   Quoted in Bray, "Hardwick: Woman of Letters."

24   RL to Elizabeth Bishop, September 18, 1958, in Bishop and Lowell, *Words in Air,* 266.

25   EH to Harriet Winslow, May 7, 1958, Lowell Papers..

26   EH to Blair and Holly Clark, October 19, 1958, Lowell Papers.

27   RL to Elizabeth Bishop, October 16, 1958, in Bishop and Lowell, *Words in Air,* 272.

28   EH to Blair and Holly Clark, October 19, 1958, Lowell Papers.

29   EH to Harriet Lowell, November 29, 1958, Lowell Papers.

30   EH to Robert Henderson, February 22, 1959. *New Yorker* Records.

31   EH to Mary McCarthy, May 9, 1959, McCarthy Papers.

32   EH to Elizabeth Bishop, June 24, 1959, Bishop Papers.

33   Axelrod, *Lowell; Life and Art,* 122.

34   Tillinghast, *Lowell's Life and Work,* 67.

35   EH to Blair Clark, July 29, 1959, Lowell Papers.

36   RL to Elizabeth Bishop, April 7, 1959, Lowell Papers.

37   Elizabeth Bishop to EH, July 23, 1959, Lowell Papers.

38   EH to Allen Tate, June 1, 1959, Tate Papers.

39   EH to Bowden Broadwater, September 6, 1959, McCarthy Papers.

40   EH to Harriet Winslow, n.d. [probably September 1959], Lowell Papers.

41   RL to Elizabeth Bishop, February 9, 1959, in Bishop and Lowell, *Words in Air,* 287. "We are just back from eight days in New York. Main event, seeing the abstract painters en masse."

42   Robert Henderson to EH, March 26, 1959, and EH to Robert Henderson, February 14, 1959, *New Yorker* Records.

43   EH, "Fantastic Voyage."

44   Saul Bellow, "The Search for Symbols, a Writer Warns, Misses All the Fun and Fact of the Story," *NYTBR,* February 15, 1959.

45   The editor of this special issue was Robert Silvers.

46   RL to Elizabeth Bishop, October 3, 1959, Lowell Papers.

47   EH to Robert Henderson, November 10, 1959, *New Yorker* Records.

48   EH to Mary McCarthy, October 5, 1959, McCarthy Papers.

49   Maximilian I ruled Mexico as emperor from 1864 to 1867, a reign marked by liberal reforms but also by the Black Decree, according to which armed

rebels were to be immediately executed—resulting in the deaths of some eleven thousand of the supporters of former president Benito Juárez.

50   EH, Oral History interview, September 20, 1979.

51   Robert Henderson to EH, April 18, 1960, *New Yorker* Records.

52   Davison, *Fading Smile*, 286. Davison interviewed Elizabeth on March 22, 1992.

53   Quoted in EH, "Hardwick Looks at Boston."

54   Wiggins, "I Don't Give the Reader . . ."

55   EH to Harriet Winslow, March 11, 1960, Lowell Papers.

56   EH to Harriet Winslow, February 16, 1960, Lowell Papers.

57   EH to Robert Henderson, November 10, 1959, and Robert Henderson to EH, November 17, 1959, *New Yorker* Records.

58   As Elizabeth explains in this piece, Berenson bequeathed I Tatti to Harvard for the research endeavors of art history students.

59   Diana Trilling to EH, May 24, 1960, Lowell Papers.

60   EH, "Faye Dunaway."

61   EH to Roger Giroux (postcard), postmarked May 14, 1960, FSG Records.

62   EH to Robert Henderson, June 19, 1960, *New Yorker* Records.

63   RL to Peter Taylor, June 27, 1960, quoted in Mariani, *Lost Puritan*, 290n4.

64   EH, "Life and Death of Chessman."

65   "Kidnapping" was deemed the appropriate charge because Chessman took the women to his car, parked more than twenty feet away. The legal definition was based on the distance between two bedrooms in a house.

66   EH, "Insulted and Injured," in *View of My Own*, 183.

67   RL to Elizabeth Bishop, November 16, 1960, in Bishop and Lowell, *Words in Air,* 347.

68   RL to Adrienne Rich, November 18, 1960, in Lowell, *Letters,* 372–73.

69   RL to Elizabeth Bishop, November 16, 1960, in Bishop and Lowell, *Words in Air,* 347.

70   Quoted in Brightman, *Writing Dangerously*, 459.

71   "American Literary Criticism Today" (symposium), Sonoma State College, 1964.

72   EH, "All Is Vanity."

73   EH to Harriet Winslow, January 10, 1961, Lowell Papers.

Chapter 7: New York

1   RL to Elizabeth Bishop, February 15, 1961, in Bishop and Lowell, *Words in Air,* 350–51.

2   Hochman, *Loving Lowell*, 6.

3   Ibid., 3.

4   Years later, after Cal published *The Dolphin*, Hochman visited Elizabeth at her New York apartment. According to Hochman's self-serving account, Elizabeth told her that she hated Caroline Blackwood and wished Cal had stayed with Hochman because she "took good care of him." Hochman, *Loving Lowell*, 239. Bizarrely, before she met Cal, Hochman had had a "brief

affair" with Israel Citkowitz, Blackwood's second husband. Hochman, *Loving Lowell*, 143.

5   EH quoted in Hamilton, *Lowell: A Biography*, 286.

6   EH to Mary McCarthy, April 3, 1961, McCarthy Papers.

7   EH to RL, June 17, 1961, Lowell Papers. Despite the date Elizabeth typed on this letter, it is unlikely that she wrote it then; the TV program was broadcast on June 18. Of course, it is possible that she misunderstood when that would occur.

8   Boris Pasternak, the Russian poet and essayist who won the Nobel Prize for literature in 1958, had died the previous year.

9   She dated the letter Monday, June 17, but that date fell on a Saturday in 1961.

10   RL to Elizabeth Bishop, June 27, 1961, in Bishop and Lowell, *Words in Air*, 366.

11   EH, "More Loveless Love."

12   EH to RL, July 12, 1961, Lowell Papers.

13   Ibid.

14   EH to RL, July 15, 1961, Lowell Papers.

15   EH to RL, n.d. [July 1961], Lowell Papers.

16   RL to Elizabeth Bishop, August 7, 1961, Lowell Papers. EH to Harriet Winslow, August 19, 1961, Lowell Papers.

17   The plays he was working on that summer—*Benito Cereno* (based on a Melville novella), *Major Molineux* (based on a short story by Hawthorne), and *Endicott and the Red Cross*—composed *The Old Glory*, a trilogy produced off-Broadway in 1964.

18   Thanks to Stephen Fitz-Gerald for identifying some of the people in this photo, a copy of which is owned by the Castine Historical Society. By early 1972, Leah had left Clark, as Elizabeth wrote to McCarthy on February 3 of that year.

19   EH, "Some Chapters of Personal History."

20   RL to Elizabeth Bishop, ca. October 3 [1961], in Bishop and Lowell, *Words in Air*, 381.

21   Rose, "Novel: An Affirmation?"

22   EH, "Riesman Considered Again."

23   Diana Trilling to EH, January 3, 1962, Lowell Papers.

24   RL to EH, April 14, 1962, in Bishop and Lowell, *Words in Air*, 404.

25   EH to Elizabeth Bishop, April 6, 1962, Bishop Papers.

26   EH to Elizabeth Bishop, February 11, 1959, Bishop Papers. On an application for State Department sponsorship of a South American tour for Cal, Elizabeth had listed British literary critic I. A. Richards as one of his references but forgot to let Richards know Cal was counting on him. He innocently wrote to the State Department that Cal would have been ideal had he not been incarcerated in a mental hospital. As a result, the tour was called off. EH to Elizabeth Bishop, June 24, 1959, Bishop Papers.

27   EH to Elizabeth Bishop, January 30, 1962, Bishop Papers.

28   Derek Walcott, interview by Edward Hirsch, *Paris Review* 38 (Winter 1986).

It must have been especially embarrassing because he and his wife, Margaret, had named one of his daughters Elizabeth after the author.

29   EH to Harriet Winslow, August 8, 1962, Lowell Papers.

30   EH to Robert Giroux, July 18, 1962, FSG Records.

31   In her letter to Giroux, Elizabeth wrote that their travel to other countries would happen in August and that they would return to New York "about Sept. 7th." Peru was no longer a likely destination because U.S. diplomatic relations with the country had been broken off after the military coup d'état that overthrew President Manuel Prado.

32   Elizabeth Bishop to EH, undated notes [1962] accompanying a letter dated September 13, 1962, Bishop Papers. Notably, this episode is *not* mentioned in Benjamin Moser, *Why This World: A Biography of Clarice Lispector* (New York: Oxford University Press, 2009).

33   Elizabeth Bishop to EH, September 13, 1962, Lowell Papers.

34   EH to Alfred Kazin, October 7, 1962, Berg Collection, NYPL.

35   Alfred Kazin, "Writers as Character," *Reporter* (October 11, 1962), 62–64. The book title was Elizabeth's choice.

36   EH to Robert Giroux, January 15, 1962, FSG Records.

37   Quoted in Robert Giroux to EH, July 9, 1962, FSG Records.

38   "People are talking about . . . ," *Vogue,* September 15, 1962.

39   John K. Hutchens, "Interesting Case of a Literary Critic Who Does Poorly on Own Medicine," *Lexington Leader,* September 16, 1962.

40   In *The 50 Year Argument* (2014), a documentary about *The New York Review of Books* written by Martin Scorsese and directed by Scorsese and David Tedeschi, Elizabeth is mentioned in the first moments, apropos the *Review* as the locus of fiercely contested views that remained civil. (She was a guest in editor Robert Silvers's home when something she said elicited the response, "I couldn't disagree with you more," and an argument ensued.) Later in the film, we see photographs of Elizabeth with Cal (and one photo of her and a young Darryl Pinckney). Elizabeth is also the penultimate voiceover speaker in this film. She says, "But perhaps what we all seem to be talking about is very casual, private criticism, which you try to write as well as you try to write a poem."

41   Quoted in James Atlas, "The Ma and Pa of the Intelligentsia," *New York,* April 4, 2017.

42   RL to Elizabeth Bishop, January 23, 1963, Lowell Papers.

43   Quoted in Nobile, *Intellectual Skywriting,* 24. Nobile's initial interview with Hardwick took place in 1971.

44   Statistics from Epstein, *Book Business,* 117. Once the *Review* began to publish biweekly, it was agreed that Robert Silvers, Elizabeth, Cal, and Barbara Epstein would hold all voting shares, and that the journal would not be dependent on donor-contributed funding. The sale of nonvoting shares for $145,000 helped keep the *Review* afloat in its early days. Ibid., 120.

45   Ibid., 119.

46   EH, "Ring," and EH, "Grub Street: New York."

47   James Baldwin, "A Letter From a Region in My Mind," *New Yorker,* Novem-

ber 17, 1962, published the following year by Dial Press as *The Fire Next Time.*

48   EH to Mary McCarthy, March 14, 1963, McCarthy Papers.

49   EH to Elizabeth Bishop, March 12, 1963, Bishop Papers.

50   EH to Richard Eberhart, May 20, 1963, Hardwick Letters.

51   EH to Harriet Winslow, July 4, 1963, Lowell Papers.

52   RL to Elizabeth Bishop, July 5 and August 12, 1963, Lowell Papers.

53   EH to Mary McCarthy, August 3, 1963, McCarthy Papers.

54   EH, "Matter and Manner in Non-Fiction."

55   The name also hints at Saint Francis Xavier, one of the first Jesuits who took vows of poverty and chastity.

56   EH to Mary McCarthy, November 30, 1963, McCarthy Papers.

57   Xavier Prynne, "Vice-Presidential Notes: (The 6th Vice-Presidential Note)," *NYRB,* November 28, 1963.

58   RL to Elizabeth Bishop, September 11, 1963, in Bishop and Lowell, *Words in Air,* 502.

59   EH, "Frost in His Letters," *NYRB,* October 31, 1963; Alfred Alvarez to EH, October 21, 1963, Lowell Papers.

60   Al Alvarez, "Keats," *NYRB,* October 31, 1963.

61   Nobile, *Intellectual Skywriting,* 102.

62   EH to Muriel Rukeyser, postmarked November 11, 1966, Berg Collection, NYPL.

63   Janet Coleman, "57th Street Rag," *NYRB,* January 15, 2013.

64   EH to Allen Tate, January 9, 1964, Tate Papers.

65   Andrew Delbanco, "Literary Journalism: A Discussion," panel discussion at the Cullman Center for Scholars and Writers, NYPL, April 3, 2013.

66   Wilson, *Sixties,* 491, entry for January 4, 1966.

67   EH to RL, December 7, 8, 10, 12, 15[?], 17, 20, and undated, 1963, Lowell Papers.

68   EH to Elizabeth Bishop, January 17, 1964, Bishop Papers.

69   Calendar of Events, 21st Annual Writing Forum, March 17, 18, 19, 1964, *Arts Forum Coraddi,* University of North Carolina at Greensboro, March 1964, 30.

70   The college is now part of the Cal State University system. It owns a reel-to-reel tape recording of this event, but the only date attached to it is "1964." Quotes are from author's transcription of an MP4 copy.

71   Jonathan Miller quoted in Hamilton, *Lowell: A Biography,* 314.

72   Howard Taubman, "Lowell: Poet as Playwright; American Place Stage Presents 'Old Glory,'" *New York Times,* November 2, 1964.

73   Nobile, *Intellectual Skywriting,* 248.

74   W. D. Snodgrass, "In Praise of Robert Lowell," *NYRB,* December 3, 1964.

75   According to Edmund Wilson, Cal visited Jean at her apartment after the dress rehearsal and kept talking to her until five a.m., telling her she probably had only two years to live. Unable to bear any more of his psychological torture, she left for New York the next day. Wilson, *Sixties,* 427.

76   Vija Vetra quoted in Hamilton, *Lowell: A Biography,* 316.

77   EH to Blair Clark, January 24, 1965, Lowell Papers.

78   EH to RL, January 30, 1965, Lowell Papers.

79   EH to RL, January 31, 1965, Lowell Papers.

80   EH to RL, "Tuesday" [February 2, 1965], Lowell Papers.

81   EH to RL, "Wednesday" [probably February 3, 1965], Lowell Papers.

82   Quoted in Hamilton, *Lowell: A Biography,* 331.

83   EH, "Apotheosis of King."

84   Ibid.

85   Andrew Kopkind, "Soul Power," *NYRB,* August 24, 1967. King's book is *Where Do We Go From Here: Chaos or Community?* (New York: Harper & Row, 1967).

86   RL to President Lyndon Johnson, *NYRB,* June 3, 1965.

87   RL to Elizabeth Bishop, July 16, 1965, in Bishop and Lowell, *Words in Air,* 582.

88   Quoted in Booth, "Summers in Castine."

89   RL to Elizabeth Bishop, February 25, 1966, in Bishop and Lowell, *Words in Air,* 601.

90   Ibid.

91   EH, "Art of Fiction 87," 32.

92   EH, Oral History interview, November 5, 1978.

93   EH, undated [probably 1970s] typescript of "Reading," Hardwick Papers. Although her papers also contain a typeset version of a portion of this essay, there is no identifying information, and I have not been able to figure out where or when it was published.

94   She might have added that our therapeutic culture believes there is a remedy for most personal problems, whereas classic literature is about seeing life as it is, with all its attendant tragedies.

95   EH, notes for a lecture on writing, undated typescript with handwritten emendations, Hardwick Papers, my italics.

96   Barbara Crampton, "Miss Hardwick Airs Views on Current Literary Affairs," *Barnard Bulletin,* November 17, 1966. This piece contains no direct quotes, just paraphrases of Elizabeth's words.

97   EH to RL, December 22, 1965, Lowell Papers.

98   In May, Miller would also direct Cal's play *Prometheus Bound* at Yale with a professional company and student chorus, supported by a grant from the National Endowment for the Humanities.

99   Sue Napier, "Worth of Theater Gets Pro-Con from UK Panel," *Lexington Leader,* April 21, 1967.

100   "Lexington Native Wins Critic Award," *Lexington Leader,* January 14, 1968.

101   After receiving the award, she published no more than one review a year— in 1968, 1969, 1970, and 1974.

102   EH, "Disaster at Lincoln Center." Unsurprisingly, the *NYRB* printed several letters attacking her point of view.

103   EH, *Sleepless Nights* (2001 ed.), 127. But by 1983 Elizabeth may have had a change of heart. In her final essay on Ibsen, she remarked that his withdrawal from theater productions was unfortunate because such practical

experience might have made him modify some "unlikely endings" and "the repetitive flatness of idea in a number of characters." EH, "Ibsen's Secrets."

104   EH, "Theater of Decadence," and EH, "Straight Play."
105   EH, "Theater of Sentimentality."
106   EH, "Word of Mouth." Elizabeth would also praise Edward Bond's much-maligned drama *Saved*, in which the violence of the British lower-class setting includes a fatal attack on a baby. In EH, "Violence Redeemed," she wrote that it was "a play of unusual beauty and intensity," establishing "a catharsis of terror around which pity hangs like a fog."
107   EH, "Critics."
108   EH, "Editor Interviews."
109   "The Second Chance," *Time* (June 2, 1967), 72.
110   Other signatories included Cal, Mary McCarthy, Barbara and Jason Epstein, Robert Silvers, Hannah Arendt, William Styron, Philip Rahv, George Plimpton, Joseph Heller, and Lillian Hellman. Earlier, in June 1964, Elizabeth signed a petition protesting the arrest of Lenny Bruce for indecency, on the grounds that it violated his constitutional guarantee of free speech.
111   EH to Mary McCarthy, March 15, 1967, McCarthy Papers.
112   EH to Mary McCarthy, May 21, 1967, McCarthy Papers.
113   Booth, "Summers in Castine." This picnic likely took place after McCarthy's purchase of the Castine house in 1967.
114   EH, "In Maine."
115   EH to Elizabeth Bishop, October 18, 1973, Bishop Papers.
116   EH, "Puritanical Pleasures: Summer in Maine." Her note on the typescript (Hardwick Papers) says this piece was published in *Vanity Fair*; actually, it appeared in the August 1987 issue of *House and Garden*.
117   EH to Jon Jewett, February 16, 1981, Jewett Collection.
118   EH, "*Little Foxes* Revived." Complaining letters about the review, and EH's reply, are in "Raising Hellman," *NYRB*, January 18, 1968. An angry letter from Penelope Gilliatt, a British novelist, theater critic, and (most relevantly) lover of Mike Nichols, and EH's reply, are in "Lark Pie" *NYRB*, February 1, 1968.
119   Elizabeth tended to stick tenaciously to her ideas about theater. She once told visiting Italian novelist Giorgio Bassani that Luigi Pirandello had changed the art form forever. When he replied that Pirandello was just one of many modern playwrights who had left their mark, she is said to have begun shouting at him. Upset, he reverted to Italian and finally walked out. Elizabeth was scornful. "Well, he was pretty disappointing," she said. Meyers, *Lowell in Love*, 96.
120   Blair Clark to EH, December 5, 1967, Lowell Papers.
121   EH to Mary McCarthy, December 27, 1967, McCarthy Papers. William Styron characterized Elizabeth's review as a "disgustingly gratuitous and mean-spirited" attack. Styron to Lillian Hellman, April 2, 1980, in Styron, *Selected Letters*, 543.
122   RL to Elizabeth Bishop, January 13, 1968, Lowell Papers.
123   Mary McCarthy to EH, February 6, 1968, Lowell Papers.

124   EH to Mary McCarthy and Jim West, March 14, 1968, McCarthy Papers.
125   Mary McCarthy to Hannah Arendt, March 7, 1968, in Arendt and McCarthy, *Between Friends*, 214.
126   Mary McCarthy to Hannah Arendt, October 20, 1969, ibid., 251.
127   EH to Mary McCarthy, March 3, 1968, McCarthy Papers.
128   EH to RL, n.d. [April 1968], Lowell Papers.
129   EH to RL, March 18, 1968, Lowell Papers.
130   RL to EH, January 9, 1969, Hardwick Papers.
131   EH to RL, March 1, 1969, Hardwick Papers.
132   Robert Lowell, "The Twentieth Wedding Anniversary 1" and "The Twentieth Wedding Anniversary 2," in Lowell, *Collected Poems*, 631.
133   Isaiah Berlin to EH, November 6, 1968, Lowell Papers.
134   EH to Mary McCarthy, February 9, 1970, McCarthy Papers.
135   EH to Elizabeth Bishop, May 29, 1970, Bishop Papers. Cal actually signed a two-year contract with the university, but he told Elizabeth that it was possible to stay for just one year.

Chapter 8: The Rift
1   Blackwood's third daughter, Ivana, was the child of her affair with screenwriter Ivan Moffat.
2   EH to Blair Clark, "about June 6, '70" added later in pencil, Hardwick Papers.
3   RL to EH, June 20, 1970, in Hamilton, *Dolphin Letters*, 57.
4   EH to Mary McCarthy, June 25, 1970, ibid., 64.
5   EH to RL, June 26, 1970, ibid., 66-70.
6   EH to Mary McCarthy, July 1, 1970, ibid., 76.
7   Mary McCarthy to Hannah Arendt, June 26, 1970, in Arendt and McCarthy, *Between Friends*, 257. Years later the poet Richard Tillinghast heard from an unnamed person that "mutual friends" found the Lowells "really unpleasant to be around" by 1970 because of their combative marriage. Tillinghast, *Lowell's Life and Work*, 52.
8   EH to Mary McCarthy, July 1, 1970, in Hamilton, *Dolphin Letters*, 76.
9   EH to Mary McCarthy, August 2, 1970, ibid., 92.
10   EH to Mary McCarthy, August 4, 1970, ibid., 93.
11   RL to EH, August 6, 1970, in Lowell, *Letters*, 542.
12   RL to Elizabeth Bishop, September 11, 1970, in Bishop and Lowell, *Words in Air*, 681.
13   RL to Elizabeth Bishop, October 5, 1970, ibid., 682-83.
14   RL to EH, October 18, 1970, in Lowell, *Letters*, 551.
15   EH to Blair Clark, October 23, 1970, in Hamilton, *Dolphin Letters*, 122.
16   EH to Mary McCarthy, September 17, 1970, ibid., 106.
17   EH to Mary McCarthy, October 29, 1970, ibid.,126.
18   EH, "Caesar's Things."
19   EH to Mary McCarthy, October 6, 1970, McCarthy Papers.
20   This is the article Cal would praise so effusively in RL to EH, July 25, 1971, in Hamilton, *Dolphin Letters*, 204.

21 EH to Robert Henderson, October 28, 1970, *New Yorker* Records. Accustomed now to writing essays, not fiction, Elizabeth wrote to Mary that it was hard "to break the junkie habit of rushing through, sending it off to Bob [Silvers] and having it in print the next morning." EH to Mary McCarthy, October 29, 1970, McCarthy Papers.

22 Robert Henderson to EH, November 4, 1970, *New Yorker* Records.

23 Robert Henderson to EH, November 24, 1970, *New Yorker* Records.

24 RL to Peter Taylor, November 1, 1970, in Lowell, *Letters*, 554–55.

25 RL to Mary McCarthy, November 2, 1970, ibid., 555–56.

26 RL to EH, November 7, 1970, ibid., 556.

27 RL to Elizabeth Bishop, November 7, 1970, in Bishop and Lowell, *Words in Air*, 686.

28 RL to Blair Clark, November 21, 1970, in Lowell, *Letters*, 559.

29 RL to EH, November 30, 1960, ibid., 560.

30 RL to EH, December 3, 1970, ibid., 561.

31 RL to EH, n.d. [December 1970], ibid., 562.

32 EH to Mary McCarthy, February 19, 1971, in Hamilton, *Dolphin Letters*, 151. Elizabeth had taken the anti-anxiety drug Librium to enable her to endure Cal's visit; she wrote to him during his stay to mention this. EH to RL, n.d. [December 1970], in Hamilton, *Dolphin Letters*, 141.

33 RL to EH, January 7, 1971, in Lowell, *Letters*, 563.

34 EH to Mary McCarthy, February 19, 1971, in Hamilton, *Dolphin Letters*, 151.

35 Mary McCarthy to Hannah Arendt, February 10, 1971, in Arendt and McCarthy, *Between Friends*, 280. Elizabeth wrote to Mary on February 19, 1971—an earlier letter she sent had been returned for insufficient postage—and offered Cal's studio as a place to stay if Mary needed one.

36 EH to RL, January 8, 1971, in Hamilton, *Dolphin Letters*, 147. In May, Elizabeth asked Cal to request money from his publisher to pay the tax bill he owed, spelling out the fact that she was paying all the rent as well as total support for Harriet. EH to RL, May 19, 1971, in Hamilton, *Dolphin Letters*, 182.

37 EH to Mary McCarthy, February 19, 1971, in Hamilton, *Dolphin Letters*, 151.

38 The Christian Gauss Seminars in Criticism, named for a former dean of the modern language department at the university, were founded in 1949 by R. P. Blackmur.

39 EH, *"Doll's House."* This piece was followed by "Ibsen and Women II: *Hedda Gabler*," and "Ibsen and Women III: The *Rosmersholm* Triangle." These three 1971 essays were published in *Seduction and Betrayal*. In 1983, in "Ibsen's Secrets," Elizabeth returned once again to the Norwegian playwright whose work she also invoked over the years when writing about other subjects.

40 Cal called her from London, she wrote, "the moment Caroline discovered she was pregnant!" EH to Peter Taylor, May 29, 1972, Taylor Papers.

41 Elizabeth had written to Caroline Blackwood in March to discuss the

planned visit, but by early April she changed her mind about bringing Harriet to England.

42   Adrienne Rich to RL, June 17, 1971, in Hamilton, *Dolphin Letters,* 187. In an earlier letter to Lowell, Rich remarked that "women like E. . . . have become more subtle, more searching" because of what they had gone through and their need to "liv[e] more autonomous lives." Rich to RL, March 21, 1971, in Hamilton, *Dolphin Letters,* 157.

43   RL to Adrienne Rich, June 23, [1971], ibid., 191.

44   EH to Mary McCarthy, April 26, 1971, McCarthy Papers.

45   EH to Mary McCarthy, May 16, 1971, McCarthy Papers.

46   EH, "Editor Interviews."

47   EH to Mary McCarthy, June 11, 1971, McCarthy Papers; Edmund Wilson, "An Upstate Diary II: 1960–1970," *New Yorker,* June 12, 1971, 43–83.

48   EH to RL, August 12, 1971, in Hamilton, *Dolphin Letters,* 213.

49   EH to RL, July 3, 1971, ibid., 197–200.

50   EH, "On Sylvia Plath." Elizabeth described her to Cal as "unattractive as a woman, so hard and cruel, with herself and with others"; her "intense burst of genius" derived from "rage and hatred." EH to RL, June 28 and August 12, 1971, in Hamilton, *Dolphin Letters,* 194.

51   RL to EH, August 3, 1971, ibid., 210.

52   RL to EH, July 25, 1971, ibid., 204.

53   RL to EH, June 23, 1971, ibid., 189.

54   Hesione, Prometheus's wife, was mournful because Zeus had chained her husband to a rock.

55   Robert Lowell, *Prometheus Bound*, typescript with handwritten emendations by Elizabeth Hardwick and Robert Lowell, Lowell Papers. The reference to the goddess Hesione was changed to Alcyone in the final version.

56   "Foxfur," in Lowell, *Collected Poems,* 699.

57   "Exorcism," ibid., 678, italics in the original.

58   EH to RL, September 27, 1971, in Hamilton, *Dolphin Letters,* 219.

59   RL to EH, n.d. [September 24, 1971], ibid., 218.

60   RL to EH, October 1, 1971, ibid., 223.

61   EH to Ian Hamilton, n.d., Hardwick Papers.

62   EH to Mary McCarthy, September 29, 1972, McCarthy Papers.

63   Mary McCarthy to EH, December 9, 1971, in Hamilton, *Dolphin Letters,* 227.

64   EH to Mary McCarthy, n.d. [December 1971], ibid., 228.

65   EH to Mary McCarthy, January 1, 1972, McCarthy Papers.

66   EH to Peter and Eleanor Taylor, March 27, 1972, Taylor Papers.

67   EH to Peter Taylor, May 29, 1972, Taylor Papers.

68   Quoted in "The New Woman, 1972," *Time,* March 29, 1972. Elizabeth remarked to Cal that she hoped the well-paying magazine would not print what she wrote, because she would receive "most of the money anyway." EH to RL, February 28, 1972, in Hamilton, *Dolphin Letters,* 239. The full extent of her contribution to this issue is unclear because *Time* articles were unsigned during this period.

69   RL to Elizabeth Bishop, March 28, 1972, in Bishop and Lowell, *Words in Air*, 713.

70   RL to EH, May 22, 1972, Hardwick Papers.

71   EH to Mary McCarthy, April 9, 1972, in Hamilton, *Dolphin Letters*, 268.

72   RL to EH, April 9, 1972, ibid., 265.

73   "For Elizabeth Bishop 3. Letter with Poems for a Letter with Poems," in Bishop and Lowell, *Words in Air*, 687, and *Collected Poems*, 594.

74   Elizabeth Bishop to RL, March 21, 1972, in Bishop and Lowell, *Words in Air*, 708. Three years after the publication of *The Dolphin*, Bishop wrote to Elizabeth "to offer you all the sympathy I can," to praise her bravery and strength, and to explain that she had tried to get Cal to make changes in the poems. Bishop to EH, August 17, 1978, Hardwick Papers. The immediate impetus for this letter was one from Cal that mentioned Elizabeth's torment, but why it took Bishop so long to express her sympathy is a mystery.

75   RL to Frank Bidart, April 10 [1972], in Lowell, *Letters*, 592. Responding to the changed order of certain poems in the book (Sheridan's birth moved closer to Cal's Christmas 1970 visit to Elizabeth), Bidart wrote that the "emotional meaning and resonance . . . is thrown out of whack." Bidart to RL, April 10, 1972, Lowell Papers. Rather than making Elizabeth appear "more restful and gracious about the separation"—as Cal had argued in his letter of April 15 (*Letters*, 592)—she now appeared "far more desperate."

76   Gunn, *Shelf Life*, 83.

77   Bidart quoted in Hamilton, *Lowell: A Biography*, 421.

78   Quoted in Chamberlain, "Not Asking for Compassion."

79   Rich, "Caryatid."

80   Tillinghast, *Lowell's Life and Work*, 55.

81   Adrienne Rich to EH, n.d. [ca. summer 1973], in Hamilton, *Dolphin Letters*, 372.

82   Stanley Kunitz to RL, April 19, 1972, quoted ibid., 422. Kunitz also would have read the poems before publication.

83   RL to Stanley Kunitz, April 25, 1971, in Lowell, *Letters*, 570. From "The Dolphin": "I have . . . / plotted perhaps too freely with my life, / not avoiding injury to others, / not avoiding injury to myself— / to ask compassion . . . this book, half fiction, /an eelnet made by man for the eel fighting." Lowell, *Collected Poems*, 708.

84   Anatole Broyard, "Naked in his Raincoat," *New York Times*, June 18, 1973.

85   Jonathan Raban quoted in Hamilton, *Lowell: A Biography*, 425.

86   EH, Oral History interview, September 20, 1979.

87   Robert Lowell, "No Hearing 1. The Dialogue," in *For Lizzie and Harriet* (1973); republished in Lowell, *Collected Poems*, 637.

88   See Sandra M. Gilbert, "Purloined Letters: William Carlos Williams and 'Cress,'" *William Carlos Williams Review* 11, no. 2 (1985): 5–15, http://www.jstor.org/stable/24564851.

89   Elizabeth Bishop to RL, June 30, 1948, in Bishop and Lowell, *Words in Air*, 38. Lowell's review was published in *Nation*, June 19, 1948.

90   Rowley, "Poetic Justice."

91 *The New Yorker* had rejected the piece because it did not fit in any of the magazine's established departments. Robert Henderson to EH, March 9, 1972, *New Yorker* Records. It was the second time a piece by Elizabeth was rejected for this reason.

92 EH to Peter Taylor, June 3, 1972, Taylor Papers.

93 I have not been able to find out who her lover was.

94 Rodney G. Dennis, curator at Houghton Library, to Michael Henshaw, July 12, 1972, Lowell Papers. The following year, after the *Dolphin Letters* controversy blew up, Elizabeth insisted on a letter of agreement that would give her control over access to letters written to and from her, which had been solely in Cal's hands according to the original document. Dennis, "A Voice from the Library: The Robert Lowell Papers at the Houghton Library," *Harvard Review* 1 (Spring 1962), 64, https://www.jstor.org/stable/27559386.

95 Adrienne Rich to EH, November 17,1972, Hardwick Papers.

96 EH to Mary McCarthy, January 27, 1973, McCarthy Papers.

97 Merkin, "Sylvia Plath." Pointing out that the poems are about suicide rather than death, Merkin stressed that Plath had a pathological illness—a fact that was not widely acknowledged at the time.

98 EH to RL, April 9, 1973, in Hamilton, *Dolphin Letters,* 326.

99 Cal, who wanted his son Sheridan to co-inherit Cousin Harriet's properties in Castine, somehow could not fathom that the "rights of descent" were valid only if the Lowells had remained married.

100 Marjorie Perloff, "The Blank Now," *New Republic,* July 7–14, 1973.

101 EH to RL, July 5, 1973, in Hamilton, *Dolphin Letters,* 356.

102 EH to Robert Giroux, July 5, 1973, Lowell Papers. She used the male pronoun because it was still considered the grammatically correct way to refer to a person of either gender.

103 RL to EH, July 10, 1973, in Hamilton, *Dolphin Letters,* 358.

104 Quoted in Meyers, *Lowell: Interviews and Memoirs,* 75. Cal quoted this question in his last poem, "Epilogue," published in *Day by Day.*

105 Perloff, "Blank Now," 24–26.

106 RL to Elizabeth Bishop, July 12, 1973, in Bishop and Lowell, *Words in Air,* 752.

107 Elizabeth Bishop to EH, July 20, 1973, in Hamilton, *Dolphin Letters,* 364.

108 RL to Robert Giroux, July 8, 1973, ibid., 363.

109 Robert Giroux to RL, July 23, 1973, ibid., 365n2.

110 Clemons, "Carving the Marble."

111 RL to EH, May 26, 1973, in Hamilton, *Dolphin Letters,* 358.

112 At least two of the photos apparently were not lost; see Chapter 9.

113 Although "When to Cast Out" was published in July, it would have been written much earlier in 1973.

114 EH to Elizabeth Bishop, July 27, 1973, in Hamilton, *Dolphin Letters,* 366.

115 EH to Mary McCarthy, August 14, 1973, ibid., 367–68.

116 EH to Elizabeth Bishop, October 16, 1973, Bishop Papers.

117 EH to Elizabeth Bishop, October 18, 1973, in Hamilton, *Dolphin Letters,* 378.

118 EH to Mary McCarthy, October 28, 1973, ibid., 379–80.

119   The quote is from "Writing a Novel," the precursor to *Sleepless Nights*. I owe this insight to Rowley, "Poetic Justice," 407.

120   EH, "Scene from Autobiography," 63.

121   EH to Mary McCarthy, December 27, 1973, McCarthy Papers. Elizabeth and Robert Silvers were among the small group of mourners who attended Rahv's funeral on Christmas Eve. Elizabeth's speech at the memorial was published as EH, "Philip Rahv." His "outstanding theme," she wrote, was "a contempt for provincialism, for the tendency to inflate local and fleeting cultural accomplishments."

122   Mary McCarthy to Hannah Arendt, March 1, 1974, in Arendt and McCarthy, *Between Friends*, 354. Mary's memorial essay about Rahv was published in *NYTBR* on February 17, 1974.

Chapter 9: Literary Splash

1   Elizabeth was one of five authors honored at a PEN cocktail party at the Hotel Pierre on May 6.

2   EH to Robert Straus, April 29, 1973, FSG Records. Elizabeth mentioned in this letter that FSG had given her an advance of $750 for a book of theater criticism; since she had no plans to write about the theater, she wondered what to do about the money. The following year the director of the copyright department wrote to Robert Bernstein, president of Random House, that Elizabeth had been asked to return the $750 "either now or from the monies [she] will receive from Random," so that she could be released from her contract. But the money had not been forthcoming, and as far as FSG was concerned, Random was not free to extend a contract to her. Rhoda F. Gamson to Robert Bernstein, April 18, 1974, FSG Records.

3   Susan Sontag to Jason Epstein, February 21, 1974, Sontag Papers.

4   Solomon, "Of Women Writers."

5   EH, "Art of Fiction," 24.

6   Merkin, "Hardwick's *Seduction*."

7   Rosenstein, "Historic Booby Prize."

8   EH, Oral History interview, April 28, 1980.

9   EH, "Election Countdown '72: One Woman's Vote," *Vogue,* August 15, 1972.

10   EH, "Is the 'Equal' Woman More Vulnerable," *Vogue,* July 1, 1972.

11   EH, undated responses to questions from Hilton Als for his *New Yorker* profile, Hardwick Papers. She misremembered her talks as being on Ibsen's heroines, the subjects of articles she wrote for the *NYRB*.

12   EH, "Caesar's Things."

13   The other members of the jury were Alfred Kazin and Benjamin DeMott, a professor of English at Amherst College.

14   Peter Kihss, "Pulitzer Jurors Dismayed on Pynchon," *New York Times,* May 8, 1974.

15   EH, "Scenes from an Autobiography," 55.

16   EH, foreword to Machado de Assis, *Dom Casmurro,* xvii.

17   Paul Levy, interview by author, June 10, 2019. Elizabeth's "Bloomsbury" essay was a review of Quentin Bell, *Virginia Woolf: A Biography* (New York:

Harcourt Brace Jovanovich, 1974), and Levy's *Lytton Strachey: The Really Interesting Question and Other Papers* (London: Weidenfeld & Nicolson, 1972).

18   Levy interview by author. Elizabeth helped him "extensively" a few years later with his book about the Bloomsbury philosopher G. E. Moore, he said: "She gave me the absolutely golden rule: Good writers never use the word *rather* as a modifier."

19   EH, *Sleepless Nights* (2001 ed.), 125. Design Research was a pioneering retail store for modern design.

20   The photo accompanies Laura Jacobs, "Vassar Unzipped," *Vanity Fair*, July 2013.

21   Mary McCarthy to Jason Epstein, April 29, 1974, Hardwick Papers.

22   EH to RL, November 20, 1974, in Hamilton, *Dolphin Letters*, 399.

23   RL to EH, December 13, 1974, ibid., 401.

24   EH to RL, January 22, 1975, Hardwick Papers.

25   Mary McCarthy to Hannah Arendt, February 17, 1975, in Arendt and McCarthy, *Between Friends*, 372.

26   Mary McCarthy to Hannah Arendt, July 20, 1975, ibid., 379.

27   Mary McCarthy to Hannah Arendt, August 5, 1975, ibid., 382.

28   During this period, Elizabeth described Mary's life as "some sort of company with a president and a chairman of the board presiding. And yet what a strange heroine she is." EH to RL, April 20. 1976, in Hamilton, *Dolphin Letters*, 427.

29   EH to RL, September 1, 1975, ibid., 414.

30   Harrower, "Smith College Grants Eight Degrees."

31   EH to Mary McCarthy, June 5, 1975, McCarthy Papers. Elizabeth apparently did not receive the Rockefeller grant.

32   EH to RL, November 16, 1975, in Hamilton, *Dolphin Letters*, 418.

33   EH to Mary McCarthy, December 30, 1975, McCarthy Papers.

34   EH to RL, January 13, 1976, in Hamilton, *Dolphin Letters*, 420.

35   Benedict, "In Memoriam."

36   Sigrid Nunez quoted ibid. Nunez graduated from Barnard in 1972 and received her MFA from Columbia in 1975.

37   Susan Minot, interview by author, August 6, 2019. Minot was a graduate student in the early 1980s.

38   Jean C. Zimmerman, Class of' '79, in Benedict, "In Memoriam."

39   Minot interview by author.

40   Quoted in Benedict, "In Memoriam." Quindlen graduated from Barnard in 1974.

41   Mona Simpson, interview by author, December 30, 2019.

42   Frances Connell, interview by author, January 15, 2019.

43   Sigrid Nunez quoted in Als, "Singular Woman."

44   Benedict, "In Memoriam."

45   White, "Talking to Mary Gordon."

46   Quoted in Benedict, "In Memoriam."

47   Benedict, *Mentors, Muses & Monsters*, 95–96.

48   Minot interview by author.

49   Elizabeth Benedict, interview by author, October 2, 2018.

50   Daphne Merkin, interview by author, September 18, 2019.

51   Epstein, "Hardwick: Form in the Voice."

52   EH, "Art of Fiction 87," 42.

53   EH, Oral History interview, November 5, 1978.

54   EH, "Conversation on a Book," 61.

55   John Cheever to *NYRB*, February 3, 1977.

56   EH, "Cheever and Ambiguities."

57   Nancy Lemann, interview by author, August 15, 2019.

58   Simpson interview by author.

59   EH, interview by Malcolm Bradbury.

60   Connell interview by author; EH to Peter Taylor, January 18, 1972, and EH to Peter and Eleanor Taylor, March 27, 1972, Lowell Papers.

61   Frances Connell's book about her family is *Down Rivers of Windfall Night* (Xlibris, 2004).

62   EH to Peter Taylor, September 10, 1971, Taylor Papers.

63   Frances Connell, *With One Fool Left in the World, No One is Stranded: Scenes from an Older Afghanistan* (AuthorHouse, 2014).

64   Margo Jefferson called it a "gripping portrait" told in "subtle and sinewy" language. "Making Generations," *Newsweek*, May 19, 1975.

65   Art Jester, "Gayle Jones: An Author Shrouded in Mystery," *Lexington Herald-Leader*, March 1, 1988.

66   EH, introduction to *Rediscovered Fiction by American Women*.

67   EH to Mary McCarthy, January 29, 1976, in Hamilton, *Dolphin Letters*, 422. The prize went to Richard Howard for his translation of E. M. Cioran's *A Short History of Decay*.

68   Quoted in Lehmann-Haupt, "Hardwick, Writer, Dies at 91."

69   EH, "Billie Holiday."

70   RL to EH, April 29, 1976, in Hamilton, *Dolphin Letters*, 429.

71   Lowell, *Day by Day*, 44–45.

72   EH to RL, February 11, 1976, in Hamilton, *Dolphin Letters*, 423.

73   EH to RL, June 20, 1976, ibid., 433.

74   RL to EH, July 2, 1976, ibid., 435.

75   RL to EH, September 4, 1976, ibid., 439.

76   Ibid., 440.

77   Hamilton, *Dolphin Letters*, xv.

78   EH to Mary McCarthy, June 15, 1977, ibid., 445.

79   EH, "Sense of the Present." In her 1985 *Paris Review* interview, Elizabeth singled out Adler's novel *Pitch Dark* and Joan Didion's *Democracy* for their intelligence and originality. EH, "Art of Fiction."

80   Francine du Plessix Gray to EH, June 16, 1976, Hardwick Papers, and Gray to editors, *NYRB*, February 3, 1977. (Elizabeth did praise Gray's nonfiction book *Divine Disobedience*, about Catholic priests who bucked the Church's stance on social issues, in a review in the August 1970 issue of *Vogue*.)

81   EH to RL, January 13, 1976, in Hamilton, *Dolphin Letters,* 421.

82   EH to Mary McCarthy, n.d. [autumn 1976], McCarthy Papers.

83   EH to RL, November 16, 1977, in Hamilton, *Dolphin Letters,* 418.

84   Schlesinger, *Journals,* 407.

85   EH to Mary McCarthy, October 21, 1975, McCarthy Papers.

86   Quoted in Rollyson and Paddock, *Sontag,* 80.

87   EH to Susan Sontag, December 23, 1975, Sontag Papers.

88   EH to Susan Sontag, June 17, 1975, Sontag Papers.

89   Jon R. Jewitt, interview by author, August 27, 2019.

90   EH, "Unknown Faulkner." In this review of a collection of previously unpublished work by Faulkner, she describes "his original union of high classical style and vocabulary with the most daring and unaccommodating experiments with form, fractured methods of narration, shifting, shadowy centers of memory and documentation."

91   EH to Susan Sontag, January 20, 1975, Sontag Papers.

92   Susan Sontag to EH, July 22, 1975, Sontag Papers.

93   EH, introduction to Sontag, *Susan Sontag Reader,* ix, xi.

94   EH, "Knowing Sontag." Italics added.

95   Quoted in Als, "Singular Woman."

96   EH to Mary McCarthy, June 15, 1977, McCarthy Papers.

97   EH to Robert Silvers, August 4, 1977, Hardwick Papers.

98   EH, Oral History interview, November 5, 1978. See also EH, "Art of Fiction." Yet Elizabeth realized there was a point of no return, telling Hilton Als that he had to learn when to stop fussing with a theater review and let it go. Als interviewed by Lisa Cohen, "The Art of the Essay No. 3: Hilton Als," *Paris Review,* Summer 2018.

99   Rilla Bray Bateman, interview by author, October 10, 2019; remarks quoted in Bray, "Hardwick: Woman of Letters," 7.

100 William Styron to Ian Hamilton, July 1, 1981, in Styron, *Selected Letters,* 549–51.

101 EH, "Solzhenitsyn." The other authors who responded included John Cheever, Lilian Hellman, Norman Mailer, Ross Macdonald, Joyce Carol Oates, Anne Tyler, Muriel Spark, and Eudora Welty.

102 EH to Robert Silvers, August 4, 1977, Hardwick Papers.

103 Frank Bidart, in Hamilton, *Lowell: A Biography,* 467.

104 For a photo of the inscription page, see Henri Cole, Twitter, https:/twitter.com/ColeHenri/status/951188477357576193.

105 Quoted in Hamilton, *Dolphin Letters,* xlix.

106 An appraisal would have been worthwhile only if this were an original painting, but Caroline's daughter Ivana Lowell claims that it was actually a *copy* of Freud's portrait of her mother. (The original, loaned by a private collector, is in the Tate Gallery in London.) Caroline supposedly requested the museum to have someone paint the copy. Lowell, *Why Not Say,* 284. The portrait in question is probably *Girl with a Kitten* (1947), though Caroline was sixteen that year, not eighteen, as Ivana states.

107 Death certificate of Robert Lowell, reproduced on page 380 of Jamison, *Setting the River on Fire.*
108 EH to Mary McCarthy, October 2, 1977, in Hamilton, *Dolphin Letters,* 452–53. Later, after finding Mary's "harmless letter" in Cal's briefcase, Elizabeth wrote to her in an apologetic mode, explaining that she had been conveying Caroline's overheated description of it rather than "what it is, an expression of sympathy." EH to Mary McCarthy, May 10, 1980, McCarthy Papers. Still, you have to wonder why Mary found it necessary to interfere at such a fraught time.
109 EH to Mary McCarthy, October 2, 1977, McCarthy Papers.
110 EH to Mary McCarthy, December 16, 1977, McCarthy Papers.
111 Adrienne Rich to EH, September 15, 1977, Hardwick Papers.
112 EH to Mary McCarthy, June 6, 1978, McCarthy Papers.
113 EH to Elizabeth Bishop, August 16, 1978, Bishop Papers.
114 Quoted in Pulliam, "Taking the Long View."
115 EH to Mary McCarthy, March 28, 1980, McCarthy Papers.
116 EH to Mary McCarthy, June 15, 1977, McCarthy Papers.
117 EH to Elizabeth Bishop, August 16, 1978, Bishop Papers.
118 EH, Oral History interview, September 20, 1979.
119 EH to Ian Hamilton, n.d. [ca. 1982], Hardwick Papers. In October 1997, when the New York Public Library presented a "Tribute to Robert Lowell," Hardwick was one of the five panelists, along with Helen Vendler, Richard Tillinghast, Frank Bidart, and Carl Phillips.
120 Nadezhda Mandelstam was a writer and the wife of the great Russian poet, persecuted by Stalin. She died at forty-seven in a labor camp. Olga Ivinskata was the longtime mistress of the married Russian poet and novelist Boris Pasternak, best known in the West for *Doctor Zhivago.*
121 See Chapter 2.
122 EH, Oral History interview, November 5, 1978.
123 Ibid.
124 EH, "Hardwick Looks at Boston."
125 EH, "Art of Fiction," 31.
126 EH, "Conversation on a Book."
127 EH to Mary McCarthy, January 30, 1979, McCarthy Papers.
128 EH, Oral History interview, April 28, 1980.
129 EH, *Sleepless Nights* (2001 ed.), 102.
130 EH, "Art of Fiction," 49.
131 This sentence was in Cal's translation of Pasternak's poem "Hamlet."
132 Elizabeth said the letters are "imaginary." EH, Oral History interview, November 5, 1978. No letters from Elizabeth to Mary McCarthy with this content can be found in McCarthy's voluminous archive at Vassar College.
133 EH, "Faithful." She received $2,455 for this piece, according to a letter of agreement dated December 1978, Kiernan Papers.
134 EH, Oral History interview, September 20, 1979.
135 EH, Oral History interview, November 5, 1978.

136 EH to Alfred Kazin, postmarked January 30, 1979, Berg Collection, NYPL. Elizabeth was referring to a passage about Cal in Kazin's autobiography *New York Jew* that she felt did not present Lowell accurately.
137 EH, Oral History interview, November 5, 1978.
138 EH to Ian Hamilton, n.d., Hardwick Papers. "In questa tomba oscura" (In this dark tomb) is an art song (*Lied*) by Ludwig van Beethoven, set to a poem by Giuseppe Carpani. The speaker/singer, heard from the grave, tells his faithless lover not to bathe his ashes "in your useless venom."
139 Although Elizabeth didn't spell it out, this character lacked the borrowed-from-life quality of the seducer in Mary McCarthy's short story "The Man in the Gray Flannel Suit."
140 EH, Oral History interview, September 20, 1979.
141 Mary McCarthy to EH, June 4, 1979, McCarthy Papers.
142 EH to Mary McCarthy, October 10, 1978, McCarthy Papers.
143 Mary McCarthy to EH, June 4, 1979, McCarthy Papers. In this letter, Mary also remarked that the "literary daring" of *Sleepless Nights* "makes my heavily plotted, semi-lifelike novel [*Cannibals and Missionaries*] seem like a bone-crusher."
144 EH, Oral History interview, November 5, 1978.
145 Ibid.
146 Didion, "Meditation on a Life." Elizabeth would write a preface for the Modern Library edition of *Slouching Toward Bethlehem*, published in 2000.
147 Mary McCarthy was among them; she included a strong mention of the book in a "Christmas roundup" that I haven't been able to locate. Elizabeth wrote to her that she was "overwhelmed with feelings indescribable, happiness and gratitude certainly." EH to Mary McCarthy, March 21, 1980, McCarthy Papers.
148 White, "Portraits Etched on Glass."
149 Johnson, "Beyond the Evidence."
150 Stone, "Hardwick's Way."
151 Ratcliff, "*Sleepless Nights*."
152 Clemons, "Blues in the Night."
153 "Lady Sings the Blues," *Time*, May 7, 1979.
154 van Galen Last, "Hardwick on the Human Comedy." The mythological Greek poet Orpheus descended into the Underworld to seek his dead wife, Eurydice. Although he was instructed not to look back until they returned to earth, he did so, and she disappeared forever.
155 Merkin, "Books and Arts: *Sleepless Nights*."
156 EH, "Fresh Way of Looking."
157 In the UK, the Book Marketing Council included *Sleepless Nights* on a list of the twenty best postwar novels by Americans.
158 Carter, "Lapidary Lady."
159 Sage, "First Person Singular."
160 Disney, "Heaven Without God." A shorter version of the interview was reprinted as "A Success No One Expected," in the Sydney, Australia, *Bulletin* on August 28, 1979.

161 EH to Sally Alexander Higgenbotham, October 26, 1980, Hardwick Papers.
162 Elizabeth received a £1,000 advance for British and Commonwealth rights, $1,500 for Swedish rights, DM 4,000 for German rights, and $500 for Danish rights. Memo to Jason Epstein, Random House, September 14, 1979, Hardwick Papers.
163 Fogel, "Hardwick: pourquoi vient-elle si tard?" Translation by the author. The title, "Why did she come so late?" refers to the fact that the French discovered her only after *Sleepless Nights* was translated (as *Nuits sans sommeil*).
164 EH, "Art of Fiction," 27. The TV show *Dallas* had debuted in 1978.
165 Hendin, "Hardwick: Reliving the Past."

Chapter 10: Literary Lion
1 EH to Mary McCarthy, January 10, 1980, McCarthy Papers.
2 EH to Mary McCarthy, February 17, 1980, McCarthy Papers. The interview with Mary was taped in October 1979 and broadcast in January 1980.
3 EH to Mary McCarthy, March 28, 1980, McCarthy Papers.
4 EH to Mary McCarthy, May 20, 1982, McCarthy Papers.
5 Elizabeth also had won an Arts and Literature Award from the academy in 1974.
6 The program, which aired in late February 1980, included footage of Cal reading from his poems and discussing them, and interviews with people who knew him.
7 EH to Mary McCarthy, March 28, 1980, McCarthy Papers.
8 She did provide commentary for *Robert Lowell*, an hour-long video, directed by Peter Hammer, which was produced in 1988 by the New York Center for Visual History.
9 Sarah L. Bingham, "Harvard Lawyer Clashes with Lowell Biographer," *Harvard Crimson*, November 11, 1980.
10 EH to Robert Silvers, August 16, 1980, Silvers Papers.
11 EH to Frank Bidart, July 20, 1980. Hardwick Papers.
12 Reynolds, "Genteel Kentuckian."
13 EH, Oral History interview, September 20, 1979.
14 EH, interview by Helen McNeil, 79.
15 Ibid., 78–79.
16 EH, "Simone Weil."
17 Sontag, *Against Interpretation*. Sontag's essay was originally published in *NYRB*, February 1, 1963.
18 EH to Susan Sontag, August 9, 1980, Sontag Papers.
19 EH to Frances Kiernan, August 24, 1980, Kiernan Papers.
20 EH to Sally Alexander Higgenbotham, October 26, 1980, Hardwick Papers. During the 1980s, Elizabeth's concerns about Harriet included her daughter's ectopic pregnancy, on which Elizabeth bullied the surgeon into operating, to save her life. Harriet Lowell, introduction to "A Solution to the Abortion War," *NYR Daily*, June 17, 2019.
21 EH to Frances Kiernan, October 9, 1980, Kiernan Papers.
22 EH to Frances Kiernan, November 5, 1980, Kiernan Papers.

23   EH to Mary McCarthy, November 18, 1980, McCarthy Papers.
24   The other finalists were Shirley Hazzard, Walter Percy, Gilbert Sorrentino, and John Kennedy Toole.
25   EH to Mary McCarthy, March 7, 1981, McCarthy Papers. A week earlier Mary had written to Elizabeth from Paris that an acquaintance spotted "a wonderful picture" of her in *The Village Voice*. Mary McCarthy to EH, February 27, 1981, McCarthy Papers. Perhaps the content of the article turned Elizabeth against the photo as well.
26   Unfortunately, UCLA does not have any documentation of these lectures.
27   "Contemporary Women Fiction Writers," n.d., typescript, Hardwick Papers.
28   EH, "Women and Arts" (lecture).
29   EH to Susan Sontag, August 11, 1981, Sontag Papers.
30   EH to Mary McCarthy, January 28, 1982, McCarthy Papers.
31   The Frances Steloff Lecture Series was conceived and endowed by Steloff, founder of the Gotham Book Mart, to bring outstanding literary and artistic individuals to the Skidmore campus. Elizabeth delivered the talk on April 20, 1982. Unfortunately, none of the typescripts in her archive at the Ransom Center can be definitively identified as this talk, and Skidmore College does not have a copy or recording of it.
32   EH to Mary McCarthy, May 20, 1982, McCarthy Papers.
33   EH, "What She Was."
34   EH, "Katherine Anne," 85.
35   EH, "What She Was."
36   John Dorsey, "Katherine Anne Porter On," *Sun Magazine*, October 26, 1969, reprinted in Joan Givner, ed., *Katherine Anne Porter: Conversations* (Jackson: University Press of Mississippi, 1987), 147.
37   EH to Mary McCarthy, April 23, 1983, McCarthy Papers.
38   EH to Alfred Kazin, March 25, 1982, Berg Collection, NYPL.
39   EH to Mary McCarthy, April 23, 1983, McCarthy Papers.
40   Rolfe, "At Home with Hardwick."
41   Darryl Pinckney, introduction to "The Art of Fiction 52: Elizabeth Hardwick," *Paris Review* (Summer 1985), 22. Elizabeth's last year of teaching coincided with this interview; the living room also contained piles of student manuscripts.
42   EH, Oral History interview, November 5, 1978.
43   Lesser, "Intelligent Preferences," 741.
44   Lee, "Firm Lines."
45   EH, "Flannery O'Connor (1925–1964)"; EH, "Romance vs. Cruelty."
46   The Melville story, published in 1853, is "Bartleby, the Scrivener: A Story of Wall Street."
47   Lesser, "Intelligent Preferences," 741; Tyler, "Civilized Sensibility."
48   EH, "Bunch of Reds."
49   EH, "Simone Weil."
50   EH, "Domestic Manners," 7–8.
51   EH, introduction to *Best American Essays 1986*, ix–xxi.
52   EH, "Perfectionist."

53   The other committee members were Renata Adler, David Kalstone, Norman Mailer, and John Updike.
54   Freedman, "McCarthy Is Recipient of MacDowell."
55   EH to Mary McCarthy, January 3, 1985, McCarthy Papers.
56   Jon Jewett, interview by author, August 27, 2019.
57   EH to Peter Taylor, January 5, 1985. Taylor Papers.
58   EH, "Art of Fiction," 50.
59   EH to Peter Taylor, October 5, 1985, Taylor Papers.
60   EH, "Dead Souls: Ernest Hemingway."
61   EH, "Wind from the Prairie."
62   EH to Peter Taylor, January 25, 1985, Taylor Papers.
63   EH, "Lion at His Desk."
64   Mary McCarthy to EH, January 14, 1986, McCarthy Papers.
65   EH to Mary McCarthy, January 23, 1096 [1986], McCarthy Papers.
66   EH, "Art of Fiction," 47.
67   The other awardees were the dancer and choreographer Honi Coles; the actor and director José Ferrer; the painter Helen Frankenthaler; the puppeteer Miguel Mike Manteo; the acting teacher Sanford Meisner; and the colaratura soprano Roberta Peters.
68   EH, Untitled talk, Hardwick Papers.
69   EH to Mary McCarthy, January 23, 1996 [actually 1986], McCarthy Papers.
70   EH, "Genius of Margaret Fuller."
71   Mary McCarthy to EH, March 30, 1986, McCarthy Papers.
72   EH, "Matter and Manner in Non-Fiction."
73   EH to Peter Taylor, August 11, 1986, Taylor Papers.
74   Constance Hunting, "The Experience of Art: The Novels of Elizabeth Hardwick," *Puckerbrush Review,* n.d., 5, Hardwick Papers. It was probably published in 1996, based on a listing of September 1996 correspondence from Elizabeth in the inventory of Hunting's papers (Box 41) at the Howard Gotlieb Archival Research Center, Boston University.
75   Lowell, *Collected Prose.*
76   EH to Robert Giroux, October 11, 1986, FSG Records.
77   EH to Peter Taylor, April 8, 1987, Taylor Papers.
78   EH to Ian Hamilton, n.d. [ca. 1982], Hardwick Papers.
79   EH, *Sleepless Nights,* part 8.
80   Ian Hamilton to EH, May 10, 1982, Hardwick Papers.
81   EH to Mary McCarthy, January 24, 1987, McCarthy Papers.
82   EH, "Gertrude Stein."
83   EH to Mary McCarthy, January 24, 1987, McCarthy Papers.
84   Ada Long, interview by author, November 18, 2019.
85   EH to Peter Taylor, April 8, 1987, Taylor Papers.
86   EH to Mary McCarthy, April 17, 1987, McCarthy Papers.
87   EH, "Fictions of America." One of Elizabeth's earlier remarks about the lack of standards in publishing can be found in a letter to Mary McCarthy written a decade earlier.
88   Trueheart, "Den of Literary Lions."

89   EH, "Heart of the Seasons." It appears that Elizabeth just browsed the catalogue rather than visiting the museum. The piece seems to be about the Terra's first show, *A Proud Century: Two Centuries of American Art,* organized with the Pennsylvania Academy of Fine Arts.

90   EH, "Art of Fiction," 43.

91   PEN Symposium on Henry James, 16, 13.

92   No doubt aware of its acuity, Elizabeth repeated it in her introduction to the Modern Library edition of *Washington Square.*

93   The original screenplay for this film, which was never produced, is in the Department of Special Collections, Memorial Library, University of Wisconsin–Madison. Karp died in 2002. (Two other films, *Grand Isle* and *The End of August,* have been based on the book.) Intriguingly, Francine Gray once mentioned the novel's heroine, Edna Le Pelletier, as an example of women who "transgress conventions *other* than sexual." Gray to editors, *NYRB,* February 3, 1977.

94   The typescript in Hardwick Papers is not dated, but the most recent film mentioned in this talk (*The Awakening*) was released in December 1990. The venue for this talk is unknown.

95   While the date of this television play is unknown, it might have been written after the Benedict archive at Vassar was updated in October 1996.

96   EH to Alfred Kazin, February 5, 1988, Berg Collection, NYPL.

97   EH, interview by Malcolm Bradbury.

98   EH, "Citizen Updike."

99   Citation, Honorary Doctor of Letters, Bard College, 1989, Hardwick Papers.

100   "Elizabeth Hardwick: 1989," Whiting Foundation, https://www.whiting.org/keynotes/elizabeth-hardwick-1989.

101   EH, "Basic Englishing."

102   EH to Alfred Kazin, September 13, 1990, Berg Collection, NYPL Other members of the American delegation included Alfred Kazin, Studs Terkel, William Gass, Louis Auchincloss, Harrison Salisury, Arthur Schlesinger, Jr., and David Halberstam.

103   EH to Jon Jewett, April 11, 1981, Jewett Collection.

104   EH to Jon Jewett, May 14, 1991, Jewett Collection.

105   Brightman, *Writing Dangerously,* 629.

106   The others were Nicholas King, Arthur Schlesinger Jr., James Merrill, William Jovanovich, and Mary's brother, Kevin McCarthy.

107   EH, speech at McCarthy's memorial, typescript, November 8, 1989, McCarthy Papers.

108   EH, foreword to McCarthy, *Intellectual Memoirs,* x, xxii.

109   EH, "Books: *Writing on the Wall.*"

110   Ginny Foote, interview by author, July 22, 2019.

111   Peter Davis, interview by author, August 16, 2019. Davis is best known for the film *Hearts and Minds.*

112   Alison West, interview by author, August 14, 2019.

113   EH, "'I Had My Pinnacle.'" The back cover of the 1993 paperback edition of *New York Days* carries a quote from the first sentence of this review.

114 Morris, *North Toward Home,* 359.
115 Ibid., 370, 400, 402.
116 EH to Jon Jewett, April 10, 1994, Hardwick Papers.
117 EH to Sally Alexander Higgenbotham, January 1, 1994, Hardwick Papers.
118 Elizabeth Kendall, interview by author, April 22, 2019.
119 EH to Jon Jewett, April 10, 1994, Hardwick Papers.
120 Quoted in Streitfeld, "Hardwick's Manhattan."
121 Hardwick gave at least one more talk, "A Writer's Personal Canon," on November 9, 1995, at New York University. Announcing this forthcoming lecture, Linda Hall praised Elizabeth's "authority," which "lends her arguments and even her isolated phrases . . . their startling force." "Queen Elizabeth," *New York,* November 13, 1995, 34.
122 Quoted in "Hardwick, Once of Castine, Dies," *Bangor Daily News,* December 6, 2007.
123 Jewett, "Hardwick Remembered."
124 Bray, "Hardwick: Woman of Letters." All quotes in this paragraph are from this article, except where noted.
125 Jon Jewett, interview by author, August 27, 2019.
126 Tolstoy's novel deals with a nobleman's guilt about his affair with a peasant girl who was forced into prostitution to survive.
127 EH, "In the Wasteland."
128 Quoted in Pulliam, "Taking the Long View."
129 Although Elizabeth didn't make the comparison in this review, she clearly valued Didion's style more highly than the accretion of details in Mary's fiction.
130 EH, introduction to Didion, *Slouching Toward Bethlehem,* xiv. A side note: in her 1977 essay "On the Road," Didion mentions bringing *Sleepless Nights* with her on a book tour. But Elizabeth's novel and Edmund Wilson's *To the Finland Station* were soon shipped home, unread. *The White Album* (New York: Farrar, Straus and Giroux, 2009), 175.
131 EH, "Grits Soufflé."
132 EH, "Family Values." This piece is ostensibly a review of four books about the Simpson trial, including Alan Dershowitz's *The Search for Justice: A Defense Attorney's Brief on the O. J. Simpson Case.* Robert Silvers had asked Elizabeth multiple questions about the issue of a "blood conspiracy," which he felt she needed to explore in more depth. Robert Silvers to EH, May 1, 1996, Silvers Papers.
133 EH, "Paradise Lost: Philip Roth"; EH, "True Confessions"; EH, *Sight Readings;* EH, "Christmas Past."
134 Oates, "American Views: Elizabeth Hardwick."
135 Ginny Foote, interview by author, July 22, 2019.
136 EH to Susan Sontag, March 2, 2000, Sontag Papers.
137 EH, interview by Helen McNeil, 81–82.
138 EH to Susan Sontag, August 24, 2001, Sontag Papers.
139 Alison West, interview by author, August 14, 2019; Kiernan, *Seeing Mary Plain,* 269.

140   EH, "Eternal Heartbreak." She explains that Melville's "miraculous plot" gets around the problematic character of John Claggart, the master-of-arms whose seemingly arbitrary bullying of Budd leads to his death. Curiously, despite her question-begging remark that the hero is "a baritone whose outstanding feature is a striking, dominating physical beauty," she does not mention the homoerotic undercurrent that runs through the opera, whose composer, Britten, and co-librettist, the novelist E. M. Forster, were both gay.

141   EH, "Son of the City's Pavements."

142   James Atlas, interview by author, May 30, 2019.

143   Paul Levy, interview by author, June 10, 2019.

144   EH, Oral History interview, November 5, 1978.

145   Da Costa, "Leviathan."

146   Michaelis, "Brief and Daring Bio."

147   Russo, "'Herman Melville' by Hardwick."

148   Leonard, "Wise Woman and Whale."

149   EH, introduction to Naipaul, *Bend in the River*, xv.

150   EH, introduction to James, *Washington Square*, xx.

151   EH, introduction to Wharton, *House of Mirth*, xiii.

152   EH, preface to Svevo, *Zeno's Conscience*, xii.

153   EH, introduction to Powers, *Morte d'Urban*, xvii–xviii.

154   EH, introduction to Schlesinger, *Unpossessed*, vii–xiv.

155   Peter Davis, interview by author, August 17, 2019.

156   EH, "Art of Fiction," 23, 42.

157   EH to Jon Jewett, April 14, 2000, Jewett Collection.

158   EH to Susan Sontag, November 16, 2000, Sontag Papers.

159   EH, "Limited Future and Frozen Past."

160   Quoted in Als, "Blocked."

161   Hall, "Literary Life Well Lived." Linda Hall is an associate professor of English at Skidmore College.

162   Jon Jewett, interview by author, August 27, 2019.

163   EH, "Barbara Epstein (1928–2006)."

164   Walcott, "Elizabeth Hardwick (1916–2007)."

165   Didion and Pinckney, "On Hardwick (1916–2007)." In October 2017, on the occasion of the publication of *Collected Essays*, the *New York Review* hosted a tribute at Barnard College; speakers included Pinckney, Susan Minot, Saskia Hamilton, and Daphne Merkin. Two additional discussions of Elizabeth's work that month were held at the Brooklyn Public Library and the Paula Cooper Gallery. *Collected Essays* are really "selected" essays; as we have seen, Elizabeth published many more pieces than are included in this book.

166   Elizabeth was cremated; her ashes are in Harriet's possession. Her papers had already been sold to the Ransom Center.

167   Michael Blumenthal, email to the author, October 10, 2019.

168   EH, "Grub Street: New York."

BIBLIOGRAPHY

AUTHOR'S NOTE: Elizabeth Hardwick's archive at the Harry Ransom Center at the University of Texas at Austin contains just one single-page, undated résumé, blurry with swaths of correction fluid. Some drafts of lectures she gave provide no date and no venue; conversely, she gave lectures for which no corresponding manuscripts appear to exist. There is no omnibus listing of her essays and short stories. For this reason, I cite not only the journal or magazine where each piece first appeared but also books in which many of them were subsequently published.

NYRB	*The New York Review of Books*
NYTBR	*New York Times Book Review*
PR	*Partisan Review*

WORKS BY ELIZABETH HARDWICK

Books (in chronological order)

The Ghostly Lover. New York: Harcourt Brace, 1945. Reprinted by Ecco Press, 1989.
The Simple Truth. New York: Harcourt, Brace, Jovanovich, 1955. Other editions: Ecco Press, 1982; Virago Press, 1987.

A View of My Own: Essays on Literature and Society. New York: Farrar, Straus and Cudahy, 1962.

Seduction and Betrayal. New York: Farrar, Straus and Giroux, 1974. Reprinted by New York Review Books, 2001.

Sleepless Nights. New York: Random House, 1979. Reprinted by New York Review Books, 2001.

Bartleby in Manhattan and Other Essays. New York: Random House, 1983.

Sight Readings: American Fictions. New York: Random House, 1998.

American Fictions. New York: Modern Library, 1999. Includes *Sight Readings* and selected essays from *Seduction and Betrayal*, *Bartleby in Manhattan*, and *A View of My Own*. Introduction reprinted in *Collected Essays*.

Herman Melville. New York: Penguin, 2000.

The New York Stories of Elizabeth Hardwick. New York: New York Review Books, 2010.

The Collected Essays of Elizabeth Hardwick. New York: New York Review Books, 2017.

Essays, Reviews, and Op-eds (in chronological order)

"Artist and Spokesman." *PR* 12 (Summer 1945): 406–7.

"Poor Little Rich Girls." *PR* 12 (Summer 1945): 420–22.

"Fiction Chronicle." *PR* 15 (June 1947): 705–11.

"Ten Years' Experiment." *NYTBR*, December 7, 1947, 26.

"Fiction Chronicle." *PR* 15 (June 1948): 705–11.

"Faulkner and the South Today." *PR* (October 1948): 1130–35.

"Fiction Chronicle." *PR* 27 (January 1950): 87–91.

"The Friendly Witness." *PR* 17 (April 1950): 340–51.

"A Florentine Conference." *PR* 17 (May–June 1950): 304–6.

"The Subjugation of Women." *PR* 20 (May–June 1953): 321–31. Reprinted in *Collected Essays*.

"Two Recent Travellers." *Kenyon Review* 15 (Summer 1953): 436–54.

"Memoirs, Conversations and Diaries." *PR* 20 (September–October 1953): 527–39. Reprinted in *Collected Essays*.

"Anderson, Millay and Crane in Their Letters." *PR* 20 (November–December 1953): 690–96. Reprinted in *Collected Essays*.

"Riesman Considered." *PR* 21 (September–October 1954): 548–57. Reprinted in *A View of My Own*.

"George Eliot's Husband." *PR* 22 (Spring 1955): 260–64. Reprinted in *A View of My Own*.

"The Neglected Novels of Christina Stead." *New Republic,* August 1, 1955. Reprinted in *A View of My Own* and *Collected Essays*.

"Way Beyond Innocence." *PR* 22 (Fall 1955): 552–55.

"America and Dylan Thomas." *PR* 23 (Spring 1956): 258–64. Reprinted in *A View of My Own* and *Collected Essays*.

"The Feminine Principle." *Mademoiselle,* February 1958.

"Theater Chronicle: Disgust and Disenchantment: New British and American Plays." *PR* 25 (Spring 1958): 282–87.

"A Fantastic Voyage." *PR* 26 (Spring 1959): 299–303.

"The Decline of Book Reviewing." *Harper's*, October 1959. Reprinted in *Collected Essays*.

"I've Been Reading." *Columbia University Forum* 2 (Fall 1959): 44–46.

"Boston: The Lost Ideal." *Harper's*, December 1959. First published as "Boston" in *Encounter*, November 1959. Reprinted as "Boston" in *Collected Essays*.

"Living in Italy: Reflections on Bernard Berenson." *PR* 27 (Winter 1960): 73–81. Reprinted in *A View of My Own* and *Collected Essays*.

"The Life and Death of Caryl Chessman." *PR* 28 (Summer 1960): 503–13. Reprinted in *A View of My Own* and in Harold Schechter, ed., *True Crime: An American Anthology* (New York: Library of America, 2008).

"William James: American Hero." *Mademoiselle*, June 1960. Reprinted in *Collected Essays*.

"All Is Vanity." *Reporter*, December 8, 1960.

"The Insulted and Injured." *Harper's*, June 1961. Reprinted as "The Insulted and Injured: Books about Poverty," in *A View of My Own* and in *Collected Essays*.

"More Loveless Love." *PR* 29 (July 1961): 702–76. Reprinted, with "Loveless Love" (*PR* 15, August 1948), as "Loveless Love: Graham Greene," in *Collected Essays*.

"Some Chapters of Personal History." *NYTBR*, August 26, 1961.

"Matter and Manner in Non-Fiction." *Harper's*, January 1962. The first section of this essay was reprinted as "Mary McCarthy" in *Collected Essays*.

"Riesman Considered Again," *PR* 29 (Winter 1962): 132–36. Reprinted in *A View of My Own*.

"Matter and Manner in Non-Fiction." *Harper's*, January 1962.

"Grub Street: New York." *NYRB*, February 1, 1963. Reprinted in *Collected Essays*.

"Ring." *NYRB*, February 1, 1963. Reprinted in *Collected Essays* as "Ring Lardner."

"Frost in His Letters." *NYRB*, October 31, 1963. Reprinted in *Collected Essays*.

"Grub Street: Washington." *NYRB*, January 23, 1964. Reprinted in *Collected Essays*.

"The Family Way." *NYRB*, February 6, 1964.

"The Disaster at Lincoln Center." *NYRB*, April 2, 1964.

"Sex and the Single Man." *NYRB*, August 20, 1964.

"Flannery O'Connor (1925–1964)." *NYRB*, October 8, 1964.

"The Oswald Family." *NYRB*, November 5, 1964.

"Bad Boy." *PR* 22 (Spring 1965): 291–94.

"Selma, Alabama: The Charms of Goodness." *NYRB*, April 22, 1965. Reprinted in *Collected Essays*.

"Sense and Sensibility." *NYRB*, August 5, 1965.

"A Death at Lincoln Center." *NYRB*, November 25, 1965.

"Theater in New York." *NYRB*, January 6, 1966.

"We Are All Murderers." *NYRB*, March 3, 1966.

"After Watts." *NYRB*, March 31, 1966. Reprinted in *Collected Essays* and in Robert Silvers and Barbara Epstein, eds., *The First Anthology: Selected Essays from Thirty Years of the New York Review of Books* (New York: New York Review Books, 1993).

"Notes on Leonardo and the Future of the Past." *Art in America* 54 (March–April 1966), 33–39.

"The Theater of Decadence." *NYRB*, April 28, 1966.

"Straight Play." *NYRB*, October 20, 1966.

"Auschwitz in New York." *NYRB*, November 3, 1966.

"The Theater of Sentimentality." *NYRB*, December 15, 1966.

"Hurrah!" *NYRB*, February 23, 1967.

"Word of Mouth." *NYRB*, April 6, 1967.

"Blow-Up." *NYRB*, April 20, 1967.

"Critics." *NYRB*, June 1, 1967.

"The Crown Jewels." *NYRB*, October 12, 1967.

"*The Little Foxes* Revived." *NYRB*, December 21, 1967.

"The Whole Hog." *NYRB*, February 1, 1968.

"The Apotheosis of Martin Luther King," *NYRB*, May 9, 1968. Reprinted in *Collected Essays* and in Joyce Carol Oates, ed., *The Best American Essays of the Century* (New York: Houghton Mifflin, 2000).

"Notes on the New Theater." *NYRB*, June 20, 1968.

"Chicago." *NYRB*, September 26, 1968. Reprinted in *Collected Essays*.

"Mr. America." *NYRB*, November 7, 1968.

"Reflections on Fiction." *NYRB*, February 13, 1969. Reprinted as "Fiction" in Louis Kronenberger, ed., *Quality: Its Image in the Arts* (New York: Atheneum, 1969), and in *Collected Essays*.

"Dead Souls: Ernest Hemingway." *NYRB*, June 5, 1969. Reprinted in *Collected Essays*.

"Books: *Four-Gated City*." *Vogue*, July 1, 1969. Review of Doris Lessing's novel.

"Going Home in America: Lexington, Kentucky." *Harper's*, July 1969.

"Scalp!" *NYRB*, November 6, 1969.

"The Theater of Grotowski." *NYRB*, February 12, 1970.

"Meeting V. S. Naipaul." *NYTBR*, May 13, 1970, 1.

"*Divine Disobedience*, 'Important Record.'" *Vogue*, August 1, 1970.

"Books: *The Writing on the Wall*." *Vogue*, September 1, 1970, 306.

"Caesar's Things." *NYRB*, September 24, 1970. Reprinted as "Zelda Fitzgerald" in *Seduction and Betrayal*.

"Militant Nudes." *NYRB*, January 7, 1971. Reprinted in *Collected Essays*.

"Violence Redeemed." *Vogue*, January 1971.

"*A Doll's House*." *NYRB*, March 11, 1971. Reprinted in *Seduction and Betrayal*.

"Ibsen and Women II: *Hedda Gabler*." *NYRB*, March 25, 1971.

"Ibsen and Women III: The *Rosmersholm* Triangle." *NYRB*, April 8, 1971. Reprinted in *Seduction and Betrayal*.

"On the Ties That Women Cannot Shake—and Have." *Vogue*, June 1971.

"On Sylvia Plath." *NYRB*, August 12, 1971. Reprinted as "Sylvia Plath" in *Seduction and Betrayal*.

"In Maine." *NYRB*, October 7, 1971. Reprinted in *Collected Essays*.

"Romance vs. Cruelty: The South Seen by Two Famous Women," *Vogue*, November 1, 1971.

"Working Girls: The Brontës." *NYRB*, May 4, 1972. Reprinted in *Seduction and Betrayal*.

"A Limited Future and a Frozen Past—Such Is the Situation." *NYTBR*, May 14, 1972.

"The Coming of Age." *NYTBR*, May 14, 1972.

"Is the 'Equal' Woman More Vulnerable?" *Vogue*, September 1, 1972.

"One Woman's Vote." *Vogue*. Six-part series, 1972: August 15, September 1, September 15, October 1, October 15, November 1.

"On the Election." *NYRB*, November 2, 1972.

"Amateurs: Dorothy Wordsworth and Jane Carlyle." *NYRB*, November 30, 1972. Reprinted in *Seduction and Betrayal*.

"Amateurs: Jane Carlyle." *NYRB*, December 14, 1972. Reprinted in *Seduction and Betrayal*.

"Bloomsbury and Virginia Woolf." *NYRB*, February 8, 1973. Reprinted in *Seduction and Betrayal*.

"Scene from an Autobiography." *Prose*, Spring 1973.

"What Is a Woman of 45 to Do?" *NYTRB*, May 13, 1973. Review of Doris Lessing's *The Summer Before the Dark*.

"Seduction and Betrayal: I." *NYRB*, May 31, 1973. Reprinted in *Seduction and Betrayal*.

"Seduction and Betrayal: II." *NYRB*, June 14, 1973. Reprinted in *Seduction and Betrayal*.

"When to Cast Out, Give Up, Let Go." *Mademoiselle*, July 1973.

"Philip Rahv (1908–1973)." *NYRB*, January 24, 1974.

"Sad Brazil." *NYRB*, June 27, 1974. Reprinted in *Collected Essays* and in Robert Silvers, ed., *New York Review Abroad: Fifty Years of International Reportage* (New York: New York Review Press, 2013).

"Sue and Arabella." *NYRB*, November 14, 1974. Reprinted in *Collected Essays*.

"Timon of Paris." *NYRB*, December 12, 1974.

"Thomas Mann at 100." *NYTBR*, July 20, 1975. Reprinted in *Bartleby in Manhattan and Other Essays*.

"Billie Holiday." *NYRB*, March 4, 1976. Reprinted in *Collected Essays*.

"Accepting the Dare: Maine," *Vogue*, Summer 1976.

"Elections: Renewal or Just Replacement?" *Vogue*, July 1976,

"The Carter Question II: Piety and Politics." *NYRB*, August 7, 1976.

"Sense of the Present." *NYRB*, November 26, 1976. Reprinted in *Collected Essays*.

"Simone Weil." *NYTBR*, January 23, 1977. Reprinted in *Collected Essays*.

"Domestic Manners." *Daedalus* 107 (Winter 1978): 1–11. Reprinted in *Collected Essays*.

"Faye Dunaway: The Face in the Dark." *Vogue*, March 1979.

"Wives and Mistresses." *NYRB*, May 18, 1978. Reprinted in *Collected Essays*.

"Knowing Sontag." *Vogue*, June 1978.

"The Portable Canterbury." *NYRB*, August 16, 1979.

"Unknown Faulkner." *NYTBR*, November 4, 1979. Reprinted in *Collected Essays*.

"Love It or Leave It!" *NYRB*, April 3 1980. Reprinted as "English Visitors in America" in *Collected Essays*.

"Master Class: Nabokov." *NYTBR*, October 19, 1980, 1. Reprinted in *Collected Essays*.

"Bartleby and Manhattan." *NYRB*, July 16, 1981. Reprinted as "Bartleby in Manhattan" in *Bartleby in Manhattan and Other Essays* and in *Collected Essays*.

"A Bunch of Reds," *NYRB*, March 4, 1982. Reprinted in *Bartleby in Manhattan and Other Essays*.

"What She Was and What She Felt Like." *NYTBR*, November 7, 1982. Reprinted as "Katherine Anne Porter" in *American Fictions* and in *Collected Essays*.

"Eye-Witness ARTnews." *NYRB*, December 2, 1982.

"Ibsen's Secrets." *NYRB*, June 30, 1983.

"Katherine Anne." *Vanity Fair*, March 1984.

"The Perfectionist." *New Republic*, March 18, 1984. Reprinted as "The Magical Prose of Poets: Elizabeth Bishop" in *Sight-Readings* and as "Elizabeth Bishop" in *American Fictions*.

"Somebody Out There." *NYRB*, August 16, 1984.

"Cheever and the Ambiguities." *NYRB*, December 20, 1984. Reprinted as "Cheever; or The Ambiguities," in *Sight-Readings* and in *American Fictions*.

"Son of the City's Pavements." *NYTBR*, December 30, 1984. Reprinted as "Son of the City's Pavements: Delmore Schwartz" in *Collected Essays*.

"The Teller and the Tape." *NYRB*, May 30 1985. Reprinted as "The Teller and the Tape: Norman Mailer" in *Collected Essays*.

"The Genius of Margaret Fuller." *NYRB*, April 10, 1986. Reprinted in *Collected Essays*.

"The Heart of the Seasons." *House and Garden*, May 1987. Reprinted in Annie Dillard, ed., *The Best American Essays 1988* (Boston: Ticknor & Fields, 1988).

"The Fictions of America." *NYRB*, June 25, 1987. Version of a talk delivered at the Wheatland Conference on Literature, April 1987. Reprinted in *Collected Essays*.

"Puritanical Pleasures: Summer in Maine." *House and Garden*, August 1987. Typescript, Hardwick Papers.

"Gertrude Stein." *Threepenny Review* 31 (Fall 1987): 3–5. Version of a talk delivered as part of the journal's Writers on Literature series, February 19, 1987. Reprinted in *Collected Essays*.

"Mrs. Wharton in New York." *NYRB*, January 21, 1988. Reprinted in *American Fictions* and in *Collected Essays*.

"Church Going." *NYRB*, August 18, 1988.

"Citizen Updike." *NYRB*, May 18, 1989.

"Basic Englishing." *NYRB*, October 28, 1989.

Mary McCarthy Memorial speech given at McCarthy's memorial, November 8, 1989. Typewritten draft, McCarthy Papers.

"New York City: Crash Course." *Granta*, Spring 1990. Reprinted in Joyce Carol Oates, ed., *The Best American Essays 1991* (Boston: Ticknor & Fields, 1992).

"On Washington Square." *NYRB*, November 22, 1990. Reprinted in *Collected Essays*.

"Wind from the Prairie." *NYRB*, September 26, 1991. Reprinted in Susan Sontag, ed., *The Best American Essays 1992* (New York: Houghton Mifflin Harcourt, 1992), and in *Collected Essays*.

"Mary McCarthy in New York." *NYRB*, March 26, 1992.

"The Eternal Heartbreak." *Opera News*, March 28, 1992.

"The Kennedy Scandals." *NYRB*, January 14, 1993.

"'I Had My Pinnacle.'" *NYTBR*, September 5, 1993.

"The Menendez Show." *NYRB*, February 17, 1994.

"A Lion at His Desk." *New Yorker,* May 8, 1995. Reprinted as "Edmund Wilson" in *Collected Essays,* with the incorrect original publication date.

"Reckless People." *NYRB*, August 10, 1995.

"Family Values." *NYRB,* June 6, 1996.

"On Behalf of the Unborn: A Celibacy Amendment" (op-ed). *Washington Post,* July 31, 1996, and *Morning Call* (Allentown, Penn.), August 5, 1996. Reprinted as "A Solution to the Abortion War: The Celibacy Amendment" in *New York Review Daily,* June 17, 2019.

"In the Wasteland." *NYRB,* October 31, 1996. Reprinted as "In the Wasteland: Joan Didion" in *Collected Essays.*

"Grits Soufflé." *New Yorker,* December 23, 1996.

"On Murray Kempton (1917–1997)." *NYRB,* June 12, 1995.

"Paradise Lost: Philip Roth," *NYRB,* June 12, 1997. Reprinted in *Collected Essays.*

"Tru Confessions." *NYRB,* January 15, 1998. Reprinted in *Collected Essays.*

"Christmas Past." *New Yorker,* December 21, 1998.

"Head Over Heels." *NYRB,* April 22, 1999.

"Far From Rome." *NYRB,* March 23, 2000.

"Melville in Love." *NYRB,* June 15, 2000.

"The Foster Father." *NYRB,* May 17, 2001. Reprinted as "The Foster Father: Henry James" in *Collected Essays.*

"Celebrities." *NYRB,* July 19, 2001.

"Pilgrim's Progress." *NYRB,* June 22, 2002.

"On *The Unpossessed.*" *NYRB,* September 26, 2002.

"Among the Savages." *NYRB,* July 17, 2003.

"Funny as a Crutch: Nathanael West." *NYRB,* November 6, 2003. Reprinted in *Collected Essays.*

"Susan Sontag (1933–2004)." *NYRB,* February 10, 2005.

"Barbara Epstein (1928–2006)" (contribution). *NYRB,* August 10, 2006.

Short Stories and Filmscript (in chronological order)

"The People on the Roller Coaster." *New Mexico Quarterly* 14 (1944).

"The Mysteries of Eleusis." *PR* 12 (Spring 1945): 207–13. Reprinted in Phillips and Rahv, *New Partisan Reader,* 3–9; and in Martha Foley, ed., *The Best American Short Stories 1946* (New York: Houghton Mifflin, 1946).

"Saint Ursula and Her Eleven Thousand Virgins." *Yale Review* 34 (1945): 524–31.

"The Temptations of Dr. Hoffmann." *PR* 13 (September–October 1946): 405–19. Reprinted in *New York Stories.*

"The Golden Stallion." *Sewanee Review* 54, no. 1 (January–March 1946): 34–65. Reprinted in Martha Foley, ed., *The Best American Short Stories 1947* (New York: Houghton Mifflin, 1947).

"Evenings at Home." *PR* 15 (April 1948): 439–48. Reprinted in Martha Foley, ed., *The Best American Short Stories 1949* (New York: Houghton Mifflin, 1949); in Hollis Summers, ed., *Kentucky Story: A Collection of Short Stories* (Lexington: University Press of Kentucky, 1954); in Morris Allen Grubbs, ed., *Home and*

Beyond: An Anthology of Kentucky Short Stories (Lexington: University Press of Kentucky, 2001); and in *New York Stories.*

"Yes and No." *New York Stories.* According to the credits, it was published in *PR* in 1949, but no story with that title appears (in any year) in the *PR* collection at the Howard Gotlieb Archival Research Center.

"Two Recent Travellers." Kenyon Review, Summer 1953.

"The Final Conflict." Written ca. 1954–1960, posthumously published in *New York Stories.*

"Portrait of a New York Lady." *Encounter,* December 1955).

"A Season's Romance." *New Yorker,* March 10, 1956. Reprinted in *New York Stories.*

"The Oak and the Ax." *New Yorker,* May 12, 1956. Reprinted in *New York Stories.*

"The Classless Society." *New Yorker,* January 19, 1957. Reprinted in *Stories from The New Yorker: 1950 to 1960* (New York: Simon & Schuster, 1960) and in *New York Stories.*

"The Purchase." *New Yorker,* May 30, 1959. Reprinted in Martha Foley and David Burnett, eds., *The Best American Short Stories 1960* (New York: Houghton Mifflin, 1960), and in *New York Stories.*

"Writing a Novel." *NYRB,* October 18, 1973.

"The Faithful." *New Yorker,* February 19, 1979. Reprinted in Stanley Elkin, ed., *The Best American Short Stories 1980* (New York: Harcourt Brace, 1980), and in Patricia Craig, ed., *Oxford Book of Travel Stories* (Oxford: Oxford University Press, 1996).

"The Bookseller." *New Yorker,* December 15, 1980. Reprinted in Stanley Elkin, ed., *Best American Short Stories 1981* (New York: Harcourt Brace, 1981), and in *New York Stories.*

"Back Issues." *NYRB,* December 17, 1981. Reprinted in *New York Stories.*

"Cross-Town." *Antaeus* 45/46 (Spring–Summer 1982). Reprinted in *New York Stories,* which incorrectly gives the original date as 1980.

"On the Eve: A Story." *NYRB,* December 22, 1983. Reprinted in *New York Stories.*

"Shot: A New York Story." *New Yorker,* October 11, 1993. Reprinted in David Remnick, ed., *Wonderful Town: New York Stories from* The New Yorker (New York: Random House, 2000), and in *New York Stories.*

The Awakening. Film script based on the novel by Kate Chopin, n.d. Typescript, Archives and Special Collections, University of Wisconsin.

Editing, Forewords, and Introductions (in chronological order)

James, Henry. *The Selected Letters of William James.* Edited and with an introduction by EH. New York: Farrar, Straus and Cudahy, 1961.

Shepard, Sam. *La Turista.* Introduction by EH. Indianapolis: Bobbs-Merrill, 1968.

Rediscovered Fiction by American Women: A Personal Selection (series). Introduction by EH. New York: Arno Press, 1977.

Sontag, Susan. *A Susan Sontag Reader.* Foreword by EH. New York: Farrar, Straus and Giroux, 1982.

The Best American Essays 1986. Edited and with introduction by EH. New York: Ticknor & Fields, 1986. Also published as "Its Only Defense: Intelligence and Sparkle," *New York Times,* September 14, 1986.

James, Henry. *Washington Square*. Introduction by EH. New York: Library of America, 1990.

de Assis, Machado. *Dom Casumurro*. Foreword by EH. Translated by Helen Caldwell. New York: Farrar, Straus and Giroux, 1991.

McCarthy, Mary. *Intellectual Memoirs: New York 1936–1938*. Foreword by EH. New York: Harcourt Brace, 1992. EH's foreword was also published as "Mary McCarthy in New York," *NYRB*, March 26, 1992, and in *Collected Essays*.

Naipaul, V. S. *A Bend in the River*. Introduction by EH. New York: Modern Library, 1999.

Wharton, Edith. *The House of Mirth*. Introduction by EH. New York: Modern Library, 1999.

Didion, Joan. *Slouching Toward Bethlehem*. Introduction by EH. New York: Modern Library, 2000.

Powers, J. F. *Morte d'Urban*. Introduction by EH. New York: New York Review Books, 2000. Also published as "Far from Rome," *NYRB*, March 23, 2000.

Svevo, Italo. *Zeno's Conscience*. Preface by EH. New York: Vintage, 2003. Originally published in 2001 by Alfred A. Knopf.

Melville, Herman. *Redburn*. Foreword by EH. New York: Modern Library, 2002.

Schlesinger, Tess. *The Unpossessed*. New York: New York Review Books, 2002. Also published as "On *The Unpossessed*," *NYRB*, September 26, 2002.

Interviews, Symposia, and Lectures (in chronological order)

"American Literary Criticism Today" (symposium). Sonoma State College, 1964. Audio recording.

EH, "The Editor Interviews Elizabeth Hardwick." Interview by Philip Rahv. *Modern Occasions* (Spring 1971), 159–67.

EH, "Solzhenitsyn," in "Writers' Writers." *NYTBR*, December 4, 1977.

EH, "Conversation on a Book." Interview by Richard Locke. *NYTBR*, April 29, 1979), 61.

EH, "Elizabeth Hardwick Looks at Boston." Interview by Robert Taylor. *Boston Globe*, May 12, 1979.

EH, "Elizabeth Hardwick: A Fresh Way of Looking at Literature—and at Life." Interview by Francine du Plessix Gray. *Vogue*, June 1979.

Disney, Anthea. "A Heaven Without God." *Observer*, August 5, 1979.

EH, Oral History. Interviews by David Farrell, October 8–9, 1977; May 8, 1978; November 5, 1978; September 20, 1979; and April 28, 1980. Audio recordings transcribed by author. Louis B. Nunn Center for Oral History, University of Kentucky Libraries.

EH, "Women and the Arts." Lecture delivered at the Creative Women Conference at Washington University in St. Louis, 1980. Audio recording. Modern Literature Recorded Multimedia Collection, Washington University Libraries.

EH, "The Art of Fiction No. 87." Interview by Darryl Pinckney. *Paris Review* 96 (Summer 1985): 20–51.

EH, Untitled talk about reading and readers, given as recipient of Mayor's Award for Art and Culture, January 1986. Typescript, Hardwick Papers.

EH and Lorna Sage in Conversation. ICA Talks, London, February 19, 1986. Audio recording, British Library Sound Archive.

EH, interview by Malcolm Bradbury. Writers in Conversation, ICA Talks, London, February 20, 1986. Video recording, Roland Collection, British Library Sound Archive.

EH, interview by Helen McNeil. In Mary Chamberlain, ed., *Writing Lives: Conversations Between Women Writers.* London: Virago Press, 1988.

PEN Symposium on Henry James, November 8, 1987. "PEN Symposium on Henry James," *PEN Newsletter* 67 (January 1989).

EH, "Places in the Mind: New York" (lecture). October 18, 1994, Folger Shakespeare Library, Washington, D.C. Video recording, Folger Library Archives.

Delbanco, Andrew. "Literary Journalism: A Discussion," panel discussion at the Cullman Center for Scholars and Writers, New York Public Library, April 3, 2013.

Wiggins, John R. "I Don't Give the Reader a Great Deal to Go on . . ." Unidentified Maine newspaper, n.d., Hardwick Papers.

Secondary Sources: Books, Articles, and Selected Reviews

Adler, Renata. *Speedboat.* 1976; New York: New York Review Books, 2013.

Aldridge, John W. "*Seduction and Betrayal,* by Elizabeth Hardwick." *Commentary,* August 1974.

Als, Hilton. "Blocked: Why Do Writers Stop Writing?" *New Yorker,* June 14, 2004.

———. "Lizzie." *New Yorker,* August 12, 2008.

———. "A Singular Woman." *New Yorker,* July 13, 1998.

Arendt, Hannah, and Mary McCarthy. *Between Friends: The Correspondence of Hannah Arendt and Mary McCarthy, 1949–1975,* ed. Carol Brightman. New York: Harcourt Brace, 1995.

Axelrod, Stephen. *Robert Lowell: Life and Art.* Princeton: Princeton University Press, 1978.

Benedict, Elizabeth. "In Memoriam." *Barnard Magazine,* Winter 2008, https://archive .org/stream/barnardmagazine971barn/barnardmagazine971barn_djvu.txt.

———. *Mentors, Muses & Monsters.* New York: Excelsior Editions, 2012.

Bishop, Elizabeth. *One Art: Letters,* ed. Robert Giroux. New York: Farrar, Straus and Giroux, 1994.

Bishop, Elizabeth, and Robert Lowell. *Words in Air: The Correspondence,* ed. Thomas Travisano and Saskia Hamilton. New York: Farrar, Straus and Giroux, 2010.

Bloom, Alexander. *Prodigal Sons: The New York Intellectuals and Their World.* New York: Oxford University Press, 1986.

Booth, Philip. "Summers in Castine: Contact Prints, 1955–1965." *Salmagundi* 37 (Spring 1977): 37–53. Reprinted in *Robert Lowell: Interviews and Memoirs,* ed. Jeffrey Meyers. Ann Arbor: University of Michigan Press, 1988.

Bray, Sharon. "Elizabeth Hardwick: Woman of Letters Who Loved Castine." *Castine Patriot,* December 13, 2007.

Brightman, Carol. *Writing Dangerously: Mary McCarthy and Her World.* New York: Clarkson Potter, 1992.

Buckman, Gertrude. "Wandering Parents," *New York Times,* April 29, 1945.

Carter, Angela. "Lapidary Lady," *Guardian,* August 9, 1979.

Chamberlain, Mark. "Not Asking for Compassion." *TLS,* January 24, 2020.

Chopin, Kate. *The Awakening and Selected Stories.* 1899; reprinted New York: Signet Classics, 1976.

Clemons, Walter. "Carving the Marble." *Newsweek,* July 16, 1973.

————. "Blues in the Night." *Newsweek,* May 14, 1979.

Cook, Richard M., ed. *Alfred Kazin's Journals.* New Haven, Conn.: Yale University Press, 2012.

Da Costa, Erica. "Leviathan." *New York Times,* July 20, 2000.

Davison, Peter. *The Fading Smile: Poets in Boston from Robert Lowell to Sylvia Plath.* New York: W. W. Norton, 1996.

Didion, Joan. "Meditation on a Life." *NYTBR,* April 29, 1979.

Didion, Joan, and Darryl Pinckney. "On Elizabeth Hardwick (1916–2007)." *NYRB,* February 14, 2008.

Dillon, Brian. *Essayism: On Form, Feeling, and Nonfiction.* New York: New York Review Books, 2018.

Dowling, David O. *A Delicate Aggression: Savagery and Survival in the Iowa Writers' Workshop.* New Haven, Conn.: Yale University Press, 2019.

Epstein, Jason. *Book Business: Publishing Past Present and Future.* New York: W. W. Norton, 2002.

Epstein, Rena. "Hardwick: The Form Is in the Voice." *Barnard Bulletin,* October 10, 1974.

Federal Writers' Project. *Lexington and the Bluegrass Country.* Lexington, Ky.: E. M. Glass, 1938.

————. *Kentucky: A Guide to the Bluegrass State.* New York: Harcourt Brace, 1939.

Fogel, Jean- François. "Hardwick: pourquoi vient-elle si tard?" *Le Point* 577, October 10, 1983,

Freedman, Samuel G. "McCarthy Is Recipient of MacDowell Medal." *New York Times,* August 27, 1984.

Givner, Joan. *Katherine Anne Porter: A Life,* rev. ed. Athens: University of Georgia Press, 1991.

Givner, Joan, ed. *Katherine Anne Porter: Conversations.* Jackson: University of Mississippi Press, 1987.

Goodman, Charlotte Margolis. *Jean Stafford: The Savage Heart.* Austin: University of Texas Press, 1990.

Gordon, Caroline. *The Collected Stories of Caroline Gordon.* 1981; reprint New York: Farrar, Straus and Giroux, 2009.

Gray, Francine du Plessix. *Lovers and Tyrants.* New York: Simon & Schuster, 1978.

Gunn, Thom. *Shelf Life: Essays, Memoirs, and An Interview.* Ann Arbor: University of Michigan Press, 1993.

Hall, Linda. "Elizabeth Hardwick: A Literary Life Well Lived." *Guardian,* December 5, 2007.

Hamilton, Ian. *Arthur Koestler: A Biography.* New York: Macmillan, 1982.

————. *Robert Lowell: A Biography.* New York: Vintage Books, 1982.

Hamilton, Saskia, ed. *The Dolphin Letters.* New York: Farrar, Straus and Giroux, 2019.

Hammer, Langdon. "The Art of Losing." *NYRB,* December 19, 2019.

"Hardwick, Once of Castine, Dies." *Bangor Daily News,* December 6, 2007.

Harrower, Vivian. "Smith College Grants Eight Degrees as Part of Its Centennial Program." *Daily Hampshire Gazette,* February 26, 1975.

Haslett, Tobi. "The Cost of Living: Elizabeth Hardwick's Political Conscience." *Harper's,* December 2017.

Heller, Anne C. *Hannah Arendt: A Life in Dark Times.* Boston: Houghton Mifflin Harcourt, 2015.

Hendin, Josephine. "Hardwick: Reliving the Past." *Esquire,,* May 22, 1979.

Hochman, Sandra. *Loving Robert Lowell.* Nashville, Tenn.: Turner, 2017.

Hulbert, Ann. *The Interior Castle: The Art and Life of Jean Stafford.* Amherst: University of Massachusetts Press, 1992.

Jamison, Kay Redfield. *Robert Lowell, Setting the River on Fire: A Study of Genius, Mania, and Character.* New York: Knopf, 2017.

Jarrell, Mary, ed. *Randall Jarrell's Letters: An Autobiographical and Literary Selection.* New York: Houghton Mifflin, 1985.

Jewett, Jon. "Elizabeth Hardwick Remembered by Jon Jewett." *Castine Visitor,* Castine Historical Society Newsletter, Spring 2008, 8.

Johnson, Diane. "Beyond the Evidence." *NYRB,* June 14, 1979.

Kachka, Boris. *Hothouse: The Art of Survival and the Survival of Art at America's Most Celebrated Publishing House, Farrar Straus and Giroux.* New York: Simon & Schuster, 2013.

Kiernan, Frances. *Seeing Mary Plain: A Life of Mary McCarthy.* New York: W. W. Norton, 2000.

Krupnick, Mark. "Elizabeth Hardwick." *Guardian,* December 6, 2007.

"The Lady Sings the Blues," *Time,* May 7, 1979.

Laskin, David. *Partisans: Marriage, Politics and Betrayal Among the New York Intellectuals.* New York: Simon & Schuster, 2000.

Lee, Hermione. "Firm Lines." *London Review of Books,* November 17, 1983.

Lehmann-Haupt, Christopher. "Elizabeth Hardwick, Writer, Dies at 91." *New York Times,* December 4, 2007.

Leonard, John. "Books of the Times." *New York Times,* April 2, 1982.

——. "The Wise Woman and the Whale." *NYRB,* July 20, 2000. Reprinted as "Elizabeth Hardwick Meets Herman Melville" in Leonard, *Lonesome Rangers* (New York: New Press, 2002).

Lesser, Wendy, "Intelligent Preferences." *Hudson Review,* Winter 1983.

Levy, Lisa. "An Original Adventure." *Believer,* May 2008.

Lopate, Philip. *Writing New York: A Literary Anthology.* New York: Library of America, 2008.

Lowell, Ivana. *Why Not Say What Happened? A Memoir.* New York: Knopf, 2010.

Lowell, Robert. *Collected Poems,* ed. Frank Bidart and David Gewanter. New York: Farrar, Straus and Giroux, 2007.

——. *Collected Prose,* ed. Robert Giroux. New York: Farrar, Straus and Giroux, 1987.

————. *Day by Day*. New York: Farrar, Straus and Giroux, 1977.

————. *The Dolphin*. New York: Farrar, Straus and Giroux, 1973.

————. "Five Poems." *PR* 25 (Winter 1958): 25–30.

————. *Letters,* ed. Saskia Hamilton. New York: Farrar, Straus and Giroux, 2015.

————. *For Lizzie and Harriet*. New York: Farrar, Straus and Giroux, 1973.

Makowsky, Veronica A. *Caroline Gordon: A Biography*. New York: Oxford University Press, 1989.

Mallon, Thomas. "Word for Word." *New Yorker,* December 16, 2019.

Marcus, James. "Perfect-Bound: On Elizabeth Hardwick." *Harper's,* January 19, 2011.

Mariani, Paul. *Lost Puritan: A Life of Robert Lowell*. New York: W. W. Norton, 1994.

Marshall, Megan. *Elizabeth Bishop: A Miracle for Breakfast*. New York: Houghton Mifflin Harcourt, 2017.

Martinson, Deborah. *Lillian Hellman: A Life with Foxes and Scoundrels*. New York: Counterpoint, 2005.

McAlexander, Hubert, ed. *Conversations with Peter Taylor*. Jackson: University of Mississippi Press, 1987.

McCarthy, Mary. *A Bolt from the Blue and Other Essays*. New York: New York Review Books, 2001.

————. *The Group: A Novel*. New York: Mariner Books, 1991. Originally published in 1954.

————. *How I Grew*. New York: Harcourt Brace Jovanovich, 1987.

————. *Novels and Stories, 1942–1963*. New York: Library of America, 2017.

Merkin, Daphne. "Books and the Arts: *Sleepless Nights*." *New Republic,* June 9, 1979.

————. "Hardwick's *Seduction*: Understanding Women Writers." *Barnard Bulletin,* April 4, 1974.

————. "Sylvia Plath: 'A Million Suckers.'" *Barnard Bulletin*, February 8, 1973.

Meyers, Jeffrey. *Married to Genius: A Fascinating Insight Into the Married Lives of Nine Modern Writers*. London: Southbank, 2005.

————. *Robert Lowell in Love*. Amherst: University of Massachusetts Press, 2016.

Meyers, Jeffrey, ed. *Robert Lowell: Interviews and Memoirs*. Ann Arbor: University of Michigan Press, 1988.

Michaelis, David. "Another Brief and Daring Bio: Teasing, Tangled Melville Yarn." *Observer,* June 2, 2000.

Miller, Brett C. *Elizabeth Bishop: Life and the Memory of It*. Berkeley: University of California Press, 1993.

Morris, Willie. *New York Days*. Boston: Back Bay Books, 1994.

————. *North Toward Home*. 1976; reprinted New York: Vintage Books, 2000.

Moser, Benjamin. *Sontag: Her Life and Work*. New York: Ecco, 2019.

Nobile, Philip. *Intellectual Skywriting: Literary Politics and* The New York Review of Books. New York: Charterhouse, 1974.

Oates, Joyce Carol. "American Views: Elizabeth Hardwick." *NYRB,* November 28, 1998; republished in *Where I've Been and Where I'm Going: Essays, Reviews, and Prose* (New York: Penguin, 1999).

O'Connor, Flannery. *The Complete Stories*. New York: Noonday Press, 1972.

————. *The Habit of Being: Letters,* ed. Sally Fitzgerald. New York: Farrar, Straus and Giroux, 1988.

Phillips, William. *A Partisan View: Five Decades in the Politics of Literature.* New Brunswick, N.J.: Transaction, 2000.

Phillips, William, and Philip Rahv, eds. *More Stories in the Modern Manner from Partisan Review.* New York: Avon, 1954.

————. *New Partisan Reader, 1945–1953.* New York: Harcourt Brace, 1953.

Pierpont, Claudia Roth. *Passionate Minds: Women Rewriting the World.* New York: Knopf, 2001.

Pinckney, Darryl. "Dancing Miss." *NYRB,* July 17, 2013.

————. "The Ethics of Admiration: Arendt, McCarthy, Hardwick, Sontag." *Three-penny Review,* Fall 2013.

————. "Master Class." *NYRB,* October 12, 2017.

Pinckney, Darryl, and Joan Didion. "On Elizabeth Hardwick (1916–2007)." *NYRB,* February 14, 2008.

Plath, Sylvia. *The Unabridged Journals of Sylvia Plath,* ed. Karen V. Kulil. New York: Anchor, 2000.

Price, Ruth. *The Lives of Agnes Smedley.* New York: Oxford University Press, 2005.

Prickett, Sarah Nicole. "A View of Her Own." *Bookforum,* September–October 2017.

Pulliam, Deborah. "Taking the Long View in Life and in Print." *Maine Times,* September 17, 1983.

Ratcliff, Carter. "Sleepless Nights." *New York,* June–July 1979.

Reid, David. *The Brazen Age—New York City and the American Empire: Politics, Art and Bohemia.* New York: Pantheon Books, 2016.

Render, Brandon J. "The Lexington, Kentucky Civil Rights Movement" (2015). Online Theses and Dissertations, https://encompass.eku.edu/etd/309.

Remnick, David. "Barbara Epstein." *New Yorker,* June 25, 2006.

Remnick, David, ed. *Wonderful Town: New York Stories from* The New Yorker. New York: Random House, 2000.

Reynolds, Sharon M. "A Genteel Kentuckian, Elizabeth Hardwick Defies Regionalism." *Lexington Herald,* May 1, 1980.

Rich, Adrienne. "Caryatid: A Column," *American Poetry Review* 2 (September–October 1973): 3442–43.

Roberts, David. *Jean Stafford: A Biography.* Boston: Little, Brown, 1988.

Robins, Natalie. *The Untold Journey: The Life of Diana Trilling.* New York: Columbia University Press, 2017.

Rolfe, John. "At Home with Elizabeth Hardwick." *Maine Sunday Telegraph,* August 7, 1983.

Rollyson, Carl, and Lisa Paddock. *Susan Sontag: The Making of an Icon.* Jackson: University Press of Mississippi, 2016.

Rose, W. K. "The Novel: An Affirmation?" *Vassar Alumnae Magazine,* February 1962.

Rosenfeld, Isaac. "In and Out of the War." *PR* 12 (Spring 1945): 256.

Rosenstein, Harriet. "A Historic Booby Prize." *Ms.* [April?] 1974.

Rowley, Hazel. "Poetic Justice: Elizabeth Hardwick's *Sleepless Nights.*" *Texas Studies in Literature and Language* 39 (Winter 1997): 399–421.

Rudikoff, Sonya. "Heroines of Literature and of Life." *Hudson Review* 27 (Winter 1974–1975).

Russo, Maria. "'Herman Melville' by Elizabeth Hardwick." *Salon*, July 26, 2000.

Sage, Lorna. "First Person Singular." *Observer,* August 12, 1979.

Schlesinger, Arthur, Jr. *Journals 1952–2000,* ed. Andrew Schlesinger and Stephen Schlesinger. New York: Penguin, 2007.

Schoenberger, Nancy. *Dangerous Muse: The Life of Lady Caroline Blackwood.* New York: Da Capo, 2002.

Simpson, Eileen. *Poets in Their Youth: A Memoir.* New York: Random House, 1982.

Smith, Gerald. *Blacks in Lexington, Kentucky: The Struggle for Civil Rights.* M.A. thesis, University of Kentucky, 1980.

Snodgrass, W. D. "A Liberal Education: Mentors, Fomentors and Tormentors," *Southern Review* 28 (Summer 1992): 445–68.

Solomon, Barbara Probst. "Of Women Writers and Writing About Women." *NYTBR,* May 5, 1974.

Sontag, Susan. *Against Interpretation and Other Essays.* New York: Farrar, Straus and Giroux, 1966.

Spender, Stephen. *World Within World.* New York: St. Martin's Press, 1994.

Spivak, Kathleen. *With Robert Lowell and His Circle.* Boston: Northeastern University Press, 2012.

Stone, Laurie. "Hardwick's Way." *Village Voice,* May 7, 1979.

Streitfeld, David. "Book Report: Hardwick's Manhattan." *The Washington Post,* October 9, 1994.

Styron, William. *Selected Letters,* ed. Rose Styron and R. Blakeslee Gilpin. New York: Random Hose, 2012.

Sutherland, John. *Stephen Spender: A Literary Life.* New York: Oxford University Press, 2005.

Tillinghast, Richard. *Robert Lowell's Life and Work: Damaged Grandeur.* Ann Arbor: University of Michigan Press, 1995.

Travisano, Thomas. *Love Unknown: The Life and Worlds of Elizabeth Bishop.* New York: Viking, 2019.

Trilling, Diana. *The Beginning of the Journey: The Marriage of Diana and Lionel Trilling.* New York: Harvest Books, 1995.

———. "Fiction in Review." *New Republic,* May 5, 1945.

Trilling, Lionel. *The Moral Obligation to Be Intelligent: Selected Essays.* New York: Farrar, Straus and Giroux, 2000.

Trueheart, Charles. "The Den of Literary Lions." *Washington Post,* April 24, 1987.

Tyler, Anne. "A Civilized Sensibility." *New Republic,* June 20, 1987.

van Galen Last, H. "Hardwick on the Human Comedy." *NRC Handelsblad* (Rotterdam-Amsterdam), June 27, 1979, Hardwick Papers. (This is a translated review of *Sleepless Nights.*)

Vendler, Helen. "Dearest Lizzie: The End of a Literary Marriage." *Harper's Magazine,* February 2020.

Walcott, Derek. "Elizabeth Hardwick (1916–2007)." *NYRB,* January 17, 2008.

Wharton, Edith. *Ethan Frome.* 1911; reprinted Mineola, N.Y.: Dover Publications, 1991.

White, Edmund. "Portraits Etched on Glass." *Washington Post Book World*, May 6, 1979.

———. "Talking to Mary Gordon," *Washington Post Book World*, April 8, 1978.

Wilson, Edmund. *The Fifties,* ed. Leon Edel. New York: Farrar, Straus and Giroux, 1982.

———. *The Sixties, The Last Journal, 1960–1972,* ed. Lewis M. Dabney. New York: Farrar, Straus and Giroux, 1993.

Wreszin, Michael. *A Rebel in Defense of Tradition: The Life and Politics of Dwight Mac-donald.* New York: Basic Books, 1995.

ILLUSTRATION CREDITS

INDEX